Greenland

Reykjavik

Baffin

Bay

Sirmilik
National Park

Davis

Baffin

Island

Auyuittuq
National Park

Strait

Melville
Peninsula

Foxe

Basin

Labrador Sea

ATLANTIC

Iqaluit

Southampton
Island

Hudson Strait

OCEAN

Hudson Bay

Peninsule
d'Ungava

Labrador

Newfoundland

page
253

Red Bay

St Anthony

Peninsula

& Labrador

Labrador City

Gros Morne
National Park

St
John's

Québec

Natashquan

Newfoundland

page
192-3

Sept-Iles

Anticosti I.

Channel-Port-
aux-Basques

Albany R.

Chibougamau

Gaspé

Ontario

Chicoutimi

Rimouski

P.E.I.

Sydney

Geraldton

page
196

New

Nova

Kapuskasing

Québec City

Brunswick

Scotia

page
224

Timmins

Val d'Or

Trois-Rivières

Saint

Halifax

Thunder Bay

Sault
Ste Marie

Sudbury

Montréal

Sherbrooke

Maine

John

Lake Superior

St Lawrence R.

Ottawa

Vt

Portland

page
180

Kings

page
156

N.H.

Toronto

Oshawa

New

Boston

Hamilton

L. Ontario

York

Mass.

Michigan

Lake Huron

page
138

Niagara

Providence

London

Falls

Syracuse

Lake Michigan

L. Erie

page
152

wisconsin

Michigan

Detroit

Pennsylvania

New York

Canada

0 ──── 250 km

0 ──── 250 miles

INSIGHT GUIDES
CANADA

APA PUBLICATIONS L
Part of the Langenscheidt Publishing Group

※ INSIGHT GUIDE
CANADA

Editorial
Project Editor
Paula Soper
Art Director
Ian Spick
Picture Manager
Steven Lawrence
Series Manager
Rachel Fox

Distribution

UK & Ireland
GeoCenter International Ltd
Meridian House, Churchill Way West
Basingstoke, Hampshire RG21 6YR
sales@geocenter.co.uk

United States
Langenscheidt Publishers, Inc.
36–36 33rd Street 4th Floor
Long Island City, NY 11106
orders@langenscheidt.com

Australia
Universal Publishers
1 Waterloo Road
Macquarie Park, NSW 2113
sales@universalpublishers.com.au

New Zealand
Hema Maps New Zealand Ltd (HNZ)
Unit 2, 10 Cryers Road
East Tamaki, Auckland 2013
sales.hema@clear.net.nz

Worldwide
**Apa Publications GmbH & Co.
Verlag KG (Singapore branch)**
38 Joo Koon Road, Singapore 628990
Tel: (65) 6865 1600.

Printing

Insight Print Services (Pte) Ltd
38 Joo Koon Road, Singapore 628990
apasin@singnet.com.sg

©2010 Apa Publications GmbH & Co.
Verlag KG (Singapore branch)
All Rights Reserved

First Edition 1978
Second Edition 2010

CONTACTING THE EDITORS
We would appreciate it if readers
would alert us to errors or out-
dated information by writing to:
**Insight Guides, P.O. Box 7910,
London SE1 1WE, England.**

insight@apaguide.co.uk

ABOUT THIS BOOK

The first Insight Guide pioneered the use of creative full-color photography in travel guides in 1970. Since then, we have expanded our range to cater for our readers' need not only for reliable information about their destination but also for a real understanding of the culture and workings of that destination. Now, when the internet can supply inexhaustible (but not always reliable) facts, our books marry text and pictures to provide those much more elusive qualities: knowledge and discernment. To achieve this, they rely heavily on the authority of locally based writers and photographers.

How to use this book

Insight Guide: Canada is structured to convey an understanding of the country and its culture and to guide readers through its attractions:

◆ Canada is an immense country, crowning the North American conti-nent with an intriguing combination of sophisticated urban living and indomitable wilderness. To under-stand Canada today, you need to know something of its past.

◆ The **Features** section, indicated by a pink bar at the top of each page, covers the history and culture of the country in a series of lively and informative essays.

◆ The main **Places** section, indi-cated by a blue bar, is a complete guide to all the attractions and areas worth visiting. Places of spe-cial interest are coordinated by number with the cross-referenced, full-color maps.

◆ The **Travel Tips** listings section, with a yellow bar, provides full infor-mation on transportation, hotels, restaurants, activities from culture to shopping to sports and a detailed

LEFT: The Dempster Highway in the Northwest Territories.

list of outdoor activities, and an A–Z section of essential practical information. A Travel Tips index is on the back cover flap, which also serves as a handy bookmark.

◆ **Photographs** are chosen not only to illustrate geography and attractions but also to convey Canada's moods and the activities of its people.

The contributors

This edition of Insight Guide Canada was updated by Toronto-based **Joanna Ebbutt** (*Central Canada* and *The East* chapters and Travel Tips) and Vancouver-based **Gael Arthur** (*The West* and *The North* chapters and Travel Tips). Arthur also rewrote the *Canada at Work* chapter. This edition builds on the original edition produced by **Andrew Eames** and **Hilary Cunningham**.

Ebbutt played a major part in re-working the previous edition. She

wrote the chapter on Toronto, the feature on living with snow and the new chapter on Nunavut. **Michael Algar**, an author of Canadian travel books, lives in Toronto. He compiled the Travel Tips and contributed features on Canadian sport, Alberta's rodeo, West Coast flora and fauna, and whale-watching. The author of the History chapters, **Hilary Cunningham**, is a native of Toronto and graduate of the University of Toronto and Yale University.

Other contributors include the culinary columnist and illustrator **Colette Copeland**, author of the Food and Drink chapter. **Charles Foran** tackled the thorny issue of French/English relations. **Geoff Hancock** wrote about Art and Performance.

The progeny of a small Ontario town, **Patrick Keyes** contributed the account of the Inuit and those of Canada's Yukon and Northwest Territories. Writer and cartoonist **Philip Street** wrote the Montréal chapter and teamed up with **Malcolm MacRury** to write about Ontario. **Matthew Parfitt**, who arrived in Montréal at the age of eight on one of the last passenger liners, has written about Québec.

In Newfoundland **John Lucas** found a special sense of humor; **Anne Matthews** discovered the smallest province, Prince Edward Island; **Diane Hall** supplied her impressions of New Brunswick and Nova Scotia; and **John Loonam** – a native of New York State who was spellbound by British Columbia – contributed the chapters on this province and Vancouver. The Prairie section is by **David Dunbar**.

The book was proofread by **Susan Howarth** and indexed by **Helen Peters**.

Map Legend

▬ ▪ ▬	International Boundary
▬ ▬ ▬	State Boundary
▬ ▪ ▬	National Park/Reserve
▬ ▬ ▬	Ferry Route
✈ ✈	Airport: International/Regional
🚌	Bus Station
❶	Tourist Information
✝ ✝ ✝	Church/Ruins
✝	Monastery
∴	Archaeological Site
🏰	Castle/Ruins
☪	Mosque
✡	Synagogue
∩	Cave
🗿	Statue/Monument
★	Place of Interest
▪	Lodge/Ranger Station

The main places of interest in the Places section are coordinated by number with a full-colour map (eg ❶), and a symbol at the top of every right-hand page tells you where to find the map.

Contents

LEFT: the Capilano Suspension Bridge in Vancouver.

Maps

The Best of Canada: Top Attractions

Here are just a few of the spectacular things to see in this diverse country – from breathtaking scenery to thrilling rodeos

△ **Québec City**. More French than Montréal, this small city is a captivating slice of Europe in North America. Wander round the Old Town and soak up Quebec City's unique atmosphere. *See page 195*

▽ **Polar Bear Capital**. Churchill, Manitoba is a very popular attraction as scores of polar bears arrive each fall until the ice on Hudson Bay is solid enough for them to continue their journey. *See page 315*

△ **Niagara Falls, Ontario**. It really is spectacular – and there is no charge for the excellent view from Table Rock of the raging waters crashing down over both Canada's Horseshoe Falls and the American Falls. *See page 164*

△ **Québec City Winter Carnival**. A celebration of winter, with activities ranging from winter sports competitions to ice-sculpture contests. *See page 383*

◁ **T. Rex Discovery Centre**. Fossil hunting is an interesting option in Eastend, Saskatchewan, where one of the world's most complete T. Rex skeletons is on display. *See page 306*

△ **The Aurora Borealis**. Even if you understand the Aurora Borealis, you will never tire of the magic. Best seen north of 60°, let these dancing lights mesmerize you in any of Canada's three territories. *See page 333*

△ **Signal Hill**, St John's, Newfoundland. The site of the first transatlantic wireless message Marconi received also affords magnificent views over the Atlantic, the harbor, and the city – well worth the half-hour hike. *See page 255*

▽ **Stanley Park**. Vancouver's jewel, a 400-hectare (1,000-acre) evergreen oasis, full of majestic cedar, hemlock, and firs – rimmed by breathtaking views from the 10km (6-mile) seawall that locals jog, in-line skate, cycle, and amble around. *See page 265*

△ **The Cabot Trail**. A spectacular 187km (303-mile) drive around Cape Breton, Nova Scotia that weaves around hairpin bends and tiny fishing villages, from cliff tops to sea level. *See page 234*

▷ **Calgary Stampede** (July). One of the biggest rodeo events in the world, with chuckwagon races and every sort of rodeo event imaginable, all surrounded by a midway, cotton candy, and fireworks every night. *See page 380*

THE BEST OF CANADA: EDITOR'S CHOICE

Fabulous winter resorts, family fun, museums, markets, and unique attractions... Here, at a glance, are our top recommendations for a visit

BEST WINTER SPORT DESTINATIONS

● **Lake Louise**
A diverse ski/snowboard area offers infinite and varied terrain in the heart of Banff National Park. *See page 296.*

● **Fernie Mountain Resort**
In B.C., renowned for its legendary powder and limitless terrain. *See page 390*

● **Whistler-Blackcomb**
Consistently ranked as the top ski resort in North America, has more than 200 trails, three glaciers, 12 alpine bowls, and unlimited backcountry. *See page 269.*

● **Mont-Tremblant**
The highest peak in Québec's Laurentians, with 94 runs and over 7 hectares (18 acres) of ramps, rails, and jumps, as well as an Olympic caliber super-pipe. *See page 193.*

● **Le Massif**
In Québec's Charlevoix region, Le Massif has the highest vertical drop in Eastern Canada, and is renowned for its snowfall, averaging almost 7 meters (22ft) per season. *See page 390.*

● **The Largest Skating Rink in the World**
In Ottawa, the 7.8km (4.8-mile) Rideau Canal Skateway winds through the capital city, attracting more than one million skaters each winter. *See page 156.*

BEST MARKETS

● **ByWard Market**
Ottawa. A traditional farmers' market that still sells all manner of foods, flowers, plants, and produce. *See page 385.*

● **City Market**
Saint John. A lively market full of New Brunswick fare including fiddleheads and dulse. *See page 217.*

● **Atwater Market**
Montréal. Capturing the spirit of Montréal's French heritage, Atwater offers an enormous selection of fruit and vegetables, cheeses, meats, breads, and pastries. *See page 386.*

● **St Lawrence Market**
Toronto. Selling everything from fish and freshly baked bread to Ontario cheese and all sorts of organic edibles. *See page 385.*

● **Granville Island Market**
Vancouver. An island in the city that combines a food market with theatres, restaurants, and artisans – a place with something for every taste. *See page 384.*

ABOVE AND RIGHT: fresh produce on display at Atwater Market. **LEFT:** a skier's paradise.

TOP VIEWS

● **Cape Enrage**
New Brunswick, just east of Fundy National Park, for its rugged, remote beauty above the pounding sea. *See page 219.*

● **Terrasse Dufferin**
Québec City, for its panoramic views from the base of the imposing Château Frontenac − over the St Lawrence river to the south shore and the distant mountains beyond. *See page 196.*

● **CN Tower**
Toronto. A favorite icon, including the famous glass floor, where kids can jump up and down, 342 meters (1,112ft) above mere mortals below. *See page 140.*

● **The Banff Gondola**
On Sulphur Mountain, offers a bird's eye view of Banff, Mount Rundle, the Bow Valley, and the Aylmer and Cascade Mountains. *See page 295.*

● **Grouse Mountain**
North Vancouver, for its stunning views over the city, and as far as the San Juan Islands on a very clear day. *See page 268.*

BEST BEACHES

● **Long Beach**
On Vancouver Island's west coast, this is a glorious stretch of golden sand between Ucluelet and Tofino, and a particular challenge to experienced surfers. *See page 281.*

● **Sauble Beach**
Gracing the Lake Huron shoreline in Ontario, this is a pristine stretch of sand cradled by the shallow warmth of the lake. *See page 170.*

● **Sandbanks Provincial Park**
Home to three of Ontario's sandiest beaches, each of them great for swimming, windsurfing, sailing, and boating. *See page 159.*

BEST MUSEUMS

● **Pier 21**
Halifax. More than one million immigrants first arrived here from 1928 to 1971, including World War II British "guest" children, post-1945 war brides and thousands of refugees. Their hopes, fears, and tears are captured brilliantly. *See page 226.*

● **Museum of Anthropology**
Vancouver. The city's most important museum, focusing on the art and culture of the region's natives. With a spectacular collection of Haida carvings and totem poles. *See page 266.*

● **Royal Ontario Museum**
Toronto. Already Canada's foremost museum, when the ROM opened its new glittering, crystal-shaped extension designed by Daniel Libeskind, it added amazing architecture to its fabulous collections. *See page 145.*

● **Musée d'Archéologie et d'Histoire de Montréal**
High-tech presentations and archeological finds bring the old city amazingly to life. *See page 183.*

● **National Gallery of Canada**
Ottawa. If pressed for time, skip everything but the indigenous gallery, which houses both are of the first peoples of Canada, and aboriginal art from other parts of the world. *See page 157.*

ABOVE: Sulphur Mountain, Banff. **MIDDLE LEFT:** the CN Tower. **MIDDLE RIGHT:** a Haida carving. **RIGHT:** surfers, Vancouver Island.

HOPE AND PROMISE

Charles Dickens once described Canada as a land of "hope and promise." Today it is that and more: a land of exuberant cities, breathtaking scenery, and diverse cultures

The writer George Woodcock said, a couple of decades ago, "The national voice of Canada is muted," and this is certainly true. Canadians are among the last people to sing the praises of their exceptionally fine land, and proclaiming its attractions has usually been left to foreigners.

"I saw a great and wonderful country; a land containing in its soil everything that a man desires; a proper land, fit for proper men to live in and to prosper exceedingly," observed British Field Marshal Lord Montgomery in 1946.

More than 100 years earlier, another traveler from Great Britain, Charles Dickens, was equally enthusiastic: "Few Englishmen are prepared to find out what it is. Advancing quietly; old differences settling down, and being fast forgotten; public feeling and private enterprise alike in a sound and wholesome state; nothing of flush or fever in its system, but health and vigor throbbing in its steady pulse; it is full of hope and promise."

Nowhere is this hope and promise better demonstrated than in the cosmopolitan cities near Canada's 5,500km (3,400-mile) border with the United States – from Montréal, with its old-world charm and new-age outlook with massive modern and postmodern skyscrapers alongside gracious red-brick mansions; to Toronto, teeming with street energy, theaters, and ethnic restaurants; to Vancouver, on the far west coast, where individuality is a valued trait, and the pioneer spirit of a young culture pervades every aspect of life.

In between, and north of the big cities, lies some of the most beautiful landscape in the world. There are more than 40 national parks, home to wild birds and grizzly bears, three national marine conservation areas, and 41 rivers totaling more than 10,000km (6,250 miles) in the Canadian Heritage Rivers System. Over half the countryside is forest, and trees soaring to a height of more than 60 meters (200ft) are not uncommon.

Theaters, art, restaurants, breathtaking scenery. Time to put all modesty aside, because Canada has a great deal to shout about. ❑

PRECEDING PAGES: red and gold fall foliage at Mactaquac Provincial Park, Vancouver; Toronto at night. **LEFT:** bungee jumping near Whistler.
ABOVE: a black bear, Ontario; carnival time.

SEARCHING FOR AN IDENTITY

With the history of its peoples spanning thousands of years and a multitude of cultures, the quest for a national identity for Canadians is elusive

For the native peoples, the Canadian identity stretches thousands of years into the past – their search is a struggle to retain elements of their ancient culture. Unlike the far more tangible character of the United States, Canada's identity is more reclusive and subtle.

The sense of antiquity and elusiveness in Canadian culture is perhaps the product of its unusual history. As the late Northrop Frye, a noted Canadian intellectual, once observed, the vast majority of early Canadians (with the exception of its aboriginals) were people who did not wish to be in Canada.

The French, abandoned by France after 1763, were left "high and dry" in Québec; the Scottish and Irish were pushed off their lands through the Highland clearances in the 16th, 17th, and 18th centuries and were shipped to Canada; thousands of Loyalists fled the American Revolution and journeyed to Canada in support of British sovereignty; others found their way to Canada because of poverty and persecution.

> Within each region there are definite qualities that demarcate Prairie folks from Maritimers, Ontarians from Québécois. The Canadian identity is an odd mixture of assertive regionalism and resigned nationalism.

In short, many of the earlier Canadians were fugitives, clinging to their culture and traditional customs, in the hope that they might be able to reproduce in Canada what they had possessed at home. In Canada one experiences echoes of different pasts, all harmonized into a Canadian score.

Multiculturalism

This is not to say that Canada has not had its own particular effect on its inhabitants. The cold, the hostile environment, the bounty of food, the availability of land – all combined to make Canada both a haven and a hell for its first immigrants. Songs, poems, and paintings of early Canada celebrate its compassion and callousness. Yet underlying these themes of survival is the notion of multiculturalism.

From coast to coast, there is no one thing that will mark a person as Canadian except perhaps for the ubiquitous "eh?" everyone seems to use without reservation as in "It's cold outside, eh?" or "The prime minister's not talking any sense these days, eh?"

In 1970, multiculturalism became an official government policy in Canada. The policy was designed to reflect one of the original principles of Confederation: that Canada become a system of coordination among different but equal parts. As a result there is a certain toleration for ethnic and religious plurality (the growing numbers of Sikhs, Hindus, Buddhists, Muslims, and Jews attest to this). Canada's international image is promoted as a "mosaic" not a "melting pot."

As a national ideology, the notion of a mosaic neatly fulfills Champlain's original wishes to found Canada on principles of justice and

group is changing. Until recently, none was a woman or an American Indian. Today, however, Michaëlle Jean is Canada's third female, and first black, governor general; James Bartleman, the lieutenant governor of Ontario from 2002 to 2007, is a member of the Mnjikaning First Nation; and Louise Arbour, a former Supreme Court of Canada justice, went on to a four-year term in 2004 as the UN High Commissioner for Human Rights. The question of a Canadian identity, then, emerges as a complex issue. The questions of "what is my culture?" and "what is my heritage?" surface at one time or another in the lives of all Canadians.

compassion. As an implemented process, however, it falls short of success. John Porter, in his classic *The Vertical Mosaic*, harshly denounced the Canadian mosaic as a highly differentiated, hierarchical structure that forced certain ethnic groups into occupational ghettos. Some critics have claimed that the cultural mosaic has only served to obscure the fact that Canada remains a rigidly class-divided society.

While statistics indicate that the financial, political, and cultural interests in Canada are controlled by a group of just 2,000 people, this

LEFT: shopping in downtown Montréal. **ABOVE LEFT:** Acadian dancers perform at Wedgeport Festival. **ABOVE RIGHT:** a young pioneer.

Native peoples

Perhaps as long as 20,000 years ago, Canada's first inhabitants crossed the Bering Strait to settle the frozen regions of the north. For many millennia, Indian life flourished in Canada. This, however, was drastically altered when European explorers, greedy for the riches of Asia, stumbled across the New World and began to colonize North America. Disease, death by gunfire, and forced settlement severely reduced the number of Canada's aboriginal population.

Comprising a little under 4 percent of the total population, Canada's Indian, Inuit and Métis peoples continue to struggle against policies that seek to stigmatize them as "non-people." Communities of Indians that have been forced to live on reserves find themselves in semi-colonial territories where government handouts, "white" schools, and running water are supposed to be accepted as improvements over a previously primitive way of life.

Visitors to Canada will frequently encounter a certain tragic pathos in the native peoples here. Reserves are often places of substandard living conditions, severe poverty, neglect and a deathly lethargy; cheap hotels and broken-down bars frequently house the inner-city Indian alcoholic or drug addict.

Responding to a renewal of sorts, since the 1970s, natives across Canada celebrate colorful ceremonies and festivals. They are determined to carve out a just existence for themselves in Canada. Powerful leaders have arisen in an attempt to synthesize divergent backgrounds and interests into a unified political entity. Increasingly, Indian groups have pressed for more economically valuable land claims – some, like the Dene, have demanded their own nation – and have made some headway with a government whose patronage has ultimately ghettoized them. The Canadian native peoples have emerged as a force to be reckoned with.

BLACK CANADIANS

Black slavery was first introduced here by the French through a royal mandate issued by Louis XIV in 1689 that permitted Canadians to fully own African slaves.

By 1783, slavery was well established in Lower Canada when around 3,500 Black Loyalists, who had fought for Britain during the American Revolution in return for freedom, fled to what is now Nova Scotia and New Brunswick. Despite the promises, Blacks continued to be denied equal status. Further west, John Graves Simcoe, Upper Canada's first Lieutenant-Governor, proposed a bill in 1793 that led to the eventual abolition of slavery in Canada. This made Canada an attractive destination for many. As news filtered down to the southern states, refugee slaves began the often-dangerous trek via the Underground Railroad, which brought thousands of fugitives *(see page 166)* to Canada. When slaves were legally emancipated throughout the British empire by the Emancipation Act in 1834, the majority of slaves in British North America had already obtained their legal freedom.

By 1960, Blacks accounted for approximately 0.2 percent of Canada's population. With immigration policy reforms in the 1960s, the doors opened to increasing numbers of Blacks from the Caribbean and Africa.

By the 2006 Census, 783,795 Canadians identified themselves as Black, around 2.5 percent of the entire population.

French Canadians

When Jacques Cartier established a settlement along the St Lawrence River at the sites of Hochelaga and Stadacona, little did he know that his fledgling community would become Canada's "black sheep of the family." Abandoned early on by France and reluctantly

> For the French Canadians biculturalism is a matter of being recognized as a founding partner of the nation, and having their children grow up in a French culture.

just about everybody else) would range from stern disapproval to outright hatred. Many English Canadians were capable of showing the same range.

While there are still, perhaps, some places in Québec and the rest of Canada where a few words in the other's language will get stony and silent stares, bicultural relations are steadily improving. Despite the naysayers, by the beginning of the 21st century, a countrywide French immersion program has more than 2 million English-speaking students studying French as a subject in school, and nearly 25 percent of the population of young people

adopted by Britain, French Canada continues to embody a fierce ethnic pride, a distinct cultural identity, and a tenacious traditionalism, especially in rural Québec.

A British-dominated Canada often treated the Québécois demands for cultural autonomy as the cries of a spoilt child. But, like dousing an already well-lit bonfire with gasoline, nothing would aggravate French Canadians more than trivializing the issue of French ethnicity in Canada. As a result, French Canadian attitudes towards *les Anglais* (which was

LEFT: aboriginal dancer performing in traditional colorful costume.
ABOVE: Fort Henry Guard musicians, Kingston.

in the country, aged between 18 and 29, are now bilingual. Between these statistics and the downfall of the separatist PQ in Québec's 2003 election, it would appear that there are many more people in Québec and the rest of Canada who are attempting to understand and respect each other's differences.

Biculturalism overshadows the quest for a cultural mosaic. For the French Canadians it is not just a matter of being a part of the puzzle but rather being recognized as a primary part, as a founding partner of the nation. Québec's separatists lost the 1995 referendum – but by just over one percent of the vote, and the quest for French integrity within Canada is far from being a settled issue.

English, Scottish, and Irish

Canada was once a predominantly "British" nation. The pomp and ceremony of public events, the ubiquitous portraits of the royal family in hallways and antechambers, the presence of a parliamentary government – all are suggestive of an English ancestry.

The history of Anglo-Saxons in Canada is much more piebald in nature than British traditions might acknowledge. In addition to those immigrants who traveled directly from England, Canada received many of its British inhabitants via the United States. Loyalist "Yankees" fleeing the American War

> The Scots in particular are proud of the Macdonald, Mackenzie, and other families who provided the first prime ministers, and dominated banking and railway management as well as the fur and timber trades.

and Scottish are almost everywhere in Canada, whether it be in the opening session of parliament or in a neighborhood pub.

Highland games, Irish folk festivals, and political ceremonies are common sights in each of the provinces.

of Independence entered Canada in droves during the latter part of the 18th century and tipped the scales in favor of an Anglo-dominated population.

English immigrants were joined by Irish refugees (many of whom were victims of the potato famine) who had come across the Atlantic in search of food and employment. Similarly, Scottish immigrants, pushed off their lands to make room for sheep farms, ventured to Canada. The combination of Irish Catholics and Protestant Scots was rarely compatible and riots, usually occurring during one of the annual parades, were common in the19th century.

Today, cultural images of the Irish, English,

A glance across a map of Canada will also reveal that many of the towns and cities have been named after a favorite spot or person in the British Isles: Prince Edward Island, Queen Charlotte Islands, New Glasgow, Oxford, Windsor, Caledonia, Liverpool.

Germans and Scandinavians

Next to the French and British, peoples of Germanic stock were among the earliest European settlers. Germans came to Nova Scotia as early as 1750 and founded the town of Lunenburg in 1753. This tiny metropolis eventually became a thriving center of Maritime shipbuilding. German Loyalists also immigrated to Upper Canada and established a (still-existing) community in a town they named Berlin, which was later changed to Kitchener during World War I, owing to fear of anti-German sentiments.

Swedes, Norwegians, and Finns have also established settlements in the west that have retained their original ethnic flavor. A group of Icelanders fostered the prairie town of Gimli, "a hallway of heaven," and have managed to thrive on the successful commercial production of two Canadian delicacies: goldeye and whitefish.

Ukrainians

The 18th century saw the influx of thousands of Ukrainians – "the people of sheep-

Columbia as miners. Others arrived in the 1880s and were recruited to work in the railway gangs that built the Canadian Pacific. Laboring under duress and in dangerous conditions, many Chinese died in the service of a country that considered them to be less than human. They were soon joined by Japanese, whose sheer endurance and a knack for frugality, enabled them to prosper in the face of racist government policies. And in 1903 the first Sikhs established a large community.

Jealousy of the Chinese success in developing lucrative commercial enterprises led to the Chinese Immigration Act of 1923, which

skin coats" as popular journalism of the time named them. Attracted by free farms in the west and undaunted by prairie fields, the first wave of Ukrainian immigrants settled in Saskatchewan, Manitoba, and Alberta. They were later joined by Polish, Czech, Slovak, and Serbo-Croatian immigrants. Canada has the world's third-largest Ukrainian population after Ukraine and Russia.

The Asians

Abandoning the exhausted goldfields of California, the Chinese first came to British

LEFT: a whale-based business in Victoria.
ABOVE: Brazilian soccer fans celebrate in Montréal.

> Next to French Canadians, Ukrainians have, perhaps, the most vocal and assertive sense of a national identity, and pursue recognition of their ethnic heritage aggressively.

effectively barred the immigration of Asians to Canada until the 1960s when immigration policies were relaxed. Joined by hundreds of thousands of immigrants from South Asia, their sacrifices are rewarded today in small commerce, and they are visible as doctors, lawyers, professors, and engineers. South Asian-Canadians have emerged as a new voice in the debate about ethnic identity. ❑

DECISIVE DATES

THE FIRST CANADIANS

70,000 BC–c.AD 1000

First arrivals are proto-Mongolian peoples, followed by several Indian cultures c.8000 BC, the Inuit in 6000 BC, and Icelandic Vikings, who establish coastal settlements in Newfoundland and Labrador c.AD 1000.

EUROPEAN EXPLORERS

1497

John Cabot arrives on Canada's east coast, believing it to be the northeast coast of Asia.

1534

Explorer Jacques Cartier claims Canada for France.

NEW FRANCE

1608

Samuel de Champlain founds Québec, capital of the colony of New France and establishes a network of trading routes across the interior.

1642

Montréal is founded.

1670

The Hudson's Bay Company, the world's largest fur trading company, is founded. England begins competing with France in North America.

ENGLISH DOMINATION

1713

England conquers Newfoundland, New Brunswick, and Nova Scotia.

1759

Battle for Québec on the Plains of Abraham. New France becomes a British colony.

1775–83

American Revolution results in United Empire Loyalists moving to Québec, Ontario, Nova Scotia, and New Brunswick.

1791

The colony is divided in two: Upper Canada (later Ontario) and Lower Canada (Québec).

1812

The United States begins a decade of skirmishes with Indians, French, and British in Canada, ending in a stalemate.

1840

The Act of Union combines Upper and Lower Canada.

1857

After gold is discovered along the Fraser River, Britain declares British Columbia a colony.

CONFEDERATION

1867

The British North America Act establishes the confederation of Canada. Ontario, Québec, Nova Scotia, and New Brunswick collectively form the Dominion of Canada.

1870

Hudson's Bay Company sells Rupert's Land to Canada, sparking an uprising by the Métis. Manitoba, created from parts of Rupert's Land, joins the confederation. The Northwest Territories are formed.

1871

British Columbia joins the confederation conditional upon forging a permanent rail link to the West Coast.

1873

Prince Edward Island joins the confederation.

1881–6

The Canadian Pacific Railroad

is built, spearheading country-wide settlement.

1905

Alberta and Saskatchewan are created from the Northwest Territories and join the confederation.

WARTIME CONFLICTS

1914–18

Canadian troops support Britain, opening up debate between English and French Canadians on national conscription.

1939–45

World War II; Canadians suffer heavy losses at Dieppe and invade Juno Beach on D-day.

POSTWAR GROWTH

After 1945

A new wave of immigration arrives, as does economic prosperity.

1949

Newfoundland joins the confederation.

1959–62

Two new transport routes stimulate Canada's economy: the St Lawrence Seaway and the Trans-Canada Highway. Toronto emerges as the country's most important industrial center.

CAMPAIGN FOR SEPARATISM

1960

Québec's separation crisis begins with the "Quiet Revolu-

EVERY CANADIAN MUST FIGHT

tion." The Parti Québécois calls for independence from Canada.

1980

In a first referendum, the majority of Québécois decide to remain part of Canada.

1982–92

Canada Act ends British control and the country receives a new constitution. An amendment, the Meech Lake Accord, emphasizing Québec's cultural and linguistic independence, fails to be ratified.

1989

Free Trade Agreement between Canada and the USA (NAFTA) leads to ever-greater prosperity.

1995

Québécois vote to remain part of Canada.

1999

On April 1, the Northwest Territories are divided, creating Nunavut, a self-governing homeland for the Inuit.

2003

A new Liberal government wins a decisive majority victory in Québec. Jean Chrétien resigns as prime minister, handing over to MP Paul Martin.

2005

Paul Martin's Liberal government is ousted, ending more than 12 years of Liberal rule.

2006

Stephen Harper leads the recently formed Conservative Party to victory with a minority government.

2008

In an unpopular election, the Conservative Party wins a second term of minority government. Québec City celebrates its 400th anniversary.

2009

The federal Liberals appoint Michael Ignatieff as their new leader, despite his many years of living outside Canada.

PRECEDING PAGES: Montréal's maritime past. TOP LEFT: Samuel de Champlain, founder of Québec. ABOVE LEFT: immigrants arrive from Europe, 1903. BOTTOM LEFT: Cartier lands in Canada, 1534. RIGHT ABOVE: World War II poster. RIGHT: Québec citizens celebrating independence, 1990.

A NATION IN THE MAKING

The steady population of Canada began around 20,000 years ago with the arrival of the Inuit

The first settlers to arrive in Canada, long before the Europeans, were nomadic bands wandering from Siberia across the Bering Strait. These robust and courageous souls sought a new life in the frozen wilds of northern Alaska and Yukon. They are thought to have arrived some 5,000 to 10,000 years ago. Their reception was not a warm one. Facing bitter temperatures and hostile winds, it is a wonder that they survived in such an unfriendly climate. These first "Canadians" developed a remarkable subsistence technology suited to the brutal environment, and traces of their ancient culture linger. They have come to be known as the Inuit.

The Inuit peoples

The ancestors of contemporary Inuit needed both intelligence and imagination to thrive in their new continent. If one word can describe the theme of life in their culture, it is survival.

> The Inuit spoke Inuktitut, a language with no word for chief or ruler – authority resided within the group. Today, around 27,000 Canadians claim it as their first language.

The Arctic Inuit are noted because of the simplicity of their hunting and cooking utensils. Bows and arrows made with tips of flint, ivory or bone were the main means of catch-

LEFT: portrait of Arctic Inuit Shulainina (left) and Tullauchiu (right). Indians inhabited Canada many years before the arrival of the Europeans.
RIGHT: Chief Duck and the Blackfoot family.

ing the family dinner. They also created special tools to accommodate the seasonal needs of hunting – and many of these practices remain today.

Archeologists celebrate the Inuit for their ingenious winter ice-spears. The spears have tiny feathers or hairs attached to one end, which the hunter holds over a hole in the ice waiting for movement that would indicate the presence of an animal. This often involves sitting over a hole in the freezing cold for several hours at a time.

Food was a major obsession and they hunted seals, walruses, whales, and caribou. Blubber, meat, and fish were staples and always eaten

When natural food supplies ran out, families would move to another area, usually on sleds made of frozen fish or hides – these could be eaten if necessary.

raw (when they are most nutritious). Partially digested lichen found in a caribou's stomach was considered a delicacy and sometimes created a little diversity in a meal.

Inuit are often associated with dome-like snow huts or igloos. Without trees (and therefore timber) the prospects of constructing even

eval Norse Viking hunters in areas around present-day Newfoundland. From 1570 to the 1850s several European expeditions looking for the Northwest Passage also encountered these resourceful people. The Inuit greatly valued the iron they acquired for harpoon points and knife blades.

Existing in a harsh and rugged world, living people needed "luck" to exist in a world full of malevolent spirits – when a person died, their "luck" had run out. As many Inuit will say, even today: "If you knew of the dangers I live through each day, you would understand why I am so fond of laughter."

a simple hut were poor – and snow was a readily available resource. Igloos, dwelling structures that are still constructed on occasion by contemporary Inuit, are made of snow blocks – the result looks much like a ski torque. The house consists of one or two interconnecting rooms. Inside, a platform for sleeping or working stands across from the entrance way; an area for animal carcasses and a heating lamp completes the layout.

Early Inuit spoke Inuktitut, a language with no word for chief or ruler. Theirs was a different understanding of authority. In these nomadic bands the underlying theme was a principle of harmony within a family group.

About AD 1250 the Inuit encountered medi-

West Coast tribes

As people traveled to other parts of Canada and spread into the plains and woodlands, many distinct languages and cultures flourished.

Throughout Canada today, one finds evidence of a remarkably rich and varied Indian history – a cultural heritage that was greatly disturbed through the process of colonization. The West Coast supported several Indian populations; among these were the Kwakiutl, Bella Coola, Nootka, Haidas, Tsimshian, Coast Salish, and Tlingit Indians. These groups found the Pacific Coast to be extremely abundant in natural resources. The sea provided salmon, halibut, and edible kelp and the forests yielded deer, beaver, and bear. The red cedar tree was the source of woven bark capes and hats, baskets, wooden implements, huge canoes, and totem poles.

Unlike the Inuit, the Northwest Coast Indians were able to make extensive use of timber: they are known for their huge dugout canoes, usually stretching to 20 meters (66ft) in length, and their 80-meter (270ft) long wooden clan houses. The ancestral fishing grounds that still lie along the rugged Pacific Coast were the sites of much activity and often a few weeks of hard work yielded enough food for the year.

Given the bounty of food and building materials, Northwest Coast cultures were able

system of trade among tribes – this network was later to become very important to the fur trade in Canada. Nootkas specialized in whale products, while the Haidas mass manufactured ceremonial canoes. The result was a fairly sophisticated practice of interchange.

Not surprisingly, the West Coast Indians show a marked preoccupation with what colonial officials considered to be "private property and material wealth."

Travelers to this area of Canada will undoubtedly hear of the famous potlatches. These were exchange ceremonies given by a chief and his local group to another chief

to devote ample time to the creation of objects. Many of their styles and techniques remain in use today and travelers to the museums and craft reserves note the omnipresence of animals, mythical creatures with protruding canines, and strangely painted human forms. Found on totem poles, houses, canoes, and bowls, the beings, depicted like European crests, became associated with particular family lineages and came to represent rank, wealth, and status.

The material wealth and artistic skills of the Northern Coastal cultures engendered a lively

and his followers. During the ceremony, huge quantities of gifts were given to each guest to assure that they bore witness to all the changes formalized during the ceremonies. Much feasting was followed by lengthy speeches. These celebrations marked a change in the status of a member of the hosting group such as the movement of an inheritor into an inheritance. Frequently, if two men were eligible to inherit one position, a series of rival potlatches were held. These often involved the destruction of valued property by burning or demolition – sometimes the slaying of a slave was a part of the procedure. The potlatches continued until one contester was "broken" financially and relinquished his claim.

LEFT: 19th-century Inuit family in front of their "snow home." **ABOVE:** Champlain's men defeat an Iroquois war party on Lake Champlain, 1609.

Plains tribes

Inhabiting yet another area in Canada's broad geographical milieu were the Plains Indians: the Blackfoot, Cree, Ojibwa, Sarcee, and Assiniboine tribes. Each group possessed a distinctive language so incomprehensible to the other that sign language was used to facilitate trade.

Yet each tribe was bound to the other through their dependency on the buffalo. The buffalo was the nucleus of life. From the buffalo came pemmican (a protein-concentrated food carried by Indians on the trail); skins that were used as blankets, clothes, and tent coverings; and hair that was dried and either woven into rope or used to stuff moccasins.

Before the arrival of the horse in the late 18th century, buffalo were hunted on foot, often by stampeding the beasts into a compound. This procedure, referred to as "buffalo jumping," involved every member of the group – a herd was chased toward an enclosure erected around a pit. One person covered himself with a buf-

> The Blackfoot tribe used to be the great hunters of the Rockies' foothills and prairies. Buffalo then satisfied all their needs, for food, clothing and shelter.

falo hide and imitated the animal's movements in the hope of drawing the herd toward the pit. Once inside the enclosure the buffalo toppled into the pit, was then shot with arrows, butchered, and later eaten. Dependency on the buffalo made the Plains peoples nomadic.

Such mobility demanded a transportable house; it is from this that the origin of the teepee can be traced. A conical-shaped hut with an aperture at the tip for smoke, the teepee was not only practical but sacred. The floor represented the earth of mortal life, and the peak the sky of the gods. The roundness of the tent symbolized the sacred circle of life.

Until the coming of the "White Man" and firearms, Plains people remained fairly loosely organized. Originally the political unit of the band was a leader; when several of these bands united, a council was formed of all the leaders. During trading ventures, wars, and celebrations the council acted as a guiding body.

One of the most famous festivals associated with the Plains Indians was their Sun Dance. A sacred pole was erected to the Great Spirit and offerings tied to it. The bands danced around the stake, recited war deeds, and prayed for guidance in their hunt of the buffalo. Plains youths would perform acts of self-mutilation, one of which involved piercing the chest with skewers tied to the pole with leather thongs, the idea being that self-inflicted torture would arouse the compassion of the Great Spirit.

Woodland tribes

Perhaps the best known, next to the Inuit, of Canada's native peoples are the Indians of the eastern woodlands. As early as 1000 BC eastern

LIVING CONDITIONS

The Jesuits and other explorers vividly describe their horror at the living conditions within the pallisaded compounds. Samuel de Champlain, aghast at what he perceived to be filth and disorder, wrote of the longhouses in which two or three dozen people lived. "The smoke from each fire in the house," he wrote, "circulates at will, causing much eye trouble, to which the natives are so subject that many become blind in their old age." Indian notions of communal sharing and sanitation offended the Europeans yet, despite their lack of "proper sanitation," Indians died of disease in huge numbers only when they became exposed to European viruses.

Canada began to be settled by semi-nomadic tribes. It is here that one discovers the contrasting lifestyles and values of the peaceful Huron, the fierce Iroquois Confederacy, and the entrepreneurial Algonquin.

Like the rest of the Indians of Canada, the people of this area made maximum use of their environment. Distinctive features of their culture were longhouses within pallisaded villages, widespread use of fired pottery, clay smoking pipes, and bundling the bones of the dead for burial. They also cultivated the land and subsisted on staples of squash, beans, sunflower seeds, and maize: the "Three Sisters." It was the

By way of contrast to the Huron, the Iroquois were a fiercer group of people who were more inclined to warfare, and developed a reputation as brutal warriors who would torture and sacrifice their captives. They were the only Indians of Canada to believe in two Great Spirits, one good and the other evil. In Iroquois religion, the two deities were constantly at odds with one another, and their myths are most frequently incidents of clashes between the good and evil gods. Before the arrival of the Europeans the Iroquois had sown the seeds of a great empire: they had developed a unified system of currency *(wampum)* that regulated trade, and

Huron who first met and baffled French missionaries to Canada.

The French discovered a people who demonstrated a partial equality between the sexes and a form of consensus rather than authoritarian government.

Walking through the woods of lower Ontario, it is easy to speculate where buried Huron and Iroquois sites might lie. These Indians chose locations for their villages on the basis of four criteria: access to water, nearness to forests for timber, nearness to rich soil for cultivation, and strategic placement for defense.

While violence was a staple in Iroquois society, the Huron were considered far more peaceful, and the Algonquin embraced a more entrepreneurial approach to life.

they had organized the confederacy for warfare against enemy tribes. Although the history of Canada is in part a history of burgeoning European society, for the Native people it is a tale of exploitation, strife and partial extinction.

Such is the stage setting, so to speak, for the arrival of the first Europeans: a vast land inhabited by highly differentiated Indian groups, each adapted to a particular lifestyle. ❑

LEFT: "Miss One Spot." **ABOVE:** *Indian Encampment,* oil on canvas by Paul Kane, 1845.

VOYAGES OF DISCOVERY

The early explorers dreamed of finding gold and gemstones;
instead they found timber, and waters teeming with fish

The first visitors to encounter Canada after the crossing of the nomadic hunters were the Vikings, whose ancestors had traveled from Norway to Iceland. From Iceland, the Vikings moved westward when Eric the Red discovered and settled Greenland. A fierce and hardy people, the Vikings were great sailors and often took to the seas in search of food and adventure. On one such voyage a seaman, Bjarne Herjolfsen, caught sight of North America and returned home to tell of the unknown land. Around AD 1000, Eric the Red's son, Leif, set out to find the new continent.

The Viking sagas tell of Leif's strange adventures and his discoveries of Helluland (Baffin Island), Markland (Labrador), and Vinland. In 1961 an archeologist, Helge Ingstad, stumbled upon the remains of a Norse settlement in L'Anse aux Meadows and decided that Vinland was probably Newfoundland. One year after the expedition, Leif's brother Thorvald returned to North America hoping to make contact with Vinland's natives. Legends tell of how "Skraelings" attacked Thorvald and his crew with bows and arrows. In other tales the illegitimate daughter of Eric the Red, Freydis the Brave and Cruel, defends the Vikings by rushing towards the Skraelings and frightening them with her wild eyes and gnashing teeth.

Who were the Skraelings? The Viking sagas describe them as dark-skinned people who wore their hair in a strange fashion. Historical anthropologists have speculated that they may have been Algonquins or early Inuit people.

LEFT: the Vikings reached Canada from Iceland around AD 1000. **RIGHT:** Martin Frobisher, the 16th-century explorer, set out in search of the Northwest Passage.

Whoever they were, they prevented the Vikings from establishing permanent settlements on the mainland. It is possible that the Vikings returned to northern Canada. The tall, blond "Copper Eskimos," so named by the explorer Vilhjalmur Stefansson in 1910, have led some to suggest that the early Norse people interbred with the Inuit of Baffin Island.

Cabot and Cartier

The dream of discovering a route across the Atlantic to the spices, jewels, and silks of the Orient became the fantasy of kings and merchants. As improvements in shipbuilding occurred, the dream became a possibility. John Cabot is the first explorer to have "officially" discovered Canada and claimed it for a king. An Italian navigator, Cabot was known for his imaginative flights of fancy and adventuresome spirit. In 1496 he persuaded Henry VII to give him leave to find a route to the Indies and claim it for England. On May 2 1497, Cabot boarded the *Matthew* with 18 men and set sail for the Americas. After 52 weary days at sea, the *Matthew* sighted land – historians are uncertain whether it was Newfoundland, Labrador, Cape Breton or even Prince Edward Island – where Cabot landed on June 24. Cabot claimed the country to be under the sovereignty of Henry VII. But where was all the gold?

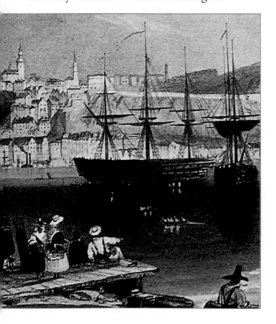

Cabot soon discovered that the soil was extremely fertile and the climate warm and friendly. He was convinced that he had found the northeast coast of Asia; further investigation could only lead him to the precious silks and gems of which he had so often dreamed. Cabot found neither but he did report banks of teeming fish and a great abundance of timber.

Upon Cabot's return, Henry VII, who had wanted gold, was singularly unimpressed with the explorer's tales of fish and paid him £10 for his efforts. In 1498 Cabot was given permission to make a second voyage. He set off from Bristol with five ships manned by 300 crew, never to be heard from again. Many explorers set out after Cabot but were not successful until Jacques

Cartier, who was sent by Francis I of France, ventured to North America in 1534. His expedition marks the origin of French and British competition for its control.

On his first trip, Cartier traveled inland until he found the Gulf of St Lawrence. Assured that the river was a water route to the Orient, Cartier sailed up the St Lawrence until he came to the Iroquois villages of Hochelaga and Stadacona (the sites of modern Montréal and Québec City respectively). Here the Indians were so friendly that he took two back with him to France. Francis I was disappointed but Cartier mollified him by telling the king that he had erected a cross in his name on Gaspé Peninsula, and had called the country New France.

The Arctic expeditions

While the early explorers devoted their time to discovering a new route to the Orient, 50 years after Cartier others became obsessed with the Northwest Passage. One such man was Martin Frobisher. With a reputation as a daredevil, in 1576 Frobisher was sent by Elizabeth I to find an ice-free route to the Americas. Despite Frobisher's inability to produce anything of consequence for British history, he still remains a cherished folk hero. No less than 300 years after Frobisher's voyages, the explorer Charles Francis Hall discovered the relics of a structure Frobisher's crew had built. Hall wrote that in 1861, three centuries later, the native peoples spoke of Frobisher as if he had just visited them.

Henry Hudson was another man drawn to the excitement of exploration. Hoping to open a passage to China, Hudson made several trips to North America, his last one ending tragically. In 1609 the *Discovery* froze in the ice of James Bay. After a long, tense winter, Hudson quarreled with a member of his crew, John Greene, who later led his shipmates into mutiny. Hudson was set adrift in the bay with his son and seven others loyal to him, and was never heard of again.

Following on Hudson's heels in 1631 was Thomas James – after whom James Bay is named – who wrote vividly of his excursions in an account titled *Strange and Dangerous Voyage*. The writings of his log later became the material upon which Coleridge based his poem *The*

LEFT: the early settlement of Québec. **RIGHT:** in 1778 Captain James Cook explored the Pacific Coast in search of a river route through the continent.

Rime of the Ancient Mariner. After James, William Edward Parry, a British naval officer, pushed through the northern icebergs to reach Melville Island in 1819 – he had come the farthest yet.

Perhaps the most heart-wrenching story of all the explorers is that of John Franklin, a Brit-

> The west coast of Canada was yet another site of interest for the ever-curious Europeans attempting to find an easy northern ocean passage to Europe.

ish rear admiral and explorer. In 1819 Franklin was put in charge of an exploration that was to mark out a route from Hudson Bay to the Arctic Ocean. He made a second trip in 1825 after the success of his first voyage and returned to North America a third time in 1845. On his last expedition, Franklin was sure he would find the Northwest Passage. His ships, *Erebus* and *Terror*, were last seen on July 26 1845. Years later a rescue mission discovered their skeletal remains and a diary of the last days of the journey. Franklin, only a few miles from success, had died of exhaustion and exposure.

From 1903–06, Norwegian explorer Roald Amundsen became the first person to successfully traverse the fabled and ever-frozen Northwest Passage in a single ship. After 1909, discouraged by the news of Robert Peary's successful foray to the North Pole, Amundsen turned his attention to Antarctica.

Travelers to the west

In 1778 Captain James Cook landed on Canada's West Coast in the course of his Pacific explorations. Cook volunteered to find a waterway through North America originating in the west but finally had to conclude that it did not exist. George Vancouver followed in 1791–5 and discovered the outlet of the Bella Coola River. Seven weeks later, Alexander Mackenzie, traveling overland, ended up at the same spot.

Such is the early history of Canada. For the Europeans, it yielded neither gold nor gems and was a disappointment. With resignation, the rulers of France and England began to make plans for the colonization of the New World. ❏

RIGHT: exploration and trade: traveling up the West Coast rivers of Canada in search of furs.

THE RISE AND FALL OF NEW FRANCE

The 17th century witnessed the development of a flourishing fur trade, continuing exploration, and bitter differences between settlers and tribes

Colonizing the New World was no easy task for the rulers of Europe in the 17th century. Cold, barren, and unexplored, Canada held little appeal for the people of England, France, and Spain. Those, however, who did venture to Canada encountered a burgeoning system of trade between the Europeans and the Indians and soon realized that the economic potential of settling in Canada was very attractive.

The fur trade

Curious and for the most part friendly, the Indian tribes that met French and British settlers in Canada became enamored of European metalware which, for them, represented a massive technological improvement over their crude stone and wooden utensils. As a result, the Indians developed a dependency on the Europeans – a dependency that was to change their lives.

The Indians never quite understood the "white man's" infatuation with the beaver. However, as the main suppliers to the fur merchants, they received various European-manufactured wares for their pelts.

At first the Indians had little to offer in return for the highly valued knives and axes, and the Europeans complained bitterly of the relative uselessness of the Indians' handcrafted

canoes and snowshoes. By the late 1600s, however, the Indians had begun to trade furs with the settlers, particularly luxury furs. When the hatmakers of Europe obtained beaver pelts from Canada, they engendered a rage for beaver hats, which they claimed were the warmest and most durable in the world. This created an immense and ongoing market for furs in the new colony. The Indians, never quite understanding the "white man's" infatuation with the beaver, became the main suppliers to the fur merchants. By the early 1700s the fur trade in Canada was booming and competition for the monopoly of the fur market in North America had begun.

LEFT: trading pelts for export to meet the demands of European fashion (1758). **RIGHT:** Samuel de Champlain, one of Canada's many progenitors.

Father of Canada

The man who was in many ways responsible for expanding the fur trade in Canada was the French explorer Samuel de Champlain. An idealist with a passion for exploration, Champlain is probably the most frequently cited "Father" of Canada and is often honored because of his wish to found Canada upon principles of justice and compassion.

Acting on behalf of the French monarchy, in 1604 Champlain established the first French colony in North America in Acadia (Nova Scotia). After Acadia, Champlain continued his explorations into the interior of Canada and on July 3 1608, on the site of an old Indian settlement called Stadacona, Champlain founded Québec. Though momentous for Canada's history as a whole, the founding of Québec for him was quite unextraordinary and, as he indicated in his diary, a location he chose more for convenience than historical importance: "When I arrived there [Québec] on July 3 I looked about for a suitable place for our buildings, but I could not find any more convenient or better situated than the point of Québec, so called by the savages, which is filled with nuts and trees... near this is a pleasant river, where formerly Jacques Cartier passed this winter." The "pleasant river" turned out to be the mighty Gulf of St Lawrence, which later became an important passageway for the export of furs to Europe.

The Hurons

One year after Champlain's settlement of Québec, a group of Indians came down from the northwest to trade their pelts with the French. Upon their arrival the Frenchmen were astonished by the appearance of their half-shaven heads and the tufts of hair that grew perpendicularly to their scalps. Likening the Indians' hair to the bristles on the back of an enraged boar (*la hure*), the French called them the Hurons. Thus began a long and tragic relationship.

One of Champlain's main objectives while in Canada was to control the flourishing fur trade and to establish stricter management of the Indians. Already allied with the Hurons, Champlain failed to see that the fur trade was exacerbating already existing hostilities among Indian tribes. Animosities of a ritualistic nature had always existed between the Huron and the Iroquois Confederation. With the fur trade the disputes acquired a mercenary element. When Champlain established an alliance between the French and the Huron, he immediately became the Iroquois' enemy.

While Champlain was organizing settlements and repelling hostile Iroquois, other colonists, mostly men from France, began to appear.

The pioneers

These early settlers, who became known as the *coureurs de bois*, or woodsmen, looked to New France as an escape from a life of drudgery – many had exchanged prison sentences for emigration papers. The *coureurs de bois* became

the backbone of Canada's trading system.

Trapping animals for a living, which involved not only a precarious existence in the bush, but also fighting off Indians, the voyagers were the intrepid entrepreneurs of Canada's early days. By the 1750s Canada had become an economically prosperous investment for France, and Britain began to take a closer look at a country she had virtually ignored for almost half a century.

When Samuel de Champlain and other explorers ventured to Canada in the early 17th century, their plans for the settlement of the new colony, although the dreams of imaginative men, were essentially expressions of the grandiose visions of European monarchs. For them, Canada was merely an addition to the ever-expanding empires of England and France. Canada was a valuable piece of property on the "Monopoly board" that the super powers of the 17th and 18th centuries ruthlessly fought to claim.

But for the others who journeyed to Canada – the farmers and fishermen, the women and children, the missionaries, and even the reckless *coureurs de bois* – Canada was much more than just a geographical acquisition. It was a very real place, empty and enormous. And at times, life was so very hard. On claiming Canada for France, Samuel de Champlain's first

The missionaries arrive

The first missionaries brought to Canada by Champlain were four Récollets, strict Franciscans who enthusiastically plunged into the bush in search of the "heathen savages." The Récollets patiently began to work on saving Indian souls – but with little success. Not long after, the Jesuits were invited to join the Canadian missions, and in 1625 Fathers de Brébeuf and de Noué left France to begin converting the Iroquois and Huron.

The Jesuits, like most Europeans, failed to understand the Indian way of life. Communally oriented, lacking hierarchical structures

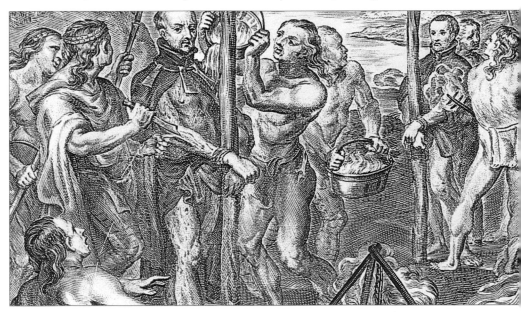

task was to regularize the fur trade. His second task was to set about Christianizing the native population so that the continent could truly become a land made for "the glory and praise of God and France."

The years 1632 to 1652 are often referred to as the "golden years" for the missions in Canada… a somewhat misleading phrase because, although it captures a sense of intense religious activity in Canada during this time, it fails to express the low success rate (in terms of conversions).

LEFT: smallpox threatens a shipload of immigrants.
ABOVE: Jean de Brébeuf, a Jesuit priest who worked among the Huron, is tortured to death by the Iroquois.

> *Samuel de Champlain's infamous Ticonderoga expedition resulted in the massacre of 300 Iroquois – an event that inspired a deep and lasting hatred for the French.*

and methods of authority, openly polytheistic and possessing different concepts of diet and sanitation, the Indians seemed to the Jesuits "barbaric."

Needless to say, the Jesuits were not always welcomed into Indian communities and many of them, given the name of "black robes" by the Iroquois, became symbols of evil and misfortune. Despite their ethnocentric attitudes, some of the Jesuit missionaries were men of great courage. Many suffered horrible deaths and became the first martyrs of Canada. Such is the story of Father Jean de Brébeuf, a Jesuit who worked among the horticultural Huron.

Brébeuf's martyrdom on March 16 1649, was recorded by a contemporary, Christophe Regnault, in *Jesuit Relations*: "The Iroquois came... took our village and seized Father Brébeuf and his companion; and set fire to all the huts. They proceeded to vent their rage on these two fathers, for they took them both and stripped them naked and fastened them each to a post. They tied both their hands and feet together.

the *habitant* the fur traders were as treacherous and vengeful as the despised Iroquois, while the farmer frightened away their game and pushed the *coureur de bois* farther into the wilderness. Although the *coureurs de bois* are often portrayed as the more robust of the two, life for the *habitants* was also very difficult. Clearing the tree-infested lands of the St Lawrence shores demanded arduous labor, crops were slow to start growing, and a year's food could be ruined instantly by bad weather. Wild beasts and hostile Indians were also constant worries.

Early homes in New France were wooden huts crudely built of rough logs; in the winter,

They beat them with a shower of blows from cudgels... there being no part of their body which did not endure this torment."

After Brébeuf's slow and painful death, the Iroquois were so impressed by his fortitude that they ate his heart, believing that by so doing they would become as brave as Brébeuf.

First French Canadians

In the early annals of Canadian history, there were two types of settlers who traveled to the New World: the *coureur de bois* and the *habitant*, the French colonist who settled on the fertile shores of the St Lawrence River and cultivated the land. From the very beginning these two lifestyles were radically different. To

ACADIA AND ACADIANS

Acadia's tiny villages set in the Maritimes became the subject of folktales and poems. Champlain's Acadian village of Grand Pré was immortalized in Henry Wadsworth Longfellow's epic poem *Evangeline*. Of Acadia and Acadians, Longfellow wrote:

Thus dwelt together in love these simple Acadian farmers...

Neither lock had they to their doors, nor bars to their windows

But their dwellings were as open as day and the hearts of the owners;

There the richest was poor and the poorest lived in abundance.

water for the household had to be drawn from a hole in the ice. Soon, however, the wooden shelters gave way to houses built of stone, with steep roofs and large heat-yielding fireplaces. As the forests were cleared, as settlements became towns, and as farmers prospered on their strips of land (called *seigneuries*), families of New

> By the 1630s the settlements of Québec and Montréal had become bustling commercial centers, although still dependent upon the fur resources of Northern Québec and Ontario.

founded schools, hospitals, and even a university (Jesuit College founded in 1636, one year before Harvard). An elaborate system of courts and litigation procedures was implemented.

In 1640 New France had 240 inhabitants – by 1685 the population had swelled to 10,000. Montréal and Québec had become lively and popular colonial capitals. The artist Cornelius Krieghoff, one of the most insightful chroniclers of early Québécois culture, portrays the French Canadians as hardworking but cheerful people.

Extremely fond of their children, the French Canadians socialized mainly through family

France eventually enjoyed higher standards of living than their European counterparts.

For the farmer of early Canada, tenant dues and church tithes were low, no taxes were paid, fertile land was available for the asking, food was bountiful, and everyone possessed the right to hunt and fish. By the 1630s the little settlements of Québec and Montréal had burgeoned into bustling centers of commerce and become bastions of French sovereignty. The French clergy, so unsuccessful among the Indians, had

LEFT: a favorite pastime of the *habitants*, card playing, was strictly forbidden by the Catholic Church.
ABOVE: Cornelius Krieghoff's portrait of the life of a French-Canadian family in the 19th century.

gatherings, card playing, dancing, and drinking parties. (By 1749 drunken horse-driving had become so serious in Québec that a strict law fining inebriated drivers six *livres* – about six dollars – came into effect.) The only ominous presence seems to have been the clergy, who sternly disapproved of dancing, cards, jewelry, and even hair ribbons. In 1700 Bishop Laval furiously chastised Québécois women for their elaborate coiffures and scandalous wardrobes.

Settlements and skirmishes

While the Jesuits continued to proselytize Catholicism, and French colonists resolutely set down roots, Samuel de Champlain and other French officials were faced with the problem of maintaining control over the new colony. Several skirmishes with other governments over territory had already occurred.

In 1627 the notorious Kirke brothers, English adventurers who supported the Huguenot effort in France, blockaded the St Lawrence River for three years and wrested the fur trade from France's charter: The Hundred Associates. At the same time Acadia (Nova Scotia) was claimed for James VI of Scotland by Sir William Alexander. Various disputes ensued until 1632 when Canada and Acadia were restored to France under the Treaty of Saint-Germain-en-Laye.

endeavored to recast French colonial policy by establishing a new administrative system. Colbert sought to make New France a province with a government similar to that of France. To this end he implemented a new structure, which consisted of a governor general, an intendant and a superior council. The Bishop of New France was made a member of the council but was more often than not engaged in bitter argument with the reigning governor.

One of New France's more colorful governors was the Comte de Frontenac, a man of great personal charm who was also extravagant and unscrupulous. From the beginning of his

Government in New France

Bitter complaints about New France were constantly arising from the colonists – one of which was the lack of a central, authoritative government. As a result, in 1647, a council consisting of a governor, the religious superior of the Jesuits, and the governor of Montréal was instituted. Although the council's role was to monitor economic activities in the colony, this model proved inefficient. Consequently New France was officially made a ward of the Crown (under Louis XIV) in 1663.

Two men in particular were instrumental in bringing a strong, centralized government to French Canada. The first was Jean Baptiste Colbert, an ambitious finance minister, who

career, Frontenac set himself in opposition to the most influential clergymen in Canada. He complained that the Jesuits exerted unreasonable control over the colonists. Scandalizing New France by his disrespectful attitude toward them, Frontenac also overlooked the aggressive presence of the British Hudson's Bay Company in the west and underestimated its importance in Canada's future.

Jean Colbert's reorganization of the colony gave New France a firmly centralized government that could efficiently deal with day-to-day problems. Jean Talon, the first intendant of Colbert's model, quickly set about reorganizing the settlement and was able to bring in thousands of new colonists, including women.

Most of the population flocked to three towns: Montréal, Québec and Trois-Rivières. Colbert and Talon hoped that settlers would establish permanency along the St Lawrence, but many traveled inland.

The transient nature of the population was a major obstacle in the settling of New France – Colbert, feeling that mobility was deleterious to French interests, subsequently forbade colonists to leave the central settlement and confined the fur trade to the areas of Montréal, Trois-Rivières and Tadoussac. Colbert's neglect of the western regions merely enabled the British to gain an even firmer foothold in the New World.

Company – the company claimed exclusive trading rights in all territories draining into Hudson Bay.

New France suddenly found herself in an awkward position: to the south were the Dutch and British-supported Iroquois and to the north was the expanding Hudson's Bay Company. Fearful of losing their new colony, New France's militia began to launch expeditions to throw the British out of Hudson Bay.

By the time the 18th century began, hostilities had increased, especially in the east where New England farmers began to covet Acadia. For several years New France was kept active by

Anglo-French rivalry

In the 1660s two malcontent trappers, Médard des Groseilliers and Pierre Radisson, decided they were going to do something about the high costs of hauling furs back to Québec (as ordered by the colonial government) and the exorbitant taxes they were paying on fur pelts. They fled to New England and were escorted to Britain. In London Groseilliers and Radisson persuaded a group of London merchants to assume control over the fur trade in the middle of Canada by forming the Hudson's Bay

> Colbert's neglect of the western regions, together with the formation of the monopolistic Hudson's Bay Company, enabled the British to gain a firmer hold on the New World.

repelling new settlers and engaging its armies in ruthless, devastating raids.

Agreement, however, was reached in 1713 when the Peace Treaty of Utrecht was signed and North America was carved up among the European powers. The French gave up much of their land. Acadia and Hudson Bay were ceded to the British and Article 15 of the treaty recognized British sovereignty over the Iroquois

LEFT: Hudson Bay Trading Store, 1888.
ABOVE: a *calèche* meanders through the frosty streets of modern Québec City.

people and permitted them to trade with western Indians in traditionally French domains.

Years of peace

Despite France's reluctance to honor the treaty, three decades of peace reigned. Canada began to prosper – the fur trade flourished; the population increased from 19,000 in 1713 to 48,000 by 1739; agriculture and fishing blossomed; and lumbering began to develop.

British imperialist economic aspirations, however, soon emerged and fighting broke out between the colonial powers again in 1744. A series of small battles followed until in 1756 a

fleets to North America since it would leave the mother country in a vulnerable position. New France's frontier was long and lightly guarded – how could Montcalm hope to defend it?

The fall of New France

Québec seemed (to both nations) to be the deciding factor in the war. In 1759 a force under General James Wolfe began an advance. Montcalm, relying upon the strategic position of the city atop formidable precipices, let the invaders come to him. After several unsuccessful frontal attacks, one of Wolfe's men suggested that he should try a flank attack. On the

> After 150 years of struggle against the harsh wilderness, New France was abandoned, the old country displaying a cruel lack of enthusiasm for what Voltaire dismissed as quelques arpens de neige – "a few acres of snow."

war was finally declared between France and Britain, which was to prove decisive.

France, characteristically nonchalant in her attitude toward the new colony, sent the Marquis de Montcalm with meager reinforcements to Québec. Lack of soldiers and food supplies made defeat seem almost inevitable. In addition, France did not wish to risk sending her

night of September 12, Wolfe and his troops crossed the St Lawrence River under the cover of darkness and scaled the cliffs. Unprepared, the French repelled the British but panicked and hastily retreated (not knowing that their attackers, too, had panicked and were about to retreat). Wolfe was killed in the exchange and Montcalm was mortally wounded.

After the fall of Québec it was only a matter of time before the rest of New France fell to the British. By 1763, under the Treaty of Paris, France lost her lands in Canada to Britain. ❑

LEFT: the death of General Wolfe at the siege of Québec (1759). **ABOVE:** competing for trade, 1879. **RIGHT:** Wolfe's troops attack the city.

ARRIVAL OF THE BRITISH

While Britain established control over the country,
its attempts to anglicize 70,000 French Canadians
proved somewhat over-ambitious

When Canada was ceded to the British, few tears were shed in France. New France had become a gnawing irritation for French officials, and its removal from France's empire was met more with relief than regret. Britain's victory in Canada began to produce major changes; one such was the shift in control of the fur trade from French hands to British ones. Although glowing from its recent economic advancement in Canada, Britain was still faced with one serious problem: the vast majority of its newly acquired colony were people of foreign descent.

From the first, Britain planned to extirpate French culture from its colony. British colonial officers hoped that American settlers would eventually move into the region and outnumber the nearly 70,000 French Canadians. For the French *habitants* the prospect of cultural defeat only added further to their already traumatized condition – they felt themselves abandoned

> Acutely aware of the rebellious rumblings to the south, Carleton urged Britain to negotiate with the French, else it might find itself faced with continental insurrection.

by France and, although not cruelly treated by Britain, in the hands of an insensitive and arrogant administration.

Britain's attempts to anglicize Québec proved futile. More than 99 percent of the white popula-

tion in Canada were French, and it soon became clear that a compromise with the French was necessary and could be advantageous.

Governor Sir Guy Carleton was one of the administrators who recognized the importance of securing the fidelity of the French Canadians. Under his guidance, the Québec Act 1774, which granted the Québécois cultural, political, and economic protection, was passed. Under the Act, British criminal law was retained but French civil law restored; the Catholic Church retained the right to levy tithes and prosecute the recalcitrant; and Franco-Catholics were no longer excluded from public office.

LEFT: British troops scale the Heights of Abraham, ready to attack Québec.
RIGHT: toe-tapping amusement in 1840.

The American Revolution

Carleton proved to be perspicacious in his treatment of the Québécois for, as American disenchantment with Britain climaxed, it became apparent that French settlers might favor British interests. Carleton's Québec Act, however, only served to accommodate the interests of the *habitants* and consequently alienated and angered British subjects. These tensions were brought to the surface with the advent of the American Revolution. The rebellion itself was, to some extent, engendered by the Québec Act – irritated by the extensions of French-protected trapping regions (which encroached

upon traditionally American lands), the American Continental Congress instituted a plot of revenge against the British in 1775. The first act of the Congress was not to declare independence from Britain but to invade Canada.

In British North America (formerly New France) sentiments about the war were mixed. The intervention of France on the American side briefly raised hopes among the Québécois. British merchants continued to sulk over what they perceived to be a betrayal of their government. The arrival of British regulars, however, in 1776, seemed to convince French and British dissenters alike that to side with Britain would be the most prudent course.

The American Revolution served to cement British rule in Canada in several ways. The relative weakness of the invaders convinced British businessmen that it was in their economic interests to support the imperial struggle.

In Nova Scotia the experience of the American Revolution possessed a more distressing component. Settlers here identified themselves with New England and found themselves caught between contradictory loyalties. In the end the war strengthened ties between Britain and Nova Scotia, again for economic reasons.

Another significant effect of the American Revolution was the influx into Canada of 60,000 United Empire Loyalists, men and women who did not support American grievances. The Loyalists radically altered the composition of Canada's population; their presence created a cultural dualism that contained all the pronounced differences existing between the French and British peoples.

Upper and Lower Canada

The aftermath of the American Revolution brought with it a renewed bitterness among the British over what they perceived to be pro-French policies in the colony. The Loyalists wanted a representative government (something denied by the Québec Act). Carleton, newly named Lord Dorchester, returned to Québec to rectify what was becoming "a delicate situation," the result being the Constitutional Act of 1791.

Under its directives the colony was to have an elected assembly that would exercise legislative authority in conjunction with a legislative council appointed by the king. Most importantly the Constitutional Act divided the St Lawrence Valley into two colonies: one named Upper Canada and the other Lower Canada. This development marked a new dawn in the emergence of French-Anglo rivalries and ushered in another act in the drama of British North America.

After the Revolution, hostilities between the British and Americans flared up in 1812 when American rebels attempted to invade Canada. They were finally routed during the Battle of Queenston Heights. Although Britain lost some of its territories to the fledgling nation, the War of 1812 formalized British North America's right to remain part of the British Empire. ❑

LEFT: Benedict Arnold's attack on the British in Quebec in 1775. **RIGHT:** General Gates leads his army during the American Revolution (1775–83).

CONFEDERATION CANADA

Disenchantment with British rule and rebellions calling
for an elected assembly led to the emergence of
a unified Dominion of Canada

The aftermath of the War of 1812 brought with it a new sense of vigor and self-determination among Canadians. As the economy flourished, Upper Canada settlers began to evaluate the political and economic role of Britain in the colonies. In Lower Canada, similar questions were being raised, although for different reasons: widespread unemployment and growing poverty engendered bitter criticism of the British among French Canadians.

Canadian settlers were mainly disenchanted with the political structure of their colony. Although the Assembly was an elected body, a Council appointed by the king of England held executive powers and frequently overruled resolutions passed in the elected legislature. Frustrated by patronage, corruption, and privilege, Canadians began to call for Responsible Government, in particular an elected Council.

The rebellions

In Québec, the Council, an elite group of wealthy merchant families, called the *Château Clique*, received the brunt of its criticisms from the acerbic Louis-Joseph Papineau, the founder of the Patriote Party. The *patriotes* drew up a list of 92 resolutions and demanded the elimination of the appointed Council.

Britain refused to accommodate their wishes. Eventually pushed beyond the point of polite discussion, the *patriotes* took to the streets in October 1837 and clashed with British soldiers.

LEFT: the radical William Lyon Mackenzie, who campaigned for "Responsible Government" in Upper Canada. **RIGHT:** Sir George Simpson establishes a council to administer British Columbia (1835).

After several deaths, the uprising was quelled and the party was left without a leader when Papineau fled to the United States.

In Upper Canada, the fight for Responsible Government was spearheaded by William Lyon Mackenzie, a fiery Scotsman who was the publisher/editor of a local newspaper. Mackenzie, known for his lacerating attacks against the Family Compact (the name for the appointed Council in Upper Canada), had been elected to the Assembly in 1828 but expelled from it in 1831 for libel.

In 1837 Mackenzie rallied several hundred angry protestors in Montgomery's Tavern on Toronto's Yonge Street. After a few shots of whiskey, discontent began to turn into active dissent and the group of rebels marched toward the government buildings. They were met by a group of 27 armed militiamen. When a colonel shot at the rebel blockade, he was killed by return fire. The mishap so flustered the protestors that they fled in panic, Mackenzie going to the United States.

Britain adopted a severe stance against the rebellions although many Canadians shared the sentiments of the insurgents. When two leaders of the Upper Canada rebellion were hanged, vexation with the British way of governing heightened.

John Ryerson said of the execution: "Very few persons present except the military and rufscruf of the city. The general feeling is total opposition to the execution of these men."

Britain, however, recognized the need to reform the colony's outmoded constitution. A royal commission was established to investigate the problems. The man chosen to direct the inquiry was a politician from one of the wealthiest families in England, Lord Durham, nicknamed "Radical Jack" by his colleagues. A man of dour intensity and a violent temper, Durham was appointed governor general.

Following six short months of investigation,

JOHN A. MACDONALD

Macdonald introduced to Canadians crucial qualifications for a prime minister: wit, articulate attack, and rebuttal. Despite his polished exterior, Macdonald's life was tragically fraught with misfortune. He had married his cousin Isabella Clark, but soon afterwards her health failed. Macdonald's first years as a politician fluctuated between attending heated arguments in the Assembly and returning home at night to watch his wife slowly die. Nine years after Isabella's death, Macdonald married Susan Agnes Bernard. Their daughter Margaret Mary was born with brain damage. Macdonald doted on his daughter, but was scarred by the event for the rest of his life.

Durham returned to England to prepare his report on the "Canada Issue." In the document, Durham complained that the five colonies were stagnating and that in order to exist alongside the dynamic and aggressive United States, Canada would have to develop a viable economy. Such an economy, he believed, could be realized through the unification of the colonies into a single province.

Durham also believed that such a union would relieve the tension between the English and French settlers by drawing the latter into mainstream British culture. French culture (which Durham privately thought was essentially backward), the report explained, had been retarded by French colonial policies.

Despite the glaring ethnocentrism of the report, it did recommend that all citizens be granted Responsible Government. Adopting, but modifying, some of Durham's suggestions, Britain united Canada West and Canada East and awarded each sector equal representation in a new joint legislature. In 1849 the new legislature formed an administration for the Province of Canada (Upper and Lower Canada).

The beginnings of Confederation

The feeling that American or British domination would always threaten Canada while the colonies remained separate geographic units

bring together a coalition of rival parties united on the one issue of Confederation. At the same time similar discussions were also taking place in the Maritime provinces. A conference of provincial ministers was held and in 1867 the British North America Act was passed by Parliament in England, creating a confederated Canada comprising Ontario and Québec (formerly Upper and Lower Canada), New Brunswick, and Nova Scotia under the title "Dominion of Canada" (see page 56).

The unlikely midwife of a unified Canada was Sir John A. Macdonald, a man who had originally opposed the concept of Confed-

pervaded political thought in the 1850s and early 1860s. Confederation, a notion that had been discussed for nearly a century, suddenly reappeared as a viable possibility.

After self-government was achieved, politics became sectional in Upper and Lower Canada. Issues such as the importance of developing an intercolonial railway and the need to acquire new territories were neglected because of conflicting party interests.

Political deadlock finally contrived in 1864 to

FAR LEFT: Scottish-born John A. Macdonald, the dominion's first prime minister, and (LEFT) his wife, Baroness Macdonald. ABOVE LEFT: Louis Riel, hanged for treason. ABOVE RIGHT: Métis rebels on the march.

eration when the Liberal newspaper magnate George Brown had proposed it, but who was to become the dominion's first prime minister. Born in Scotland, in the year of Napoleon's Waterloo, and brought to Kingston, Ontario, when still a small boy, Macdonald was perhaps the most improbable person in public life to nurture a fledgling Canadian territory.

Macdonald, a tall, gangly figure with a careless but stinging sense of humor, didn't seem to fit the mold of a Canadian prime minister. An audacious alcoholic and a bit of a dandy, he lacked the prim reserve of a British politician. But what he lacked in demeanor and appearance, he compensated for through his sharp intelligence and keen powers of insight.

The Dominion of Canada is Born

Throughout the early 1800s the idea of uniting the five British colonies in North America was discussed on both sides of the Atlantic

Unification, it was argued, would not only strengthen the economy, it would provide a solid force against any future aggression by

the United States. A joint legislative Assembly for Upper and Lower Canada had been established in Ottawa in 1849. But rather than tackling major issues, activity centered around petty political bickering. Governments lasted a few months, then a few weeks, until in 1864 political deadlock emerged.

With the American Civil War raging to the south, Canadians were chilled by the prospect of renewed Anglo-American conflict. Confederation seemed to be a timely way to get the colonies going again. In the same year as the deadlock, a coalition of rival parties (the Blues led by George Étienne Cartier, the Conservatives headed by John A. Macdonald, and the Liberals by the powerful newspaper magnate, George Brown) was formed. Their union was based upon a platform of Confederation.

In the Maritimes a similar discussion of uniting the coastal provinces had surfaced. The provinces had called for a conference to draw up a strategy for Confederation, when the governments of Upper and Lower Canada heard of their plans. A delegation consisting of John A. Macdonald, George Brown and six other ministers decided to "crash" the conference and push for their own proposals.

The *Queen Victoria* was chartered in Québec City and, loaded with $13,000-worth of champagne, set sail for Prince Edward Island. Although somewhat disconcerted by the fact that they were met by only one official in an oyster boat, the delegation was able to persuade the Maritime governments that Confederation should include Upper and Lower Canada. The rough terms of Confederation were drawn up at "the great intercolonial drunk" (as one disgusted New Brunswick editorial described it) and received ratification a few weeks later at the Québec Conference.

At the London Conference in London in 1866, final discussions were held with the Colonial Office, (Prince Edward Island and Newfoundland had withdrawn from the talks at the last minute), leading directly to the most important statute in Canadian constitutional history.

On July 1 1867, Confederated Canada became a reality when the British North America Act divided the British Province of Canada into Ontario and Québec (formerly Upper and Lower Canada) and united them with New Brunswick and Nova Scotia. The new nation was called the Dominion of Canada. An extract from the Act read as follows:

Whereas the provinces of Canada, Nova Scotia and New Brunswick have expressed their Desire to be federally united into One Dominion under the Crown of the United Kingdom of Great Britain and Ireland, with a Constitution similar in Principle to that of the United Kingdom;

And whereas such a Union would conduce to the Welfare of the Provinces and Promote the interests of the British Empire;

And whereas on the Establishment of the Union by Authority of Parliament, it is expedient, not only that the Constitution of the Legislative Authority in the Dominion be prepared for, but also that the Nature of the Executive Government therein be declared;

And whereas it is expedient that Provision be made for the eventual Admission into the Union of other parts of British North America. ❑

LEFT: the fathers of Confederation in debate.

The Métis rebellion

Confederation, once approved by London, was not distinguished by a smooth transition. One of the first omens of trouble to come was the acquisition of Rupert's Land from the Hudson's Bay Company for £300,000.

Unwisely, the government regarded the territory as the sole property of the company and neglected to take into account the indigenous population living there, namely the Métis of the Red River Colony. Trouble soon followed. The Métis, who spoke French and practiced Catholicism, were homesteaders who had long thought of themselves as a sovereign but autonomous

Scott (who had been captured by the Métis), had not tried to throttle Louis Riel. Riel had the prisoner court-martialed and shot. Much to Macdonald's dismay, Scott had been a citizen of Ontario; worse, he was a Protestant murdered by a Catholic. Predictably the affair became politically "delicate." It was finally settled when the colony entered the Confederation as the province of Manitoba. Riel fled to the United States. Despite its promises, the Canadian government did not respect the integrity of the Métis community and, over a decade after the first rebellion, Riel returned to begin a second one, this time in Saskatchewan. Eventually captured by

FORT GEORGE, OR ASTORIA, COLUMBIA RIVER.—THE HUDSON'S BAY COMPANY'S ESTABLISHMENT.

nation of neither European nor Indian extraction, but one of both. When Rupert's Land was acquired without their consultation, the Métis organized under the leadership of Louis Riel, a man of charismatic eloquence. They seized Fort Garry, a British outpost, and set up a provisional government. No blood was shed during the insurrection.

Supported by an American fifth column of infantrymen, the Métis were in a strong position and the Macdonald government knew it. Negotiations had commenced and all might have ended peacefully if a young upstart, Thomas

ABOVE: Hudson's Bay trading post. The company's sale of Rupert's Land to the government enraged the Métis.

British troops, Riel was put on trial for treason. Perhaps the blackest stain on Macdonald's otherwise illustrious career was his decision to have Louis Riel hanged. Responding to indignant French cries of opposition, the prime minister remarked: "He shall hang though every dog in Québec should bark in his favor." Riel's death only served to entrench the old, bitter hatred between the French and the English.

The railway scandal

A second slight on Macdonald's political record occurred through the Pacific Railway scandal. By the time a second election was due in Canada, Prince Edward Island, the Prairies, and the Pacific Coast had been added to the Confederation. The problem of connecting the provinces became a major issue in the elections of 1872. A national railway stretching from coast to coast seemed to be the natural solution.

The Canadian Pacific Railway was a project proposed by Macdonald's party and was organized by Sir Hugh Allan, a prominent Montréal shipping magnate. The railway was backed by large American and Scottish investments and Macdonald bluntly told Allan that foreign capital must be eliminated from the project. Allan agreed, but deceived Macdonald by retaining his American partners and keeping them in the background.

Six weeks before the election day, Macdonald found himself desperate for campaign funds; he asked Hugh Allan for support. Mysteriously, $60,000 appeared; another $35,000 soon followed. In a moment of fatal foolhardiness Macdonald wired Allan for a final amount: "I must have another ten thousand. Will be the last time of calling. Do not fail me."

Macdonald's ticket won the election. At the moment of his relief, however, others were planning his demise. The offices of Sir Hugh Allan's solicitor were ransacked, and stolen documents were sold to ministers of Macdonald's rival party, the Liberals, for the sum of $5,000.

The Liberals exposed the scandal: it seemed that Prime Minister Macdonald had given Hugh Allan the Canadian Pacific Railway project in exchange for election funds. Eventually forced to resign, Macdonald left office in disgrace. The railway was later completed, but it would always lack the luster of accomplishment of which Macdonald had dreamed.

The close of a century

When Macdonald left office, the task of shaping Canada's future was taken up by Alexander Mackenzie. Macdonald later returned as prime minister, then others followed: Sir John Abbott, Sir John Thompson, Sir Mackenzie Bowell, Sir Charles Tupper. By 1900 Canada was well on its way as a nation.

Continually facing new challenges and reconciling divergent interests, Canada saw the advent of the 20th century as the beginning of a future of golden promise. ❏

RIGHT: the coming of the railways was – despite this storybook representation – fraught with hardship and scandal, which led to the prime minister's resignation.

TORONTO'S
GRAND SUMMER
CARNIVAL

INDUSTRY INTELLIGENCE INT

JARVIS ST PROMENADE

30th JUNE

SETTLEMENT AND WAR

The Canadian government is obliged to back British war efforts, but the Canadian people are not convinced

A tentative prosperity and progress ushered Canada into the 20th century. Under Prime Minister Wilfrid Laurier's government, railway construction continued apace and by 1914 the Canadian-Pacific extended from one coast to the other. Although diplomatic relations began to be forged with the rest of the world, most international ties were organized through Britain, and Canadians began to grumble about being ruled by a tiny island thousands of miles away. Further resentment erupted over the "Alaska Boundary Fiasco."

To settle a dispute between the US and Canada over the Alaska/Yukon boundary, a commission of three Americans, three Canadians and one British minister was formed. The Americans issued a proposal that was overwhelmingly in their own favor. Lord Alvertone, for Britain,

> To attract immigrants to the country's unpopulated West, advertisements reading "The Last Best West; Homes For Millions; 160-Acre Farms In Western Canada; Free", were distributed throughout Europe.

voted with the US, which was seen by Canada as a betrayal of their interests and further evidence of British duplicity.

Britain was also contributing to the burgeoning influx of Europeans. Canada's immigration policy favored Anglo-Saxon migrants,

---

PRECEDING PAGES: Toronto's Yonge Street, June 1901.
LEFT: celebrating progress and prosperity.
RIGHT: a poster encourages British families to emigrate.

but the influx was not enough and the west, in particular, loomed large and empty.

Laurier's Minister of the Interior, Clifford Sifton, initiated a widespread advertising scheme designed to attract other European settlers to the prairies. The result was the mass migration of Ukrainians, Czechs, Slovaks, Poles, Hungarians, and Serbs to Alberta and Saskatchewan (provinces created in 1905).

Like the French *habitants*, prairie homesteaders faced difficult beginnings. The tough prairie scrub had to be cleared, and soil, dried for thousands of years under a blazing sun, had to be plowed. Winter temperatures, so cold they could freeze human flesh within five seconds, and torrid summers were difficulties offset only by successful harvests. Canada's unique brand of democratic socialism was born of the rugged lives of prairie farmers struggling to survive in the early 20th century. It is from this era that one discovers the roots of populist, radical, and progressive movements in Canadian politics.

Women had a voice, too. Nellie McClung and Emily Murphy led a movement in the famous "Persons Case." The frontier women objected to the chauvinistic interpretation of the "persons clause" in the British North America Act, which specified that "persons" could be nominated to the Senate.

The Canadian parliament understood this to mean men only. McClung's and Murphy's petition was turned down by the Supreme Court but an executive committee in London overruled its decision. As a result, the Senate was opened to both sexes in 1929.

The rise of industrialism

With the development of new businesses and industries, many Canadians experienced radical changes in their lifestyles: for the entrepreneur, commercial development meant assured affluence, but for many others it meant a life of drudgery and exploitation.

In the east, the factory became the oppressive environment of the urban immigrant. Twelve-hour days, six-day weeks, and low wages were standard practices. The hiring of women and children at lower rates of pay was also common.

When questioned by a Labor Commission in 1910 about the appropriateness of brutally whipping six-year-old girls in his textile factory, one Montréal merchant replied that just as training a dog required strict forms of punishment, so, too, did the hiring of children necessitate rigorous discipline. In 1905 David Kissam Young, a writer for the *Industrial Banner*, described the Canadian Factory owners' creed as: "Suffer little children to come unto me; for they pay a bigger profit than men you see." This led to the rise of trade unions and labor organizations. In 1908 Ontario passed the first child-labor law in Canada – the minimum age at which a child could work was 14 years.

World War I

The 1914–18 war in Europe had profound consequences for Canada. Still considered a loyal subject of the British Empire, Canada felt duty-bound to enter the war in support of Britain. The decision was not without its own advantages. When Russian wheat exports were hindered by fighting, Canada became the main agricultural supplier of Britain and its allies. Canadian munitions industries sprang up overnight and fortunes were made. But these economic benefits were gained at the expense of many lives.

Robert Borden was prime minister of Canada for the duration of World War I. His main task was to ensure that Canada found the 500,000 men it had promised in support of Britain.

Efforts to actively support the war in Europe began to pervade Canadian society. Appeals to civic pride were made by political leaders, ministers preached of Christian duty, army officials advertised the glamour of wearing complete highland regalia, and women wore badges reading "Knit or Fight."

Unmoved by loyalty to either France or Britain, French Canadians were reluctant to join the war effort, and Québec inhabitants responded cynically to the government's patriotic propaganda. Tensions eventually led to anti-conscription riots in 1918. In one skirmish, soldiers from Toronto opened fire on crowds in Québec and killed four civilians. Ottawa warned that future rioters would be conscripted on the spot.

On August 18 1918, Canadian and Australian troops broke through a German battalion near Amiens. The German soldiers were pushed farther back until the final day at Mons on November 11 when the German army was defeated. By the time the war was over, Canada had lost 60,611 lives – thousands of others returned home severely and permanently mutilated, both physically and mentally.

> To mirror glamorous silent film stars, women shed several pounds of clothing, cut their hair and fought for new gender identities.

Like Americans, Canadians were thrilled by the glamorous Toronto-born Mary Pickford and flocked to see Douglas Fairbanks and Rudolph Valentino in their latest silent films: but Canada was still a land of small towns. As such, it bolstered a small-town conservative attitude – an attitude given a literary form in Stephen Leacock's *Sunshine Sketches* (1914).

There were new Canadian directions to be taken as well, early in the century. In the arts, the Group of Seven created a stunning but scandalously different visual image of the Canadian landscape. Using the techniques of Cézanne, the Impressionists, and art nouveau, Lawren

The purring Twenties

If the 1920s roared in the United States, they at least purred in Canada. In the States, a modern equivalent of the Inquisition, the Big Red Scare, swept across the country and sought to purge America of any "suspected or real communists." The movement never made any serious headway in Canada. Radical parties in the prairies, union organizers, and the handful of self-avowed communists experienced mild to severe harassment, but Canada lacked the fanatic allegiance to "democracy" of the US.

FAR LEFT: registering immigrants.
ABOVE: around 105,000 Canadian soldiers lost their lives in World Wars I and II.

Harris, A.Y. Jackson, Arthur Lismer, Frederick Varley, J.E.H. MacDonald, Franklin Carmichael, and Frank Johnston re-explored Canada as bold iconoclasts – their works distinguished Canada internationally and had a lingering effect on the country's visual arts for many decades.

Grain drain

When the Depression hit Canada in 1929, it hit hard, exacerbated by the collapse of the world grain market – a wheat glut had made it more economical for Canada's clients to buy from Argentina, Australia or the Soviet Union.

R.B. Bennett's Conservative government quickly rallied to address the problems of a faltering economy. Relief programs and social services (which became expert at detecting "fraud and waste") were swiftly established. Callous in their lack of understanding of the hardship the Depression caused, politicians claimed that "jobs were there to be found," and they created work camps in British Columbia for single men. Hundreds of workers either froze to death on the trains or were murdered on their way to find work. Those who made it to the camps were paid 20 cents a day. In Toronto, a team of men would shovel snow from the driveway of a wealthy Rosedale family for seven hours, only to be paid 5 cents. However, widespread unemployment sent men

to become Canada's socialist party, the NDP (New Democratic Party).

As the Depression deepened throughout Canada, radio sets became the main means of escape and, in what the government claimed was an attempt to allay the misery of millions, the Canadian Radio Broadcasting Commission was set up. Sports events, radio dramas, the lively commentaries of Gordon Sinclair, and reporting of events such as the Dionne quintuplets born in Calendar, Ontario, served as diversions for many Canadians. When the Depression ended, a decade of hardship had produced a thrifty generation.

and women into the streets, and nowhere was destitution greater than on the prairies. Out west it seemed as if the forces of nature had collaborated with the vagaries of the economy to make life as miserable as possible. In 1931 raging winds swept away the fertile topsoil; in 1932 a plague of grasshoppers devoured the crops; and 1933 marked the beginning of a series of droughts, hailstorms, and early frosts. Even Newfoundland, barely surviving itself, sent prairie families dried cod cakes. (Not sure what to make of the cod, some westerners used it to plug up holes in their roofs.)

Prairie hardship influenced the development of the Cooperative Commonwealth Federation (CCF), a farmers' labor movement that was later

World War II

Just days before Britain declared war on Germany, the pervading mood throughout Canadian society was a belief that the war would just go away. But on September 3 1939, Canadians had their heads pulled out of the sand. Newspaper headlines this time read: "British Empire At War – His Majesty Calls To Britons At Home And Overseas."

Canada's involvement was complicated by the fact that in 1931 the Statute of Westminster had made it an autonomous community within the British Empire. Legally Canada could remain out of the war – but morally there seemed to be no alternative but to enter it.

In French Canada the politician Maurice

Duplessis challenged the government's right to speak for *all* of the people of Canada. Québec, Duplessis argued, ought to remain independent of any European struggles. Then, in the spring of 1940, when the German *blitzkrieg* began, Duplessis' calls for neutrality were lost amid the scrambling of French Canadians to register for overseas service.

Prime Minister Mackenzie King maintained support for the war by promising that conscription would never be thrust upon them. Soon the country was spending $12 million a day on the war effort; by 1943, 1.5 million were employed to work in munitions factories.

the draft; in its ranks was the young Pierre Elliott Trudeau, later to become one of Canada's most popular prime ministers. Fortunately for King, it was not necessary to conscript soldiers until the final months of the war. In 1942 in Dieppe it was mostly Canadian men who suffered the huge losses of that debacle and on D-Day, under the banner of "Allies," it was the

> *The Québécois voted against conscription and a fierce nationalist movement rose up to resist the draft.*

When Japan attacked Pearl Harbor in 1941, Canada, in recognition of the growing bonds being forged between itself and the US, promptly declared war on Japan.

As the war raged on, Britain began to experience severe manpower problems. King decided to see if the Canadian people would agree to conscription, through a national plebiscite. The majority of voters agreed, but the vast majority of Québécois voted against conscription and a fierce nationalist movement rose up to resist

Canadians who landed at Juno Beach. By the time the fighting was over, Canada had lost 45,000 lives. The troops had fought bravely and had played a vital role in the war's deciding battles. But like other nations, Canada's record was not unblemished. Using the pretext that angry neighbors might harm Japanese Canadians, the government had interned 15,000 in camps and had auctioned off their property.

Under Minister of Justice Ernest Lapointe, Canada refused to admit all but a few Jewish refugees, both during and after the war. With these blots to its copybook, and with a returning army of displaced and tired soldiers, the Canadian nation set about the task of building a new future. ❑

LEFT: settlers travel west on the Canadian-Pacific (1915). **ABOVE:** the Depression, compounded by freak weather conditions, almost destroyed life on the prairie homesteads in the 1930s.

LE DEVOIR

FAIS CE QUE DOIS

Rédacteur en chef : Omer HEROUX

MONTREAL, VENDREDI, 1er JUILLET 1949

Directeur : Gérard FILION

...UME LX — No 151

S. Gall, évêque.

BEAU ET CHAUD 67

Minimum 83

FIN DE LA GRÈVE DE L'AMIANT

Augmentation de 10 cts; pas de représailles

L'entente a été signée tôt ce matin après une assemblée des grévistes — Le juge Thomas Tremblay présidera le tribunal d'arbitrage — Le retour à l'ordre d'ancienneté sera respecté — Le retour au travail débutera demain pour se continuer au travail à mesure que la production l'exigera — ... à mesure de MM. Picard et Foster

SON EXC. MGR ROY

Les instituteurs sont en faveur subsides fédéraux à l'éduc...

À la condition que soit respectée l'autonomie provinciale

Recherches interrompues à Val-d'Or

POSTWAR PROSPERITY

The conclusion of World War II left Canada in a position of relative strength and its standard of living soared

World War II, along with integrating Canada's investment and trading systems into the North American grid, had brought to new levels of success the old "National Policy" of Sir John A. Macdonald. Central Canada's industrial wealth was promoted, through federal policy, by harnessing the resources of the country's region. The result was a spectacular continent-wide prosperity. And in 1949, Canada welcomed its tenth province into the Confederation: Newfoundland.

At the same time, the federal government's power increased to historic highs. Armed with taxing and spending powers gained from the provinces during the crisis of the war, the Liberal government of Mackenzie King laid the foundations of the Canadian welfare state. Old-age pensions were increased, unemployment insurance was expanded, and federal-provincial welfare programs grew rapidly.

Throughout the 1950s, with a population of just over 14 million, the basics of Canadian

The face of Canada began to change as its population grew by 50 percent between 1946 and 1961, transforming bland cities into multi-cultural mosaics.

public life remained stable. A seemingly permanent Liberal government in Ottawa, now under the stewardship of Québec's Louis St-Laurent, continued to win elections with a coalition

LEFT: industrial disputes such as this one in 1949 were a feature of development.
RIGHT: Prime Minister, Lester Pearson.

anchored in Québec and the west. US investment combined with Canadian enterprise to expand industry and resource sectors rapidly. Future Prime Minister Lester Pearson levered Canada's international status to give it a voice in international bodies such as the United Nations. His proposal for the first use of UN peacekeeping troops – the now familiar "blue helmets" of the world's hot spots – in the 1956 Suez Crisis, won him the Nobel Peace Prize.

Powerful forces were reshaping Canadian society. The population increased by 50 percent between 1946 and 1961, to 18 million people, with 2 million coming in the greatest immigration in the nation's history. The face of urban

Canada began to change, as Mediterraneans and Eastern Europeans transformed dull cities. The country became one of the world's most urbanized nations, with 77 percent of Canadians living in towns by 1961. Television and other mass-communications, mass-merchandising, and suburbanization were accelerating social and cultural mobility, and women's roles were changing, with an increase in female participation in the workforce.

The political and cultural upheavals of the 1960s were pre-figured by the upset victory of John Diefenbaker's Progressive Conservatives in 1957. His minority-government election, based

on eroding Liberal support in urban Ontario and the west, became a majority triumph a year later, when Québec's right-wing provincial government delivered the province to Diefenbaker, creating a national landslide. Although Diefenbaker's period in office, which lasted until 1963, was unable to reorder the political dynamics of Canada, it was a harbinger of an accelerating transformation.

The Quiet Revolution

In 1960, a pivotal provincial election in Québec brought to power a new Liberal government with a new vision of the province.

For decades, Québec's political development had followed its own path, in many respects separate from the currents of change afoot throughout the western world. The pillars of Québec society – a parochial government, a powerful Catholic Church, and a dominant Anglo-Saxon business elite – were to be dramatically transformed in what became known as *la révolution tranquille*. With the slogan, "*maîtres chez nous*" (masters in our own house), the government of Jean Lesage transferred responsibility for the health and education systems from the church to the provincial government, and promoted the development of a French-speaking state sector as a competitor to the Anglo business establishment. The social energies released by the Quiet Revolution ran in two opposing directions, both with deep roots in Québec's political tradition. Some sought to parlay Québec's self-assertion into a greater role in national politics, to bring "French Power" to the federal government in order to secure for Québec all of the benefits of modern Canada rising around it. Montréal intellectual Pierre Trudeau, who abhorred what he saw as the inward-looking character of Québec nationalism, would become the exemplar of this current. Others saw Canadian federalism as incapable of responding to Québec's unique imperatives of cultural survival, and sought to fulfill Québec's aspirations through the growth of a separate nation-state.

The separatist movement

The separatist movement began among radical intellectuals and traditionalist folk singers, but would gain credibility as more powerful adherents joined, most notably René Lévesque, who had a been a minister in the Lesage government and would become the first separatist premier of Québec from 1976 to 1983. This crystallization of the federalist and separatist tendencies in Québec politics dominates the life of the province to this day.

The growing assertiveness of Québec clashed with the increasing activism of the federal government, Liberal once again under Lester Pearson from 1963 to 1968 and ambitious to continue building the welfare state through such initiatives as a national medicare system. Perhaps the greatest boon to Canadian prosperity was in 1965 when Canada and the US signed the Auto Pact allowing free trade in automobiles and parts.

Québec's social ferment was probably more politicized than that of the rest of Canada during the early 1960s. Through much of the decade, English-speaking Canada – along with the United States – reveled in sustained prosperity and a growing sense of sophisticated modernity. This culminated in two events: 1967's World's Fair in Montréal at which a 100-year-old Canada played host to an approving world; and, in 1968, the election as prime minister of the urbane, even hip, Montréal intellectual, Pierre Trudeau. Simultaneously, the current of philosophical discontent found fertile ground in Canada – from student radicalism to the sexual

federal government responded, at the request of Québec's provincial government, by imposing the War Measures Act – a move widely supported at the time and seemingly vindicated when Laporte was found murdered, but since believed by many to have been a panicked overreaction. The episode concluded with the release of Cross

> In the 1970s the rising oil- and gas-rich western provinces began to challenge the federal government's national policies and its preference for central Canadian industry.

revolution, widespread divorce, and the awakening of feminism.

The key popular-music figures of the period in Canada were singer-songwriters such as Joni Mitchell, Leonard Cohen, and Neil Young; not as loud as their contemporaries in the US – Jimi Hendrix or Janis Joplin for example – but certainly more reflective.

As elsewhere, the ferment culminated in tragedy when radical separatists, the *Front de la Libération du Québec*, kidnapped a British diplomat, James Cross, and Québec's Minister of Labor, Pierre Laporte in October, 1970. The

LEFT: Pierre Trudeau led the nation, while his wife Margaret (**ABOVE**) created national scandal.

and flight of the terrorists to Cuba. Throughout Canada there was a genuine sense of innocence lost as the legacy of the "October Crisis."

The cracks widen

The 1970s were a pivotal decade for Canada. Backdropped by "stagflation" (low growth, high inflation, and unemployment), politicians and pundits argued such topics as "the limits of growth," the "revolution of rising expectations," and Trudeau's aggrandizement of the state, while public tastes rummaged furiously through a wild assortment of fads. The national longing for the Big Time was bizarrely fulfilled when Margaret Trudeau, the Prime Minister's wife, abandoned her first-lady role for a life of frolic with the likes of Keith Richards and the environs of New York's Studio 54.

Three crucial events shaped and echoed this sense of dislocation, cracking the basic pattern of Canada's national life and threatening her very existence. The first was the oil shock of 1973, and the end of the "Long Boom" that had transformed the country and the world in the postwar years. The Canadian economy slowed through the 1970s, distorted by double-digit inflation. Chronic unemployment began. Taxes continued to rise, as did spending, but a gap began to appear between the government's revenues and expenditures, which continued to

was elected on a good government platform that downplayed separatism, Lévesque pressed ahead with a province-wide referendum in May 1980. The result seemed conclusive: 41 percent of voters cast a *Oui* ballot and 50 percent said *Non* to the government's request for a mandate to negotiate separatism.

Prime Minister Trudeau campaigned actively in the referendum contest. His promise took the form of a crusade to "repatriate" the Canadian Constitution so that it could be amended without British consent, and to add to it a Charter of Rights and Freedoms. This proposal carried considerable support, and Trudeau used it to

widen until Paul Martin, as minister of finance, introduced cost-cutting policies to eliminate the country's chronic fiscal deficit. In time, federal-provincial politics became a contest over who could shift the blame for declining service levels and chronic budgetary deficits.

The second critical development came with the oil shock. The rise of western Canada, for generations an economic hinterland, fundamentally altered the nation's politics. Oil and gas-rich western provinces began to join with a still-more-assertive Québec in a drive to transfer powers to the provincial governments.

The third key event was the election in 1976 of a separatist Parti Québécois (PQ) government in Québec under René Lévesque. While the PQ

fashion a Constitution Act that was proclaimed in 1982, over the angry protests of Québec.

On his resignation in 1984, despite some important achievements in his 16 years of power, Trudeau's desired legacy of a strong federal government with a united country seemed farther away than ever. Federal-provincial relations were rancorous, westerners increasingly alienated from national affairs, and Québec sullen over its exclusion from the constitutional deal. Moreover, the Canadian economy had stagnated badly.

Prosperity and provincialism

The disastrous financial performance of the last Trudeau government was largely due to the recession that rocked the Canadian economy in

1981 and 1982. With unemployment reaching 11 percent, English Canada turned to the Progressive Conservatives under their new leader, Québécois Brian Mulroney. The result was the greatest federal election victory in Canadian history, with 211 out of 295 seats in the House of Commons going Conservative. The 1980s boom allowed Mulroney greater scope to tackle Canada's deficits.

For most of the country, the classic images of the 1980s were smart cars, chic restaurants and soaring property values. But for many Canadians the boom never really happened. Unemployment remained considerable, rural and Atlantic

a 168-seat majority for the Tories. Although it never became a campaign issue in 1988, many Canadians were now growing insecure with Mulroney's Québec policy. His promise to amend the constitution had been, it seemed, fulfilled in the April 1987 Constitutional Accord signed at Meech Lake in Québec.

At Meech Lake, all 10 premiers and the federal government had agreed to amend the constitution to meet five specific demands of Québec, including legal recognition of the province as a "distinct society." But trouble arose because women feared their rights would be compromised. Natives complained that their consti-

> Mulroney promised Québec constitiutional amendments to allow it to "re-enter the Canadian family with honor."

tutional issues had been ignored and recent immigrants worried that their rights would be undermined. Then, in 1989, Premier Bourassa bowed to separatist pressures in Québec and introduced a law banning the use of English on signs. This was a catalytic event in crystallizing English Canadians' opposition to the Accord.

Canada stayed in decline, and in the cities, homeless people became a feature of urban life.

Optimism was sufficient, however, for the Mulroney Government to win re-election on a platform of free trade with the US, securing

A new deal for the nineties

If the brinkmanship and back-room deals of the Meech Lake process soured the national mood, the economic events of 1990 curdled it. A recession longer and deeper than any since the Great Depression engulfed the country's economy. Unemployment soared to 11 percent, property values tumbled and businesses folded.

LEFT: René Lévesque, Premier-elect, 1976.
ABOVE LEFT: Lévesque casts his vote at the ballot box.
ABOVE RIGHT: the use of the English language on outdoor signs in Québec was banned in 1989.

In this troubled context, Québec reacted angrily to the failure of the Meech Lake Accord. Premier Bourassa embarked on a two-year review of Québec's political options, including separation. Slowly, however, the elements of a new deal emerged, to include: replacing the appointed Senate with an elected body, modifying five of Québec's Meech Lake demands, reconfirming the rights of immigrants and women, and self-government for natives. This ambitious project culminated in a second Accord, in August of 1992 at Charlottetown, P.E.I. To pass, the Accord needed majority support in a national referendum from all provinces. Six provinces

the Bloc Québécois. Although a Québécois, Jean Chrétien underestimated the strength of the separatist movement and was shocked when, in a 1995 referendum, the proposal to grant Québec independence was defeated by a margin of 1.12 percent.

Federally, Chrétien and his Liberal Party were re-elected in 1997, and again in 2000, while the right-wing Canadian Alliance – which in 2003 merged with the Progressive Conservatives to become the Conservative Party of Canada – remained the official Opposition. With a mutiny within the Liberals' rank and file becoming more imminent, Chrétien

passed it; four, including Québec, rejected it. In the wake of the defeat, all talk of constitutional amendment was abandoned, and Brian Mulroney resigned.

His successor, Kim Campbell, went on to lead the party into another general election after just four months as leader. Her defeat, which left the Progressive Conservatives with just two seats instead of 153, entered the record books as the worst ever suffered by a ruling party.

The Liberals, under Jean Chrétien, took power, with the separatist Bloc Québécois the second-largest party. The result boosted the fortunes of Lucien Bouchard, a former Progressive Conservative minister who had quit over the failure of Meech Lake and founded

SOCIAL ISSUES

Canada has managed to remain reasonably steadfast in its liberal approach to social issues. Those who are terminally or chronically ill have been allowed to use medical marijuana since 2001. In July 2005, the Civil Marriage Act, which legitimized same-sex marriages countrywide, was introduced by Paul Martin's Liberal government, and passed. And in June 2008, Stephen Harper apologized in the House of Commons to former students of native residential schools for the wrongful policy of assimilation that had been run by a federally financed program – one that had a deeply damaging impact on First Nations, Métis and Inuit peoples – until as recently as 1996.

resigned at the end of 2003, and was replaced by Paul Martin, his minister of finance for many years. Martin's reign was brought down – by a sponsorship scandal that revolved around promoting federalism in Québec – in the 2006 election. The Conservative Party, led by Stephen Harper, won with a minority government that included significant gains in Québec. Martin was replaced as the Liberal leader by Stéphane Dion, a former academic whose passion for "green" policies never won over his party or the country.

Through much of 2008, Canadians were entertained – or appalled – by various political

Divided we stand

If there is a cause for optimism in assessing Canada's political and economic prospects, it probably lies in the country's historic ability to muddle through. As one commentator pointed out, the 1995 vote in Québec was in its way a vindication of the country's strong democracy since, in 90 percent of the world's countries,

> Building a prosperous, humane society on such unpromising ground was a formidable achievement.

shenanigans. These included the machinations by leadership aspirants within the Liberal party, and an unpopular general election in October won again by a minority Conservative government, followed in a matter of weeks by an unprecedented suspension of Parliament called by Stephen Harper, to avoid a non-confidence vote on the government's economic plans. Two months later, Parliament resumed in January 2009, and Michael Ignatieff was finally ratified as the Liberal leader, and therefore of the Opposition, in May.

LEFT: animal activists protest against the slaughter of seals. **ABOVE:** Prime Minister Stephen Harper meets Queen Elizabeth II and Prince Philip.

the leaders of such a forceful secessionist movement would have ended up in jail. Moreover, the last two recessions have taught Canadians some painful lessons about taking prosperity for granted. Those who wish the country to remain together in the future have at their disposal some powerful economic arguments. For the rest of the world, the drama seems baffling. Why should Canadians be putting at risk what is an enviable prosperity? But the forces that tug at Canada's unity are, after all, part of the nation's heritage. Building a prosperous, humane society on the unpromising ground once described by Voltaire as *quelques arpents de neige* ("a few acres of snow") was a formidable achievement, and one that won't lightly be discarded. ❏

NEW ARCHITECTURAL HEIGHTS

Today, Canada stands at the forefront of modern architecture and its architects are sought after the world over for their flair and expertise

From the log cabins of the frontiersmen to the vibrant skyline of modern Toronto, Canada has an eclectic array of architectural styles. In the early days of colonization, settlers simply built replicas of their home-country buildings. The French, for instance, erected the simple stone houses they had been familiar with in Normandy, while the Ukrainians constructed onion-domed churches across Manitoba.

Architects – sometimes military engineers – drew on their own design heritage and by the late 19th century a form of building etiquette had evolved: parliament buildings and churches tended to be designed in the Gothic style, banks and railway stations were Classical, legislative buildings looked to the Renaissance, the French chateau-style was reserved for hotels, while houses, particularly in the Atlantic provinces, drew on English Georgian influences.

Futuristic Design

As the 20th century progressed, Canadian design began to take on its own distinct identity. Montréal's Expo '67, with Moshe Safdie's "Habitat" of stacked dwellings, and the 1976 Montréal Olympics, characterized by Roger Taillibert's circular stadium, attracted international recognition.

Since then the country hasn't been afraid to commission buildings on a large scale, and a number of influential architects have emerged including Moshe Safdie (National Gallery of Canada, Ottawa), Douglas Cardinal (Musée Canadien des Civilisations, Hull, Québec), Patricia and John Patkau (Canadian Clay and Glass Gallery, Kitchener, Ontario), and in the Maritime provinces Brian MacKay-Lyons is making an impact with his designs for urban living.

LEFT: sculpture at the Simon Fraser University, Vancouver.

ABOVE: many of the world's significant architects have contributed to Toronto's skyline, including Frank Gehry and I.M. Pei.

BELOW: the Esplanade Riel is a pedestrianized bridge spanning the Red River in Winnipeg. Have lunch at the Salisbury House restaurant, located on the bridge.

STYLE MAKER OF THE MUSEUMS

For an architect who was asked to withdraw from his architectural studies at the University of British Columbia, partly because his designs were thought too radical, Douglas Cardinal has not done too badly. He now ranks among the world's top practitioners.

After graduating with honors from the University of Texas in the 1960s, Cardinal practiced in his home town of Red Deer, Alberta, and then in Edmonton, pioneering the use of the computer in structural calculations with his award-winning St Mary's Church, and gradually gaining recognition for his distinctive approach.

In 1983 he won the prestigious commission to build the Musée Canadien des Civilisations in Hull, Québec *(pictured above)* to house the nation's collection of native artifacts.

Combining both nature and technology, Cardinal describes the museum's curving shape as symbolizing the emergence of a continent sculpted by winds, rivers, and glaciers.

Following on from the success of this project, Douglas Cardinal Architects went on to design the Smithsonian's National Museum of the American Indian, in the heart of Washington DC.

ABOVE: the Edmundston-Madawaska steel bridge, in New Brunswick, connects Canada with Maine in the US.

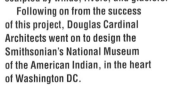

LEFT: a traditional hunting and fishing lodge on Tagish Lake, British Columbia.

RIGHT: the neo-Classical City Hall in Kingston, erected in 1843, pays due homage to an illustrious past.

THE FRENCH AND THE ENGLISH

Historically, the relationship between the French- and English-speaking peoples has been uneasy, if not explosive. But bridges are being built across the cultural divide

Eight hundred kilometers (500 miles) separate Québec City from Toronto. Situated between these two cities are cosmopolitan Montréal and Loyalist Kingston; in between these two cultural focal points lie 300 years of Canadian history, tradition, and circumstance. Québec City is archetypically French, politically resistant, insular, its visual splendor and old worldliness reminding one of Europe, of the ancient towns in Normandy or along the Rhine. Toronto is both typically English Canadian and North American. The city serves as an economic center for the entire country. Everything from its skyline, waterfront and endless suburban sprawl to its professional baseball team locates Toronto squarely in the mode of a North American urban center. These two cities share in common a vast country called Canada. But what else do they share? One city communicates in French, the other in English. One city looks to France for its cultural heritage and for much of its music, film, and literature. The other city combines the vestiges of British custom, an indigenous literary community, with strong leanings toward American popular culture.

The Confederation of Canada in 1867 did not guarantee that these two worlds would unite. Economically, Québec and English Canada do communicate on a regular basis. The St Lawrence Seaway, the Trans-Canada Highway, the tourist charms of Montréal and Québec City serve to maintain a steady flow of traffic between the two communities. Economic ties, along with political commitments (through the federal government in Ottawa), remain strong. Canada is a country – a viable and functioning nation noted for its size and natural wealth. Yet a fragmentation exists. Once beyond economic

and political considerations, the ties between the French and English grow more tenuous, more problematic. Eventually a difficult question must be asked; culturally, spiritually, what do these two worlds share in common?

The weight of history

Any understanding of French-English relations today must begin deep in North America's past. The weight of history was upon the New World from its inception. North America was a battleground for the English and French to wage imperial war. In Canada, the French arrivals tended to settle along the banks of the St Lawrence, in the area now known as Québec, with the English establishing themselves farther inland, initially in the Great Lakes region. By the 1750s, less than 100 years after the first influx of population, the lines were already drawn between French and English areas. With the rapid growth of the English community to the south, which was soon to be called the United States of America, the French were in a very real way already isolated and defeated.

The population of New France was less than a tenth of that of the English colonies. From the very beginning, the French in North America were a visible minority. What consolation they found derived largely from the "safety net" of mother France, watching over their interests. After 1759, however, this too disappeared. The subsequent English military possession of Québec virtually ruled out hope of reconciliation between the two communities.

What Confederation gave Québec was a political framework for change – the provincial government. The decentralized nature of the agreement, allotting considerable power to each province, should have provided the Québécois with a means to reassert themselves. For many reasons this did not really happen for almost 100 years. The seeds were planted, however, the very same day the country was born.

English bosses

The first half of the 20th century saw little overt change in the situation. English Canada expanded, solidified its borders, with Ontario coming quickly to dominate the economic scene. Naturally the markets of Montréal and Québec City were worth preserving. Statistic after statistic from this period suggests basic problems: companies located in Québec with an entirely French-speaking work staff but entirely English-speaking management; blatant instances of discrimination against French-Canadians; English-Canadian businessmen earning huge profits from the province without reinvesting it in the economy.

Provincial politicians – especially the looming figure of Maurice Duplessis – found themselves supporting English hierarchies to maintain their political lives, seeking outside investment, inadvertently suppressing the aspi-

rations of the Québécois to strengthen the province's financial status.

In English Canada the French were seen as backward, remote, a society of Catholic farmers and blue-collar workers with little to offer the rest of the country except the brilliant hockey players of the Montréal Canadiens. English was simply not spoken in most parts of the province. Even in Montréal, where the anglophone community ignored the Québécois culture around it, the majority of the inhabitants were unable to function in the economic and political language of Canada. Ottawa and Toronto controlled the lives of most Québécois, dictated their

THE DECISIVE BATTLE

After the battle on the Plains of Abraham, the British were the conquerors; the Québécois the defeated. Consequently, the French settlers were abandoned by their country and left to fend for themselves on an English continent. A pattern emerged in 1759 that persists to this day; a largely English-speaking government dictating to a largely French-speaking population. By 1867, a fairly rigid socio-economic relationship had developed. The English-speakers in Québec were the bankers, the power brokers; the French were the workers who created and sustained a rich folk-culture. So the English continued to play the role of victors, and to reap the spoils.

PRECEDING PAGES: festival performers, Montréal; Frontenac County Court House. **LEFT:** a piper at Fort Hill, Kingston. **ABOVE RIGHT:** face to face in the Promenade des Artistes, Montréal.

social and economic position, yet had relatively little to do with their day-to-day existence.

In 1964 Montréal writer Hugh MacLennan published his novel *Two Solitudes*, a bleak if honest account of relations between the two communities. MacLennan portrayed both English and French Canada as inward looking, defensive, unwilling to take the necessary step to end the "solitude" in which each exists.

This phrase, "two solitudes," has come to be an important part of the Canadian vocabulary. To some extent the term is as applicable today as it was 40 years ago. Yet the period between 1955 and 1980 saw a remarkable change in the *révolution tranquille*, which developed into the separatist movement of the 1970s, had its root in cultural change is important. These artists were demanding that the Québécois take pride in their culture, their language, themselves. Québec was something quite different from the rest of Canada, it needed to be vigilant and protective of its identity.

The October Crisis

From the enlightened leadership of premiers Jean Lesage and Daniel Johnson, to the rise of René Lévesque and the Parti Québécois (PQ), the movement's political wing grew in prominence.

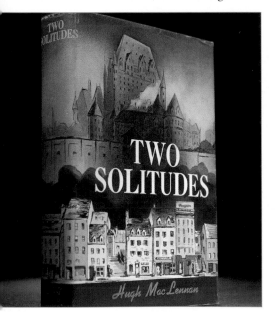

fabric of both groups. In particular, the cultural and political awakening in Québec has altered completely the dynamics of the relationship. In the last 30 years tremendous upheaval has come close to dissolving the Canadian experiment.

A quiet revolution

In the late 1950s a group of artists, journalists, and political figures – Pierre Trudeau among them – began to assert the cause of Québec. Known in retrospect as the *révolution tranquille*, this movement sought to create an autonomy entirely known as Québec, by strengthening the cultural fabric of the society. Song-writers, poets, playwrights, painters, film-makers, historians all rallied around the concept. That the

A dark manifestation of this impulse, the terrorist group Front de Libération du Québec (FLQ), gained much attention in the English-Canadian press. While Albertans or Torontonians were oblivious to the cultural excitement in Québec, to the music of Gilles Vigneault, the writing of Hubert Aquin or Jacques Godbout, they were more than well aware of the bombings in Montréal. For them Québec's struggle for selfhood consisted of denunciations of English Canada, cries for independence, and a terrorist group running amok. This distortion was disastrous to the cause of French-English relations.

The assassination of Pierre Laporte in 1970 – the so-called "October Crisis" – proved to be a decisive moment. For a few days English

Canadians witnessed with horror a brief and extremely exaggerated period of social unrest.

Suddenly all the news reports were filled with images of soldiers, of house-to-house searches, and of army checkpoints, not in Northern Ireland or Chile but in Québec, Canada.

The image of Prime Minister Pierre Trudeau declaring a state of emergency from Ottawa,

> Québec's growing pains forced people to examine their priorities, their sense of self. What if Québec separated? Would Canada survive?

as a force to be reckoned with. Assertive, self-possessed, the province now had a mind of its own and, because of the nature of provincial governments, a mandate within the Confederation to exert considerable control over its internal affairs. In a sense the gauntlet had been thrown at the feet of English Canada.

In the meantime, immigration to urban centers, in particular Toronto and Vancouver, had altered the social make-up. The "WASP" (White Anglo-Saxon Protestant) dominance of commerce in central Canada, while still unquestionable, was being flavored by new influences, new faces. Just as Montréal was no longer sim-

did more to bring the cause of Québec's self-assertion to the surface than did any of the more positive events of the previous 20 years. The October Crisis was indeed a baptism of fire.

The proud province

The remainder of the decade saw the strengthening of the PQ, their assumption of power in 1976, and the referendum on sovereignty-association of 1980. By the summer of that year, Québec, while apparently unwilling to sever its ties with the rest of Canada, had emerged

ply English controlled and French populated, so was Toronto no longer simply a city of English money, and Anglo-Saxon temperament. Québec's growing pains greatly affected the economics of Canada. They also forced people to examine their priorities, their sense of self. Québec's struggle had initiated a kind of collective debate across Canada on the nature of its national being.

After the close-run referendum of 1995, Québec remains a partner in the Confederation. At times, difficult economic conditions have relegated questions of independence to a secondary position, but the issue will not go away and the final outcome is still uncertain. To some extent the Québécois' point has been

LEFT: *Two Solitudes*, a novel by Hugh MacLennan. **ABOVE LEFT:** Raymond Villeneuve, a founding member of FLQ. **ABOVE RIGHT:** "non!" to Québec independence.

made; ownership of business is again largely internally (or US) controlled, French is the language of commerce and politics, while the cultural life of the province continues to thrive.

The exodus from Montréal of many English-language businesses offered – for the media, anyway – graphic representation of the isolation of the communities. Legislation brought in by the PQ, especially the controversial Language Bill 101, left a bitter taste in the mouths of non-French-speakers in Québec, along with frequent charges of discrimination against the government. Indeed many of the policies had the effect of further entrenching the country's

over the next five years on boosting bilingualism in schools, community programs, and the federal civil service. And surveys repeatedly show there is support for two official languages. The support is strongest among young Canadians, to whom the value of knowing and using both English and French is increasingly obvious, from a global as well as a patriotic perspective.

Québécois' willingness to give federalism another chance was resoundingly demonstrated in the April 2003 provincial election. Jean Charest (a former Progressive Conservative cabinet minister under Prime Minister

"two solitudes." In its bid to fortify, Québec seemingly added bricks to the considerable wall that already existed between itself and English Canada.

What then is to be said of Canada's bilingual experiment? While there are still those who ask why someone in Calgary should be expected to learn French, or why Manitoba should have its laws written in French as well as in English, many more people are realizing that, in today's world, speaking only one language poses a considerable disadvantage.

The federal government felt sufficiently strongly about the need for ongoing support for bilingualism to announce, in March 2003, that it would invest more than $750 million

Brian Mulroney) led the province's Liberals to victory, taking 76 of the 125 seats. Charest won again, with a minority government, in 2007, but was returned with his third mandate and a majority government on December 8, 2008. His party's success may have been partly due to the lead-up to the federal election held in October of that year. Stephen Harper and his Conservatives went to great lengths to curry favor with Québec, but once word got out that his government planned to cut $45 million from the budget for arts funding – something very close to the heart of the most Québécois – support for the federal Conservative party evaporated, leading to yet another minority government in Ottawa.

Until not so long ago, Québec's culture was all but ignored. English Canada had almost no exposure to the wealth of literature, film, and visual art that was flourishing throughout the province. But with the success of wunderkind Robert Lepage from Québec City, Cirque du Soleil's reinvention of the circus, Michel Tremblay's widely translated and acclaimed plays, La Bottine Souriante's wild folk music, and the films of Denys Arcand, to name but a few, Québec is making its mark on the rest of Canada and around the world. There is no longer any question of Québec being viewed by English Canada as impoverished and backward.

city – with what, until 2002, was known as Hull. It, too, was merged with other municipalities, to form the city of Gatineau. It used to be that Hull, with its late night cafes and bars, was a lively night out for the citizens of Ottawa. But changes were made on both sides of the border around the turn of the 21st century. After

> While English Canada can no longer patronize Québec, French Canada can no longer complain of inequality. Each are equal, siblings in a challenging experiment in nationhood.

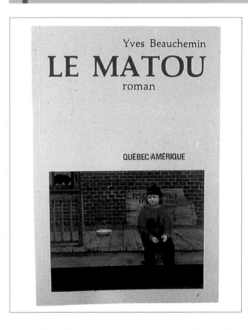

Across the bridge

The city of Ottawa is regal, stately, in the image of an old English town. Home to the country's Parliament, Ottawa was once the quintessence of English Canada. Now, however, it is one of the most bilingual cities in Canada and has a strong and vocal Franco-Ontarian population. On any street, in any store, French is as likely to be spoken as English.

Five bridges cross the Ottawa River, linking Ottawa – which, in 2001, amalgamated with 10 other municipalities to become a much larger

years of battling seedy bars and clubs, Hull City Council decreed that their bars should close at 2am. At the same time, Ontario changed its law to allow bars to stay open until 2am. While Gatineau still has a lively nightlife, Ottawa's visitors and residents have no special reason to cross a bridge to party. Indeed, the clubs around Ottawa's ByWard Market or along Elgin Street are packed most nights of the week.

There was a time when Ottawa and Hull represented the reality of Canada's "two solitudes." Today, so many people who live in Ottawa work in Québec, and vice versa, that is no longer the case. Contact between the communities has transformed from infrequent and ill at ease to frequent and perfectly comfortable. ❏

LEFT: in Québec, it is normal for signs to be in French.
ABOVE LEFT: Cirque du Soleil perform the Skeleton Dance. **ABOVE RIGHT:** literary evidence of bilingualism.

THE INUIT

For 5,000 years the Inuit and their predecessors have inhabited the Arctic region. Only now are their culture and way of life earning the respect they deserve

I t was just a few years ago that Canadians living south of the 60th parallel were surprised to learn that Eskimos have always called themselves Inuit, the "only people." The name is quite apt when you consider that the Inuit were the only people who had lived in the Arctic for thousands of years. The "Eskimo" is not Inuit but Cree, meaning "eaters of raw meat."

It is hardly a name that fairly describes these resilient soft-spoken people. The fact that for so long Euro-Canadians called the Inuit "Eskimo" speaks volumes of the silence that has existed between the two.

The Arctic environment has not always been static; it has undergone both warming and freezing trends, with a variety of life living in the region at different periods. The north's nomadic inhabitants have had to adapt accordingly.

The first group to live in the north migrated across the Bering Strait during a relatively warm period. This nomadic group, known as the pre-Dorset, spread north into the Arctic Archipel-

> With the growth of the ice pack, the Thule adapted; breaking into smaller nomadic groups, they depended less on the huge bowhead whale, more on belugas, narwhals, seals, and caribou.

ago and east to Greenland. These people hunted seals and fished the waters of the Arctic Ocean.

Around 1500 BC a cooling trend began in the north that forced them to move south onto the mainland. It was during this period that the

LEFT: Arctic entertainment – a community trampoline.
RIGHT: you can't beat the taste of home cooking.

pre-Dorset culture evolved into the indigenous Dorset culture. These people now stalked the caribou herds instead of hunting on the sea ice. Their cultural links with their cousins west of the Bering Strait were broken.

Yet the Dorset are not the direct ancestors of the Inuit. Starting in AD 900 another warming trend began that heralded the migration of the Thule from Alaska. The Thule hunted sea mammals. With the retreat of the permanent ice pack on the mainland, the whales, seals, and walruses swam through the Bering Strait and into the Beaufort Sea. The Thule were quick to follow.

The Thule differed from the Dorset in several respects: one was that they lived in fairly large settlements along the coastline, unlike the Dorset, who lived in small family groups. Secondly, the Thule were technically more sophisticated hunters. Ironically, about AD 1500, the Thule found themselves in a position similar to that of the Dorset 3,000 years earlier; yet another mini-ice age had set in. This period saw the ice pack grow so large that the number of sea mammals passing through the Bering Strait to the Arctic Ocean decreased and the migration patterns of the caribou shifted southward. The Thule broke into smaller groups and became more nomadic. It is these people who are called the Inuit.

for centuries becomes even more remarkable when one considers that despite the technological sophistication that Euro-Canadians have brought with them, they still encounter tremendous emotional upheaval in adjusting to the isolation of northern climes. The Inuit do not have that sense of isolation; for them the wind, the snow, the seasons of light and darkness are a part of their life.

European contact

In 1576 the isolation of the Inuit ended when Martin Frobisher, an Elizabethan explorer and privateer, sailed into a large bay on Baffin Island

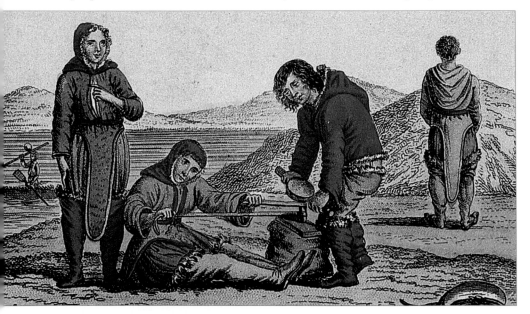

Arctic home

The Inuit chose to make the Arctic their home, in spite of the adversity they encountered. Their history, culture, and language are unlike that of the Indians, who moved south soon after crossing the Bering Strait.

In that harsh unforgiving land they perfected the building of igloos and airtight kayaks; they became experts in tracking polar bear and seal on the Arctic ice. Although they suffered from famines and exposure, the Inuit stayed.

Forged with their innate ability for innovation was a humility that made the Inuit a tolerant, stoic society, who accepted their limitations in a land where darkness reigns for six months of the year. The fact the Inuit have endured

in search of gold and the Northwest Passage to India. He was met by Inuit who circled his vessel in their kayaks. In a bid to coax them closer he rang a bell, the sound of which had probably never been heard in the Arctic before.

One curious Inuit was close enough to reach for the bell. Frobisher, with both hands, pulled the man and kayak up and into the ship and stowed him away, like booty, in the hold. After the search for gold and the passage both proved fruitless, Frobisher returned to England, where the north's "ambassador" was put on display for royalty. The grief-stricken man soon died in captivity of European disease, and ever since the Inuit have traditionally distrusted foreign involvement in their affairs.

Apart from Frobisher's expedition, the Inuit of the high Arctic seldom had contact with any Europeans until 1818, with the arrival of whaling vessels in the eastern Arctic Ocean. These whalers risked navigating through the treacherous iceberg-laden Davis Strait in search of the bowhead whale. In the 1830s there was a series

William Penny noted on his arrival in Baffin Island in the 1840s that there were 1,000 Inuit. By 1858 there were only 350 due to the prevalence of tuberculosis and influenza.

so successful by the 1880s, the bowhead whale population in the Arctic was greatly reduced. In spite of the decline in the whaling industry, the contact with the southerners, or *Kabloonat*, continued because of the growing presence throughout the Arctic of the Hudson's Bay Company, Canada's largest fur-trading company. Although the Inuit maintained their semi-nomadic life, they began to rely upon trapping and trading to provide for themselves.

This shift away from living solely off the land to a barter and then cash-based economy provided them with guns, butter, cooking utensils, and foodstuffs. For some, the Hudson's Bay

of whaling disasters, with vessels becoming trapped by the Arctic ice.

A solution to these problems was to establish whaling stations. In the 1840s William Penny, a typically shrewd Scottish whaling captain, began to employ local Inuit at his station on Baffin Island. He found that they were exceptional whalers, hardly surprising when you consider that the Inuit had been whaling for centuries. Soon Penny and other astute whalers began to adopt the warm clothing, harpoons, and other paraphernalia of Inuit technology.

Unfortunately, because the whaling proved

LEFT: a spear-hunting expedition. **ABOVE:** captured on film beside the Great Whale River (*c.*1920).

stores became a base or second home.

However, this arrangement changed when, in the 1840s, the price of furs fell dramatically. Suddenly they could no longer purchase ammunition or other goods that had become essential. On Baffin Island, two-thirds of the Hudson's Bay stores closed their doors.

A long period of starvation and deprivation began. Except for missionaries who struggled to aid the Inuit, the "only people" discovered how alone they were. While the Inuit economy was collapsing, missionaries were filing reports to medical authorities that tuberculosis (TB) and influenza epidemics were annihilating the Inuit. One anthropologist studying at Coronation Gulf found in the 1920s that 30 percent of the Inuit population had died from influenza over a 14-year period. Similarly in Coppermine in 1931, 19 cases of TB among a population of 100 were found.

The government intervenes

For the most part, until the late 1940s the Canadian government had ignored the Inuit. However, after prodding from the churches, it began to take action. In 1950 medical authorities ordered 1,600 Inuit, or 14 percent of their population, to sanatoriums in Edmonton and Montréal. This action, though medically necessary, was devastating for the Inuit, the vast

majority of whom had never left the north. As well as treating tuberculosis, the health authorities were startled by the high rate of infant mortality. In 1958 infant mortality was at 257 per 1,000 live births. By 1970 it had dropped to 100 per 1,000, and in 2000 it was 6.4 per 1,000 – still 22 percent higher than the Canadian rate.

The federal government introduced more than a medical plan for the Inuit; they coupled together policies that would rocket the Inuit into Canadian society. The central tenet of all these policies was to encourage them to abandon their nomadic life and move into government-built permanent settlements. These artificial communities provided housing, medical facilities, churches, and schools.

However well intentioned policy-makers were, they failed to understand that the Arctic tundra and ocean is home for the Inuit. From the beginning of this resettlement period the Inuit struggled to retain their identity. The first step was made in 1959; in that year the Cape Dorset Artists Co-op was formed on Baffin Island.

A sense of community

Over the centuries the Inuit have worked with ivory, stone, bones, and skins to make clothing, utensils, hunting tools, toys, and religious amulets. Often intricate designs were patterned onto these objects. When whalers arrived, trading

began to take place, with the resourceful Inuit even manufacturing ivory cribbage boards for trade. It was in the 1950s that southerners began to rediscover the Inuit's remarkable skill in carving and other traditional crafts, and funding was made available to develop these skills.

As a result the Inuit co-ops have flourished, receiving international recognition for their work in several mediums, including stonecut prints, stencil, sculpture, and carving.

The co-op system has evolved to become more than enclaves for artists. In many communities it manages hunting expeditions, municipal services, and trading posts. The philosophy behind the co-ops reflects the Inuit concept of community and what western thinking might call egalitarianism. For this reason, Inuit town meetings tend to be excruciatingly long and are filled with long meditative silences. Generally, the Inuit will not leave a local meeting before a well-thought-out consensus has been forged.

The next generation

In a society where the line between nuclear family, extended family, and community is blurred, the importance of children cannot be overestimated. Traditionally, Inuit women are encouraged to have many children; many start from puberty and still bear children into their mid-forties. If for whatever reason the parents of

in the south. The pursuit of personal wealth is for the most part played down. The respect one can earn in the eyes of the community is important. For men this respect has traditionally been earned through becoming a good hunter or trapper, although this is now changing. Carving, despite its lucrative nature, is not regarded as such a worthy occupation.

It is this intrinsic relationship with the land that has made the Inuit, particularly the older Inuit, ambivalent towards higher education and the learning of "southern skills." Mandatory school attendance was seen by the Inuit as a method of either forcing them to follow

a child are unable to support it, the child will be adopted by the grandparents or by some other member of the family. Illegitimacy is less of an issue here than in other societies, which is partly attributable to a sense of communal responsibility for children. In the 1960s the Inuit were baffled when social workers first attempted to formalize adoption procedures. Social workers were equally puzzled when they attempted to unravel whose children belonged to whom.

Within the Inuit community there is clearly a different set of values operating from those

Because of their isolation – for them the wind, the snow, the seasons of light and darkness are a part of their life – the Inuit have developed into a self-sacrificing people who are tolerant of community goals.

their children into government-built communities, or separating them from their children by sending them away to school. Many Inuit questioned the relevance and importance of their children learning subjects like English, science, and math.

The federal government has attempted to integrate the educational system into the com-

LEFT: celebrating Inuit heritage at the Moosehide Gathering. **ABOVE LEFT:** whale bone carving of Inuit family. **ABOVE RIGHT:** keeping up traditions.

munity. A program was introduced to recruit and train Inuit to become teachers. It failed in part because few Inuit were willing to leave their community for eight months at a time to train.

Over the past 15 years it has been the young adult Inuit population that has been the most affected by the complications of living in a world with two divergent cultures. These Inuit are the product of a "baby boom" that swept across the Arctic in the 1950s and 1960s. This boom was in part created by the lowering of infant mortality and generally improved health.

The question that faces this group of people is how they will support themselves in the com-

ing years. As part of government policy many left home to attend regional high schools. That isolation had a disorienting effect. They failed to learn, as their parents had, how to live off the land, how to keep warm while out in the cold, how to build an igloo. Knowledge of survival techniques forms the basis of their culture. Yet, if the young are not familiar with traditional skills and their implicit philosophy, they also have not acquired the skills necessary to compete for management positions in government or in industry.

The continuity in passing down the knowledge and communal values from one generation to another has been broken. The resulting problems have manifested themselves in alcoholism, vandalism and suicide.

Adopting new technology

There can be little doubt that technology has brought about a safer and more comfortable life for the Inuit. They ride on snowmobiles, watch TV with VCR attachments and hunt with high-powered rifles. They have running water. They no longer live in snow houses. The question that many would ask is: has technology made the Inuit more or less Inuit?

The Inuit have traditionally been eager to adopt new technology. In their environment they had to be great innovators. It is what the technology represents that bothers the Inuit. The challenge for the Inuit is to make technology their own; then they will be rulers in their own land. In adopting this technology, the Inuit must look to their knowledge of how they lived in the past if they are to avoid becoming strangers in their own land.

For more than 5,000 years the Inuit and their predecessors have politically, aesthetically, and socially been building and rebuilding a society that has allowed them to live independently in an environment where others could not bear the physical and psychological pressure.

It is their unique culture that has allowed them to make the north their home. If the young are not permitted to capture that spirit, if they are overwhelmed and bullied by western society, then they will no longer be Inuit. And Canadian society will lose a fragment of its colorful mosaic.   ❏

TEN YEARS ON

In 2009, Nunavut marked its 10th anniversary. Those ten years saw an extraordinary transition that has taken its toll on the Inuit and their culture. Education will be key to resolving many of Nunavut's problems, from poor housing to substance abuse, poverty, and inadequate job skills. On a promising note, high school graduation has increased by 50 percent since 1999. As well, Inuit artists – from painters and sculptors to filmmakers and musicians – are increasingly making their mark far beyond their own territory. The remarkable growth in mineral development could also kick-start Nunavut's economy.

LEFT: an Inuit celebration.
RIGHT: bags packed and "ready to go."

ART AND PERFORMANCE

Canadians have worked with great determination to create a vibrant artistic, dramatic, and literary scene that reflects the talents of its multicultural population

Although artistically Canada is a young nation, its contribution to the arts world is impressive. It has renowned writers, respected literary events and drama festivals, and boasts much-admired theater and dance. In the world of music, it has leaders on all fronts, having spawned exceptional classical performers, along with mainstream and alternative composers and performers. Its French language films have won international accolades and Toronto and Vancouver vie for the title of Hollywood North, having initially gotten the chance to compete as locations in the filmmaking world thanks to a low Canadian dollar. Now, the fluctuation of the dollar is less a consideration than the ready supply of skilled professionals who call these two cities home.

Given that most Canadians live within 240km (150 miles) of the US border, with saturation from North American cable television, newspapers, books and magazines, fast-food, and shopping malls, the influence of American culture and lifestyle has always been strong. A quick browse through the daily papers makes one wonder what constitutes Canadian culture.

Since World War II, artists' efforts to develop a sense of identity have been backed by government protection of "cultural industries" in its negotiations with the US.

In spite of this intervention, after the war many serious Canadian artists went abroad, to England, France, and America. That changed in the 1960s, in part thanks to Canada's anti-

American sentiment amplified by the Vietnam War, when Canada was identified with the distinctive voices of Leonard Cohen, Joni Mitchell, and Neil Young. Government grants at that time made it possible for the next generation of artists to have more successful careers at home, or at least to promote themselves as Canadians and be recognized as talented.

Regional strengths

The search for a cultural identity is also an attempt to unify a vast land. Canada's most popular authors and artists are often identified with specific regions.

In literature, Québec is historically associated

PRECEEDING PAGES: performance of *The Drowsy Chaperone* in Vancouver. **LEFT:** Canadian-born Nelly Furtado. **RIGHT:** *Blunden Harbour, c.*1928–30, by Emily Carr, who painted in British Columbia.

with Mordecai Richler, Michel Tremblay, and Gabrielle Roy; Nova Scotia with Hugh MacLennan and Antonine Maillet; Manitoba with Margaret Laurence; The Yukon with Pierre Burton; and rural Ontario with Stephen Leacock and Alice Munro.

Early Canadian society, with its long winters and agricultural industrial base, presented many limitations. Nineteenth-century artists in a sparsely populated country were isolated and without an audience. In the colonial period, Canadians turned to France, Britain, and the US for inspiration and approval. This trend continued in the 20th century. In a country suspicious of the arts, Canadians found fuller expression of their talent, and public recognition, abroad.

The tough, demanding industries such as mining, forestry, and fishing ("rocks, logs, and fish," as the poets say) and hardships of the pioneers left them little time for artistic creativity. Pioneering writers such as Susannah Moodie considered that escape was to be found only in the grave. Even today many writers and artists continue to explore subject matter provided by their ancestral pasts, their immigrant backgrounds, and the pioneering days of their forebears.

CREATIVE CANADIANS

Creative Canadians have had to struggle to be heard for the simple reason that they are outnumbered by American and British competition. The world media is controlled elsewhere, so making a name in many artistic endeavors requires leaving home. Indeed, when a humorous commentator explained that Canada's fourth largest city is Los Angeles, the statistician in the crowds wonders aloud if that might not be true. Certainly, it has long been recognized that to succeed financially, an artist has to leave Canada.

Given that most Canadians live within 240km (150 miles) of the US border, the influence of American culture and lifestyle has always been strong.

But nowhere is the difference of experience more defined than between the English speakers and the French speakers of Québec, the "two solitudes," as the novelist Hugh MacLennan described it. The constant tension between the two communities has given a demanding dynamic to the country, which can be seen reflected in the arts.

Such 19th-century movements as the Canada First movement and the Confederation Poets (or Maple Leaf school) drew inspiration from the landscape. Lucy Maud Montgomery's (1874– 1942) still popular *Anne of Green Gables* novels and Mazo de la Roche's 16 impossibly romantic *Jalna* (1927) novels would sell millions of copies around the world. The short stories of Morley Callaghan; the pioneer novels of Frederick Philip Grove; the struggle of pioneering artists in the poems of E.J. Pratt; tales of shipwrecks and seal hunts, and epics of rail building and missionaries – all of these were serious efforts at coming to terms with the Canadian experience.

The Stratford Shakespeare Festival in Ontario attracts an audience of 500,000 to its annual six-month season. Popular summer Shakespeare festivals include those held in St John's, Halifax, Saskatoon, Calgary, and Vancouver.

economy, funding is stripped out of the government's budget. The result is that artists live with uncertainty which occasionally sparks amazing prolific spurts of creativity, occasionally sends them out of the country, and occasionally forces them to abandon their dreams altogether. The lack of stability has had a huge impact on the development of a sustainable artistic underpinning to the Canadian identity.

Theater

Ceremonials and ritual drama are central to Aboriginal and Inuit social and religious activities, which use masks, costumes, and properties

Policy changes

When Prime Minister Lester Pearson gave the country a flag in the early 1960s, it was a time of optimism for Canada's creative class. The Centennial in 1967, and the famed Expo fair in Montréal, "Man and His World," generated a new-found nationalism, stimulating a cultural revolution, supported by direct funding through the Canada Council.

When the economy is good, Canada Council funding increases. The other side of this coin is that, as soon as there is a downturn in the

LEFT: *To Prince Edward Island*, the disturbingly realistic art of Alex Colville. **ABOVE:** *Mamma Mia* at the Prince of Wales Theatre, Toronto..

to enhance dialogue. Great ritual drama, like the Kwakiutl, takes five months to perform. Most Canadians are not familiar with these traditions. Native theater and dance companies and a Native Writing School are now addressing centuries of neglect.

Since the mushrooming of theaters in the 1970s, Canadian audiences have had a choice of regional theaters and the summer festivals that take place across the country. The most prominent of these events is the Stratford Shakespeare Festival in Stratford, Ontario, founded in 1953. With a budget of close to $60 million, and attendance of a half a million people, it presents a six-month season of Shakespeare's plays, a variety of musicals, and contemporary classics in four separate theaters. It is fair to say that Stratford is in large part responsible for the other summer Shakespeare festivals that have sprung up in virtually every province across the country. As a training ground for performers, directors and stage technicians, Stratford sets the standards that other companies aspire to, or sometimes react against.

Next in prominence is the Shaw Festival, at Niagara-on-the-Lake, founded in 1962 to showcase the plays of George Bernard Shaw. Charlottetown, on Prince Edward Island, is home of the longest-running Canadian musical, *Anne of Green Gables*, first performed in 1965.

It has taken time for Canadian plays to emerge. In the 1960s and 1970s some small alternative theaters opened, including Vancouver's Savage God; Toronto's Theatre Passe Muraille, Factory Theater, Tarragon Theater; and Halifax's Neptune Theater. The challenge has always been to attract an audience with a relative unknown playwright, particularly when the material being addressed was often controversial. But more and more Canadian plays are being written and performed, including noteworthy work by First Nations playwrights Tomson Highway (*The Rez Sisters* and *Dry Lips Oughta Move to Kapuskasing*) and Drew Hayden Taylor (*Toronto at Dreamer's Rock* and *Only Drunks and Children Tell the Truth*).

A major challenge to the nearly 90 smaller theaters in Toronto during the 1990s was the success of the blockbuster international musicals, such as *Les Misérables* and *Phantom of the Opera*. The Princess of Wales Theater in Toronto was built especially for *Miss Saigon*. Now, however, the long-running shows have closed or moved on, to be replaced by more touring productions.

In financially difficult times, special-interest theaters have grown. Comedy cabarets, theaters for senior citizens and children, feminist and gay theaters, and experimental media such as Videocabaret, demonstrated a lively approach. Toronto's comedy club acts are broadcast worldwide, and have nurtured such talents as Dan Ackroyd, John Candy, and Martin Shortt.

Dance

The Canadian Ballet Festival movement, launched in Winnipeg in 1948 to give dancers a sense of what their colleagues were doing elsewhere in Canada, soon developed into a strong regional ballet movement across the country. Four years later the first experimental dance company, Les Grands Ballets Canadiens, was established in Montréal, while Celia Franca established Toronto's National Ballet of Canada, developing international ballet stars such as Karen Kain and Veronica Tenant.

With freedom to create non-literal and abstract dance, modern dance experiment companies, such as the Paula Ross Company and Anna Wyman Dance Theater of Vancouver, the Toronto Dance Theater, Robert Desrosiers of Montréal as well as dozens of independent choreographers, challenged the classics of the larger companies and, by the 1980s, classical ballet and modern dance companies were eager to learn from each other.

According to Canadian arts advocate Max Wyman, Canada's professional dance scene today reflects the country's emergence as a modern nation. Whether working in classical or contemporary styles, their dance is enriched by the traditions of aboriginal people, influenced by European and American cultures and inspired by generations of immigrants who have come to Canada from around the world.

Painting and sculpture

Prior to Confederation, documentary tradition dominated Canadian painting. Painters were usually inspired by European trends. But landscape painting changed immeasurably in Canada in 1920 with the first exhibition of the modernist Group of Seven (1920–33). The painting tended to post-Impressionist mannerisms, with great dabs of mysticism. It caught the public interest, and their claim to be Canada's national painters aroused furious debate among critics. An associate of the group, Tom Thomson, became romanticized after his mysterious drowning in 1917. His paintings of pine trees and lakes are among Canada's most famous images and one even sold at auction for close to $1 million.

the Automatists, after their 1947 exhibition. The most prominent of the younger painters was Montreal-born, Jean-Paul Riopelle. Québec painting would soon show the new dynamics of color, abstract expressionism, and non-figurative forms.

The painter Borduas' 1948 manifesto *Refus Global* advocated spiritual and artistic freedom and attacked the repressive government and Church in Québec culture.

The manifesto effected change in all the artistic disciplines, including dance, music, theater, painting, and sculpture. Despite his own personal hardships, Borduas' paintings

Most early 20th century artists worked in isolation and were disregarded, experiencing success posthumously. Emily Carr (1871–1945), for example, worked on the west coast, painting forests, native villages and totem poles with bold strokes and color. David Milne (1882–1953) introduced modernist techniques and he, too, found success only in his later years.

Montréal painters took a different path. Alfred Pellan, Paul Emile Borduas and John Lyman returned from France inspired by the example of modern European art, especially cubism and surrealism, and called themselves

The work of Inuit artists has achieved the recognition it long deserved. In some villages, soapstone carving and printmaking are the most important sources of revenue for the community.

and manifesto represent one of the major achievements of Canadian art.

Toronto dominated artistic expression in the 1950s. Jack Bush, Harold Town, and William Ronald were the major painters of a group who took the name Painters Eleven and promoted the new American abstractions of the 1950s. In the west, Gordon Smith, John Koerner, and the

LEFT: open-air ballet in Ottawa. **RIGHT:** abstract expressionism from Jean-Paul Riopelle.

late Jack Shadbolt experimented with a variety of styles and techniques. The late Toni Onley's distinctive and mystical representation of the beauty of the Pacific Northwest became synonymous with the landscape.

Today the dominant painter of the Atlantic region is Alex Colville, who has set a new standard for realistic art with his enigmatic images.

Painting is now being challenged as the leading edge of the visual arts by conceptual art, sculpture, video, performance, and the work of the First Nations people.

Since the mid-20th century the work of Inuit and West Coast native artists has earned the

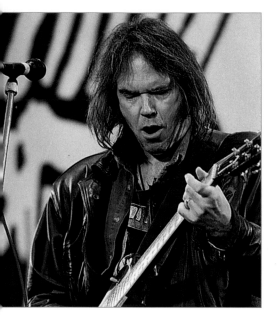

recognition it deserves, winning international acclaim, and becoming an important force in the country's culture. In the 1950s and 1960s, with the help of the Hudson's Bay Company and Canadian Handicrafts Guild, Inuit-owned co-operatives were set up in many Arctic communities, as much as a source of income for the people as to encourage local skills.

One of the most prominent Inuit sculptors is David Ruben Piqtoukun, whose work in stone is inspired by his concern for the loss of his culture, and the spiritual beliefs of his ancestors. Art galleries countrywide, including Québec's fine Musée Canadien des Civilisations in Hull, are devoting space to First People's art.

Music

From the classics to pop, the music scene in Canada has been consistently and extraordinarily varied. It has a strong lyric quality and is never afraid of breaking new ground. Outdoor concerts are an important part of the summer in every part of the country.

After the 1967 Centennial a remarkable flourishing of compositions explored new directions; chance music, electro-accoustic music, with R. Murray Schafer and Harry Somers pre-eminent among the *avant garde*.

Canada has more than 100 professional or community orchestras, although the classical orchestras face funding issues, as they do in many parts of the world. In its intensity and diversity, the country's music has assumed great proportions. Toronto has become a center for new and alternative music in North America and a leader in Caribbean-influenced pop.

In the summer, live rock concerts feature the best of national and international performers. Canadian hard-rock groups such as Nickelback and The Tragically Hip, and singers such as Bryan Adams or Céline Dion, stage sell-out concerts. Most towns in Canada have rock clubs and bars.

There is a long history of singer-songwriters who have found international fame since the 1960s, including Leonard Cohen, Paul Anka, Joni Mitchell, Neil Young, Rita MacNeil, k.d. lang, and Diana Krall. Perhaps the best example of this is David Foster: while most people are not aware that he is Canadian, he is the epitome of a Canadian performer – diverse, equally adept at writing, performing, arrang-

MUSICAL MILESTONES

Among those who made their mark in music, but have died, are Glenn Gould (whose interpretation of Bach's Goldberg variations in 1955 and again just a year before his death in 1982 are still referred to as landmark recordings) and jazz wizard Oscar Peterson (whose 1962 *Hymn to Freedom* became a rallying song for the American civil rights movement and was played at the Obama inauguration in January, 2009).

In the classical world, individual performers on the world stage today include pianists Angela Hewitt and Jon Kimura (Jackie) Parker, along with an astonishing number of singers: Nancy Argenta, Elizabeth Bayrakdarian, Russell Braun, Judith Forst, and Ben Heppner.

ing, and producing music. His extensive list of compositions includes *I Have Nothing*, sung by Whitney Houston in the film *The Bodyguard* and nominated for both a Grammy and an Academy Award.

The CRTC (Canadian Radio-Television and Telecommunications Commission) regulatory agency ensures at least 35 percent of music played on the radio is Canadian and that 50 to 60 percent of broadcast television is of Canadian content – a policy that has helped to give many popular Canadian performers a start to their careers.

A national party station, MUCH-Music, takes popular music seriously, showcasing the political, social, and artistic side of contemporary performers from England, France, and multicultural Canada. Though jazz clubs have short histories in most Canadian cities, the summer jazz and blues festivals have up to 25 acts crisscrossing the country, as far north as Dawson City in the Yukon.

Modern writing

While prose and poetry have a long history in Canada, historically readership was small; most works were not published until accepted by a US or British company. Toronto's Harborfront Reading Series, founded by poet Greg Gatenby in 1974, is pre-eminent in the world for its festival of national and international literary celebrities. In the 1960s, writing communities flourished coast-to-coast.

By the 1970s, with federal and provincial government support, publishing houses were in every province. It is fair to say that the past decade has wrought havoc on both the book publishing and magazine industries in Canada, but equally fair to say that many have simply embraced the internet not as the instrument of their demise, but as an opportunity to attract new readers. Like most businesses dealing with intellectual property, they are struggling to find an economic approach to the challenges.

Major literary critics, such as George Woodcock, Marshall McLuhan and Northrop Frye set new standards for the appreciation of Canadian letters. Toronto is still important, but it is no longer the place for writers to make their mark. Indeed, the diversity of the country supports

LEFT: veteran rock star Neil Young.
ABOVE: Canadian author Alice Munro.

their staying "home" and allowing their writing to reflect their place in the world.

Film and television

Canada is considered part of the American domestic film market, and Canadian films have limited opportunities to be shown in Canadian theaters and on television. World War II changed the Canadian film industry, with the formation of the National Film Board (NFB), which began to train and develop Canadian film-makers. The NFB is practically synonymous with quality documentary film. Beginning with documentary film needed for

the war effort, the NFB expanded into areas of ethnic groups, Canadian art, and social problems. The 1974 development of a women's studio at the NFB led to the making of many good films on a variety of topics from a woman's perspective.

As film-makers began to turn their interest from educational and informative films to the fiction feature film, Hollywood moved to protect its interest. Despite complex talks of quota systems, there was virtually no feature film-making in English Canada until the 1960s. However, Canada did command worldwide respect for work in short-film animation. Nearly all the films were produced by the NFB. Especially outstanding is the work of Norman McLaren, who dazzled millions around the world with such films as *Neighbours*, which won an Academy Award (1952), and *Pas de Deux* (1969), with its haunting dance sequence developed with an optical printer.

The development of the 16mm camera and the influence of French "new wave" film-making led to a more personalized cinema. By 1970 such films as Don Shebib's *Goin' Down the Road* and Gordon Pinsent's *The Rowdyman* were commercial and artistic successes. An important figure was David Cronenberg, whose low-budget horror films created a cult following at home; he has since become a major

international director with such films as *The Fly*, *M. Butterfly*, *Crash*, and *Spider*.

In the 1980s, there were notable successes by such filmmakers as Anne Wheeler, Philip Boros, Patricia Rozema, and Atom Egoyan, who won a Director's Prize at Cannes. The world-famous Toronto International Film Festival held each September is considered as important as Cannes. In fact, it has been ranked by the *Los Angeles Times* as number one in the world.

Québec film-making likewise has had its share of challenges, but it has produced some exceptional prize-winning films: Denys Arcand was twice nominated for an Academy Award for *Jesus of Montréal* and *The Decline and Fall of the American Empire*. Claude Jutra and Jean

Beaudin made significant titles such as *Mon Oncle Antoine* and *J.A. Martin, Photographe*.

While the early 1990s saw the Québec film industry again in crisis, with less money and fewer productions, in the late 1990s there was a significant resurgence. On the international stage, Denys Arcand won the Best Foreign-Language Oscar for *The Barbarian Invasions* at the 2004 Academy Awards, and Jean-Marc Vallée's *C.R.A.Z.Y.* won Canada's own annual Genie Awards for best motion picture in 2006. A testimony to the courage and inventiveness of the Québec film industry is the 2006 comedy thriller buddy cop film *Bon Cop, Bad Cop*, a film that mixes French and English indiscriminately, bringing out the sharp differences between life in Toronto and Montréal.

If there have been hard times at home, actors have sought fame further afield. From the early days of Mary Pickford and Lorne Greene, through the era of television (where William Shatner boldly dared to go and Michael J. Fox inhabited *The West Wing*) and on to Pamela Anderson, Jim Carrey, and Jason Priestley, Canadian actors, producers, and writers have found success in Hollywood. Larger-than-life heroes Superman, Ghostbusters, and Rambo originated from Canadian-born authors. Ottawa-born comedian Dan Aykroyd even made a tongue-in-cheek feature film about the Canadian plot to take over the Hollywood empire. More recently, Ontario-born Mike Myers launched Austin Powers at the world. Such figures are recognized internationally, just as many of Canada's writers and musicians have made their names outside the country. Sometimes it is a surprise to discover that such

> *The list of important Canadian writers alive today is too long to enumerate, but a few worth exploring include Margaret Atwood, Joseph Boyden, Douglas Coupland, Rohinton Mistry, Alice Munro, and Michael Ondaatje.*

well-known people are Canadian, and not American after all. But their roots are the same as those who have stayed at home, where local arts are still active day after day. There is no lack of opportunity for attending a performance. ❏

LEFT: Canadian actor Mike Myers as Austin Powers.
RIGHT: the Princess of Wales Theatre, Toronto.

ANCIENT INUIT ART

Canada's galleries and museums now give full recognition to its rich heritage of native art dating back to the Dorset peoples of 600 BC

Traditionally there was no word for "art" in the Inuktitut language. Early carvings tended to be functional – tools, weapons, and utensils – or they were used for spiritual purposes, such as amulets and masks. The sculptures of animals, birds, sea creatures, and human figures simply represented daily life.

The first people to produce what is now recognized as "art" belonged to the Dorset culture (*c.*600 BC–AD 1000). They used ivory, bone, and wood and, like today's artists, kept as close as possible to the original shape of the material. The items were often small and remarkably smooth.

Inuit Ancestors

Thule people, the ancestors of today's Inuit, migrated east from northern Alaska around AD 1000, and replaced the Dorset inhabitants. Their art was more feminine and less ritualistic. It consisted of decorated everyday items such as combs, needlecases, pendants, and female figurines, harpoon toggles, and gaming pieces. In the 16th and 17th centuries a colder climate led to the demise of the Thule culture. European exploration was beginning and the Inuit started to barter their carvings with the traders and explorers who made their way across the north.

In the 1940s, the federal government began to encourage the development of Inuit art as a means to bring much-needed income to the isolated communities. With the help of the Hudson's Bay Company and the Canadian Handicrafts Guild, Inuit-owned co-operatives were set up across the Arctic. Contemporary Inuit art has achieved international status, and across Canada museums and galleries devote considerable space to its exhibition.

ABOVE: in 2005 the Musée National des Beaux-Arts du Québec acquired the extraordinary Raymond Brousseau collection of Inuit art, consisting of over 2,500 works (mostly sculptures) throughout the Canadian Arctic.

BELOW: a finger mask used by women during dance entertainments, representing the moon spirit.

LEFT: a shaman's mask in the form of a whale.

CONTEMPORARY ARTISTS AT WORK

Inuit art comprises a great number of regional styles determined by tradition, available materials, and the artists themselves.

Many of today's artists have experienced life away from their communities, and combine the various cultural influences in their work. David Ruben Piqtoukun, whose sculptures have been exhibited widely, was born in 1950 north of the Mackenzie River Delta. His father was a hunter and trapper. At the age of five, Piqtoukun, like so many of his generation, was sent away to school and forced to come to terms with an English culture. His work has a strong spiritual element on the one hand, while also exploring the impact of outside influences on his culture. He lives outside Toronto and regularly returns to his home community of Paulatuk.

Ovilu Tunnillie also experienced life in an alien world, which is reflected in her carving. She was born on Baffin Island in 1949. As a child she contracted tuberculosis and spent three years in hospitals in Manitoba. On her return she had to relearn both her language and way of life. Taught by her father, Tunnillie began carving in 1972. She now lives in Cape Dorset and her sculptures are exhibited worldwide.

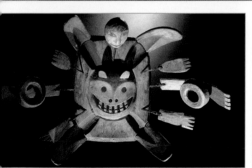

ABOVE: a mask symbolizing a shaman's spirit flight; the face in the centre represents the shaman's soul.

RIGHT: animals, birds, and fish are often the subject of Inuit sculptures. This small carving (8cm/3in tall) of two polar bears wrestling was made in the 19th century on the northwest coast.

LEFT: an inukshuk (stone landmark) stands guard over Whistler Mountain, British Columbia.

CANADA AT WORK

A well-educated population and the realities
of geography and language make for a business
scene that is as diverse as the country itself

The Canadian economy is as diverse as its geography, in part because of its geography and in part because of its sparse population. Its total population is about 10 percent less than California, mostly located along a thin strip to the north of its 6,400km (4,000-mile) border with the United States. Its people are generally well-educated, but how do they earn a living and how has this changed over the more than four hundred years since the first French explorers set up a permanent settlement and established the fur trade?

Historically, Canadians were thought of as – and thought of themselves as – hewers of wood and drawers of water. The evolution of Canadian industry followed a path determined by explorers and entrepreneurs who were more interested in either adventure or personal fortune than creating a vision for the country. As explorers opened up the country, through contact with First Nations people, they learned what riches each corner had to offer and determined

Oil is the main resource that provides jobs for Canadians. In Alberta, there are the massive tar sands to be "mined" – bitumen-rich ore is extracted by open-pit mining, crushed, processed, ultimately creating synthetic crude oil.

whether these were useful for the purposes of trading or for sending back to Europe.

The resources that found favor progressed beyond the fur trade through gold, silver, forestry, coal, and oil. Each of these industries needed large numbers of unskilled or semi-skilled workers, willing to perform hard physical labor. After the initial flush of the gold rush faded, and there were no more nuggets to be harvested by panning the creeks and rivers, gold mines were required. The daily grind of earning a living wage by digging and blasting away the rock that encased a vein of gold held little appeal for those who craved excitement and adventure. They moved on, to chase the next dream. New immigrants arrived, willing to take on this brutal work to get a foothold in a new country, and save enough money to send for their families.

Traditional and contemporary industries: a mineworker (**LEFT**) and optical cables (**RIGHT**).

Land division

Other waves of immigrants arrived, with a different plan. In 1870, the Hudson's Bay Company (which was granted initial right to most of what is now Canada by Charles II of England in 1670) ceded its interest in the territory between Ontario and British Columbia to the newly created Canada.

The land was divided in square mile (2.6 sq km) sections. One section was made up of 640 acres (close to 260 hectares). Similar to the American plan to attract settlers, much of this land was made available to immigrants to "homestead." That is, in exchange for the

Primary industries

Today, oil is the main resource that provides jobs for Canadians. Off the coasts of Nova Scotia and Newfoundland, offshore drilling attracts the adventurers of today, who are willing to work under intense and risky conditions for a few years, often hoping that the money they accumulate (there isn't a lot of opportunity to spend money on an oil rig) will give them a nice nest egg for their future.

Another less-publicized industry is diamond mining – while the Northwest Territories has the first diamond mines in North America, it appears that there are other locations in north-

promise that they would build a house and cultivate a small portion of the land, they were granted a quarter-section of land (160 acres/65 hectares). The program triggered immigration from Britain, the United States, and numerous other countries, which explains varied pockets of Ukranian, Danish, Swedish, and Dutch Mennonnites (who came from Russia) across Manitoba, Saskatchewan, and Alberta.

The legacy of that settlement and images of the vast prairie wheat fields create a misleading picture of Canada as an agricultural economy. Statistics for 2006 show that less than 1 percent of the Canadian population is involved in farming, and that this number is dropping.

> The 1989 free trade agreement with the United States had a major impact on Canadian industries and the subsidies and tariffs that had governed their operation.

ern Ontario, Québec, and Nunavut that have commercially viable quantities of diamonds. Like the tar sands, massive capital investment is required to set up the initial facilities (when De Beers set up its Snap Lake mine, the cost came close to one billion dollars).

But primary industries such as mining and forestry employ only a small percentage of Canadians. Beginning early in the 20th century, the government, looking to build a stable and independent economy, recognized that Canada did not have sufficient economies of scale to survive. In the absence of a large investment class, government stepped in and helped create industry. When two other rail lines became insolvent after World War I, the government stepped in and created CN Rail.

Often, the approach was for the government to simply create an entity, like the airline, Air Canada, in 1937 and Petro-Canada, the state owned oil company in 1975. Once created, these companies (or "crown corporations" as they were generally called) operated as busi-

steel and automotive industries in Ontario.

Falling trade barriers, first with the US and then with Mexico in the mid-1990s have forced a critical element of Canada's economy, state enterprise, to undergo major restructuring.

The old way of government stepping in where private capital was unwilling to invest simply couldn't work any more, and the reasons extended beyond free trade agreements. Although its debt load was not as catastrophic as that which led to the 1980s New Zealand crisis, during the 1990s, the Canadian government had to take serious steps to reduce its debt to maintain its standing internationally. The solu-

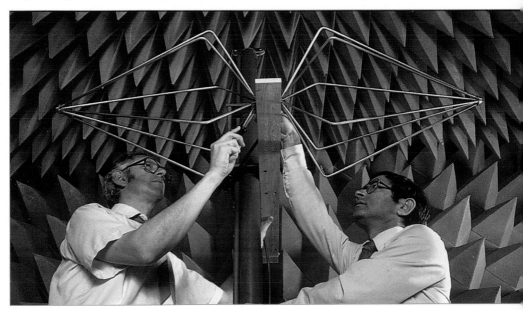

nesses, with an important exception, If they were not profitable, the government stepped in to cover the shortfall. While these operations helped achieve national political and economic objectives, they rarely operated with the same strict criteria imposed on private companies.

Over time, government assistance also took the form of subsidies to certain industries and trade barriers (tariffs) for others.

Public policy was designed to compensate for the country's shortfalls in population and expertise. Industries that benefited included the shoe and clothing industries in Québec and the

tions were twofold: in order to avoid massive tax increases, it had to cut spending and sell off assets. Air Canada, Canadian National Railways, and Petro-Canada were all privatized. Anything that the government could eliminate, it did, which meant reductions of civil servants.

Infrastructure

The next phase in government efforts to maintain a strong infrastructure in Canada has been the much lauded "Public-Private-Partnership" approach to financing new initiatives. They include contracts to maintain existing facilities, as well as contracts for developing, building, financing, and operating new facilities. One of the early examples was the construc-

LEFT: downtown Vancouver from Stanley Park.
ABOVE: engineering research in Ottawa.

tion of the third terminal at Toronto Pearson airport; a more recent example is the new Canada Line in Vancouver, the rapid transit line built between the airport and downtown Vancouver as part of the preparation for the 2010 winter Olympics.

> Bombardier, the world's rail equipment manufacturing and servicing industry, now has manufacturing facilities in close to 30 countries, but still maintains a significant part of its workforce in Canadian plants.

These partnerships result in Canada getting much-needed infrastructure – often related to transportation in this vast country – without raising taxes. Taxes in Canada are high, in part to maintain a universal health care system and a comprehensive welfare system, including legislation providing for extended maternity leave (at least partially paid through the unemployment insurance program).

Highly specialized

The manufacturing that still exists in Canada is often highly specialized. Research in Motion is an example of a tremendously successful Canadian company. The creator of the BlackBerry® has managed to create a whole category of mobile communication. While it operates internationally, RIM has maintained a large Canadian operation, attracting the brightest new graduates in every field from engineering to finance to marketing.

The massive shift of production of goods overseas – everything from shoes and clothing to automobiles – has left more and more Canadians working in the service sector. In fact, three out of four Canadians work in the service sector.

An important part of this sector which arose in parallel with the resource, agricultural, and manufacturing industries is the financial services industry. Canadian banks have long provided a stabilizing influence on the economy, serving a conservative, risk-averse population. Regulations imposed by the Canadian government resulted in a banking sector dramatically different than its American counterpart. For decades, five large banks controlled the lion's share of Canadian banking, all the while keeping the savings of the people secure, their publicly traded stocks offering secure dividends to pensioners. The relatively conservative approach and diversified holdings meant that in the aftermath of the 2008 financial meltdown, they suffered less than American and European banks and rebounded more quickly.

The next wave

As industries such as the automotive industry, once virtually the foundation of Ontario's economy, experience continued downsizing and restructuring exercises, Canadians must be adept at moving on to the next new wave. Fortunately, they still have the pioneer spirit and face adversity with optimism, firm in the belief that something else will come along. It's a people that can draw on its strengths and adapt to the next wave of technology, grabbing it and modifying it to suit its own needs.

A phrase attributed to Sir Wilfred Laurier, Canada's prime minister of the day, in 1904 that "the 20th century belonged to Canada," may have been overly optimistic. However, the fact that Canada not only survived but thrived during that tumultuous century bodes well for the future of a people who have proven they can adapt quickly in order to survive. The future for Canadians remains bright,   ❑

LEFT: Hydro Québec power cables. **RIGHT:** engineer for Bombardier, the mass-transit specialists.

FOOD AND DRINK

Canadian cuisine is a combination of influences from the native peoples to recent immigrants, using the country's own abundant food resources

Early settlers faced many challenges and the first Canadian cuisine consisted of eating what you could hunt, fish, and forage – most of it learned from the native peoples, saving many a fur trader and explorer from certain starvation.

As a result, there is no single cuisine that defines Canada but one made up of several components. There are more than 80 cultural communities, and some 5,000 restaurants at any given time in a city such as Toronto, where the Italian population rivals a mid-size Italian city and Chinatown is one of the busiest in North America. If a food or ingredient exists, it's probably available somewhere in Canada, and definitely in the larger cities.

Foreign visitors can be forgiven for thinking that mainstream Canadian food is interchangeable with American. Hamburgers and French fries are standard fare at any Canadian shopping mall, just as in any American city. But a closer look reveals Japanese sushi, Korean

Over the past 400 years, successive streams of immigrants have brought their recipes and ideas with them, each contributing to Canada's food culture.

bulkokee, Chinese stir fry, Ukranian perogies, and Greek souvlaki. Canadians are used to combining foods from four or five cultures on the same plate and see nothing unusual about this approach to eating.

LEFT: Canadian corn on the cob.
RIGHT: time for coffee in Toronto.

The 100-mile diet

The various trends and obsessions with fresh and organic are at home in Canada. First Nations cultures all across the country evolved diets and favorite foods that were directly related to what was available and what could be stored for the winter. As a country of abundant game, fish, corn, squash, beans, berries, and greens, the cuisine was varied in summer, but very limited during the long winters. Much of the food eaten by settlers and colonials was an attempt to recreate food from the countries they had left behind; this not being practical, they began to adapt to the land and learn a new way of eating.

Now, modern technology has helped farmers cultivate more exotic foods in Canada profitably, so the bounty that can come out of a local Canadian garden is truly astonishing.

Food for all tastes

The sheer volume of immigrants brought with it all manner of food styles and tastes. The country is almost pathologically receptive to whatever is going on in the outside world, so what you can expect in Canada is a cuisine that's like an orchestra, with native and colonial strands and a plethora of richly varied imports. Churrasco-style (Portuguese) barbe-

beef on the continent; and in British Columbia, cedar plank salmon.

There are few exclusively Canadian foods. However, butter tarts are so prevalent in Canada that they deserve special mention. The doyenne of Canadian cuisine, Elizabeth Baird, in confirming their unique position, even recommends them as a great treat for Canada Day (July 1). Their origin is unclear but one theory claims they are an adaptation of the southern US pecan pie. These little pastry shells, filled with a sticky mixture of butter, brown sugar, corn or maple syrup, and sometimes raisins or pecan nuts, are the subject of endless debates:

cued chicken can coexist with Jamaican ginger beer, as can Armenian *lahmajoon* (flatbread spread with ground lamb) with Thai salad and real ale from a microbrewery. The idea of melding all these cuisines into one distinct Canadian school of cookery has largely failed: simply put, Canadian cuisine focuses on the best of all its constituent cultures.

Of course there are the regional specialties that the whole country enjoys and that people use as a shorthand to define a region and its culture. In the Maritimes, lobster, mussels, oysters, and fiddlehead greens (ostrich fern), along with Prince Edward Island's famous potatoes; in Québec, maple-sugar pie, Oka cheese, and old-style bagels; in Alberta, possibly the best

PICK OF THE WINES

Ontario and British Columbia wines consistently win major international awards. The quality assurance program, VQA (Vintner's Quality Assurance) ensures that labeled wines come from specified lands as well as pass sensory tests to confirm varietal characteristics. Every winery has something special to offer, but here are a few of the highlights:

• In British Columbia, Black Hills Winery, Lake Breeze Vineyards, Sandhill, Sumac Ridge Estate Winery and Tinhorn Creek Vineyards.

• In Ontario, Cave Spring, Château des Charmes, Jackson Triggs Niagara Estate, Malivoire, Thirty Bench winemaker.

should they be runny or chewy, is sugar or syrup or both the best, where are the best butter tarts in the country?

Creating a Canadian cuisine

Today Canada is home to some of the finest chefs in the world, many of whom create "market-inspired" cuisine, relying on the excellence and abundance of local ingredients to craft inspired dishes with blueberries, fiddlehead greens, wild rice, maple syrup, bison, and seafood. One well-known Canadian chef, Michael Stadtlander, abandoned Toronto to move operation to a farm in the country,

tious, they aren't – people here genuinely care about their food and are interested in knowing everything about it, even its provenance.

In the **Atlantic provinces**, the first French settlers have left a lasting and treasured legacy. Although most of those settlers, the Acadians, were forcibly removed by the British in the 18th century (and transported south to Louisiana, today's Cajuns), many managed to return. Their influence is very evident in Nova Scotia and New Brunswick, in *galettes* (oatmeal and molasses cookies), *fayots au lard* (pork and beans), and *poutines* (delectable fruit pastries). Halifax became the center of British social life, German

where he could move to the 5-mile (8km) diet for his patrons.

Canadians are keenly aware of their country's gastronomic resources, and are using more homegrown foods and produce. Indeed, menus have become longer, not because there are more items, but because the descriptions include the provenance of the main ingredients. In Vancouver, the duck will be Polderside, the pork Sloping Hill Berkshire, the oysters Fanny Bay, the lamb from Salt Spring Island or perhaps Peace River. While the descriptions may seem preten-

LEFT: salmon dried in the traditional way.
ABOVE LEFT: wine for sale at Blasted Church Vineyards.
ABOVE: that finishing touch makes all the difference.

farmers settled in Lunenburg, and the Loyalists brought with them the flavors of New England and the South. In the 19th century, Irish and Scottish immigrants introduced oatcakes and shortbread, along with traditional stews.

Some of North America's oldest culinary traditions are found in Newfoundland, settled by Irish and English fishermen. Salt cod, salt beef, pork, molasses, and root vegetables are still staples today, although many of the recipes have been updated.

Most of **Québec**'s early settlers came from northeastern France, some from the Charente-Maritime region north of Bordeaux. Today, its cuisine draws gourmands from all over the continent, not only with its traditional fare, such as *tourtière* – a meat pie with ingredients that vary according to region – and contemporary French cuisine, using locally produced products including foie gras, cassis, and shockingly good cheeses.

Long before the first European settlers arrived in southern **Ontario**, the Huron and Iroquois nations were cultivating corn, pumpkins, and beans. The United Empire Loyalists who came north after the American Revolution were mostly of British stock. The province's culinary contribution today rests on its agricultural produce, its wines from Niagara vineyards, and Toronto's unbelievable array of ethnic cuisines.

Manitoba, **Saskatchewan** and **Alberta** have come a long way since immigrant Scottish crofters to the prairies survived on little more than oatmeal, and the Métis cooked in the way of their Indian and French-Canadian heritage. Mennonites, Scandinavians from the Dakotas, and American ranchers moved north, and cowboys lived on steak, beans, flapjacks, and raisin pies. Ukrainians, Eastern Europeans, Icelanders, European Jews, and Chinese, with their own culinary traditions, contributed to shifting the emphasis from a heavily British one to a brave new multicultural world.

British Columbia enjoys the flavors of Asian

A QUICK GUIDE TO CANADIAN BEERS

Part of the Canadian stereotype is beer, along with back bacon, hockey, and winter. While the rest may be questionable, the beer part has a ring of truth. Canada has a long brewing tradition, initially dominated by Molson and Labatt's. There were some smaller regional breweries, but nothing really exciting until microbreweries took off in the mid-1980s. Microbreweries focus on offering natural beers of distinction and taste, and brewpubs across the entire country now produce an array of specialty beers, from ales and lagers to bitters and stouts.

The big breweries have formed alliances with (or been bought outright by) international consortiums, so the concept of a truly "Canadian beer" leads the discerning drinker

to the craft breweries. Passionate beer devotees now make the discovery of each town's best beer an exciting adventure as important as any museum, park or historic site. Forget Molson, Labatt's and all the multi-national brands: choose the local beverages and compare across the regions. Here are a few producers and beers to watch for:
• Big Rock – Grasshopper Wheat Ale
• Les Brasseurs du Nord – Boréale Rousse
• Gahan House – Iron Horse Dark Ale
• Nelson Brewing Company – Paddywhack India Pale Ale (organic)
• Propeller – India Pale Ale
• Yukon Brewing Company – Yukon Red

cuisines as well as the initial British penchant for joints of meat and hearty stews. Vancouver enjoys a restaurant scene that is hard to beat: its environmentally aware populace have supported sustainable programs, including Green Table, whose member restaurants commit to reduced waste and more recycling, more eco-friendly practices and more products that benefit the local economy.

The gourmet influence has even begun to extend to the **Yukon**, the **Northwest Territories** and **Nunuvut**, at least as far as serving tourists is concerned. The sparse population of First Nations and Inuit peoples is augmented

in cities across the country, so vodka rules, but more as a statement of identity.

Whether it's an espresso martini in Vancouver's Yaletown, (equal parts of chilled espresso coffee, vanilla-infused vodka. Kahlua, and Frangelico) or the Companions of the Quaich at a regular meeting to nose and savor the most exclusive Scotch whiskies, Canadians like to make statements with their choice of drink. Canada, despite high taxes on alcohol, boasts some of the most ardent supporters of the highest quality products. For visitors, it's a great opportunity to taste magnificent wines from all over the world.

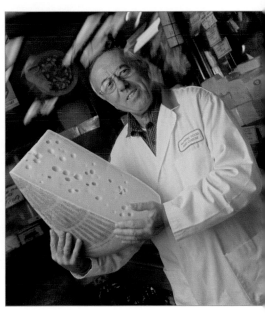

by outsiders working in government and business. Here the introduction of canned and packaged foods has resulted in the loss of many of the traditional ways of eating, such as caribou, moose, seal, and wild fowl.

Drinking in Canada

Wine and beer are mentioned in separate panels – suffice to add that there are amazing selections of both. Aside from beer and wine, Canadians like their share of spirits. Globalization has had its influence on the bar scene

On the non-alcoholic front, the European-style cafe, complete with croissants and pains-au-chocolat, was once to be found only in Montréal, but cafes are readily found in all cities and many smaller towns. While Starbucks outlets abound, there are plenty of independents offering a quality personalized experience as well. Even the Canadian doughnut chain Tim Hortons has embraced its version with its iced cappuccino (not something that would appeal to a die-hard Italian coffee-lover, but a step up from drip coffee with a scoop of ice cream…).

It's also not surprising that it's relatively easy to find a properly steeped cup of tea here as well. After all, the British did rule here for a few centuries. ❑

LEFT: Canada has a long brewing tradition.
ABOVE LEFT: a fine selection of freshly-baked bread.
ABOVE RIGHT: cheese at St Lawrence Market.

PLACES

A detailed guide to the entire country,
with principal sites cross-referenced by
number to the maps

anada is the second-largest country in the world, stretching over 5,500km (3,400 miles) from the Atlantic Ocean to the Pacific and over 4,600km (2,900 miles) from the northern tip of Ellesmere Island to the United States border.

This sprawling country is not, of course, fully inhabited: 89 percent of the land has no permanent population. In sharp contrast are the urban areas, where nearly 80 percent of Canadians live in large centers located within a few hours' drive of the southern border, mostly in Ontario, Québec or British Columbia.

The country is dominated by its three principal cities: Toronto, Montréal, and Vancouver – places that have elicited comment for centuries. Toronto, for instance, invited the observation by Charles Mackay in 1859 that "there is a Yankee look about the place… a pushing, thrusting, business-like smart appearance." Montréal, on the other hand, "conveys the idea of a substantial, handsomely built European town, with modern

improvements of half French, half English architecture." Vancouver is a different kind of place altogether, looking neither to America nor to Europe for its inspiration.

Rural Canada is divided into 10 provinces and three territories. Newfoundland and Labrador is the most easterly province, bordering the North Atlantic; Prince Edward Island is the smallest; Nova Scotia is a peninsula; New Brunswick is nearly rectangular with a gentle, undulating land; Québec's and Ontario's cities and high-octane profiles make them the best known – although Alberta is fast catching up; while the Prairie provinces of Manitoba and Saskatchewan are less exuberant.

Rudyard Kipling was particularly pleased with the clean air and pioneering spirit of British Columbia, observing in 1908 that "such a land is good for an energetic man. It is also not so bad for the loafer." Energy is certainly needed for exploring Canada's three territories: the Yukon, the Northwest Territories and, its newest one, Nunavut. You can loaf here, too. Or anywhere in Canada, for that matter.   ❑

PRECEDING PAGES: Miscou Island lighthouse, New Brunswick; Basilique
Notre-Dame, Montréal; Toronto Caribbean Carnival. **LEFT:** the Rockies, Alberta.
ABOVE: the village of Arcadia, Nova Scotia; the bright lights of Toronto.

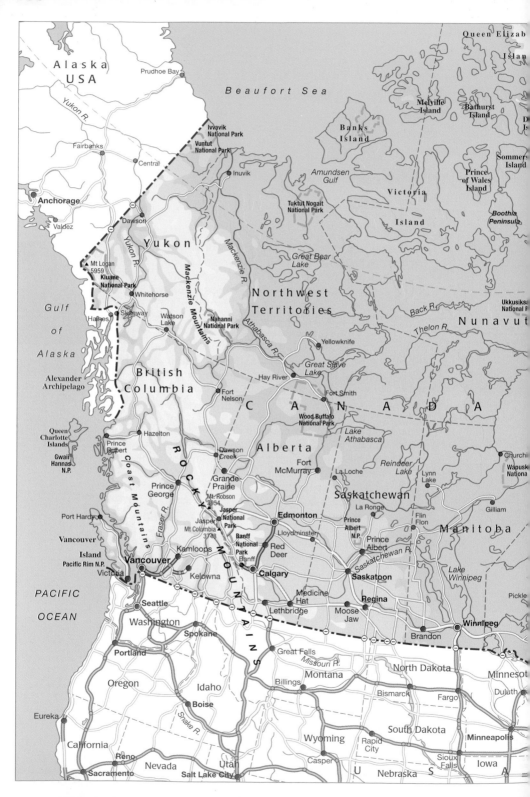

Canada

0	250 km
0	250 miles

CENTRAL CANADA

Heartland of Canada's colonial history, Ontario and Québec offer a wealth of different experiences for the traveler

To the considerable displeasure of the other provinces, Québec and Ontario house not only Canada's most prosperous cities, but also more than half its population. Rich in their cultural traditions, these provinces represent the origins of colonial Canada and contain remnants of the historic tension between their British and French forebears.

They also have the most tourists – 57 percent of all Canada's international visitors, who generate 54 percent of the country's tourism revenues. Toronto, with its lakeside setting and bubbling nightlife, is an obvious starting point. The nation's capital, Ottawa, is on the eastern edge of the province of Ontario, which extends north and west into the Arctic.

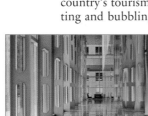

Often overlooked, northern Ontario is a vast but accessible region of pristine lakes and quiet townships. The chapter on the province is designed to give a feel for the area by walking through its cities, towns, rural communities, and parks. Ottawa is highlighted, as well as gems such as Stratford, Elora, Goderich, Kingston, Picton, and Algonquin Park.

Québec is the other historical center of Canada. Here the emphasis is on Québec's uniquely French nature, its cultural institutions, its festivals, and its conflict with British customs, and the efforts of the province's inhabitants to retain their heritage. A detailed account of everything Montréal has to offer is followed by a visit to Québec City, and a trip up the St Lawrence River into the countryside, ending at the Gaspé Peninsula in the estuary of the St Lawrence River. ❏

LEFT: the unmistakeable Flatiron Building, Toronto.
ABOVE: Kingston boating docks; brightly colored stained glass at Palais de Congres, Montréal; fresh berries in a Montréal market.

TORONTO

The multicultural city of Toronto has a dazzling assortment of ethnic neighborhoods, a vibrant waterfront, theaters, concert halls, clubs, galleries, and some of the best shopping in North America

The largest city in the second largest country in the world is best approached by car and at night. Toronto is cradled within small hills that roll down gently to the calm north shore of Lake Ontario. A sheltered Great Lakes port, it has a magnificent downtown skyline when viewed from the highways that hug the lake shore. In the dark, the glowing office buildings and the trademark CN Tower have an alien beauty.

A meeting place

From around 1000 BC, natives gathered here to trade, socialize, and relax. In fact the name Toronto comes from a Huron Indian word meaning "Place of Meeting." In 1615 an explorer called Etienne Brûlé discovered an Iroquois village here on the Humber River, and later a fur-trading post was established by the French in 1720. The British became the ruling power after the defeat of the French on the Plains of Abraham in 1759, and in 1787 they purchased the land Toronto now stands on from local Mississauga Indians – who by then had replaced the Iroquois. Gradually a settlement grew around the natural harbor.

In 1793 Toronto, renamed York, became the new capital of Upper Canada (today's southern Ontario). Throughout the War of 1812, York remained loyal to Britain, although in 1813 it was briefly occupied twice by the Americans.

After incorporation in 1834, the city was renamed Toronto. From the early 1800s, waves of British immigrants arrived, and later 40,000 Irish immigrants, as a result of the potato famine in 1847. The first Jewish immigrants arrived from Europe in the 1830s, and another wave came in the 1880s.

Loyal royal subjects

Until the end of the 19th century, British immigrants were the largest group by far, and their loyalty to Queen Victoria and to everything the British

Main attractions
ROGERS CENTER
CN TOWER
HOCKEY HALL OF FAME
ST LAWRENCE MARKET
DISTILLERY DISTRICT
HARBOURFRONT CENTRE
TORONTO ISLANDS
ROYAL ONTARIO MUSEUM

PRECEDING PAGES:
Equinox Festival.
LEFT: a street
performer at
Buskerfest.
BELOW: the iconic
CN Tower.

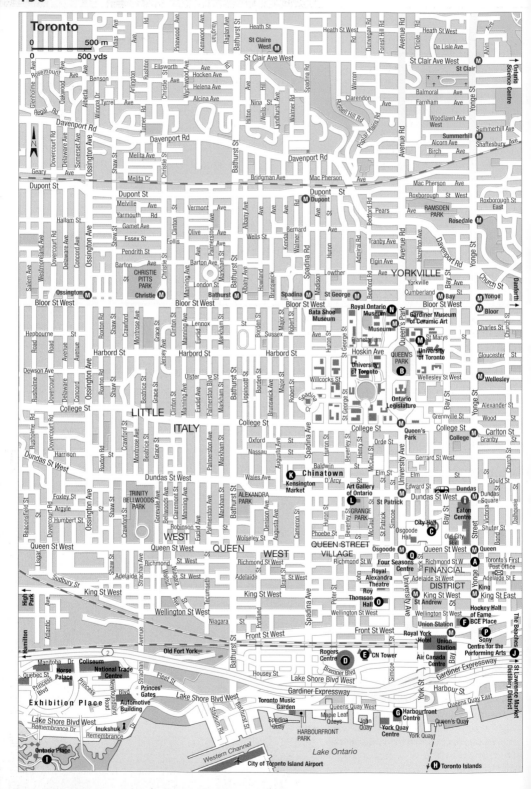

Toronto

0 — 500 m
0 — 500 yds

St Claire West

St Clair Ave West

St Clair Ave West

St Clair

Ontario Science Centre

Heath St

Heath St West

Heath St West

De Lisle Ave

Alvin

Rosemount Ave

Benson

Ellsworth Ave

Hocken Ave

Wychwood Ave

Helena Ave

Alcina Ave

Warren

Clarendon

Balmoral Ave

Farnham Ave

Woodlawn Ave West

Summerhill

Alcorn Ave

Shaftesbury Ave

Birch Ave

Atlas Ave

Arlington

Rushton

Hilton

Wells

Lyndhurst Ave

Walmer Rd

Russell Hill Rd

Poplar Plains Rd

Davenport Rd

Davenport Rd

Davenport Rd

Davenport Rd

Bridgman Ave

Mac Pherson Ave

Mac Pherson Ave

Roxborough St West

Roxborough St East

Dupont St

Dupont St

Dupont St

Dupont

Pears

RAMSDEN PARK

Rosedale

Melville Ave

Yarmouth Rd

Vermont Ave

Clinton

Albany Ave

Bernard Ave

Kendal

Walmer

Bedford Rd

Tranby Ave

Hazelton Ave

Gamet Ave

Essex St

Olive Ave

Wells St

Huron

Admiral Rd

Elgin Ave

Avenue Rd

YORKVILLE

Barton

Barton Ave

Howland Ave

Brunswick

Lowther Ave

Yorkville

Cumberland

Bay

Church St

CHRISTIE PITTS PARK

Christie

Ossington

Bloor St West

Bloor St West

Bathurst

Spadina

St George

Bloor St West

Royal Ontario Museum

Museum

Bloor St West

Gardiner Museum of Ceramic Art

Yonge

Bloor

Bata Shoe Museum

Planetarium

St Marys

Hepbourne

Roxton

Crawford

Montrose Ave

Grace Ave

Clinton St

Lennox

Major St

Robert St

Sussex Ave

Hoskin Ave

QUEEN'S PARK

University of Toronto

Charles St

Gloucester

Harbord St

Harbord St

Harbord St

Wellesley St W

Wellesley

Dewson Ave

Ulster

Borden St

Willcocks St

Ontario Legislature

Grenville St

Wood

Alexander St

College St

LITTLE ITALY

College St

College St

Queen's Park

College St

College

Carlton

Granby

Oxford St

Baldwin

Nassau St

Gerrard West

Gerrard West

Elm

Wales Ave

Chinatown

Kensington Market

D'Arcy

Art Gallery of Ontario

St Patrick

Edward St

Dundas

Dundas Square

Dundas St West

Dundas St West

TRINITY BELLWOODS PARK

ALEXANDRA PARK

Denison Ave

Augusta Ave

Cameron St

GRANGE PARK

City Hall

Eaton Centre

Old City Hall

Osgoode Hall

Queen St West

Queen St West

WEST

Queen St West

QUEEN WEST

QUEEN STREET VILLAGE

Osgoode

Queen St West

Queen

Foxley St

Argyle

Humbert St

Robinson

Wolseley St

Richmond St W

Richmond St W

Four Seasons Centre

Richmond St W

FINANCIAL DISTRICT

Toronto's First Post Office

Queen St West

Adelaide

Richmond

Adelaide St West

King St West

Wellington St West

Adelaide St West

Royal Alexandra Theatre

Roy Thomson Hall

Adelaide St East

King St West

St Andrew

Wellington St W

King St East

Hockey Hall of Fame

Union Station

Royal York Hotel

Union Station

BCE Place

Sony Centre for the Performing Arts

High Park

Sudbury St

King St West

Wellington St West

Niagara St

Front St West

Front St West

Air Canada Centre

Gardiner Expressway

The Beaches

St Lawrence Market Distillery District

Hamilton

Old Fort York

Rogers Centre

CN Tower

Bremner Blvd

Lake Shore Blvd West

Harbour St

Harbourfront Centre

Queen's Quay

Coliseum

National Trade Centre

Princes' Gates

Horse Palace

Lake Shore Blvd West

Gardiner Expressway

Toronto Music Garden

Maple Leaf Quays

Queens Quay West

Harbourfront Centre

York Quay Centre

Exhibition Place

Automotive Building

HARBOURFRONT PARK

John Quay

York Quay

Ontario Place

Inukshuk

Remembrance

Lake Ontario

Western Channel

City of Toronto Island Airport

Toronto Islands

Empire stood for meant that Toronto life was firmly shackled by a code of rigid moral values, including draconian Lord's Day legislation that prohibited most working, sporting, and entertainment activities on the Sabbath.

This did not, however, deter immigration. Following World War II, Toronto's population swelled with the arrival of refugees from Europe. In the 1970s, as a result of relaxed federal immigration laws, fresh waves came from Asia, Latin America, Africa, and the Caribbean. By the 1990s, Toronto's population of 3.8 million included hundreds of thousands of Caribbeans, Chinese, Italians, Greeks, and South Asian immigrants and their descendants, along with substantial groupings from most other parts of the world. Today more than 140 languages are spoken by the city's 90 (and counting) different ethnic groups. One result of this vibrant mixture, layered over the solid British underlay, is that Toronto became, de facto, the political, cultural, and financial juggernaut of Canadian accomplishment.

Subways, streetcars, and buses

Among Toronto's attributes are three subway lines, with all-night buses taking over after the trains stop rolling around 1.30am, 11 streetcar routes, and more than 140 bus routes. Despite the system's convenience and safety, Torontonians have been switching to automobile use over recent years. Efforts by the Toronto Transit Commission to lure them back to the trains sometimes result in commuters being jolted out of their early morning reverie by droll quips from a conductor over the PA system.

Toronto's longest street

Yonge Street divides the east and west sides of the city, stretching 1,896km (1,178 miles) north from the lakeshore in Toronto to Rainy River on the Ontario/Minnesota border. The underside of Toronto's thriving economy

becomes apparent as you walk along the **Yonge Street Strip** , between King and Bloor Streets, but it's worth investigating – not least because the bizarre mix of restaurants and stores offers some excellent bargains.

Power play

Usually a peaceful haven in the heart of Toronto, **Queen's Park** 🅑 is home to the Ontario Legislature Buildings. Built between 1886 and 1892, the imposing sandstone building has a historic Legislative Chamber and an impressive collection of 19th-century and early 20th-century Canadian art. After the landslide victory of the Progressive Conservative Party in the 1995 provincial election, and its re-election in 1999, legislation with far-ranging consequences on Ontario's social and municipal infrastructures – that reflected the party's so-called "Common Sense Revolution" – was pushed through the legislature. Conservative rule came to an end in 2003, with a

Transport is key to the city; from Union Station an "Underground City" has 27km (16 miles) of passages, with around 1,200 shops.

BELOW: try today's specials.

On September 5 1914, the Blue Jay baseball player, Babe Ruth, hit the first home run of his professional career at Hanlan's Point on Toronto Islands.

BELOW: Topol performs *Fiddler on the Roof*. **RIGHT:** modern art in the Financial District.

sweeping victory for the more moderate Liberals. Under Premier Dalton McGuinty, the Liberals won a second majority in October 2007.

Heart of the matter

What distinguishes Toronto from most North American cities is the vibrancy of its Downtown. Running through its center is **Bay Street**, the main artery of the country's financial capital. Most Canadian head offices and a huge stock exchange are on or close to it.

At the corner of Queen and Bay Streets, Toronto's newest **City Hall ⓒ**, which was designed by the Finnish architect Viljo Revell in 1965, is striking. Its vast rotunda and two curved towers, which flank the central dome, lord it over Nathan Phillips Square, where visitors can admire the sculptures. Henry Moore's sculpture, *The Artist*, was a controversial addition in the square's early years.

Minutes away are sizeable clusters of residential housing, from exclusive condominiums to Government-funded co-operative housing, the **Entertainment District** (Toronto claims to have

the world's third-largest live theater industry, after London and New York) with its attendant restaurants and clubs, and some of the city's most famous attractions.

Toronto's Downtown is also grail for thousands of sports fans. The Toronto Blue Jays and the Toronto Argonauts play baseball, and football, according to the season, at the 56,000-seat **Rogers Centre ⓓ**. The world's first retractable domed stadium squats besides another record-breaking building. A couple of blocks east, the **Air Canada Centre** is home to the Toronto Maple Leafs hockey team, the Toronto Raptors basketball team, and the Toronto Rock lacrosse team. The **CN Tower ⓔ** (www.cntower.ca; daily except Christmas Day until 11pm; charge) is, at 553 meters (1,815ft), the world's tallest freestanding structure, and an ever-present exclamation above the city. There are eateries cheek by jowl in this part of town, from the lofty **360** revolving restaurant at the top of the tower to cheerful Italian at **Kit Kat** on King Street West. A few blocks east, in BCE Place, at the corner of Front and Yonge

Street, is the **Hockey Hall of Fame** ❻ (www.hhof.com; seasonal opening hours; charge). It's a mecca for hockey buffs, with its collection dedicated to the history of Canada's national game; grown men have even been seen to weep in front of the hallowed Stanley Cup.

At the intersection of Front East and Jarvis Street is the **St Lawrence Market** (Tue–Sat), where the tradition of shopping goes back to 1803, although not in the same building. Torontonians still come in droves, every Saturday. The site was also home to Toronto's first two city halls. In this historically preserved neighborhood, old warehouses have been transformed into offices, studios, and restaurants. Between Parliament and Cherry Streets, the Gooderham and Worts Distillery has become a cultural hotbed.

The Distillery District (55 Mill Street; tel: 416-364-1177; www.thedistillerydistrict.com) occupies what was once the largest distillery in the British Empire. Founded in 1832, the 44 buildings of this site comprise the best-preserved collection of Victorian industrial architecture in North America. The business closed in 1990, and a little over ten years later, a local development company acquired the entire complex and proceeded to turn it into Toronto's newest art center. Today it houses art and dance studios, galleries, performance spaces, boutiques, restaurants, cafes, and even a microbrewery.

Down on the waterfront

Summers are special on Queen's Quay at **Harbourfront Centre** ❼ (daily 10am–11pm, Sun until 9pm; some events ticketed, many events free). The former warehouse has been converted into specialty stores, restaurants, and a theater. Patios overlook the lake, where sailboats, dinner cruises circling Toronto Islands, and the occasional tall ship grace the waterfront. World-class dance companies perform in the Fleck Dance Theatre, and in nearby York Quay Centre a dynamic range of cultural ventures takes place year round,

including the International Festival of Authors – a 10-day celebration of the world's best-known writers of fiction, poetry, drama, and biography.

Toronto Islands ❽ are actually a 5km (3-mile) strip of sandbar with several names, jutting out into the city's harbor. The island community is a unique aspect of Toronto, with a group of residents intent on preserving their simple way of life. In summer the choice land swarms with picnickers and, on occasion, youths with ghetto blasters, while the bitter winters bring winds that sweep mercilessly across Lake Ontario. Food and other supplies have to be ferried across or delivered to the airport at the island's west end. It's not what you'd call easy living, though most islanders wouldn't change it for the world. However, in 2006, the controversial launch of Porter Airlines, a small but growing airline that uses the Toronto Islands' airport as its base, continues to be viewed as a threat to their way of life.

It's a lovely haven in summer, and only about 10 minutes away by leisurely ferry. Once there, the 600-acre

BELOW: looking down on the Distillery District.

Fashion conscious in the city.

(243-hectare) park offers secluded beaches, meandering bicycle trails, the village community, and an amusement park. You can transport a bike across or rent one there for some of the nicest riding in the city. The **Rectory Cafe** is a hidden gem on the southside board-walk of Ward's Island, although it's difficult to beat the tranquility of an evening picnic amid the trees border-ing the north shoreline, watching the sun set over the city.

Parks and boardwalks

Toronto's waterfront has become increasingly accessible to walkers, cyclists, and in-line skaters, as lakeside trails are extended and widened. They stretch from **Scarborough Bluffs** in the east to the **Humber Bay Park** in the west, with its butterfly habitat and stunning memorial to the victims of the Air India crash. Well worth a detour is **High Park**, the city's largest park and home to a rare stand of black oak savannah and unusual plants such as blazing star and the sassafras tree. More manufactured leisure time can be had at **Ontario Place ❶** (mid–end

May and Labor Day–mid-Sept Sat–Sun, June–Labor Day daily; charge), a spacey lake-front attraction that offers prime viewing for the annual fire-works competition, the Canada Dry Festival of Fire. One of the most imagi-native arrivals on the waterfront, the **Toronto Music Garden** (475 Queens Quay West; daily) was conceived by internationally renowned cellist Yo-Yo Ma and is based on Johann Sebastian Bach's Suite No. 1 for Unaccompanied Cello. Each of the six dance move-ments within the suite corresponds to a different section in the garden.

The **Beaches ❶** are a favorite haunt on Toronto's east side. The best time to stroll along the boardwalk is on weekdays and evenings. Sailboats and seagulls skim the waves of Lake Ontario on one side, while joggers and strollers enjoy wooded parkland on the other. You can cut up to Queen Street, where an assortment of cafes, restaurants, and pubs caters to most palates and budgets. Among them are **The Beacher Cafe**, a Queen East mainstay, where you can sample eggs Benjamin (eggs Benedict with smoked

salmon), and the **Remarkable Bean**, which serves limited-edition coffees at chessboard tables.

Exploring Toronto's "villages"

Toronto's neighborhoods reflect the city's vibrant history, from the early Anglo-Saxon, pro-monarchist immigrants to the Afro-Caribbeans, Italians, Greeks, Chinese, Portuguese, Ukrainians, Poles, Indians, and Irish – among many others – who have all come to the city, each group carving out a neighborhood or two for its own.

You'll find Greeks on the Danforth, Italians and Portuguese on College Street and St Clair Avenue, the Chinese on Dundas Street, East Indians on Gerrard Street, Jamaicans on Bathurst Street, and Eastern Europeans on Roncesvalles Avenue or in Bloor West Village.

Kensington Market ❻, with its old-world boisterousness and scruffy charm, has witnessed much of this, since it began with Jewish immigrants in the 1920s and 1930s, who were later supplanted by Portuguese, Chinese, and West Indians.

The main thoroughfares are Augusta and Kensington Avenues, and their connecting streets, Baldwin and Oxford. Here you'll encounter frail, elderly Chinese ladies haggling with the Portuguese women who sell fruit and do incredible mental arithmetic in lieu of a cash register; leisurely Rastafarian merchants hawking spicy beef patties and sharp ginger beer; and black-clad Italian widows carrying home several tonnes of fresh fruit or vegetables on one arm. Drop by **Amadeu's**, a popular Portuguese eatery that specializes in seafood and Portuguese wines at reasonably modest prices, at the south end of Augusta.

At Augusta and Dundas Street West, **Chinatown** and Kensington Market meet. With the massive growth of its Chinese population, the greater area of Toronto now has six distinct Chinatowns. This one is the biggest, and

bustles with shoppers and hawkers all day and long into the night. Sprawling along Dundas and north up Spadina are overflowing fruit and vegetable stands, Chinese herbalists, and grocery stores. Mouthwatering smells wafting through open doors may well prompt you to search out some of the city's best Chinese restaurants – places like **Happy Seven** and **Sang Ho**.

Presiding on the threshold of Chinatown is the **Art Gallery of Ontario** ❶ (Wed–Fri 10am–9pm, noon–9pm in winter, Sat–Sun year-round 10am–5.30pm; charge). The AGO commenced a three-year, $500 million expansion in 2005.

The doors to the transformed art gallery re-opened in 2008, with more than 68,000 visitors streaming through in its opening week, eager to visit the new glass-fronted galleries with their additional 10,000 works of art. The AGO has the world's largest public collection of Henry Moore sculptures, most of them a direct gift from the sculptor, and an impressive collection of Inuit work. The permanent collection ranges from 15th-century

Worth the Wait

For three years, visitors to the AGO made do with a much-reduced gallery amidst massive reconstruction. Their patience was amply rewarded with its re-opening in November 2008. Reaction to the innovative design of celebrated architect Frank Gehry – particularly to the Douglas fir-clad curving staircase rising from the Walker Court and to the Galleria Italia, a powerful, soaring space that fronts AGO's north-facing facade – has been ecstatic. Although Gehry was born in Toronto this was his first work in Canada.

Close to half of the permanent collection of some 73,000 works of art documents Canada's art heritage from pre-Confederation to the present, with pivotal works by Cornelius Krieghoff, James Wilson Morrice, Tom Thomson, the Group of Seven, David Milne, and Emily Carr and an impressive collection of Inuit work.

Of these, 2,000 came from Ken Thomson's (Lord Thomson of Fleet, Canadian art collector) extraordinary collection; among them, an important group of First Nations objects spans two millennia, from around 200 BC to the late 19th century, greatly enriching the gallery's holdings of historical First Nations art.

One highlight is Ruben's masterpiece *The Massacre of the Innocents* – purchsed for a record $117 million.

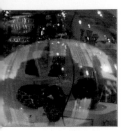

Time to reflect in Yorkville.

European paintings to international contemporary works of art.

Another of the city's livelier neighborhoods is **The Danforth**. For about 10 blocks, from Broadview to Coxwell, the Greeks have taken over the main east-west artery of the city. Even the street signs are bilingual, while every other restaurant is a taverna. At the long-established **Asteria Souvlaki Place** patrons enjoy bouzoukis and souvlakis on the outside patio in summer, while a highly touted, more elegant addition to the scene is **Pan on the Danforth**.

The Italian community is the city's largest non-Anglo ethnic group, numbering considerably more than 420,000 people. Long popular with students and artists, **Little Italy** is one of the earlier communities, centered on College Street between Grace and Ossington Streets.

A perfect evening begins at **Souz Dahl**, a romantic, candlelit bar that pours magnificent martinis; continues at **Grappa**, for its cheerful atmosphere and excellent food; and ends at the **Sicilian Ice Cream Company** for *gelati* and cappuccino.

Close to the **University of Toronto ⓜ**, The Annex is a well-established student hangout, stretching along Bloor Street West from Spadina Avenue to Bathurst Street. To the north, gracious buildings on shady streets are either student fraternity houses or the elegant (and pricey) homes of professionals and artists. Housing south of Bloor is usually of a more modest scale, built to accommodate the waves of Jewish, Chinese, Italian, and Portuguese newcomers as they arrived in Toronto.

Inexpensive eateries offering an enticing variety of ethnic cuisines are an integral part of the Annex. Two popular longtime fixtures are **By The Way Café** for its Middle Eastern-inspired dishes, and **Pauper's**, a pub housed in a former bank, with a lively piano bar downstairs and a romantic sundown rooftop patio above.

Three remarkable museums border the Annex. The **Bata Shoe Museum** (Mon–Sat 10am–5pm, Thur until 8pm, Sun noon–5pm; charge), at Bloor and St George Streets, houses an extraordinarily comprehensive collection of shoes and related arti-

BELOW LEFT: Little Italy, home to Toronto's Italian community.
BELOW RIGHT: fancy footwear at the Bata Shoe Museum.

facts in a dramatic "shoebox" structure designed by renowned architect Raymond Moriyama. Spanning some 4,500 years, its collection explores the extent to which shoes reflect the living habits, culture, and customs of the people who wore them.

A few minutes' walk away, on University Avenue, is the **Royal Ontario Museum** (daily 10am–6pm, Fri until 9pm; charge). Known locally as ROM, the museum is one of the world's few multidiscipline museums – which means its exhibits range from science to art to archeology. ROM's East Asian collection is world-renowned, and includes an impressive collection of temple art. A stunning crystal addition composed of five interlocking prismatic structures, designed by Daniel Libeskind, houses seven new galleries.

On the other side of University Avenue is the **Gardiner Museum of Ceramic Art** (daily 10am–6pm, Fri until 9pm, Sat–Sun until 5pm; charge). It's another one-of-a-kind in North America, with a spectacular collection of pottery and porcelain treasures spanning some 3,000 years.

Abutting the Annex is **Yorkville**, a couple of trendy blocks delineated by Cumberland Street and Yorkville Avenue, where – in red-brick, Victorian houses – Yorkville's designer boutiques and trendy art galleries are all the rage. The neighboring streets of Hazelton and Scollard are fertile territory for collectors of North American Native Indian artifacts and Inuit sculpture and prints.

Amid the glitz is **The Coffee Mill**, a basement-level eatery that dishes up marvelous Hungarian fare in a thoroughly unpretentious fashion.

In the city's West End, two up-and-coming neighborhoods are grabbing attention. **West Queen West** was once a down-at-heel extension of Queen Street West, but inexpensive rents have led to an influx of art galleries, eclectic boutiques, and trendy eateries and bars. In **Roncesvalles Village**, Polish newcomers took over from the original very British community.

Today its Old World ambience has become more edgy. Jazz and cabaret-style clubs and pubs, as well as several acclaimed restaurants, sit amongst the

The family-friendly Ontario Science Centre (daily 10am–5pm, Thur until 8pm; charge) has nine exhibition halls packed with interesting displays. Past exhibits have ranged from comic book superheroes to bird-watching.

BELOW:
the Royal Ontario Museum.

Map on page 138

BELOW: Toronto
Symphony
Orchestra.
RIGHT: the drop
zone at the
Canadian National
Exhibition.

fruit and veggie markets, and the Polish butchers, bakers, and delis.

The Anglo-Saxon roots of Toronto still hold dominion in one neighborhood. **Rosedale** is where the reticent, affluent people who run the financial and legal district centered on Bay Street continue to live – often with a BMW or two in their garage. The tour buses detour here from time to time for a quick, wish-it-were-me-living-here gawk.

When night falls

For decades, it seemed, Torontonians were accustomed to their city being disparagingly referred to as "Toronto the Good" by other Canadians. Indeed, Toronto nightlife used to be plagued by a Victorian carry-over, enforcing tight restrictions on the city's bars. Today's legislation permits them to stay open until 2am, so between that and the city's all-night dance clubs, night owls have more time to party.

The live-music scene is eclectic and very good, offering jazz, rock, funk, folk, or almost anything else you might be into. Toronto has a good underground of amateur bands and it's a habitual stop on most music tours, especially for European bands. Prices and quality vary hugely from place to place so it's best to consult the advertisements in either *Now* or *Eye*, two free entertainment weeklies.

Multiculturalism, naturally, has an imprint on Toronto entertainment. Each October, in Little India, Diwali – or the Festival of Lights – is the largest festival celebrated in the city's South Asian community, while Caribana, the annual Caribbean festival, is an exuberant affair that's one of the city's biggest summertime draws.

On a more erudite note, the Toronto Symphony Orchestra, the Canadian Opera Company, and the National Ballet of Canada are all world-class outfits based in Toronto, with extensive fall and winter seasons. Those able to meet the pecuniary demands of the box offices of the **Roy Thomson Hall ⓞ**, **Sony Centre for the Performing Arts ⓟ** (currently being renovated), and the sparkling new **Four Seasons Centre for the Performing Arts ⓠ**, will undoubtedly be suitably impressed by the performances at these venues.

A cultured city

Toronto is one of the world's greatest theater cities, with more than 200 professional theater and dance companies. Since 2007, local, national, and international artists take to Toronto's stages, streets, and public spaces for ten days each June, offering theatre, dance, classical and contemporary music, film, literature, and visual arts during Luminato. On the literary scene alone, with its annual International Authors Festival and year-round Harbourfront Reading Series, Toronto has been compared with Paris in the 1920s. Toronto writers and filmmakers are recognized as international trendsetters.

And yet Toronto manages to retain, with its varied population, both a small-town aura and healthy dollops of European charm. With enough of whatever it takes to make a great city, it's something of a joy to visit. ❑

ONTARIO

Ontario is one of the world's most urbanized regions, with towns standing like high-tech sandcastles by the Great Lakes. Venture north, however, and you'll discover a wilderness of water and forests

The most American of Canada's provinces, thrust down into the industrial heartland of the United States, Ontario remains profoundly suspicious of the Great Republic, and even now is still somewhat attached to the British monarchy. It is a highly modernized region, but it is also a wilderness with 90 percent of its area under forest.

But it is a land, a country, a home. Underlying the exotic diversity of Ontario's population is a common love of place, whether that place be a Gothic revival farmhouse at Punkeydoodles Corners or a New Age zucchini plot on Toronto's Markham Street. In 1844 J.R. Godley, a traveler from Great Britain, described Upper Canada as a place where "everybody is a foreigner and home in their mouths invariably means another country." Today Ontario is still a land of many peoples, but its residents have found their home.

The voyageurs' heartlands

Although home to the Canadian Indians for millennia, and a corridor for the fur trade, the living essence of modern Ontario isn't found in the longhouse or canoe portage, but in the limestone homes of the United Empire Loyalists that stretch along the St Lawrence River.

More than any other region of Ontario, **Eastern Ontario** remains devoted to the Loyalist traditions of "peace, order, and good government." The stolid farmhouses, regal court-

houses, and towering Anglican spires proclaim that no matter what the "democrats and levelers" in western Ontario may do, the East will be faithful to the province's motto: "loyal she began, loyal she remains."

There's no more historically resonant place to begin a tour of Ontario than in the counties of **Prescott-Russell** and **Glengarry**, wedged between the Ottawa and St Lawrence rivers. The lower Ottawa countryside appears more Québécois than Upper Canadian. Barns boldly decked out in orange and green,

Main attractions
UPPER CANADA VILLAGE
OTTAWA
NIAGARA FALLS
NIAGARA-ON-THE-LAKE
POINT PELEE NATIONAL PARK
SANDBANKS PROVINCIAL PARK
ALGONQUIN PROVINCIAL PARK

PRECEDING PAGES:
Thousand Islands
Parkway. **LEFT:**
Changing of the
Guard. **BELOW:**
Algonquin
Provincial Park.

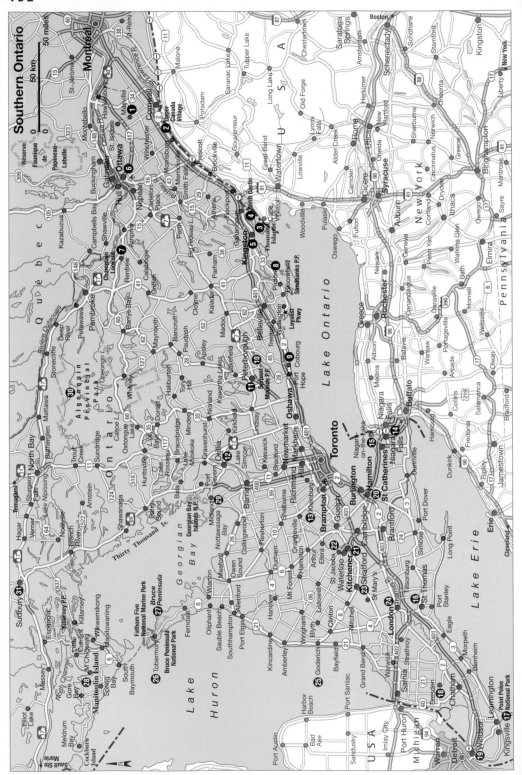

silvery "ski-jump" roofs, and towns centered on massive parish churches reveal a distinct French-Canadian character.

But this is Ontario, not Québec. Surveyed by British army engineers, all of Southern Ontario is rationally divided into little blocks (lots) within big blocks (townships) dissected by concession roads that irrationally ignore such non-Euclidian features as rocks, boulders, hills, lakes, and swamps.

Driving southwest from the Ottawa River, the French place names give way to towns named Dunvegan, Lochiel, Maxville, and Alexandria, telltale signs that this is now Glengarry County. Glengarry was the first of the hundreds of Scottish settlements in Ontario.

Beginning with the arrival of the loyalist Royal Highland Emigrant Regiment in 1783, the hill country north of the St Lawrence became the destination of thousands of emigrant Scots. Entire parishes from Glengarry, Scotland, emigrated for the promise of free land and the chance to escape the oppression of their landlords.

Each year in early August former residents are drawn back for the Glengarry Highland Games at **Maxville** ❶, 60km (37 miles) east of Ottawa, to throw a caber or toss back a scotch.

River of empire

At **Cornwall**, Ontario's easternmost city, 30km (18 miles) south of Maxville, the **Robert Saunders St Lawrence Generating Station** stretches across the river to harness the thrust of the Great Lakes as they are funneled towards the Atlantic. Appropriately, an abstract mural by the artist Harold Town adorns the observation tower. For this is a triumph of the modern technological age over the defiant, age-old barrier of the Long Sault and International Rapids. With the opening of the **St Lawrence Seaway** in 1959, the interior of the continent was made accessible to the ocean-going giants and the St Lawrence superseded the Rhine as the world's foremost river of commerce.

It is a river of empire. The French and English struggled for 150 years to determine control of the Great Lakes waterway, and when they were done the Canadians and Americans took up the cudgels. Indeed, it is a ripe irony typical

At Dunvegan, near Maxville, one of Glengarry Museum's prize exhibits is a cooking pot used by Bonnie Prince Charlie at Glengarry, Scotland, 1746.

BELOW:
a traditional Scottish event, tossing the caber.

of Canada that in order to remain British the American loyalists emigrated to share this river with the ancient enemy of the British Empire: *Les Canadiens*.

At **Morrisburg**, upriver from Cornwall, **Upper Canada Village ②** (mid-May–mid Oct daily 9.30am–5pm; charge) presents an historical recreation of what life was like for these loyalist immigrants. Early log cabins are juxtaposed with spacious American classical revival houses, illustrating the changing fortunes of the first political refugees to find a Canadian haven.

Iroquois legend tells of two potent spirits, one good the other evil, who battled for control of the mighty St Lawrence. In their titanic struggle, huge boulders were tossed across the river in a great cannonade, many to fall short into the narrows leading into Lake Ontario. With the triumph of the good spirit, a magical blessing fell upon the land bringing rich forests of yellow birch, red and white trillium, silver maple, and winged sumac to life upon the countless granite chunks scattered about the river. Today they are called the **Thousand Islands ③**.

Brockville, 85km (53 miles) southwest of Cornwall, a stately loyalist city with early architectural treasures along Courthouse Avenue, serves as the eastern gateway to the islands. Cruises around the numberless islands leave from nearby **Rockport** and **Gananoque**, a more rambunctious resort town 53km (33 miles) closer to Kingston. The Thousand Islands have long been a playground for the very rich who, no matter how bad their taste in architecture, always seem to have an eye for the world's most extraordinary real estate. The most famous of the millionaire "cottages" is an unfinished one named **Boldt Castle ④** (mid-May–mid-Oct daily from 10am; charge), which broods over Heart Island. As it is on American soil, visitors who are not American must bring proper identification, generally a passport.

Begun in 1898 by George Boldt, king of the Waldorf Astoria, it was never completed due to his grief over his wife's death. Today it stands open to the elements and to the curious, and a major on-going restoration is underway to restore this piece of island history. A more lasting monument to Boldt is the Thousand Islands salad dressing that his chef concocted in honor of the region.

The once and future king

Briefly the capital of the United Provinces of Canada (1841–3), the city of **Kingston ⑤** has never quite recovered from Queen Victoria's folly in naming Ottawa the new capital of the Dominion of Canada in 1857. Kingston certainly meets all the requirements of a capital city: a venerable history stretching back to 1673 and Fort Frontenac; a quiet dignity redolent in the weathered stone houses that line its streets; and a grandiose, neo-Classical **City Hall**, erected in 1843 in expectation of Kingston's greater destiny. The Martello towers strategically placed around the town's harbor, and the great limestone bulwark of **Fort Henry** (mid-May–mid-Sept daily 10am–5pm; charge) are testi-

BELOW: John H. Fulford memorial fountain, Brockwell.

mony to the enduring fear of invasion that the War of 1812 engendered.

Apparently, the spirit of 1812 lives on at **Queen's University**, the pride of Kingston, founded as a Presbyterian seminary in 1841. In 1956 the student body invaded the nearby town of Watertown, New York, under cloak of night, replacing the "Stars and Stripes" flying at public buildings with Union flags.

The memory of Sir John A. Macdonald, the first prime minister of Canada, is as permanent a fixture in Kingston as any fort or college. **Bellevue House** (daily, Apr–May and Sept–Oct 10am–5pm, June–Labor Day 9am–6pm; charge), an Italianate villa occupied by Macdonald in the late 1840s, is now a museum filled with memorabilia of the Old Chieftain. More importantly, Macdonald's unofficial political headquarters, the **Grimason House** (now the **Royal Tavern**), is still standing and open for business in the city center.

Just to the east of Kingston, between the harbor and old Fort Henry, lies the southern entrance of the **Rideau Canal**. Built between 1826 and 1832, the canal follows the path of the **Rideau River** route northeast through 47 locks, numerous lakes, and excavated channels until it emerges beside **Parliament Hill** on the Ottawa River. Today the canal region is a pleasure-boat captain's delight. Sleek-lined yachts and flat-bottomed cabin cruisers play snakes and ladders with the great stone locks, many of which are as they were over a 150 years ago.

To the thousands of Irish laborers brought to Canada to construct the canal, the route was a foul, mosquito-ridden wilderness and their British Army taskmasters nothing less than Pharaoh's satraps. Rapids were dammed, boulders blasted, and huge stone blocks hauled through roadless forests. The cost in human life was terrific. Construction in the 30km (18-mile) long Cranberry marsh took 1,000 workers through yellow fever.

The purpose of the canal was military, not economic. The British Army wanted a second, more secure route connecting Upper and Lower Canada in the event of an American seizure of the St Lawrence. The military character of the canal is evident at **Merrickville**, 48km (30 miles) southwest of Ottawa, where the largest of the 22 blockhouses that were built to protect the route still looms over the river.

Many of the canal's laborers settled in the region. A bevy of Scottish master stonemasons, lured across the water to build the locks, stayed on to build the town of **Perth** on the Tay River, 41km (25 miles) west of Merrickville. Perth today is a feast of exquisite Georgian, Adamesque-Federalist, Regency, and Gothic residences – one of the most photogenic towns in Ontario.

Ottawa

Queen Victoria's choice of **Bytown**, then newly renamed **Ottawa ❻**, as her capital in the Canadas was greeted with

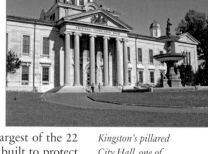

Kingston's pillared City Hall, one of Canada's finest classical buildings.

BELOW: grazing in the Kingston countryside.

Sir John Macdonald, Canada's first prime minister, was a wily boozer. On vomiting once midspeech he claimed that his opponent always made him feel ill.

shock by her trusting subjects. Today's equivalent would be commanding all the capital's stenographers, pollsters, and politicos to pack up their bags and begin working in Tuktoyaktuk in the Northwest Territories.

But the indignity wasn't limited to just moving to a backwater, for Bytown in the mid-1800s was also the most notorious work camp in North America. Lumber was king of the region and Bytown was its capital. Rival shantymen gangs the size of regiments set up shack towns here. Worked like machines, ill-fed, isolated, and racially divided, the lumbermen spent their recreational hours in drunken bouts of kick fights and eye gouging. It was in these muddy, dangerous streets that the **Parliament Buildings Ⓐ** (daily; tours, free) were erected between 1859 and 1865, rather like the proverbial pearl in a pigsty.

The contrast between these savage shantymen and their descendants – well-ordered, conformist civil servants – is wonderfully absurd. It is the contrast between settlement and wilderness, between convention and epic

adventure that runs through Canadian history. The contrast has not quite vanished from Ottawa today. In the **Gatineau Hills** that rise up behind Ottawa to the east, wolf packs still gather to howl. And at the **Royal Canadian Mint Ⓑ** (Victoria Day–Labor Day Mon–Fri 9am–7pm, Sat–Sun 9am–5.30pm, Sept–May daily 9am–5pm; small charge), Canada's moneymakers still churn out coins depicting wild birds, moose, and beavers.

For Ottawa will never be a capital city in the style of Washington or Brasilia, fashioned around a grandiose design that reorders the world along geometric lines. Initiated in 1937, the Capital Region Plan of designer Jacques Greber emphasizes the area's natural beauty and molds the city around it. Consequently, pleasure craft wend their way through the downtown center's parks in summer, while winter turns the Rideau Canal into an ice-skating promenade. The annual gift of thousands of tulips by the Netherlands, in gratitude for Canada's wartime hospitality to the Dutch Royal Family, makes spring in the city a visual delight.

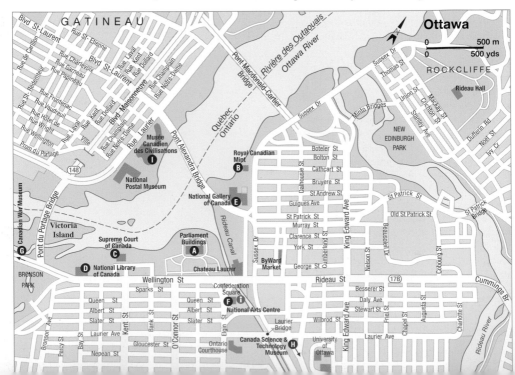

Because of its national stature, Ottawa has more cultural resources, museums, and galleries than a population of 300,000 would normally allow. Besides the Parliament Buildings, the Art Deco **Supreme Court** ❸ (guided tours May 1–Aug 31 Mon–Fri 9am–5pm, reservations required Labor Day–Apr 30; free), the **National Library** ❹, and the residences of prime ministers, governors general, and foreign ambassadors, Ottawa boasts the **National Gallery of Canada** ❺ (May–Sept daily 10am–5pm, Thur until 8pm, Oct–Apr Tue–Sun 10am–5pm, Thur until 8pm; free), the country's foremost gallery, made primarily out of glass; the **National Arts Centre** ❻, comprising opera house, theater, and studio, and home to the acclaimed National Arts Centre Orchestra; the **Canadian War Museum** ❼ (daily, mid-Oct–Apr Tue–Sun; charge, free Thur 4–8pm), which traces Canada's wars or involvement in wars from the 17th century; and the **Canada Science and Technology Museum** ❽ (May–Labor Day daily 9am–5pm, Sept–Apr Tue–Sun 9am–5pm; charge), containing an impressive display of steam locomotives.

Across the river in Hull, in the province of Québec, stands the outstanding **Musée Canadien des Civilisations** ❾ (daily, mid-Oct–Apr Tue–Sun; charge, free Thur 4–8pm), featuring the history of Canada, the art and traditions of the native cultures and ethnic groups.

The unknown river

Author Hugh MacLennan, in *Seven Rivers of Canada*, describes the Ottawa as the "unknown" or "forgotten" river of Canada. As the St Lawrence superseded it as the principal trade route, the image of the Ottawa was dimmed and it took on the status of a short tributary linking the cities of Ottawa and Montréal. To the *voyageurs* and the lumbermen of early Canada, however, the Ottawa river was *la grande rivière*, the main route to the Upper Great Lakes and the western prairies beyond.

In the **Ottawa Valley**, running north of the capital to **Pembroke** and **Deep River**, the character of the old Ottawa River comes alive. Here at **Champlain Lookout** ❼, high above the town of **Renfrew**, you can see the power of the

A lighthouse from Nova Scotia, hands-on displays, and a vast refracting telescope attract visitors to Ottawa's Museum of Science and Technology.

BELOW:
the glass-roof interior of the National Gallery of Canada.

Cobourg lighthouse.

river's current as it bursts over narrows, and understand why the journey either up or down the Ottawa was dreaded by the *voyageurs*. The Ottawa Valley is full of tall tales of the bigger-than-big lumberjacks like Joe Mufferaw, who waged war on the forest to provide the British Navy with white pine masts. These are best heard in the Valley dialect, which is a complex mix of Gaelic, Polish, French, and Indian idioms.

Prince Edward County

Hwy 33 leads south from Hwy 401 to Prince Edward County, which locals simply call "the County." A peninsula that juts into Lake Ontario, south of Belleville, it was settled by Loyalists in the 1780s. Though more and more people are discovering its charms, there is still an island-like sense of remoteness to this area. The highway becomes the Loyalist Parkway, the County's main east–west artery, with lovely vistas of New England-style clapboard houses, brick homes with gingerbread trim and of Wellington Bay.

In **Wellington**, many older homes have been converted into restaurants and bed-and-breakfast places. **The Wellington Historical Community Museum** (Victoria Day–July 1 and Labor Day–Thanksgiving Fri, Sat and Mon, 2 July–Labor Day Tue–Sat 10am–4.30pm; small charge) is housed in a former 1895 Quaker meeting house and focuses mainly on the area's Quaker history.

Antiques are big business along the main street of **Bloomfield**, as are gift and craft stores, artist galleries, and bed-and-breakfasts, mostly housed in historic buildings. The County is ideal for exploring by bike, which can be rented from the Bloomfield Bicycle Company on Main Street. Nearby, Slickers County Ice Cream offers all-natural ice cream that is made daily by hand, using fresh County products.

Picton ❽ is the County's main town, with several historic buildings, including the County Courthouse and Jail on Union Street, where Sir John A. Macdonald, Canada's first prime minister, began practicing law. Prince Edward County Museum (May–June, Sept–mid-Oct daily 1–4.30pm, July–Aug Tue–Sun; small charge) is housed in the old St Mary Magdelene Church – part of the Macaulay Heritage Park complex – and provides an excellent overview of the County's bygone days, including a fascinating presentation on Sir John and detailed exhibits on the town's Loyalist connection.

Restored theatre

When the **Regent Theatre** opened in Picton in 1922, it was a rare example of an Edwardian opera house with a stage equal in size to that of Toronto's Royal Alexandra Theatre. Barely surviving the whims of the entertainment industry during the 20th century, it too has been restored as close to its original state as possible, and is now the County's center for the arts, with a year-round program of theater, first run movies, and alternative films, as well as festivals for chamber music and jazz.

The County has been attracting artists and artisans for years, drawn by its

Cultural Gems

Ottawa's National Gallery of Canada and, across the river, Hull's Musée Canadien des Civilisations, stand out both for their architecture and for their remarkable collections.

The airy glass-and-steel turreted National Gallery by architect Moshe Safdie (1988) houses Canadian painting from the 18th to the 20th centuries, including the Group of Seven; European and American works from Filippino Lippi to Francis Bacon; the reconstructed, fan-vaulted, Rideau Street Convent Chapel; and, since 2009, the Canadian Museum of Contemporary Photography's collection, dedicated to work by Canadian photographers.

The photographic collection covers the history of the art from William Henry Fox Talbot through Eugène Atger, Walker Evans and August Sander to the contemporary work of Diane Arbus and Man Ray. It is worth spending at least half a day at the gallery.

Dedicated to the human history of Canada, the Musée Canadien des Civilisations, designed by Douglas Cardinal (1989), features the world's largest collection of totem poles. All aspects of life in Canada, from the earliest native peoples to the arrival of Norsemen and successive waves of Europeans, are shown in eye-catching displays. Exhibitions of native art make this a museum not to be missed.

inspiring surroundings (and, perhaps, by the lower than big city prices). Studios of photographers and woodcarvers, weavers, sculptors, and painters are found down many a country backroad. Every year Picton hosts **Art in the County** (June–July), a juried art show and sale, the Prince Edward County Studio and Gallery Tour (end Sept) and the Marker's Hand (early Nov).

One of its most popular attractions is **Sandbanks Provincial Park**. Formed by a vast fresh-water sand dune system, it's a laid-back, family-orientated park, with giant sand dunes, three wide golden sandy beaches, and shallow waters that are perfect for windsurfing, sailing, and canoeing, as well as swimming in warm weather. Every spring, birdwatchers arrive in droves. The County's sandy shoreline, limestone outcrops, lakes, forests, and wetlands attract over 300 species of birds.

Just east of Picton, there are over 20km (12 miles) of hiking trails in **Macaulay Mountain Conservation Area**, through both lowland and wooded escarpment. Birdwatchers come to see the likes of great crested flycatchers and winter wrens, others to see the quirky folk art of Macaulay's Birdhouse City, in which many of the 100 birdhouses are colorful reproductions of local historic buildings.

Central Ontario

There are no firm borders separating eastern from western Ontario, let alone the east from the middle. But when classical limestone gives way to red brick Victorian, and billboards advertise the pleasures of Toronto Hilton Jacuzzis over free TV and hot water in Cornwall, the nebulous line has been crossed. Firmly within the orbit of Toronto, whose fatted-calf suburbs have gobbled up rich farmland with alacrity, the hamlets and towns of the region struggle to maintain their own character and traditions.

The town of **Cobourg** ➒, 96km (60 miles) east of Toronto, is just far enough away to remain relatively unscarred by bedroom dormitory blight. It, like its neighbors **Port Hope** and **Colborne**, was once a bustling lake port in the age of Great Lake steamers. The harbors are filled with pleasure sails now, but these small lakeside ports are the best places to appreciate the vistas offered by Lake Ontario.

The center of Cobourg is dominated by the neo-Classical **Victoria Hall**. Completed in 1860, it contains a courtroom replica of London's Old Bailey, and one of only two acoustically perfect opera houses in North America. In its time it served as a marvelous statement of Canadian pretensions to cultural superiority over the rebel Yankees. Here, the colonial elite had something solid to point to in explaining why they chose to remain impoverished British North Americans while Uncle Sam boomed.

Finger lakes with bones

To the immediate north of Cobourg the long, thin **Kawartha Lakes** are strung like pegs on a clothesline tied to **Lake Simcoe** in the west. The Kawarthas have a pastoral appeal in contrast to the

By the time boaters reach Lake Simcoe from Lake Ontario they will have negotiated 43 locks and ascended 180 meters (590ft).

BELOW: on the Trent-Severn Canal.

Window of a pioneer church, Hay River.

rugged beauty of the more northerly Canadian Shield lakes. **Rice Lake**, the most southerly of the lakes, is especially beguiling. Framed by gently sloping drumlins bearing Holstein dairy farms on their elongated backs, Rice Lake is dotted with forested islands. Two thousand years ago, a little-known Indian civilization buried their dead by these shores in 96km (60-mile) long, snake-like ridges. **Serpent Mounds Provincial Park** ❿ (May–Thanksgiving; charge) 30km (19 miles) southeast of Peterborough, offers a cutaway viewing of the largest mound's bones and burial gifts.

The Kawartha Lakes form the basis of the **Trent-Severn Canal System**, which allows houseboats and cabin cruisers to sail uphill from **Trenton** on Lake Ontario to **Port Severn** on Lake Huron's Georgian Bay.

Peterborough ⓫, the center of the Kawarthas region, is the star attraction along the canal. Here the **Peterborough Hydraulic Lift Lock**, the world-champion boat lifter since 1904, boosts a boat up with one hand, while sinking a second vessel with the other.

Settled later than the counties along Lake Ontario, the Peterborough district was reputed in the 1830s to have the "most polished and aristocratic society in Upper Canada." British army officers granted free land, and younger sons of the English gentry gave the backwoods of Peterborough and Lakefield a tone uncommon in earlier settlements.

Not that gentility made the hardships of pioneering any more bearable. Susannah Moodie, an early pioneer of Lakefield, and of Canadian literature, described in *Roughing It in the Bush* her feelings on being condemned to a life of horror in the New World, from which the only hope of escape was "through the portals of the grave." Today, Peterborough seems to have found a middle ground between aristocracy and poverty, for it is a favorite testing ground for the arbiters of middle-class taste – the consumer-marketing surveyors.

Sunshine sketches of every town

There isn't much of tourist interest in the town of **Orillia** ⓬, situated on

the narrows between Lake Couchiching and Lake Simcoe, 96km (60 miles) north of Toronto – and that's what makes it so interesting. To be sure, there's a statue of Samuel de Champlain, noting the fact that he stopped nearby on his own Great Ontario Tour of 1615, but every town has a monument to someone or other.

No, the appeal of Orillia lies in the very ordinariness of the town: shady maples leaning over spacious side streets; wide front porches for socializing and spying; photographs of local hockey heroes in the barbershop-cum-agora. Stephen Leacock caught the flavor of the place – the flavor, for example, of Mr Golgotha Gingham, town undertaker who "instinctively assumes the professional air of hopeless melancholy" – in his book, *Sunshine Sketches of a Little Town*. A work of irony (one part affection, one part castigation), *Sunshine Sketches* won Leacock praise throughout the world when it was published in 1912. Everywhere, except Orillia. Now, Orillia has adopted the humorist as a favorite son and turned his home on Brewery Bay into a literary museum,

the **Stephen Leacock Museum** (Mon–Fri 10am–5pm; charge).

South of Lake Simcoe, 40km (25 miles) north of downtown Toronto, lies another shrine to Canadian artists: the **McMichael Canadian Art Collection** (daily 10am–4pm; charge) in the village of **Kleinburg** ❸. Started as a private gallery, the collection has grown into the finest display of the Group of Seven's canvases in Canada, along with works by Tom Thomson, Group of Seven contemporaries, First Nations, Inuit, and other Canadian artists. The McMichael Collection, with more than 13 exhibition galleries housed in log and stone buildings, is the perfect place to feast on their labors.

Southern Ontario

The excellent system of roads in Southern Ontario is a sign of its long-accustomed prosperity. The Macdonald-Cartier Freeway, more widely known as the 401, spans the distance between Windsor in the west and the Québec border in the east. But it's on the country roads that travelers begin to encounter Southern Ontario: the rolling fields

The Group of Seven stood the Canadian art establishment on its head in the 1920s as they sought to portray the Canadian wilderness in all its Nordic harshness.

BELOW LEFT: flora in Kleinburg.
BELOW RIGHT: a "pioneer" makes maple syrup in the Kortright Centre for Conservation, Kleinburg.

EAT

Sample the sweet taste of rural Canada: the Maple Syrup Festival is held every spring, in Elmira, 10km (6 miles) north of Waterloo.

of corn, wheat, or grazing livestock; the majestic elms and maples that line the town streets and shady farm lanes; the graceful houses, ranging from the earliest log and stone dwellings in "American vernacular" style to stately Victorian and Edwardian homes in red and yellow brick; and the rivers. It's difficult to drive anywhere in Southern Ontario without crossing a creek, stream or honest-to-God river.

West of Toronto lies some of the richest farmland anywhere. And strung along those smooth roads are towns that sometimes seem to have forgotten how they got there. But fast food and video rental outlets notwithstanding, the pioneer experience has made a deep impression. Almost every town and village blossoms annually with a fair or festival. Maple syrup festivals. Apple cider festivals. Bean festivals. And everywhere are people who are determined to remember how they got there and what it was like before there were roads.

A rich history

With the capture of Fort Detroit in 1759, the British finally wrested con-

trol of the North American frontier from the French. But the settlement of the vast peninsula, bounded by Lakes Ontario, Erie, and Huron, lagged behind that of the booming colonies south of the Great Lakes. It wasn't until those colonies declared their independence from Britain in 1776 that the wilderness that would one day be Ontario became inviting to settlers. These were the loyalists, whose impact on Eastern Ontario has already been noted. Their contribution to the western part of the province is even more fundamental. They gave up established homesteads to start all over again in the bush, simply because that bush remained under British law. Yet these people were Americans, and the egalitarian sentiments and pioneering spirit they brought with them helped to shape Ontario.

Southwestern Ontario was sculpted into its present shape by retreating glaciers at the end of the last Ice Age. In the late 18th century this rich soil lay under a different kind of sea: a green, rolling swell of dense forest. The French had not seriously attempted to settle the land. Clearing away the giant

BELOW: harvesting tomatoes in Leamington.
BELOW RIGHT: rural retreat at Elora.

trees and draining the swamps would have driven back the beavers whose pelts were so lucrative to the fur traders. For a time the British adopted this attitude as well.

The American War of Independence changed all this. Thousands of settlers from the Thirteen Colonies who feared or distrusted the new regime poured across the Niagara River. John Butler, the son of a British army officer, led a group of loyalists north to Niagara. In 1778 he recruited a band of guerrilla fighters, which became known as Butler's Rangers, and until the end of the war the group harassed the American communities in the area. Butler was stationed at Fort Niagara and charged with keeping the Six Nations, whose territory was south of Lake Ontario, friendly to the British. At this he succeeded, even persuading the Seneca and Mohawks to engage in fighting the rebels.

The leader of the Mohawks was Joseph Brant, who had received an English education and was committed to the British tradition. When the former Six Nations' lands were ceded to the Americans in the 1783 treaty that ended the war, Brant appealed to the British for redress. He and his followers were given land beside the Grand River to an extent of 10km (6 miles) on either side. Part of that land took in Elora, where the Grand River has carved a canyon that has become one of the most popular retreats in Ontario. The only land that remains in the hands of the Six Nations of the Grand River is at Ohsweken, on the southeast outskirts of Brantford. Today it is one of Canada's largest native settlements and is currently engaged in a controversial claim over land in nearby Caledonia.

Famous Falls

The **Niagara Escarpment**, a rolling slope which falls away in a rocky bluff on its eastern face, is another legacy of the last Ice Age. It rises out of New York State near Rochester, follows the shore of Lake Ontario around to Hamilton, snakes overland to the Blue Mountain ridge south of Collingwood, divides Lake Huron from Georgian Bay as the Bruce Peninsula, dips underwater, resurfaces as Manitoulin Island, disappears to emerge again on the western shore of Lake Michigan, and finally peters out in Wisconsin. The first farmers in the Niagara region had no idea of the extent of this formation, but they and their heirs discovered that the soil between the escarpment and the lake was very fertile.

Perhaps the best way to fully appreciate the richness of the land is to follow the **Wine Route** (www.winesofontario. org). From Country Road 24, some of the most glorious lake views are seen as the road descends into Vineland. The route eventually leads to St David's and Niagara-on-the Lake. Some of Canada's best wines are produced on the Niagara Peninsula, and the area's 65 wineries are easily accessed by following the Wine Route signs; most offer tours and tastings, and several have acclaimed restaurants.

The **Niagara Falls** ⑭, where Lake Erie overflows into Lake Ontario at the rate of 14 million liters of water

Niagara Falls have attracted many a daredevil, but none so bold as Blondin, whose high jinks on a tightrope above the cataract included stilt-walking.

BELOW: Blondin, a Frenchman, crosses Niagara Falls on a tightrope, 1859.

per minute, have always been the most celebrated feature of the escarpment. Of his pilgrimage, Charles Dickens wrote: "We went everywhere at the falls, and saw them in every aspect... Nothing in Turner's finest watercolor drawings, done in his greatest days, is so ethereal, so imaginative, so gorgeous in color as what I then beheld. I seemed to be lifted from the earth and to be looking into Heaven." Most would agree with Dickens and not with Oscar Wilde, who, noting the popularity of the Falls for honeymooners, remarked that "Niagara Falls must be the second major disappointment of American married life."

The Falls, or rather the crowds that swarm around them, have attracted a host of sideshows over the years. But the greatest carnival draw was Blondin, the French daredevil who first crossed over the cataract on a tightrope in 1859. In 1901, Annie Edson Taylor became the first person to plunge over the Falls in a barrel and live. These and other "daredevils" are remembered in the **Niagara Daredevil Exhibition** within the Imax Theater (6170 Fallsview Boulevard; daily 9am–9pm; free).

The most popular way to approach the Falls is on the *Maid of the Mist*, which brings you to the very edge of the cascading wall of water. Wearing complimentary hooded raincoats for protection, visitors are boated up to the Table Rock Scenic Tunnels under the Falls for a spectacular, if not intense, encounter with water.

Niagara-on-the-Lake

John Butler and his Rangers founded the town of Newark at the mouth of the Niagara River after the American revolutionary war. In 1792, when John Graves Simcoe arrived, the place was called "Niagara-on-the-Lake." It was the capital of Upper Canada, a province newly created out of the English-speaking portion of Québec. One of the first things Simcoe did was to choose a new capital, for Niagara-on-the-Lake was uncomfortably close to the US. He selected a site at a fork of the river, which he named the Thames. The capital would be called London (naturally). But Dundas Street was no sooner hacked out of the bush than Simcoe moved the capital to Toronto

BELOW: Niagara Falls, a natural wonder.

– which he promptly renamed York. The Mohawk Chief Joseph Brant once remarked: "General Simcoe has done a great deal for this province, he has changed the name of every place in it."

Niagara-on-the-Lake ⑮ was blessed by its fall into political obscurity. It is one of the most well-preserved colonial towns in North America. It's also home to the annual **Shaw Festival**, a major theatrical event featuring the plays of George Bernard Shaw as well as works by other writers.

The War of 1812–14

Canadian fears of American aggression were justified in June 1812 when the US took advantage of Britain's preoccupation with Napoleon to declare war. Many Americans thought Canada would be a pushover. Isaac Brock, the military commander of Upper Canada, wrote of his predicament: "My situation is most critical, not from the disposition of the people… What a change an additional regiment would make in this part of the province! Most of the people have lost all confidence – I, however, speak loud and look big." He acted swiftly and decisively. His troops captured Fort Michilimackinac in northern Michigan and repulsed an attack at the Detroit River. These early victories won the native peoples in the area to the British cause and galvanized the settlers.

The Niagara region figured prominently in the war. The Americans attacked **Queenston**, just down river from the Falls, in October 1812. Isaac Brock was killed in the Battle of Queenston Heights, though the town was successfully defended. The war dragged on, but without the example of Brock's boldness, the heavily outnumbered colony might not have held out at all.

The War of 1812–14 gave Canada a stronger sense of community identity, though it did not end the political divisions between Tories and those calling for democratic reform in the province. It also gave a signal to Britain that this colony was still too sparsely settled for its own security.

Southwestern Ontario

Today the highway that hugs the northern shore of Lake Erie is designated **The Talbot Trail**. **St Thomas** ⑯, founded in 1817 between London and Lake Erie, was also named after Colonel Thomas Talbot, who had been granted 19,600 hectares (48,500 acres) to start a settlement in 1803. But Talbot was no saint. He ruled his "principality," as he called it, with stern efficiency. He laid down stringent rules for his settlers. Those who defaulted on the agreed conditions he evicted – a rare procedure on any frontier. And the reason why the Talbot Road was the best in Upper Canada was that farmers were held responsible for maintaining some parts of the road that fronted their properties.

The Talbot Trail rolls through dairy farms and fishing villages, tobacco farms and beaches. West of St Thomas it bends south with the lakeshore into mixed-farming country. This, the westernmost tip of southern Ontario, is the southernmost part of Canada.

A legendary figure of the 1812–14 war is Laura Secord, who overheard American soldiers planning an attack and walked through enemy lines to warn the British.

BELOW: Battle of the Thames, 1813.

Point Pelee National Park (daily; charge), a peninsula jutting south of **Leamington**, 50km (30 miles) southeast of Windsor, is the southernmost part of mainland Canada. Lying at the same latitude as Rome and northern California, Point Pelee is home to plants and animals that are rarely seen in Canada. A trail through the woods and a boardwalk over the marshlands make it a living museum of natural history. The **Jack Miner Bird Sanctuary** at **Kingsville** (Mon–Sat 8am–5pm; free), 10km (6 miles) west of the park, is one of the earliest and most famous waterfowl pit stops in Canada. This haven is free to migrating birds and migrating humans alike. Jack Miner said: "In the name of God, let us have one place on earth where no money changes hands." The sanctuary is run by his family as a public trust.

The Underground Railroad

The southern border of Ontario played an unusual part in history: as one terminus of the "Underground Railroad." In the early 1800s, runaway slaves from the American South were sheltered by sympathizers along several routes that led to Canada.

Reverend Josiah Henson, a self-educated slave from Maryland, made the trip with his family in 1830. He settled in **Dresden** ⑱, 90km (56 miles) northeast of Windsor, and subsequently devoted himself to helping other fugitives. Henson was the prototype for "Uncle Tom" in Harriet Beecher Stowe's novel *Uncle Tom's Cabin*. His home in Dresden is part of **Uncle Tom's Cabin Historic Site** (mid-May–June, Sept–Oct Tue–Sat 10am–4pm, Sun noon–4pm, July–Aug Mon–Sat 10am–4pm, Sun noon–4pm; charge) that focuses on his life and works.

Chatham, 80km (50 miles) east of Windsor, was another terminus of the "railroad." Here, the abolitionist John Brown plotted the 1859 raid on the government arsenal at Harper's Ferry, Virginia. He hoped to spark a general uprising of slaves, but he was caught, convicted of treason, and hanged.

The city of **Windsor** ⑲ is the biggest urban center on Canada's border, a kind of half-sister to Detroit. Windsor is also an automobile industry town but, unlike Detroit, has a pleasant Downtown with extensive parks and gardens on the riverfront. It is noted for its casino.

Lake Ontario

In the 1820s the growing towns and farms positioned along the western curve of Lake Ontario continued to nibble at the wilderness around them. **Ancaster**, **Dundas**, **Stoney Creek** and **Burlington** all eventually lost their bids for supremacy at the lakehead to the town of **Hamilton** ⑳, the "ambitious little city," 70km (43 miles) south around the lake from downtown Toronto.

The Niagara Escarpment, referred to locally as "the mountain," divides Hamilton into split levels. The city's steel mills and other heavy industries have given Hamilton a grim image in the minds of many. But the somewhat

BELOW: Point Pelle National Park.

misleadingly named **Royal Botanical Gardens** incorporate a wildlife sanctuary called **Coote's Paradise**, with trails winding through 1,200 acres (485 hectares) of marsh and wooded ravines (indoor Mediterranean Garden: daily 10am–5pm; outdoor gardens seasonal: daily 10am–dusk; charge).

Hamilton's architectural jewel is **Dundurn Castle** (July 1–Labor Day daily 10am–4pm, Sept–June 30 Tue–Sun noon–4pm; charge). Sir Allan Napier MacNab – landholder, financier, all-round Tory, and Hamilton's first resident lawyer – had it built in 1835 as a lavish tribute to himself. The finest home west of Montréal at the time and named for MacNab's ancestral homeland in Scotland, it is now restored as a museum to reflect the 1850s when MacNab was premier of pre-Confederation Canada. Every mid-July, Hamilton hosts the Highland Games – a weekend of bagpipes, dancing, and caber tossing.

The first thing to note about nearby **Kitchener** ㉑, 40km (25 miles) north of Brantford, and **Waterloo** is how prosperous they are. Kitchener is one of the fastest-growing municipalities in Canada. The second thing to note about the Twin Cities is how German they are. The original settlers in the area were members of the austere Mennonite sect transplanted from the German communities of Pennsylvania in the 1780s. The Mennonites soon had German neighbors of various creeds and today Kitchener and Waterloo host the biggest **Oktoberfest** (week-long in mid-Oct) this side of the Rhine. "Good cheer" is spelled *Gemütlichkeit* in this part of the country.

Ten kilometers (6¼ miles) north of Kitchener, the Mennonite village of **St Jacobs** ㉒ was settled in the 1840s by German Mennonites. Many heritage buildings along Front Street have been converted into artisan studios and attractive stores. Among the casually attired shoppers, local Mennonites are solemnly dressed in black, the women in bonnets and the men sporting dark, broad-brimmed hats. They come here to sell their farm produce and handmade quilts, and are often seen speeding along the country roads in their horse-drawn buggies.

Hamilton installed the first telephone exchange in the British Empire in 1878, only four years after Alexander Graham Bell invented the device. It was at his parents home in Brantford that Bell dreamed up the idea.

BELOW:
Dundurn Castle, Hamilton.

For the Oktoberfest, Kitchener and Waterloo sprout 15 "festhallen" where sauerkraut, sausage, and beer are enjoyed to the beat of oompah music.

On Front Street, **Telling The Mennonite Story Visitor Centre** (Mon–Sat 11am–5pm, Sun 1.30–5pm; small charge) explains the history, culture, and religion of the Mennonite people. Founded in 1525 in Switzerland during the Reformation, they established the first "free church" and introduced the now widely accepted principle of separation of church from state. Considered revolutionaries, they were severely persecuted for several generations, before migrating first to Pennsylvania and then, after the American Revolution, to this corner of southern Ontario.

A few miles west of the village, **St Jacobs Country Market** (year-round Thur and Sat 7am–3.30pm, mid-June–early Sept Tue 8am–3pm) is a huge farmers' market that attracts shoppers from as far away as Toronto. Besides stalls overflowing with fresh Ontario produce, it peddles all things maple – syrup, butter, fudge, even lollypops – and old country specialties such as homemade perogies, butter tarts, German apple cake or raspberry apple cobbler. Somewhat incongruously, the St Jacobs Outlet Mall across the street

BELOW: celebrating the Oktoberfest at Kitchener.

offers a 21st-century shopping experience, with more than 30 stores selling discounted top name brands.

The Huron Road

In the 1820s, the land between Lake Huron and the modern site of Kitchener was a piece of wilderness called the **Huron Tract**. The development of this, and other bits of Crown land, was the target of the Canada Company. The company's success can be attributed to its first superintendent of operations, the Scottish novelist and statesman John Galt, and to his chosen lieutenant, Dr William (Tiger) Dunlop. Galt's first task was founding a city on the edge of the wilderness. **Guelph**, 15km (9 miles) northeast of Kitchener, was inaugurated in April of 1827 and it is a striking blend of 19th-century architecture. The Roman Catholic church of **Our Lady of the Immaculate Conception** dominates the skyline with twin Gothic towers.

After surveying the Huron Tract, the exuberant Dunlop had pronounced: "It is impossible to find 200 acres together which will make a bad farm."

Art, the Environment, and War

L ong known as Steel City because of its steel industry, Hamilton is a place that few people, especially Torontonians, would have considered as a great day out. Today, however, this gritty steel town is transforming into a cultural hub – partly as cheaper rents and properties have attracted many Toronto-area artists.

Downtown, the **Art Gallery of Hamilton** is Ontario's second-largest art gallery. Within its striking gold-and-glass exterior, an exceptional collection of Canadian art can be viewed. The city has also overseen a massive environmental clean-up of its harbor and waterfront, to create a much-loved outdoor playground. On Pier 8, the **Canada Marine Discovery Centre** introduces visitors to Canada's national marine conservation areas, which encompass 243,000km (151,000 miles) of coastline and another 9,500km (5,900 miles) along the Great Lakes, with a special section devoted to Hamilton Harbour. Through riveting interactive displays – such as tests on navigating the Great Lakes – and lively guides, visitors can absorb the importance of conserving Canada's marine heritage. On the periphery of Hamilton International Airport, the **Canada Warplane Heritage Museum** captures the magic of flight with displays on Canada's aviation history. One of its biggest attractions is the only operational Lancaster bomber in North America, and one of only two in the world.

Galt wanted a road so that settlement could begin in earnest. In 1828, Dunlop directed the construction of that road, through swamps, dense forest, and tangled brush. Work was slow and fever plagued the work camps. It was a stupendous achievement that is not diminished by the many improvements the road has seen since. Now Highway 8, the Huron Road became the spine of settlement in the tract.

Eighteen kilometers (11 miles) into the bush, the first Huron Road curved at an attractive meadow by a river. Before long the settlement that sprang up there was called **Stratford ㉓**, and the river the **Avon**. The connection to Shakespeare was strengthened in the naming of wards and streets (Romeo, Hamlet, Falstaff) while Stratford boomed in the 1850s by virtue of being the county seat and at an intersection of railway lines.

In the years after World War II, Stratford native Tom Patterson was persistent, and finally successful, in peddling his dream of a Shakespearean theater for the city. On July 13, 1953, Alec Guinness stepped onto a stage in a riverside tent as Richard III, and the rest, as they say, is history. The tent-like (but permanent) **Festival Theatre** was opened in 1957, and its "thrust stage" has influenced a generation of theater-builders. The Stratford Festival now includes three other stages (the **Avon Theatre**, the **Third Stage** and the **Studio Theatre**) and features music as well as plays. Over 500,000 people are attracted to the town annually.

Another road which helped to open up the Huron Tract is the one north from **London ㉔**, 60km (37 miles) south of Stratford. Or south to London, if you like, because all roads in southwestern Ontario eventually lead to London. Failing to become the capital of Upper Canada, London stayed small until it became the district seat in 1826. British tradition and the American feeling of wide open spaces are in harmony here. On the street signs of London such names as Oxford and Piccadilly mix with names from Ontario's history like Simcoe, Talbot, and, of course, Dundas Street. Other names, like Wonderland Road and Storybook Gardens, may lead visitors into thinking that they have

A red double-decker bus in London.

BELOW: market day in St Jacobs.

stumbled into a kind of Neverland. The impression will be reinforced by the squeaky cleanness, and greenness, of this relentlessly cheerful city. It isn't called "the forest city" for nothing; from any vantage point above the tree-tops, London visually disappears under a leafy blanket. The River Thames flows through the campus of the **University of Western Ontario**, a school whose presence is definitely felt in town. Also in London is the **Fanshawe Pioneer Village** (Victoria Day–Thanksgiving Tue–Sun 10am–4.30pm; charge), a fascinating reconstruction of a pre-railway, 19th-century town, equipped with log cabins, a general store, a weaver's shop, and a carriage-maker's quarters.

Western Ontario and Lake Huron

In Ontario Ministry of Tourism language, the Lake Huron shoreline is called Bluewater Country. It is a glorious lakefront with cottages, beaches, and places like **Bayfield**, 75km (46 miles) north of London. This village, with its intact 19th-century main street, shady beach, and fine marina, is a gem.

Twenty-one kilometers (13 miles) farther north is **Goderich** ㉕, Tiger Dunlop's town. Not merely planned, Goderich was designed; the **County Courthouse** sits on an octagonal plot (called The Square) from which streets radiate in all directions.

The Square is probably the world's most leisurely traffic circle (or octagon). Whether or not Goderich really is "The Prettiest Town in Canada," as the signs proclaim, this spot regularly displays some of the most spectacular sunsets on earth. In fact, that goes for the whole of the Huron lakeshore, including popular resort towns such as Southampton and Sauble Beach, whose wide sandy beaches have been attracting generation after generation of Ontario families.

When they saw how quickly the Huron Tract was being gobbled up, the British Government threw open for settlement the Indian territory immediately to the north of it. The Queen's Bush, as it was called, was not as fertile as land farther south, and some of the boom towns soon went bust. Those that remained on the stony soil turned

to raising beef cattle. Several railroads snaked into Ontario between 1850 and 1900. Towns along the routes prospered, especially those where lines crossed. But as the rail lines fed city factories, industries in small towns declined and the smallest towns focused solely on the needs of the surrounding farming communities.

Small towns

In the 1970s there was a swell of interest in the history and architecture of Ontario's small towns. A good illustration of this is the **Blyth Festival**. A community hall was built in 1920 in **Blyth**, 33km (20 miles) east of Goderich. Upstairs in the hall is a fine auditorium, with a sloping floor and stage, which lay unused from the 1930s until the mid-1970s when it was "discovered" and refurbished as the home for an annual summer festival dedicated to Canadian plays, most of them new, and most of them celebrating small-town and farming experiences. That the Blyth Festival has become a favorite with Canada's urban drama critics indicates both its theatrical quality and the potency of its subject matter, namely the history and people of rural Canada.

About 17km (11 miles) south of Blyth on the literary map lies **Clinton**, the home of writer Alice Munro. Her beautiful stories transcend regional interest and "local color." There is no better introduction to the life of small-town Ontario.

This region has always been sparsely settled; the soil is thin, and navigation on the lake hereabouts can be treacherous. But many people make the effort to reach **Tobermory** ㉖, the resort that looks like a fishing village at the tip of the 80km (50-mile) long **Bruce Peninsula** ㉗. The peninsula is bordered by Lake Huron's warmer and shallower waters to the west, while the Georgian Bay side is dominated by the Niagara Escarpment – a rugged wall of limestone that climbs to 100 meters (328ft) in places. On Colpoy's Bay, Wiarton

is the gateway to the peninsula. Steep cliffs flank the harbor, providing a striking setting and sheltered waters for sailing and fishing. Across the peninsula are Oliphant and Red Bay, neighboring communities where families come for good beaches and safe waters. Farther north, 11km (7 miles) beyond Dyer's Bay, the **Cabot Head Lighthouse** (Victoria Day–Thanksgiving daily 10am–7pm; donation) houses a small museum of local history, while the adjacent Wingfield Basin Nature Reserve is frequented by 120 species of birds, ranging from the snowy owl to the great blue heron.

Bruce Peninsula National Park encompasses the northern tip. Its dense forest cover is a botanist's delight. Birders are also handsomely rewarded here, and the hiking is exceptional. Just off Tobermory lies **Fathom Five National Marine Park**. Encompassing 19 islands and at least 22 shipwrecks, it is one of North America's premier diving sites.

Through the season, Tobermory is action-packed, especially when Little Tub Harbour is jammed with dive

Winter transport.

BELOW: at home in Algonquin Provincial Park.

Studded by islands, Georgian Bay is a popular sailing area. Its coastline varies from the white sands of Wasaga Beach in the south to the rocky northern shore.

and cruise boats. Some visitors are heading north for **Manitoulin Island** ㉘, the largest freshwater island in the world, on board the giant ferry *Chi-cheemaun* (big canoe). Measuring 176km (110 miles) long with more than 80 inland lakes, Manitoulin is known for its tranquility and natural beauty. **Wikwemikong** is an unceded Indian reserve that is known for hosting North America's largest Pow Wow each August and its rich cultural heritage (a high number of internationally known First Nations artists hail from here, including Daphne Odjig, Leland Bell, and Jim Mishibinijima).

M'Chigeeng (formerly West Bay) is the second largest native community on the island. Here, the **Ojibwe Cultural Foundation** (Mon–Fri 9am–6pm, Sat 10am–4pm, Sun noon–4pm) showcases the work of many local artists. Over the road, the **Immaculate Conception Church** is a striking circular building that blends traditional Christian and Native cultures. Little Current is the island's largest town and a popular port of call for Georgian Bay's extensive yachting community.

South of **Georgian Bay**, on the eastern ridge of the escarpment, a range of large hills provides the best ski-runs in Ontario. Ontarians call these the **Blue Mountains**, but not too loudly in the presence of anyone from the Rockies.

Ste Marie Among the Hurons

To visit the small peninsula poking out into Georgian Bay is to step a little farther back into history than most places in rural Ontario permit. This area is called **Huronia**, where 350 years ago French Jesuit missionaries traveled and preached among the Huron Indians.

When the lonely fortified mission of **Ste Marie Among the Hurons** was established in 1639, it was the only inland settlement of Europeans north of Mexico. It prospered for 10 years; but the Huron nation was eventually destroyed in wars with its enemies, the Iroquois, who also tortured and killed the Jesuits. The movie and novel *The Black Robe* tell this story. Ste Marie was not attacked, but the fort was burned by retreating Jesuits to keep it out of Iroquois hands. After much research,

BELOW: Georgian Bay coastline.

the mission and its everyday life have been re-created on a site 5km (3 miles) east of **Midland ㉙** (mid-May–mid-Oct daily 10am–5pm, early–mid-May and mid–end Oct Mon–Fri 10am–5pm; charge). It was in this area that Fathers Jean de Brébeuf and Gabriel Lalament were tortured and then brutally killed by the Iroquois in 1649. Their remains were housed across from the mission in the Martyrs' Shrine, a towering edifice that commands a spectacular vista over the surrounding country. Nearby is **Wye Marsh Wildlife Center** (daily 9am–5pm; charge) with boardwalks extending over the marshlands. A visitors' center explains the ecology of the area and features guided tours.

The many thousands of lakes in Ontario and, particularly, those in the Canadian Shield region, just to the north, provide a cherished escape for city dwellers. The settlers' war of extermination against the trees has given way to a desire to preserve the woodlands and waters of the near north for recreational purposes.

However, the **Georgian Bay**, **Muskoka**, and **Haliburton** regions

can no longer be described as forested wilds, dotted as they are by thousands and thousands of cottages. For Ontario is one of the few places in the world where seemingly everyone, rich and not so rich, has a country estate even if it's only a humble cabin.

A museum in the woods

To the north of Haliburton and the northeast of Muskoka lies the last real expanse of wild land in Southern Ontario – the 7,600-sq-km (2,934-sq-mile) **Algonquin Provincial Park ㉚** (Visitor Center, see www.algonquinpark. on.ca for hours). Set aside as a provincial park in 1893, Algonquin preserves the primordial, aboriginal, and pioneer heritages of Ontario as a kind of natural museum.

Loons, the oldest-known birds, abound in the park's 2,500 or more lakes as they did 10,000 years ago after the last Ice Age. Algonquin Indian "vision pits" can be found in the northwest corner of the park. Here, in these rock-lined holes, a young Algonquin would fast for days waiting for the vision of a spiritual guardian who

TIP

Entry to Algonquin Provincial Park is by permit (arrive early or book ahead, tel: 1-888-668-7275). Avoid peak vacation times if you plan to explore by canoe.

BELOW LEFT: snowboarding is a national pastime. **BELOW:** colorful fall foliage.

The Monarch butterfly migration in Point Pelee National Park.

BELOW: a canoe with a view in Algonquin Provincial Park.

would draw the rite of passage to a close. In the park's interior, east of **Opeongo Lake**, lies the last stand of great white pines in Ontario. These few dozen ancient pines are all that is left of the huge forests cut to provide masts for the British Navy.

Algonquin should be seen by canoe. Heading north on **Canoe Lake** away from the access highway, it is only one or two portages before the motorboats and "beer with ghetto-blaster" campers are left behind. In the interior, porcupines, beaver, deer, wolves, bear, and moose can all be seen by canoeists. In August, park naturalists will even organize wolf howls, where campers head out *en masse* at night to try and raise the cry of the great canines. The loons, however, need no such encouragement. Their haunting cry, which the Cree believed was the sound of a warrior who had been refused entry to paradise, can be heard on every lake.

Each season brings its own character to Algonquin. Spring is the time of wild-flowers, mating calls, white water, and blackflies as thick as night. Summer brings brilliant thunderstorms, mosquitoes in place of blackflies, acres of blueberries, and water actually warm enough to swim in. In the fall, Algonquin turns into a Group of Seven canvas. The funeral for the forest's leaves is as triumphant and colorful as that of any New Orleans jazz singer. Uniform green gives way to a kaleidoscope of scarlet, auburn, yellow, and mauve, while in the winter, in total contrast to the rest of the seasons, the park falls deathly silent as it waits for the resurrection under a mantle of snow.

Algonquin, however, is not without its problems, problems typical of an urban society unable to control its effect upon the natural environment. Not only is most of Algonquin under license to logging interests, whose long-term effect on the ecosystem cannot be gauged; it is also being scarred by the ever-increasing effects of industrial pollution.

Northern Ontario

Highway maps of Ontario divide the province in two: one side showing

southern Ontario, the other northern. **Sudbury** ㉛, 390km (242 miles) north of Toronto, is called "the gateway to the north" and it marks the boundary between the two. It is a city of 150,000, known for its copper and nickel mines, and its cultural focus points include **Science North**, an interactive museum for families (daily; charge), and a lively summer music event, the **Northern Lights Boréal Festival**.

Most travelers never give the north of Ontario a look, never turn over the map. Myth has it that northern Ontario is an endless tract of conifers, lakes, bogs, mining camps, moose, and mosquitoes. Like all myths it's true in part, but only in part.

Just north of Algonquin Park is the Near North region of lakes and pristine wilderness areas, such as **Temagami** toward the Québec border. Not far from North Bay, the region's largest center, is **Temagami Station**. Here, Grey Owl, the Englishman who successfully posed as a native environmentalist writer in the 1930s in the UK and US, lived and wrote.

Cars taper off along northern highways, and settlements are further apart. Every second vehicle is a logging truck. One of the most popular routes into the wilderness, which Canadians call "bush," is aboard the **Polar Bear Express**. It leaves every day but Saturday, late June to late August, from **Cochrane**, a place of fishing poles and down vests, to the Arctic tidewater towns of **Moosonee** and **Moose Factory**. The adventurous bring their own canoes and paddle on to the isolated James Bay outposts.

Lying 296km (184 miles) west of Sudbury, Sault Ste Marie is a cultural and sporting center, whose attractions include the 114-mile (183km) Agawa Canyon train tour and, for the angler, the largest fish hatchery in Ontario.

Located at the top of the Great Lakes, some 700km (435 miles) north of Sault Ste Marie, Thunder Bay's location is hard to beat. Surrounded by unspoiled wilderness – a constant source of inspiration to the city's many artists – it is

backdropped by the Nor'Wester Mountains. On its doorstep, a string of islands entice kayakers, sailors, and hikers. The Sleeping Giant, a massive series of mesas at the tip of the Sibley Peninsula, forms an impressive guardian to Thunder Bay's harbor. With more than 80km (50 miles) of hiking trails, the Sleeping Giant Provincial Park's backcountry offers a world of peace and solitude.

Farther west still is the **Lake of the Woods** district and **Kenora**, a pulp and paper center, near the Manitoba border. This land rivals the Muskokas for resorts and bluewater camping. For those whose idea of Canada is a place where you contract a bush pilot and sea plane and fly in to an isolated cabin for a week or two, Lake of the Woods fits. "Fly-in" resorts are extremely popular, with loons, sunsets, a moose or two, and ads that read, "Ask for Don or Lynn." Now that's Northern Ontario.   ❑

The Comfort Maple tree, in the Niagara Conservation Area, is said to be the oldest sugar maple tree in Canada.

BELOW: pathway through the snow in Temagami.

MONTRÉAL

The second-largest French city in the world after Paris, Montréal has extraordinary personality. Worldly but romantic, perhaps a little extravagant, it is earnest in its aim to enjoy life

The Québécois have a proud and often obsessive attitude towards their language and culture, and the 6.8 million French speakers of the province are deeply aware of being surrounded by almost 300 million anglophones whose culture seems to impinge upon their own. But there is also a tinge of North American culture, with a refreshingly lively approach to both work and play, and a *joie de vivre* is evident on Montréal's rue St-Denis, rue Crescent, boulevard St-Laurent or l'avenue Mont-Royal.

Despite one of the city's most tenacious myths, **Mont-Royal** Ⓐ is not the result of a volcano, but in fact one of eight Monteregian hills, formed millions of years ago. At 233 meters (764ft) high, and with a park on its crest, its central location makes it Montréal's main landmark. And so today, from parking lots on rue Camilien Houde, to the lookout with its splendid view of the city, it's still the ideal place to begin a visit to Montréal.

Surrounded by the waters of the St Lawrence, centering on the mountain, and penetrated by a maze of subterranean shopping plazas and passages, Montréal is an unusually three-dimensional city. Everyone refers to Mont-Royal as "the mountain" despite its being more of a hill. The surrounding terrain is so flat, however, that the view from the summit is excellent. In the distance lie the other mountains of the Monteregian group. On a clear day,

you can see as far as New York State's Adirondacks and the Green Mountains of Vermont.

The city spreads out down the mountainside to the St Lawrence. The view of the downtown core has changed rapidly over the last two decades, but the cruciform tower called **Place-Ville-Marie** on Boulevard Réne-Lévesque and, to the right, the slightly taller **Bank of Commerce** building, still dominate. Between them is the **Sun Life** building, once the tallest building in the British Commonwealth.

Map on page 180

Main attractions
MUSÉE DES BEAUX-ARTS DE MONTRÉAL
PLACE DES ARTS
VIEUX-MONTRÉAL
BASILIQUE DE NOTRE DAME
LE VIEUX-PORT
ORATOIRE ST-JOSEPH
BIOSPHÈRE
JARDIN BOTANIQUE DE MONTRÉAL

PRECEDING PAGES: cold snap, Québec. **LEFT:** summer in the city. **BELOW:** *The Illuminated Crowd*, BNP Tower.

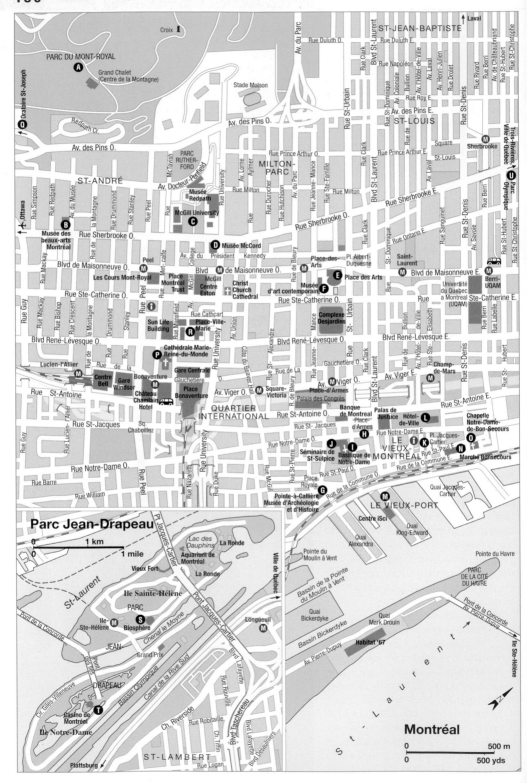

Croix

PARC DU MONT-ROYAL

Grand Chalet
(Centre de la Montagne)

Oratoire St-Joseph

A

Laval ↑

ST-JEAN-BAPTISTE

Rue Duluth O.   Rue Duluth E.

Av. du Parc   Rue Clark   Blvd St-Laurent

Rue Napoléon   Rue de l'Hôtel-de-Ville

Rue Rachel O.   Av. Coloniale   Bullion

Rue Roy E.

Stade Molson

Av. des Pins O.   Rue St-Urbain

ST-LOUIS

Rue de   Av. des Pins E.

Av. Henri-Julien   Av. Drolet

Rue St-Denis

Square St-Louis   St-Louis

Sherbrooke   M

Rivard   Av. de Châteaubriand   Av. St-Christophe

Trois-Rivières,
Ville de Québec

Redpath Cr.

Av. des Pins O.

PARC RUTHER-FORD

McTavish

ST-ANDRÉ

Av. Docteur-Penfield

Musée Redpath

McGill University   B   C

Rue Simpson   Rue Redpath   Av. du Musée   Rue de la Montagne   Rue Drummond   Rue Stanley   Rue Peel   Rue University

MILTON-PARC

Rue Prince Arthur O.   Rue Prince Arthur E.

Rue Lorne   Rue Aylmer   Rue Durocher   Rue Hutchison   Rue Jeanne-Mance   Rue St-Famille   Rue Clark

Rue Milton   Rue Milton

Rue Sherbrooke E.

Rue Sherbrooke O.

Rue Sanguinet   Rue St-Denis   Rue St-Hubert

Berri   Sherbrooke   M

ST-LOUIS

U   Parc Olympique

Ottawa →

Musée des beaux-arts Montréal

B

Rue Sherbrooke O.

Blvd de Maisonneuve O.

Rue Ste-Catherine O.

Rue Guy   Rue Mackay   Rue Bishop   Rue Crescent   Rue de la Montagne   Rue Drummond   Stanley   Rue Peel   Rue Met. calfe

Peel   M

Les Cours Mont-Royal

Place Montréal Trust

McGill Centre Eaton

Musée McCord   D

Av. Collège du Président Kennedy

Blvd de Maisonneuve O.

McGill   Christ Church Cathedral

Place-des-Arts

Pl. Albert-Duquesne

Place des Arts   E

Musée d'art contemporain   F

M   Blvd de Maisonneuve E.

Saint-Laurent   M

Rue St-Dominique   Rue St-Laurent

Rue Ontario E.

Université du Québec a Montréal (UQAM)

Ste-Catherine E.

Berri-UQAM   M

Rue Berri   Rue Labelle   Rue St-Denis   Rue St-Hubert   Rue St-Christophe

Sun Life Building

i

Place-Ville-Marie

Rue Ste-Catherine O.

Rue Cathcart

Rue University   Rue Mansfield

Rue Metcalfe

Complexe Desjardins

M   Mance   St-Urbain   Bullion   Rue de l'Hôtel-de-Ville   Elisabeth

Rue Berri

Blvd René-Lévesque O.

Cathédrale Marie-Reine-du-Monde

P

Blvd René-Lévesque E.

Gare Centrale

Luclen-l'Allier

Centre Bell   Gare Windsor   M

Château Champlain Hotel

Bonaventure   Place Bonaventure   M

QUARTIER INTERNATIONAL

Av. Viger O.   Square-Victoria   M

Place-d'Armes   M

Palais des Congrès

Champ-de-Mars   M

Av. Viger E.

Rue St-Antoine E.

Chapelle Notre-Dame-de-Bon-Secours

Rue St-Antoine O.

Banque de Montréal   Place-d'Armes

Séminaire de St-Sulpice   J

Basilique de Notre-Dame   I

Palais de Justice   Hôtel-de-Ville

H

i   k   L

LE VIEUX-MONTRÉAL

Pl. Jacques-Cartier   O

Marché Bonsecours   N

Rue Notre-Dame O.   Rue St-Pierre   Rue Notre-Dame E.   Rue St-Paul E.

Rue St-Jacques

Place Royale   G

Rue de la Commune O.

Pointe-à-Callière Musée d'Archéologie et d'Histoire

LE VIEUX-PORT   M

Centre iSci

Quai King-Edward

Quai Jacques-Cartier

Parc Jean-Drapeau

0   1 km

0   1 mile

Vieux Fort

Lac des Dauphins   La Ronde

Aquarium de Montréal

La Ronde

Île Sainte-Hélène

PARC

Île-Ste-Hélène   S   Biosphère

JEAN

Grand Prix

DRAPEAU

Casino de Montréal

Île Notre-Dame

ST-LAMBERT

Plattsburg →

Pont Jacques-Cartier

Ville de Québec

Longueuil   M

Pointe du Moulin à Vent

Bassin de la Pointe du Moulin à Vent

Quai Alexandra

Quai Bickerdyke

Bassin Bickerdyke

Av. Pierre-Dupuy

Habitat '67

Pointe du Havre

PARC DE LA CITÉ DU HAVRE

Quai Mark Drouin

Pont de la Concorde   Av. Pierre-Dupuy   Île Ste-Hélène

St-Laurent

Montréal

0   500 m

0   500 yds

French first

French is the language of business as confidently as it is the language of road signs and storefronts, but visitors still find the city conveniently bilingual. Although, after the 1976 election of the separatist Parti Québécois, many English-speaking Montréalers left, many of their children, now adults, have since returned – eager to embrace the French language and a collegial relationship with the Québécois. Reciprocally, young French-Canadians are generally more comfortable speaking English than their parents, a pragmatic response to the realities of globalization.

Downtown Montréal

Côte des Neiges and rue Guy bring you down into the heart of the downtown shopping district. The finer grade of stores and hotels such as the **Ritz-Carlton** run along this section of rue Sherbrooke, being the lower limit of the "Golden Square Mile," the old domain of the wealthiest anglos. The **Musée des beaux-arts de Montréal ❸** (Tue 11am–5pm, Wed–Fri 11am–9pm, Sat–Sun 10am–5pm; charge), known for its

exclusive exhibitions, is here. It houses an extensive permanent collection of works by both Canadian and European masters. A few blocks east is **McGill University ❸**, former home of Ernest Rutherford, Stephen Leacock, and, many insist, Jack the Ripper. Its **Musée Redpath** (Mon–Fri 9am–5pm, Sun 1–5pm; charge) features fossils, minerals, and zoological exhibits. Opposite the university stands the **Musée McCord ❹** (Tue–Fri 10am–6pm, Sat–Sun 10am–5pm, June–Sept daily 10am–5pm; charge) with its emphasis on the social history of Canada.

Rue Ste-Catherine, two blocks south, is livelier. It is lined with boutiques, cafes, department stores, fast-food joints (especially *croissanteries* and smoked-meat delis), and arcades. Intersecting this bustling artery is rue Crescent, one of the concentrations of bistros and restaurants that give Montréal its reputation for nightlife and table-hopping.

Underground travel

Farther east, the largest department stores, and a nexus of multi-story shopping centers – **Complexe Les Ailes**,

Fiddling away on Rue Ste-Catherine.

BELOW: downtown Montréal from Mont-Royal.

Plateau Mont-Royal

Plateau Mont-Royal has been labeled one of the coolest neighborhoods in North America. Predominantly francophone, the mix of artists, students, young families, and yuppy professionals live in the shadow of Mont-Royal, surrounded by the buzz of activity from boulevard St-Laurent, the designer boutiques of St-Denis, the "it" spots of l'avenue Mont-Royal, and the casual, bring-your-own-bottle eateries of rue Prince Arthur. Trendy stores share sidewalk space with butchers, bakeries, and delicatessens, yet the tranquility of parc Lafontaine grounds them all. By night, people from near and far flock to the Plateau to catch the latest opening – theater or art – or to check out a martini lounge or relax in the microbrew pub. For a compact neighborhood, the options are plentiful.

The February Fête des Neiges is followed through the year by fireworks, jazz, comedy, gastronomy, film, and dance.

BELOW: water features at the Place des Arts.

Place Montréal Trust, Les Cours Mont-Royal, Centre Eaton – are joined by underground passages to the Métro, Montréal's subway system. Trains on rubber wheels thread their way between "designer" stations, each having its own bold architecture. Opened in 1966, with its quiet, high-speed trains, it's still the most efficient and pleasant way to get around.

Arts and cultures

Still farther east are the **Complexe Desjardins**, another dramatically conceived shopping center, and the **Place des Arts E**, comprising five concert halls, housed on top of one another in the step-pyramid style building, and the **Salle Wilfred Pelletier**, with elegant, sweeping curves, the home of Montréal's orchestra, opera, and ballet.

L'Orchestre Symphonique de Montréal (OSM) has emerged as one of the world's great orchestras and is often called "the world's first and finest French orchestra," drawing rave reviews on tours and prizes for many of its recordings. Its home in the Place des Arts also houses Montréal's modern

art museum, the **Musée d'art contemporain F** (Tue–Sun 11am–6pm, Wed until 9pm; charge).

Beyond the Place des Arts on Boulevard St-Laurent, there emerges an eclectic jumble of small businesses representing the ethnic communities who have made this their neighborhood: Jewish, Italian, Portuguese, Greek. Within this area lies another focus of Montréal's nightlife: **rue Prince Arthur**. Closed to motor traffic, Prince Arthur frequently fills up with hundreds of people lining up to eat at its popular Greek or Vietnamese restaurants. Most of Montréal's Greek restaurants allow patrons to bring their own wine, which makes an excellent dinner easy to afford. The crowds may appear daunting, but the lines move quickly.

Around the corner from Place St-Louis, the historic square at the east end of Prince Arthur, is rue St-Denis. One stretch of road here has been known for many years as the "Latin Quarter" of Montréal: bohemian, a little ramshackle, politicized. Today it equals rue Crescent as the hub of Montréal's night-time activity although it is

more frequented by locals than visitors. The annual **International Jazz Festival** revolves around St-Denis and Place des Arts, but throughout the year St-Denis has a particularly Québécois vibrancy and charm.

Vieux-Montréal

Although Jacques Cartier discovered an Indian settlement called Hochelaga (near the site of McGill University) when he landed in 1535, Montréal was not permanently settled until a century later. The founders' purpose was to save the pagan "savages" by converting them to Christianity. The project began when the Société de Notre Dame de Montréal commissioned Paul de Chomedy, Sieur de Maisonneuve, to establish a settlement in this remote wilderness far from "civilization" – 70 recruits and young Jeanne Mance, a nurse, accompanied him.

The settlement of Ville-Marie in that year, 1642, was having a bad time defending itself against the brutal attacks of the Iroquois but, for whatever reason, the Iroquois ignored the new settlement. Once winter came, the settlers were able to erect a few huts and a log palisade.

The late 17th-century European vogue for hats made of beaver pelt gave Montréal a secondary purpose, the fur trade, which became its primary object, with greater organization and profits. The accommodation of business and religion as twin forces in Montréal's history is visible everywhere, particularly in Vieux-Montréal. Archeological finds from the city are on display at the fascinating **Pointe-à-Callière Musée d'Archéologie et d'Histoire de Montréal** Ⓖ (Sept–June Tue–Sun, June 25–Aug 30 daily; charge) on Place Royale.

North up rue St-Pierre and east along rue Notre Dame leads to the hub of Vieux-Montréal, **Place d'Armes** Ⓗ. Banks surround the square on three sides; it was once the heart of the Canadian financial establishment, dominated by anglo-Montréalers. On the south side stands the **Basilique de Notre-Dame** Ⓘ, the symbol *par excellence* of Québécois Roman Catholicism.

The facade of Notre-Dame is plain because stone workers were rare in

BELOW: Basilique de Notre-Dame.

In the 18th century, rue St-Jacques vied with New York City's Wall Street for banking supremacy. See mechanical piggy banks at Banque de Montréal's museum.

Québec when the church was built around 1829. In stark contrast its interior is a magnificently ornate tribute to the importance of woodworking and decoration in Québécois tradition.

Everywhere there is paint laced with real gold leaf, and the reredos gleams in a vivid blue. Ironically, Montréal's finest church was designed by an Irish American, James O'Donnell, but the interior is the inspiration of a French Canadian, Victor Bourgeau. Neither ugly nor the epitome of subtle elegance, it is what it was meant to be: simply overwhelming.

Adjacent to the west wall of the basilica stands Montréal's oldest building, the **Séminaire de St-Sulpice ❶**, built in 1685. The Sulpicians became the seigneurs or landlords of all Montréal when they took over missionary responsibilities from the Societé de Notre-Dame in 1663. More than 300 years after its construction, the seminary still serves as the residence for the Sulpicians.

Across the square stands the English businessman's retort to Notre-Dame's assertion of indomitable French-Cana-

dian values: the serene neo-Classical **Banque de Montréal**, built in 1847. During banking hours, the main hall is open to visitors, as is a tiny interesting museum.

Walking east past the shops and cafes on rue Notre-Dame, you encounter on the north side the old Napoleonic-style **Palais de Justice** with its silver dome, and on the south side the less graceful "new" Palais de Justice with its august pillars and heavy doors. Both buildings are government offices today.

Opening off the south side of rue Notre-Dame lies **Place Jacques Cartier ❿**, a center of much less serious activity than Place d'Armes. Cobblestoned, floriated, peopled, and surrounded by restaurants and terrace cafes in buildings a century-and-a-half old, it preserves the charm, the human scale, of another era. At the top of the square stands **Nelson's Column**, the city's oldest monument and the first in the world to be dedicated to Admiral Nelson. Lest the monument should be thought a rather diminutive replica of the column in Trafalgar Square, know that Montréal's predates London's by 34 years.

BELOW: stairway to Oratoire St-Joseph.

Oratoire St-Joseph

One of the greatest of Montréal's monuments is the Oratoire St-Joseph on Mont-Royal. It was the dreamchild of Alfred Bessette, Brother André, who was porter at the nearby Collège Notre Dame when he developed a reputation as "the miracle worker," because of the many cures he performed. The secret of his cure was the application of "oil of St Joseph" to the bodies of the sick. Soon the sick were flocking to him by the thousands.

People were asked to donate money to its construction and the church began to take shape in 1924. When money ran out during the Depression, Brother André recommended that a statue of St Joseph be placed in the center of the roofless church. "If he wants a roof over his head, he'll get it," he said. Two months later money was found to continue with the building.

Facing Nelson across rue Notre Dame is the **Hôtel de Ville** ⚫ (city hall), an elegant Second Empire-style building with its slender columns and mansard roofs. Opposite, on the south side, stands the **Château de Ramezay** (1705), looking like a sturdy farmhouse, but nevertheless the focal point of more than a century of early Canadian history. Today, the château is a private museum (daily, June–Thanksgiving 10am–6pm, Oct–May 10am–4.30pm; charge) with some impressively equipped 18th-century living quarters and many fascinating artifacts. Look out for North America's first paper money: playing cards authorized as legal tender when a cargo of coins was delayed on its way across the Atlantic.

Yet another site to see here is **Le Vieux-Port** ⓜ, now an entertainment area that offers summer evenings of music, dancing, and beer under the stars with the city skyline as a backdrop. The port also provides the best view of the **Marché Bonsecours** ⓝ, which served as the Lower Canada Parliament during its construction (1849–52), but for almost a century was Montréal's principal marketplace. Its long, classical facade and silver dome greeted thousands of immigrants and travelers in the 19th century. Now it houses café-terrasses and boutiques that showcase Québec artists, designers, and artisans.

Besides the Marché Bonsecours, and overlooking the river, stands the **Chapelle Notre-Dame-de-Bon-Secours** ⓞ, also known as the Sailors' Church as sailors have traditionally come here to give thanks for being saved from a shipwreck. Built in 1658, it is Montréal's oldest stone chapel. Within it, the **Musée Marguerite Bourgeoys** (May–Thanksgiving Tue–Sun 10am–5.30pm, mid-Oct–mid-Jan and Mar–Apr 11am–3.30pm) is dedicated to the history of the chapel and the life of Marguerite Bourgeoys, Montréal's first teacher.

Until the 1960s, religion as much as language set French Canada apart from the rest of North America. In the mid-dle of the anglo business district Monsignor Ignace Bourget built **Cathédrale Marie-Reine-du-Monde** ⓟ, a one-third scale replica of St Peter's in Rome. But nowhere is the role of religion more obvious than at **Oratoire St-Joseph** ⓠ, the church that rises 152 meters (500ft) above the street on the western summit of Mont-Royal. It rose up out of a wave of popular devotion to St Joseph, the patron saint of the worker, led by the humble Brother André who became famous for his curative powers during the first half of the 20th century. If the exterior is more remarkable for its size than its beauty (only the dome of St Peter's in the Vatican is larger), the austere simplicity of the modern interior is more lovely. Impressive in quite a different way is the crypt with its rows of crutches, donated by the miraculously healed, and banks of devotional candles. Brother André's tiny living quarters still stand in the shadow of the oratory.

The buildings of the 1960s in Montréal are monuments not to the church but to modernity. **Place-Ville-Marie** ⓡ, perhaps the most successful creation of the famous urban architect I.M.

TIP

Visit Maison Sir Georges-Etienne Cartier, 458 Notre-Dame Est, for a peek into the life of a 19th-century statesman of Québec (mid-June–Labor Day daily, end Apr–mid-June and Labor Day–end Dec Wed–Sun; charge).

BELOW: café life in Le Vieux-Port.

Map on page 180

Ile Notre-Dame is a haven for picnickers and cyclists; it even sports an artificial beach and fresh-water swimming lake.

Pei (responsible for the pyramid outside the Louvre in Paris), with its cruciform tower and underground plaza, pioneered the concept of the shopping mall in 1962. For Expo 67 Moshe Safdie, a student at McGill University, designed **Habitat 67**, a sort of cubist representation of the mountain made out of 158 concrete apartment units.

Parc Jean-Drapeau

The site of **Expo 67**, on two man-made islands in the St Lawrence, is now Parc Jean-Drapeau. **Ile Ste-Hélène** and **Ile Notre-Dame** can be identified by Buckminster Fuller's geodesic dome, built to house the US pavilion. The **Biosphère** **S** (June–Oct daily 10am–6pm, Nov–May Tue–Sun 10am–6pm; charge), on Ste-Hélène, is now home to an environmental observation center focusing on the St Lawrence-Great Lakes ecosystem. An amusement park, **La Ronde**, (June–late Aug daily, mid-May, Sept and Oct Sat–Sun only; charge) is on the island's eastern tip. Nearby is the **Vieux Fort** (1822), with summer re-enactments of maneuvers by the Fraser Highlanders. The **Musée Stewart au Fort de L'Ile**

BELOW: the Biodôme de Montréal. **RIGHT:** Cirque du Soleil entertainers.

Ste-Hélène provides insight into early European exploration and the settlement of New France. (Currently the museum is closed for extensive renovations.) By night on the Île Notre Dame, Montréalers and visitors try their luck at the **Casino de Montréal** **O** with its river and city views (daily 24 hrs; free).

Hochelaga-Maisonneuve

On the eastern end of the island, Hochelaga-Maisonneuve was Canada's fifth largest city before it was annexed to Montréal in 1918. Known for its striking collection of Beaux-Arts architecture, one of the best examples is the **Maisonneuve Market**, which opened in 1912 and is now popular for its organic and regionally grown products.

The neighborhood's most prominent and modern monument is the **Parc Olympique O**, one of the world's most ambitious sports complexes, located on rue Sherbrooke Est. Designed by French architect Roger Taillibert, the stadium was built for the 1976 Summer Olympic Games and is famous for its suspended retractable roof and for the **Montréal Tower**, the highest inclined tower in the world. It has one of the best views in the city (daily 9am–5pm, mid-June–Labor Day until 7pm, closed early Jan–mid-Feb; charge). At its base, the impressive sports center includes six huge swimming pools.

Next to the stadium is the **Biodôme de Montréal** (mid Feb–early Mar daily 9am–5pm, Mar–mid-June and Labor Day–mid-Feb Tue–Sun 9am–5pm, mid-June–Labor Day daily until 6pm; charge), featuring flora and fauna from four different ecosystems: rainforest, polar, marine, and forest.

Opposite the Parc Olympique are the **Botanical Gardens**, considered among the world's best, with 73 hectares (180 acres) of flora (the **Arid Regions** greenhouse is the best place to escape from a Montréal snowstorm). More than 250,000 species are housed in the **Insectarium** (daily 9am–5pm in winter, until 6pm in summer, until 9pm Sept 8–Oct 31; free). ❑

THE GREAT OUTDOORS

The country's huge land and water masses and varied climate provide countless opportunities for outdoor pursuits and sports – not just ice hockey

Canadians are avid tourists in their own country. Some families spend entire summer vacations in their favorite national and provincial parks in pursuit of outdoor activity. Others have vacation homes, known as "cottages," regardless of their size. Boaters head for the waters, tenters to the back-roads. Bird-watchers, fishermen, and canoeists, too, find plenty of space for these gentle pursuits. If all that sounds too tame, there is plenty of scope for whitewater rafting, heli-hiking, even heli-fishing. Parks have campgrounds, supervised beaches, hiking, and cycling trails.

Even city-dwellers can enjoy walking and cycling trails cut through municipal parks well endowed with wooded areas, rivers, and lakes.

Participant Sports

In the realm of participant sports, golf and tennis are summer's favorites, but cricket and soccer also have their adherents. Lacrosse, which originated as a rough native tribal contest, has been tamed to a seven-a-side game.

In winter, ice and snow are welcomed by many. That's when city walking and cycling paths are transformed into cross-country ski and snow-shoeing trails, fishermen cut holes in the ice, dog-team enthusiasts have race meets, amateurs enjoy sleigh rides, while alpine skiers head for the mountain slopes.

ABOVE: Canada's magnificent scenery and wildlife are often best observed from the water.

LEFT: this is a very popular activity in the west and on the prairies, where novices can improve their technique on a ranch holiday. Best of all is trail-riding in the Rockies' national parks.

RIGHT: around Emerald Lake, Banff Lake Louise and Jasper in the Rockies, the skiing, both cross-country and downhill, is world-class.

ABOVE: hiking takes you to the true heart of the country and parks have well-marked trails, graded for most abilities.

SPORTS WORTH WATCHING OUT FOR

Baseball, ice hockey, and Canadian football all have amateur and professional teams and hordes of enthusiastic supporters. In summer youngsters play "little league" baseball. A treat for the kids around Toronto is to visit the Rogers Centre to watch the Toronto Blue Jays play American opponents.

In winter little-leaguers trade baseball mits for hockey skates and take to community ice rinks. While the origins of ice hockey (known in Canada simply as "hockey") are murky, there is no doubt it is Canada's sporting gift to the world. This is a major spectator sport, with teams competing from all over North America. If the Edmonton Oilers, Montréal Canadiens or Toronto Maple Leafs arrive at the annual Stanley Cup game in late spring, the entire country comes to a halt to watch.

Canadian football, which has its origins in 19th-century English rugby, is played by high-school and university teams as well as commercial league teams. Football's high point is the Gray Cup in late November or early December. Parades and post-game festivities bring Gray Cup fever to a high pitch; the game itself often has well-fortified fans cheering their teams on.

ABOVE: Canada's lakes, rivers, and coastlines provide haven for fishing enthusiasts. Permits are required.

BELOW: the South Nahanni River, which flows through Nahanni National Park in the Northwest Territories, offers some of the most thrilling white water in the country.

QUÉBEC

Fiercely proud of its French-speaking traditions, the province of Québec, from the frozen north to the fertile land along the St Lawrence, has developed its own distinct culture

A t 1,504,687 sq km (594,860 sq miles), Québec is the largest eastern province, lying between Ontario and New Brunswick, Hudson Bay and the Gulf of St Lawrence. Montréal, Québec City, and the other main population centers are along the St Lawrence River and on the east coast. The 7.6 million Québécois are deeply aware of being surrounded by almost 300 million anglophones whose culture seems to impinge on their own. Don't be surprised if you sometimes encounter a protective and proud attitude towards language and culture, two great local preoccupations.

The Eastern Townships

For hundreds of years, the Eastern Townships have been a place of refuge and of peace. Once predominantly English, the region is now 90 percent French (though the majority can speak both languages) and is now known as *Cantons-de-l'Est*. During the American War of Independence, many who preferred to stay loyal to the British Crown settled in these parts, and it has retained an English and American flavor throughout its history. It also drew benefit from the American Civil War, when southerners who felt uncomfortable in the northern states would spend holidays in one of the Townships' many fine old hotels. But no friction between the Townships and New Englanders survives, and today they are the closest of neighbors.

Highway 10 from Montréal will get you into the Townships in about one hour. **Granby**, just north of the highway, 84km (52 miles) east from Montréal, is known for its zoo and collection of fountains.

Head on for another 45km (37 miles) towards **Mont Orford ❶** (a ski resort with a chairlift to the summit year-round) and **Magog** for the most beautiful country. The gentle hills and valleys are an extension of the ancient Appalachian mountain range, and with its intricate network

Main attractions
MONT ORFORD
MONT TREMBLANT
PLACE ROYALE, VIEUX QUÉBEC
MUSÉE DE LA CIVILISATION
LA CITADEL
PLAINS OF ABRAHAM
SAGUENAY
PERCÉ ROCK
JARDINS DE MÉTIS

LEFT: Mont Tremblant.
BELOW: canoes at sunset.

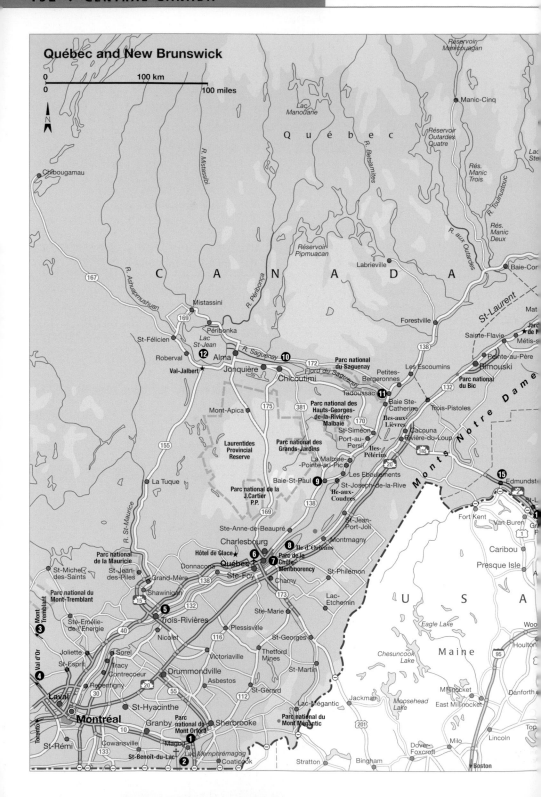

Québec and New Brunswick

0 ————— 100 km
0 ————— 100 miles

N

Reservoir
Manicouagan

Manic-Cinq

Q u é b e c

Réservoir
Outardes
Quatre

Lac
Manouane

Rés.
Manic
Trois

Lac
Ste

R. Mistassibi

Chibougamau

Réservoir
Pipmuacan

Rés.
Manic
Deux

R. aux Outardes

R. Besiamites

Baie-Cor

C   A   N   A   D   A

Labrieville

St-Laurent

R. Péribonca

Forestville

Sainte-Flavie

Jard
de N

Mat

167

R. Ashuapmushuan

Mistassini

169

Péribonka

St-Félicien

Lac
St-Jean

Roberval

12 Alma

R. Saguenay

172

10

Jonquière

Chicoutimi

Fjord du Saguenay

Parc national
du Saguenay

Les Escoumins

Petites-
Bergeronnes

Métis-l

Pointe-au-Père

Rimouski

138

Parc national
du Bic

132

Val-Jalbert

Mont-Apica

175

381

Parc national des
Hauts-Georges-
de-la-Rivière-
Malbaie

170

Tadoussac   11

Baie Ste-
Catherine

Îles-aux-
Lièvres

Trois-Pistoles

Monts Notre Dame

155

Laurentides
Provincial
Reserve

Parc national des
Grands-Jardins

St-Siméon

Port-au-
Persil

Cacouna

Rivière-du-Loup

185

20

La Tuque

Parc national de la
J.Cartier
P.P.

169

La Malbaie
-Pointe-au-Pic

Baie-St-Paul   9

Îles-
Pélerins

Les Eboulements

St-Joseph-de-la-Rive

15 Edmundst

2

St-L

R. St-Maurice

Ste-Anne-de-Beaupré

138

Île-aux-
Coudres

St-Jean-
Port-Joli

Fort Kent

Van Buren

Gr

1

Charlesbourg

Hôtel de Glace

Parc national
de la Mauricie

St-Michel-
des-Saints

St-Jean-
des-Piles

Grand-Mère

138

Donnacona

6 Québec

7

Ste-Foy

Charny

173

8 Île d'Orléans

Parc de la
Chute-
Montmorency

St-Philémon

Montmagny

Lac-
Etchemin

Caribou

Presque Isle

U   S   A

Parc national du
Mont-Tremblant

Mont Tremblant   3

Shawinigan

15

5

132

Trois-Rivières

Ste-Emélie-
de-l'Energie

Ste-Marie

Ste-Marie

Eagle Lake

Woo

Houlton

95

Nicolet

40

116

Plessisville

St-Georges

M a i n e

Chesuncook
Lake

Val d'Or   4

Joliette

St-Esprit

Sorel

Tracy

Contrecoeur

Victoriaville

Thetford
Mines

St-Martin

Drummondville

Asbestos

Moosehead
Lake

Millinocket

Danforth

Repentigny

30

20

55

St-Gérard

112

Lac-Mégantic

Jackman

East Millinocket

Top

Laval

Montréal

St-Hyacinthe

Granby

Parc
national du
Mont Orford

Sherbrooke

Parc national du
Mont Mégantic

201

Dover-
Foxcroft

Milo

Lincoln

Toronto

10

1

Cowansville

133

Magog

St-Rémi

St-Benoît-du-Lac

2

Lac Memphrémagog

Coaticook

Stratton

Bingham

Boston

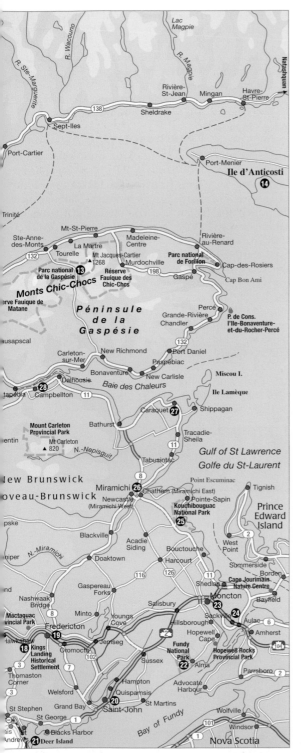

of lakes and streams, its country villages, dairy cattle, sheep, and strawberry fields, this part of Québec has a bucolic charm that is unusual in the often rugged terrain of the province. Indeed, **North Hatley** (on Route 108 at the north end of Lake Massawippi) rests in a shielded valley, warmed by sunlight reflected from the lake, giving it a "microclimate" that prolongs summer and softens winter enough to make it the home of hummingbirds and flora normally found far to the south.

Long, slender **Lac Memphrémagog ❷** is the largest in the area; boat cruises and a variety of water sports are available at the town of Magog on its northern tip. On its west shore, the beautiful hillside Benedictine monastery of **St-Benoît-du-Lac** (Nov–May Mon–Fri 9–10.45am, 1.30–4.30pm, Sat 9–10.45am, 11.45am–4.30pm, late June–mid-Oct Mon–Sat 9–10.45am, 11.50am–6pm, Sun 12.15–6pm) manufactures cheese and chocolate.

The Laurentians

Spring, which in Québec lasts about a day and a half, is the only season in which Montréalers avoid the Laurentians. It is the playground just beyond the backyard of the metropolis; though its wooded lakes and hills are still lovely, the difficulty is often where to get away from it all when everyone has come to do just that.

Winter is ski season; almost everyone in Montréal skis either cross-country or downhill. In summer, families pack up the car and head to the cottage for swimming, sailing, windsurfing, and waterskiing. In fall, the leaves turn those deep shades of red and orange that draw hikers parading over the hills and valleys.

Not all the Laurentian towns are equally picturesque. Prettiness tends to be in proportion to size, though **St-Sauveur-des-Monts** and **Ste-Adèle**, 60km (37 miles) northwest of Montréal are worth visiting for their restaurants and character.

The best bet, however, is to take Autoroute 15 or the more scenic and slow Rte 117 to **Mont-Tremblant ❸**. About 140km (87 miles) from Montréal, the town of Mont Tremblant is both the Laurentians' largest resort and one of eastern North

For an introduction to the dominant pulp and paper industry of the region, visit the Centre d'Exposition sur l'industrie des pâtes et papiers in Trois-Rivières.

America's foremost all-year travel destinations, with 94 ski and snowboarding runs and four top-ranking golf courses for summer visitors. The Laurentians are among the oldest mountain ranges in the world, so for the most part erosion has softened peaks into gently rounded hills perhaps 300 meters (1,000ft) high. Mont Tremblant is the region's highest mountain at 875 meters (2,870ft); chairlifts operate year round to transport visitors up to the summit.

The resort sits beside Parc national du Mont-Tremblant, a vast 1,500-sq-km (579-sq-mile) expanse in which the area's tranquility and natural beauty are easily appreciated. More than 400 lakes and hiking trails are scattered throughout the park, with facilities available for windsurfing, canoeing, white-water rafting on the Rivière du Diable, fishing, and swimming.

Val d'Or ❹ means Valley of Gold and it lies at the eastern extreme of the Cadillac Break, a gold-rich fault that extends west to Kirkland Lake in Ontario. The glittering metal was first discovered in 1914, and high gold prices still keep the miners working. A village called

Bourlamaque – first built by the mining company for its employees – is now a well-preserved historic quarter of 75 pinewood houses and a small museum. More recently, the town found another source of prosperity: its strategic location on the road north from Montréal to the vast James Bay hydroelectric project.

Paper town

Ten percent of the world's newsprint, 2,500 tons a day, once came from **Trois-Rivières ❺**, 142km (88 miles) northeast of Montréal. Though still important commercially, it struggles to overcome its image as a lackluster industrial town. It has prospered since 1610, but the fires that regularly swept through all Québec's communities have left little to show from the town's first two centuries. In rue des Ursulines, the **Manoir de Tonnancour** (Tue–Fri 10am–noon and 1.30–5pm, Sat–Sun 1–5pm; free), housing temporary art exhibitions, the **Maison Hertel-de-la-Fresnière** (also used for visiting exhibitions) and the **Musée-des-Ursulines** (Mar–Apr Wed–Sun 1–5pm, May–Nov Tue–Sun 10am–5pm, Nov–Feb closed;

BELOW: the city of Trois-Rivières.

The Other Townships

Unsurprisingly, the most frequented part of the Eastern Townships is closest to Montreal. Sherbrooke is the stepping stone into lesser-known le Haut-St-François, which describes itself as "the other Townships."

In its eastern reaches, Mégantic is the Townships' most mountainous region and spectacularly beautiful. Granite has been quarried here since the 1890s. At 1,100 meters (3,609ft), Mont-Mégantic is said to be the highest mountain in the province that can be climbed by car. At the summit, astronomical research is conducted in the Mont-Mégantic Observatory, which houses a 24-tonne telescope, the eastern seaboard's largest. The multimedia AstroLab (www.astrolab-parc-national-mont-megantic.org) looks at all things Universe-related.

small charge) survive, at least in part, from the early 18th century.

The town's attractions are modern: the **Grand Prix** races through the streets in August, the **International Poetry Festival** takes place in October, the **Laviolette Bridge** spans the St Lawrence. The revitalized area at the port is also well worth a visit.

Nowhere in the vicinity draws as many visitors as the shrine, 10km (6 miles) north of Trois-Rivières, called **Notre-Dame-du-Cap**, in the small town of Cap-de-la-Madeleine. The little church of Notre-Dame-du-Rosaire was built in 1714 and drew a moderate number of pilgrims until the day in 1883 that Father Frederic Jansoone and two others saw the statue of the Virgin open her eyes. Trois-Rivières stands at the confluence of the St-Maurice and the St Lawrence rivers, begging the question: where is the third river? In fact, there isn't one. If you travel up the St Lawrence by boat, as Jacques Cartier and Samuel de Champlain did, the two delta islands at the mouth of St Maurice give the impression that *trois rivières* end here. The name survives from then.

Ville de Québec

"The impression made upon the visitor by this Gibraltar of North America: its giddy heights; its citadel suspended, as it were, in the air, its picturesque streets and frowning gateways; and the splendid views which burst upon the eye at every turn: is at once unique and everlasting."

Remarkably, Charles Dickens's comment on the **Ville de Québec ❻** is still appropriate more than a century after his visit. It retains its 18th-century ambience with narrow, winding streets, horse-drawn carriages, and fine French cooking behind charming facades. The only dramatic change in the old town is the construction at the turn of the 19th century of a castle-like hotel that perches on its promontory overlooking the St Lawrence River: the **Fairmont Le Château Frontenac ❹**.

The province's cryptic motto, *Je me souviens* (I remember), insists upon the defense of Québécois tradition, language, and culture. Here in the provincial capital, reminders are everywhere that this was once performed by soldiers with guns from turrets and

Rooftops of old Québec.

BELOW: Fairmont Le Château Frontenac.

The Basilica of Notre-Dame-du-Cap, a Catholic sanctuary that attracts hundreds of pilgrims every year.

bastions. Today, the politicians and civil servants of Québec City have taken over the job, using the milder instruments of democracy, but are hardly less ardent in their purpose. Québec City still stands sentinel over the St Lawrence, the only walled city on the continent north of Mexico. The views are as lovely as ever: from the **Terrasse Dufferin ꓐ** in front of the Château Frontenac, one looks out at the blue Laurentian hills and Mont St-Anne, the rolling countryside and the boats passing on the shimmering St Lawrence 60 meters (200ft) below.

An archeological dig is currently taking place beneath the Terrasse Dufferin, revealing the remains of the St-Louis Fort and Château St-Louis, the residence of colonial French and British governors. While the archeologists are still making their discoveries, guided tours are offered (early May–mid-Oct daily).

Diagonally opposite **Place d'Armes ꓚ**, the former drill and parade ground, rue du Trésor runs down to rue Buade. This lane, named after the building where colonists used to pay their dues

to the Royal Treasury, is today the artists' row; hung with quite decent watercolors, etchings, silkscreens. Rue Buade winds downhill to **Parc Montmorency**, opposite the grand **Ancien Bureau de Poste** with its rather pompous monument to Bishop François-Xavier de Laval-Montmorency, first bishop of Québec and founder of its largest university.

Côte de la Montagne drops steeply to the left, winding down into the Lower Town, following the ravine that Québec's first settlers used to climb from the Lower Town to the Upper. Just beyond the **Porte Prescott**, a recent reconstruction of the original erected here in 1797, is **L'Escalier Casse-Cou**, the "Breakneck Stairway." This staircase, not quite as daunting as it sounds, leads to the narrow Petit-Champlain, which is lined with crafts shops.

From the foot of L'Escalier Casse-Cou, **Place Royale** is just around the corner. Thus one tumbles from the Château Frontenac into the cradle of French civilization in North America.

Place Royale, where the first settlement in America stood, was the business center of Québec City until about

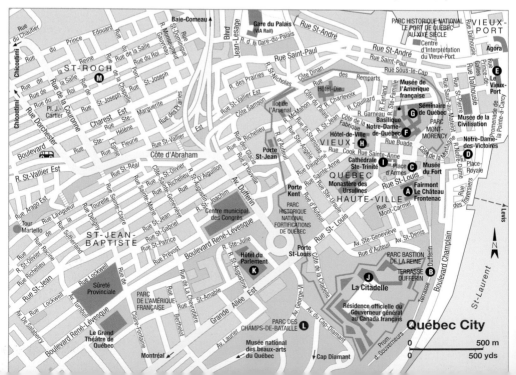

Québec City

1832. Its name derives from the bust of Louis XIV, the great Sun King of Versailles, that was erected here in 1686. Today it is the scene of constant play and concert performances, usually recreating the culture of the 17th and 18th centuries. **Eglise Notre-Dame-des-Victoires ➊**, dominating the square, was built in 1688 and reconstructed after Wolfe's devastation of the Lower Town in 1759. The church is named for two early victories against the Anglo-Americans – or rather, one great victory and one lucky accident. A Bostonian, Sir William Phips (knighted for discovering 32 tons of shipwrecked bullion), sailed to Québec with 34 boats and 2,000 men in October 1690, and demanded its surrender.

Governor Frontenac promised to reply with his cannon, and during six days of fighting his guns hammered the fleet. By land, snipers, fighting Indian-style against Phips's troops drawn up in formal battle-order, killed 150 men with only one loss to their own party. Phips withdrew on the sixth day, unaware that the French had just run out of ammunition. The lucky accident – or to the French, Our Lady's victory – was the storm in the Gulf of St Lawrence that destroyed the enormous British fleet of Sir Hovendon Walker in 1711, saving Québec from almost certain defeat. Both these events are depicted in little scenes above the odd, turreted altar.

Crossing the road on the waterfront, rue Dalhousie, you leave the 18th century behind and enter the more modern world of the port. On the right is the entrance to the government-operated ferry services to **Levis** on the other side of the river, while straight ahead the MV *Louis-Jolliet*, a colorful and popular cruise boat, docks.

Walking north beside the river leads to the new commercial and community complex, called **Le Vieux-Port ➋** despite its thoroughly contemporary design: overhead walkways of red and silver tubing and plexiglass walls connect spacious, functional pavilions. The complex surrounds the **Agora**, a 6,000-seat amphitheater used for cultural events, particularly evening concerts throughout the summer. The award-winning modern **Musée de la Civilisation** (mid-June–early Sept daily

A monument to Sieur de Maisonneuve, founder of Montréal, stands in Québec's Place d'Armes. Legend has it that he killed an Indian chief here in battle in 1644.

BELOW:
Québec City port.

The Musée de la Civilisation, designed by the contemporary Canadian architect Moshe Safdie, incorporates Maison Estèbe, a merchant's house, circa 1752.

9.30am–6.30pm, early Sept–mid-June Tue–Sun 10am–5pm; charge, Nov–May free on Tue, Jan–Feb free on Sat 10am–noon) in the center of Le Vieux-Port has exhibitions on such subjects as language, thought, the body, and society.

The easiest way to get back to the Upper Town is by taking the little funicular at the head of rue Sous-le-Fort, which is worth the small charge to save wear and tear on the feet in this city-made-for-walking. It shinnies up the cliff from the house of Louis Jolliet (the explorer of the Mississippi River) to the Terrasse Dufferin (daily, end Oct–early Apr 7.30am–11pm, Apr–mid-June and Labor Day–end Oct until 11.30pm, mid-June–Labor Day until midnight).

At the intersection of rue Buade and Côte de la Fabrique is the baroque cathedral of Québec City, **Basilique Notre-Dame-de-Québec** ❻ (daily 8.30am–4pm; guided tours May–Nov daily, Dec–Apr Sat only). The city's main church has been here since 1633 when Samuel de Champlain built Notre-Dame-de-la-Recouvrance in gratitude for the recovery of New France from the British. Next door stands the **Séminaire de Québec** ❼ and the **Université Laval**. The Jesuits established a college here in 1635, a year before Harvard opened, but the Seminary was officially founded only in 1663 by Bishop Laval (guided tours in summer; charge).

The university still exists, though its modern campus is now in the suburb of **Ste-Foy**, and these buildings serve their original purpose as a seminary and high school. The seminary's museum, known as the **Musée de l'Amérique française** (June 24–Labor Day daily 9.30am–5pm, Labor Day–June 23 Tue–Sun 10am–5pm; charge) is the oldest museum of history in Canada. Now part of the Musée de la Civilisation, its permanent exhibition looks at the economic and social role the Seminary played, as well as the religious and educational aspect. Across the street from the cathedral is the monument to **Cardinal Taschereau**, looking formidable, as if ready to carry out his threat to excommunicate any worker who joined a union. Behind is the gray, ample **Hôtel-de-Ville** ❽.

BELOW: rue du Trésor, Québec City.

Around the corner stands the only rival to the Château Frontenac on the city's skyline, the **Price Building**. With 17 stories, it just about qualifies as the old town's only skyscraper. One is enough, and fortunately the 1937 art deco style is not out of keeping with the neighborhood. Straight on, however, stands the **Cathédrale Ste-Trinité ⓘ**, the first Anglican cathedral built outside the British Isles and thoroughly English from its design (on the model of St Martin-in-the-Fields in Trafalgar Square) to its pews made of oak imported from the Royal Windsor Forest.

Lively **Rue St-Louis**, with its snug little restaurants and *pensions*, slopes up from the end of Rue Desjardins to the Porte St-Louis, rebuilt in a grand neo-Gothic style (complete with turret and crenellated gun-ports) to replace the 17th-century original. Just in front of the gate is the lane that leads to **La Citadelle ⓙ**, the star-shaped bastion on the summit of **Cap-Diamant** (tours Apr–Oct daily; Nov–Mar bilingual guided tour daily at 1.30pm; charge), 100 meters (400ft) over the St Lawrence.

The citadel, with its Changing of the Guard ceremony (June 24–Labor Day daily 10am) and Beating of the Retreat (July–Aug Fri–Sat 7pm), appeals to childhood notions of soldierly glory and adventure. But however colorful, it continues to play a military role as the headquarters of Canada's French-only Royal 22e Régiment, known as the "Vandoos" (the nickname a corruption of *les vingt-deuxième*).

Built by the British in the early 1800s according to plans approved by the Duke of Wellington, with double granite walls and a magnificent position above a sheer cliff, it was considered one of the most impregnable strongholds in the Empire.

Beyond the wall's confines, the city becomes suddenly roomy, opening out onto the **Grande Allée** and the lawns of the **Hôtel du Parlement ⓚ**, the seat of the National Assembly, Québec's provincial government. Though not old by the city's standards (building began in 1881), the elaborate French Renaissance design by Eugène-E. Taché does seem to embody Québec's distant roots in the court of Louis XIII. Its symbols,

A throne in the apse of the Cathédrale Ste-Trinité is called the King's Bench – rather ironical since, though it has been graced in its 200 years by queens, princes, princesses, and governors-general, it has not, so far, been the seat of a king.

BELOW: Changing of the Guard at the citadel.

Québec City thrives on festivals: early February is Carnival, with parades and canoe racing on the frozen St Lawrence. In July its streets are alive with music.

BELOW:
the chic streets of Québec City.

however, are purely Québécois; the important figures of her history are all there, each trying to outdo the other's elegant pose in his alcove on the facade: Frontenac, Wolfe, Montcalm, Lévis, Talon… Below, Louis-Philippe Hébert's bronze works include dignified groups of Indians, the "noble savages" of the white man's imagination.

Outside, the terraces of the Georgian houses that border the Grande Allée west from the National Assembly are cluttered with tables where visitors and civil servants enjoy the cuisine, the wines, and the serenading violins of some of Québec's liveliest restaurants. A block south, there is gentle peace. **Parc des Champs-de-Bataille ❶**, or the **Plains of Abraham**, runs parallel to the Grande Allée with spectacular views across the St Lawrence to the Appalachian foothills. Its rolling lawns and broad shade trees have known far more romance than fighting, many more wine-and-cheese picnics than violent deaths, but however incongruously, it commemorates a vicious 15-minute battle in which Louis-Joseph, Marquis de Montcalm,

lost half of North America to the British. It wasn't quite that simple, but the fact remains that the Indian fighting style of the Canadians had won them success after success against the British until the Marquis de Montcalm, a traditionalist and a defeatist, became head of the land troops. Always ready to retreat even after a victory, and rarely pressing an advantage, Montcalm steadily reduced the territory that he had to defend.

General Wolfe, who sailed down the St Lawrence with half as many troops as Montcalm held in the fortress of Québec City, never really hoped to succeed in taking it and so he destroyed 80 percent of the town with cannon fire.

Montcalm would not emerge to fight a pitched battle and, in a last-ditch, desperate attempt, Wolfe took 4,400 men up the cliff in silence by cover of night to the heights where there was no hope of turning back. Montcalm had been expecting Wolfe at Beauport, north of the city, and he rushed back to fight on the plains. Throwing away every advantage, time, the possession of the city stronghold, and the sniping

skills of his men, Montcalm fought the kind of European-style set battle that his troops were improperly trained for. Wolfe was killed, Montcalm mortally wounded and, though the British held only the plains at the battle's conclusion, the French surrendered the city.

At the far end of Parc des Champs-de-Bataille, just beyond the now vacant jail called the **Petit Bastille**, stands the **Musée national des beaux-arts du Québec**, (early June–early Sept daily 9am–6pm, Wed until 9pm, early Sept–May Tue–Sun 10am–5pm, Wed until 9pm; charge) the imposing neo-Classical home of a large proportion of the best Québec art. Painters such as Alfred Pellan, Marc-Aurèle Fortin, and Jean-Paul Riopelle are not quite household names throughout the world, but the work of these modern artists has a wide range from expressionistic landscapes to frenetic abstracts.

A 15-minute walk west from Vieux-Québec, the neighborhood of **St-Roch** Ⓜ, offers sharp contrast to a city steeped in hundreds of years of history. Reclaimed by cutting edge entities in art, technology, food, fashion, and music, it has become one of the hippest parts of the city.

Pack your bathing suit when you head east for 10km (6 miles) either by the upper Route 360 or the lower road, Route 138, to **Parc de la Chûte-Montmorency** ❼ (daily; free). These falls at 83 meters (272ft) are considerably higher than Niagara Falls, though less dramatic because they are so much narrower. Here, however, instead of looking at the falls from the top down, you approach the base, which means that the closer you get, the wetter you get from the spray. The province has thoughtfully built a large granite platform at the base of the falls so that visitors can actually stand inside the chilly cloud of spray. In winter, the spray forms a solid block that grows up from the bottom into a "sugarloaf" of ice and snow, providing a splendid slope for tobogganing.

Fertile island

Just a mile (2km) south of the falls, the bridge over the **Ile d'Orléans** ❽ turns off the autoroute. In 1970, the provincial government declared the

On the Plains of Abraham, two robust little Martello Towers (June 24–early Sept) were built as outposts of the British defense system between 1804 and 1823, with walls up to 4 meters (13ft) thick on the side facing the enemy.

BELOW:
Parc de la Chûte-Montmorency.

Discover St-Roch

The emerging district of **St-Roch**, in the Lower Town, has fluctuated dramatically in terms of popularity and fortune. In the early 1900s it thrived as the shopping and industrial center of the city, but by the 60s, suburban shopping malls were luring locals away in droves. A desperate attempt to revive the area saw several blocks along Rue St-Joseph – one of the neighborhood's main arteries – covered to create a protected mall that would bring back the shoppers. It was a disaster, resulting in even more bankruptcies and empty buildings. Thanks to the efforts of a visionary mayor, Jean Paul l'Allier, along with the discovery by artists of low-cost warehouse space for studios and lofts, St-Roch is now a fine example of urban regeneration, home to countless galleries, avant-garde restaurants, and trendy boutiques.

> **TIP**
>
> The best observation points for spotting whales in the St Lawrence are in the area of the Parc du Saguenay at Pointe-Noire Promontory and Cap-de-Bon-Désir.

island a historic district to prevent the encroachment of the city and the tourist trade from destroying the milieu of one of Québec's most picturesque and historic regions. The exceptionally fertile soil brought prosperity early to the island. In the 1600s there were as many inhabitants here as in Montréal or Québec, and farming is still the vocation of most of the families here.

Few visitors can resist indulging themselves at the roadside stands that offer fat strawberries swimming in lakes of thick, fresh cream topped off with maple sugar. **Ste-Anne-de-Beaupré**, a nearby town on the St Lawrence's north shore, houses a cathedral that millions of Catholics have visited. The fountain of St Anne, in front of the church, is said to have healing powers.

Charlevoix, Saguenay, and Lac St-Jean

Stretching over 200km (124 miles) along the north shore as far as the Saguenay River, the Charlevoix region's immediate selling point is its sheer beauty. Here, the Laurentian mountains plunge sharply down to the St

Lawrence. Dense forests, fertile valleys, racing streams, and cascading waterfalls backdrop picture-perfect towns of silver-spired churches and steep, red-roofed houses. In the early 1900s, Canadian artists such as A.Y. Jackson, Clarence Gagnon, and Jean-Paul Lemieux came to capture its magic on canvas – and painters, photographers, and writers continue to come here for inspiration. Many of them stay in historic **Baie-St-Paul** ❾, where the Musée d'art contemporain de Baie-St-Paul (Tue–Sun; charge) hosts an international symposium of contemporary art in August.

Among all Québec's uncountable lakes and waterways, perhaps none can match the splendor of the **Saguenay** ❿, its ragged cliffs looming hundreds of meters over the broad, blue river. Vikings and Basque fishermen came and went long before Jacques Cartier named it "the Kingdom of the Saguenay" when he came seeking the Orient in 1535. Its spectacular beauty survives today, and the whales never fail to gather in the deep estuary each July, staying until December, when they swim away

BELOW: the Saguenay River.
RIGHT: maple leaves in the fall.

to unknown destinations. The cruise boats that leave from the wharf at **Baie-Ste-Catherine**, 71km (44 miles) north of Québec on Route 138, can virtually guarantee whale sightings.

A ferry takes passengers and cars across the river to **Tadoussac ⓫**, where North America's oldest wooden church, **Petite Chapelle de Tadoussac** (mid-June–Labor Day daily 9am–8pm, Labor Day–mid-June daily 9am–6pm; charge), has stood since 1647, and New France's first fort, built in 1600, has been reconstructed. If the **Tadoussac Hotel** looks familiar, it's because the movie *Hotel New Hampshire* was filmed here.

Farther inland, the terrain levels out onto the fertile plain of the **Lac St-Jean ⓬** region. Fur-trading companies held a monopoly on the area until the mid-19th century and it was barely settled until railroads brought pulp and paper developments after 1883 followed by large hydroelectric and aluminum smelting plants.

For visitors, however, the industry is relatively insignificant except in the commercial centers of Chicoutimi, Jon-quière, and Alma. The rich soil produces 4.5 million kgs (10 million pounds) of blueberries a year and, coupled with award-winning local cheeses, these provide the materials for an endless supply of mouth-watering blueberry cheese-cakes. Less decadent regional specialties include various *tourtières* (spiced meat pies) and a dried-bean soup called *soupe à la gourgane*. Local fish – trout, pike, doré, and plentiful freshwater salmon – complete the menu.

Beyond the commercial centers, several beautiful small towns cluster around Lac St-Jean, such as **Péribonka**, the setting of Louis Hémon's novel *Maria Chapdelaine*, and **Mistassini**, the blueberry capital. **Val-Jalbert**, a ghost-town since 1927, has been partially restored, preserving its original character and buildings. The old mill stands against the 72-meter (236ft) **Ouiatch-ouan Falls**.

Péninsule de la Gaspésie

Route 132 loops around the **Péninsule de la Gaspésie**, beginning and ending at **Ste-Flavie**, in a 560km (348-mile) circle that strings together the sleepy

30 minutes northwest of Québec City, the Hôtel de Glace is North America's only Ice Hotel; made entirely of snow (15,000 tons) and ice (500 tons), each year's design is different. Generally operating January to April, the 36-room hotel is also open for public tours.

BELOW: sightings of whales are guaranted.

The mountains, meadows, limestone cliffs, and sandy beaches of Gaspésie's Parc national de Forillon are home to a wealth of flora and fauna (daily).

fishing villages of the eastern coast. The Mi'kmaq called it *Gespeg*, "the end of the earth." Though the Gaspé has been settled since Shakespeare's time, it has suffered almost no industrial development. Even the roads and trains that came with the later part of the 19th century left its rural tranquility and Acadian culture largely the same as ever.

From Ste-Flavie, the road cuts southeast down the Matapédia Valley, following the "river of 222 rapids," which cascades through a deep gorge at the edge of the Chic-Choc mountains. At the village of **Matapédia**, 150km (93 miles) south, the road turns northeast and follows the Baie des Chaleurs. Once known as the "Canadian Riviera," the bay is thankfully too wild and unspoiled to merit the name today. The road weaves among coves and villages, some with English names such as New Carlisle, New Richmond, and Douglastown, given to them by loyalists who settled here to escape the American War of Independence. Eventually the coast wends northward and meets the red, rocky cliffs where the Chic-Chocs

veer down to the sea. Rounding a curve, suddenly the **Percé Rock** appears, a 400-million-ton block of limestone jutting improbably out of the sea. Roughly oblong in shape, there were once as many as four arches driven by the tides through this treeless crag, which also goes by the name "pierced rock." Nearby, the bird sanctuary on **Ile Bonaventure** is home to 50,000 gannets.

The north coast of the Gaspé is more rugged: the road winds along the bluffs at the edge of the highest mountains in eastern Canada. **Mont Jacques-Cartier** rises 1,268 meters (4,160ft) a few miles inland at the edge of the **Parc national de la Gaspésie** ⑬. This stretch along the south St Lawrence shore provides perhaps the most dramatic scenery on the Gaspé: the road hugs the steep cliffs that the sea washes below. At **Mont-St-Pierre,** near Ste-Anne-des-Monts, a hang-gliding festival is held each July, its competitors jumping like Icarus over the St Lawrence.

A number of families who live along the shore are descended from Irish immigrants whose boats were destroyed on the coast. Some remem-

BELOW:
Percé church with the spectacular Percé Rock in the background.

ber the day in 1914 when the *Empress of Ireland* collided with another boat and sank in 15 minutes, with the loss of 1,014 lives. A gentler civilization reappears at **Jardins de Métis** (formerly Reford Gardens) near Métis-sur-Mer where Lord George Stephen built **Reford House** in the last century with its beautiful English garden displaying more than 3,000 floral varieties (June–early Oct daily; charge).

The round trip from Québec City covers 1,600km (1,000 miles) – not exactly a Sunday afternoon drive, but worthwhile if you can afford a couple of Sundays, and the week between.

Anticosti Island

Like something coughed up out of the mouth of the St Lawrence, the 8,000 sq-km (3,000-sq-mile) **Ile d'Anticosti** ⑭ may seem a little remote. Surrounded by steep cliffs and treacherous reefs, Anticosti was known as "the graveyard of the gulf." About 400 shipwrecks scatter the coast, some of them quite recent. These days, populated by 300 people, Anticosti is an ecotourist's haven. It is home to the fourth-

largest population of bald eagles in North America.

The island is now divided between four outfitters (SEPAQ Anticosti, Pourvoirie du Cerf-Sau, and Pourvoirie du Lac Geneviève), with the exception of the village of **Port-Menier**. Reservations with an outfitter are definitely recommended for hunting and fishing (mainly sea trout, salmon, and speckled trout), and permits are required for fishing and hunting anywhere in Québec. Access is convenient: daily flights leave from **Havre-Saint-Pierre**, and a ferry boat, the *Relais Nordik*, takes passengers from Rimouski or **Sept-Iles** to Port-Menier.

There are two hotels in Port-Menier, **Hotel de l'Il** and **Auberge Port-Menier**, and another, **Auberge de la Pointe Ouest**, at Pointe Ouest, approximately 20 minutes from Port-Menier. There are also six campgrounds offering around 170 campsites. Though a vast area is untouched by humans, centuries of occasional habitation have left their mark: ghost towns, overgrown cemeteries, an old railroad, and the 4,000-year-old remains of its earliest inhabitants. ❏

A wealthy French chocolatier named Henri Menier, who bought Anticosti for its hunting and fishing potential in 1895, imported the first white-tailed deer; those 220 deer have proliferated impressively ever since, and now exceed 100,000.

LEFT: Pointe Carleton lighthouse on Ile d'Anticosti. **BELOW:** a floral window display.

THE EAST

Canada's four Atlantic provinces are bound
by seafaring traditions, yet each has its
own rich cultural identity

The host to Canada's first European visitors, and with the freshness of air laden with sea spray, the east coast is perhaps one of the most startlingly beautiful regions of Canada. Here are the achingly lonely beaches of Nova Scotia, the distinctive sense of humor and charming friendliness of the people of Newfoundland and Labrador, the old-world, unembarrassed potato obsession of the Prince Edward Island farmers, and the graceful elegance of New Brunswick's towns.

The four provinces that constitute Canada's eastern region are bound together by their proximity to the Atlantic Ocean – nowhere is more

than 160km (100 miles) from the sea, and most of the land is much closer – yet each possesses its own singular charm. On one side, Atlantic waves crash against soaring cliffs; on the other, the more sheltered waters of the Gulf of St Lawrence are calmer and warmer. New Brunswick's rugged coastline begins the section and reveals the province's unusual blend of eastern reserve and wanton wildness in its towns and landscape. Nova Scotia, "New Scotland," is explored by following its circuitous coastline and stopping to examine some of its unusual cities and delightful towns.

Newfoundland and Labrador is perhaps the most quirky of all the provinces, and its rugged beauty and remoteness serve as a background to a portrait of the area's friendly inhabitants.

The East section ends at Prince Edward Island, Canada's tiniest province. Surrounded by singing ocean and covered with potato fields, it offers some of the area's most beautiful beaches.

PRECEDING PAGES: the Acadian coast. **LEFT:** burnished colors in the fall make a spectacular sight. **ABOVE:** houses in Saint John; an iceberg in Trinity Bay; boats docked at Port Dufferin.

NEW BRUNSWICK

New Brunswick serves as a perfect beginning to experiencing the east coast lifestyle. Settled by French-Acadians and Anglo-Loyalists, it is a province rich in traditions

ere in New Brunswick the pace is slow and the friendly people take the time to talk. Magnificent wild forests cover 85 percent of the land, supporting a substantial pulp and paper industry. Under these lie lead, copper, and zinc, providing a healthy mining industry. And then there is the mining of the sea: fishing.

The Acadians and Loyalists

The first people to settle in this region after the Mi'kmaq and Maliseet First Nations were the French in 1604. They arrived with Samuel de Champlain and called the land they worked Acadie; it covered the Atlantic provinces and Maine. The Acadians were constantly fighting battles with the British during the Anglo-French wars of the 17th century. French rule ended in 1713 and mainland Nova Scotia was controlled by the British. In 1755 the British Governor, Charles Lawrence, delivered an ultimatum to the Acadians – take an oath of allegiance to the British Crown, or face deportation. The Acadians did not want to take the oath for fear of being forced to fight fellow Frenchmen on behalf of Britain. The infamous Deportation Order forced 14,600 Acadians into exile. Many settled in Louisiana where the Cajuns survive to this day. When peace was declared between England and France in 1763, most of the Acadians returned to Nova Scotia, only to find their land had been occupied by new English col-

onists. Once again they moved on and settled in what is now New Brunswick. Today almost 33 percent of the province's population is French-speaking, and the province is Canada's only officially bilingual province.

For the descendants from the British Isles, the deportation was a windfall that started a trend. Many New Englanders moved, and during the American Revolution even more crossed the border. They were known as the Loyalists. With them they brought the maritime traditions of the seafaring colonies.

Main attractions
KINGS LANDING HISTORICAL
  SETTLEMENT
HISTORIC GARRISON DISTRICT,
  FREDERICTON
FUNDY ISLANDS
FUNDY NATIONAL PARK
HOPEWELL ROCKS
VILLAGE HISTORIQUE ACADIAN

PRECEDING PAGES: Grand Falls Gorge. **LEFT:** fresh lobster. **BELOW:** living history at Kings Landing.

Summertime in New Brunswick.

BELOW: the covered bridge at Hartland.

St John River Valley

The St John River is New Brunswick's lifeblood. It was the route traveled by Maliseet and Mi'kmaq, Acadians and Loyalists, Scots, and Danes. In the northwestern region of the province it creates a border with Maine and from there the waterway can be traced along its winding course to Saint John.

New Brunswick's westernmost outcrop, a thumb-like parcel of land bordered by Québec, Maine, and the St John River, is popularly known as the Republic of Madawaska. The region's inhabitants created this mythical realm in the 1800s because they were fed up with being pawns in border negotiations between Canada and the United States. With their own leader (the mayor of Edmundston) and their own flag, the Madawaskans (mostly francophones) are both proud and exuberant. At no time is their spirit more in evidence than during the festival called *La Foire Brayonne* (the French in this region are known as Brayons, after a tool used in processing flax). The midsummer event features both folk dancing and lumberjack competi-

tions. **Edmundston** ⓯, an important pulp and paper center and the capital of Madawaska, is situated where the St John and Madawaska rivers converge. Of particular interest to visitors is the Church of Our Lady of Sorrows, containing woodcarvings (The Stations of the Cross) by New Brunswick artist Claude Roussel.

To the south, the beautiful and productive St John River Valley has always been a major thoroughfare. The northern segment of the valley, from Saint-Léonard to Woodstock, is known as the "potato belt." This tuber is a major regional crop, celebrated each year at the Potato Festival in **Grand Falls** ⓰, during which flower-strewn boats are sometimes launched over the town's waterfalls. The gorge into which the water plunges is one of the largest cataracts east of Niagara Falls. Eighty km (50 miles) downstream is the small agricultural town of **Hartland** ⓱, known for its majestic covered bridge, which spans the St John River. This is not just any covered bridge, but the world's longest with seven spans, traversing 391 meters (1,282ft).

Covered Bridges

The covered bridge at Hartland is one of 63 still standing in New Brunswick. Built like old barns from hand-hewn timbers, they capture the essence of bygone times. They were first erected in the late 19th century, to assist those traveling from A to B, with rivers to cross. New Brunswick had an ample supply of rivers, lumber and skilled labor eager to connect the ever-expanding settlements. By protecting the bridge from the elements, the wood did not rot as quickly, which could extend the bridge's lifetime to 50–60 years longer than the more typical 10 years of a conventional structure. Many of them had colorful names such as The Bridge to Nowhere (built to service a community that was ultimately not built) or the Plumwessweep Bridge, a Maliseet word for salmon river.

Just south is Woodstock, whose residents pride themselves on their tradition of hospitality. A landmark here is the restored Old Courthouse, which over the years has served not only as the seat of justice, but as a social hall, a coach stop, and a political meeting house. It's only fitting that such a busy little town should be the birthplace of Canada's first dial telephone system in 1900.

For a look at Loyalist life in the valley throughout the 1800s, visit **Kings Landing Historical Settlement** ⓲ (early June–mid-Oct daily 10am–5pm; charge), 37km (23 miles) west of Fredericton. This reconstructed village, built on the banks of the St John River, depicts daily life among the Loyalists of that era. In 1783 Loyalists exploring the valley came upon the area and, realizing its natural advantages, settled here the same year. After enduring the hardship of a very severe first winter, they proceeded to build a town whose spirit exists to this day – **Fredericton** ⓳, "Atlantic Canada's Riverfront Capital." It is an appellation that befits this provincial capital.

Fredericton is the cultural center of the province, thanks in large part to the generosity and high profile of the publisher and statesman Lord Beaverbrook, who never forgot his boyhood home. The **Beaverbrook Art Gallery**, Queen Street (June–Dec Mon–Sat 9am–5.30pm, Thur until 9pm, Sun noon–5.30pm, Jan–May Tue–Sun; charge), houses a marvelous collection from the 15th century on, including the work of Dalí, Constable, Gainsborough, Botticelli, Henry Moore, and even Winston Churchill.

The Legislative Building (Mon–Fri; free) displays portraits by Joshua Reynolds as well as a rare copy of the *Domesday Book*. The city's most elegant structure is Christ Church Cathedral. Completed in 1853, it is considered one of North America's best examples of decorated Gothic architecture.

The Historic Garrison District beside the river, is the hub for museums, art galleries, outdoor concerts, and heritage walking tours. It incorporates the **York-Sunbury Historical Society Museum** (Apr–June Tue–Sat 1–4pm, July–Labor Day Mon–Sat 10am–5pm,

Mactaquac, near Kings Landing, is the site of a provincial park. People flock to this area for what is reputed to be the best bass fishing in North America.

BELOW LEFT: the water-powered saw mill at King's Landing.
BELOW: fountains in Fredericton.

Sun noon–5pm, Labor Day–Nov Tue–Sat 1–4pm, Dec–Mar by appointment; charge), which chronicles Fredericton's military and domestic past. Reenactments of the Changing of the Guard (July–Aug Tue–Sat 11am and 7pm; free) take place in Officers Square. Modern military life can be found by following the St John River southeast from Fredericton to Oromocto, home of Canada's largest military training base and a military museum.

First city

Weathered **Saint John** ⑳, Canada's oldest city, sits along the Bay of Fundy at the mouth of the Saint John River. Samuel de Champlain landed here in 1604 and gave the location its name, but its true birth came in 1783 with the arrival of 3,000 Loyalists from New England.

"The Loyalist City," as it is known, celebrates its heritage each July during Loyalist Days. The festivities include a three-day jazz and blues festival, the annual Buskers on the Boardwalk Festival, and various summer theater presentations.

Determined, energetic, and ambitious, the Loyalist citizenry catapulted their new home into the forefront of wooden shipbuilding. The thriving port city declined following a disastrous fire in 1877 along with the eventual obsolescence of wooden ocean-going vessels. Recent waterfront development and urban renewal have provided Saint John with a much-needed transfusion. It claims the first police force in North America, and the first newspaper and bank in Canada.

To catch up with the city's past there are four walking tours: Prince William's Walk, a Victorian Stroll, the West Side Walk and Drive, and the Loyalist Trail. One attraction the tours are sure to include is **Barbours General Store** (mid-June–mid-Sept daily 10am–6pm), a restored and fully stocked 19th-century store in which thousands of artifacts, including 300 "cure-all or kill-alls," bring the past to life.

Saint John's Loyalist roots are nowhere more evident than at King Square (opposite the Loyalist Burial Ground), landscaped in the form of the Union flag; and at **Loyalist House**

BELOW: jazz at Saint John.

(mid-May–end June Mon–Fri, July–mid-Sept daily, rest of year by appointment; charge), a Georgian mansion completed in 1817 after taking seven years to build. Occupied for about a century and a half by Loyalist David Daniel Merritt and his descendants, it is the oldest structurally unaltered edifice in the city; indeed one of the few buildings to survive the Great Fire of 1877. With most of its original furnishings still intact, Loyalist House is a tribute to the fine craftsmanship of 19th-century Saint John.

Saint John's City Market is another survivor of the Great Fire. This institution has provided unflagging service since 1876, making it Canada's oldest market. Then, as now, the market clerk rings a bell to close commercial proceedings. The building, filled with New Brunswick produce, is a pleasure to the eye, with its ship's-hull roof, its big game trophies, and its ornate iron gate.

The gem of Saint John's revitalized downtown waterfront district was officially christened Market Square in 1983. Its success has brought business, tourism, employment, and pride back to the city. An early 19th-century brick facade serves as an invitation to a warm and lively center for shopping and dining. There is a boardwalk by the sea, a grand Food Hall and a regional library with a fine collection of early Canadian printed work.

In Market Square, the country's oldest museum, the New Brunswick Museum (mid-May–Oct Mon–Fri 9am–5pm, Thur until 9pm, Sat 10am–5pm, Sun noon–5pm, Nov–mid-May Tue–Sun; charge), has treasures from around the world, and particularly artifacts pertaining to the history of New Brunswick. Its Hall of Great Whales is one of the most arresting displays.

For a panoramic view of the city and its waterfront, visit Fort Howe and the Carleton Martello Tower.

The Fundy coast

West of Saint John, the idiosyncratic Fundy coast is characterized by picture-perfect fishing villages. This is where United Empire Loyalists settled en masse after the American Revolution.

Carved out of the Bay of Fundy, between Maine and New Brunswick,

BELOW LEFT: wood carvings in the Loyalist Plaza, Saint John. **BELOW:** the City Market.

At Reversing Falls Rapids, the twice-daily high tides of the Bay of Fundy meet the St John River and spectacularly force the river to flow back upstream.

BELOW: puffins can be seen on the Fundy Trail.

is Passamaquoddy Bay. At its eastern edge sits **Blacks Harbor**, famed for possessing the Commonwealth's largest sardine factory.

Rounding the bay takes you through **St George**, where visitors can meander about one of the oldest Protestant graveyards in Canada, while nearby Oak Bay is the site of a beachfront park and campground.

Probably the best-known community on the bay is **St Andrews**, a fishing village, resort, and marine biological research center, studded with 18th- and 19th-century mansions. Founded by Loyalists following the American Revolution, some families floated their homes here (one piece at a time) when the border with Maine was determined in 1842 – hence the New England atmosphere. St Andrews is home of the Algonquin Hotel, one of Canada's oldest resort hotels; but its most distinctive landmark is **Greenock Church**. This pristine structure, encircled by a white picket fence, is embellished with a carved oak tree design, a clock, and a weathervane.

The multi-award winning **Kings-brae Garden** (mid-May–mid-Sept daily 9am–6pm; charge) was created from the grounds of several of St Andrew's grand old estates, offering a delightful mix of old and new gardening styles. The village also houses the Huntsman Marine Science Centre (mid-May–end-Sept daily 10am–5pm; charge), which gives visitors a chance to see just what swims around the Bay of Fundy.

St Stephen, New Brunswick, stands face to face with **Calais**, Maine. These border towns have traditionally been the best of friends – even during the War of 1812 when St Stephen loaned Calais gunpowder for its Fourth of July celebration. Today, the towns hold joint festivities each summer. The world's first chocolate bar is thought to have been invented here at the Ganong candy factory in 1910.

Roosevelt's paradise

A paradise for birdwatchers, whale-watchers, fishermen, and other outdoor types exists on the **Fundy Islands** where Passamaquoddy Bay widens into the Bay of Fundy. The beauty and natural riches of the islands have attracted

Fundy Trail

Linking Fundy National Park and Hopewell Rocks, the 11km (7-mile) Fundy Trail offers access – by car, bike or on foot – to one of the last remaining wilderness coastlines between Florida and Labrador. Carved out of the Fundy escarpment, the trail hugs the top of 250-meter (820ft) cliffs, high above the Bay of Fundy's famously high tides, and connects to paths and stairways leading to pristine beaches and tumbling waterfalls. As these waters are the breeding habitat for Right Whales, this is one of the best places for viewing marine and wildlife. A suspension footbridge above the Big Salmon River Interpretive Center crosses to the start of the rugged Fundy Footpath – a separate entity to the Fundy Trail – that winds some 41km (24 miles) through thick forests to the boundaries of Fundy National Park.

nature lovers, from James J. Audubon to Franklin Delano Roosevelt.

Grand Manan Island is the largest and farthest from the coast. It is a particular favorite of ornithologists, with about 230 species of birds, including the puffin, which has become somewhat of a symbol here. For the artist there are lighthouses and seascapes to paint or photograph. Campobello, the "beloved island" of F.D. Roosevelt, is accessible by bridge (from Lubec, Maine). It brings you to the **Roosevelt-Campobello International Park** (daily sunrise–sunset; free), a natural preserve in the southern portion of the island. Visitors can see round Roosevelt's 34-room "cottage," (end May–mid-Oct daily 10am–6pm; free), built in the Dutch Colonial style, from where he viewed so many sunrises.

Located smack on the 45th parallel (and proud of it), **Deer Island ㉑** is a mere 12km (7½ miles) long. It compensates for its size by having the world's largest lobster pond and, offshore, the world's second largest whirlpool, "Old Sow," named because of the auditory experience it provides.

The southeast

The southeast region of New Brunswick, from Saint John to Moncton, reveals the cultural texture of the province; towns and villages gradually reflect a transition from areas settled by Loyalists to those settled by Acadians.

Beyond the seacoast village of St Martins is **Fundy National Park ㉒**, 80km (50 miles) east of Saint John, a showcase for the spectacularly dramatic Fundy tides and coastal terrain. It once reverberated with the clamor of a thriving lumber industry which, along with intense trapping in the area, nearly destroyed its natural gifts. By 1930 the population of Alma, on the eastern edge of the park, once a roaring lumber town, was reduced to two struggling families.

Thanks to Parks Canada, the region is now being returned to a wilderness state, with protection of its forests and reintroduction of its wildlife and fish stocks, particularly salmon.

Hopewell Rocks, 40km (25 miles) east of Alma, is perhaps better known than the national park, and it is also better known as home of the "Flower-

Fundy National Park, Alma, covers an area of rugged shoreline, forests, and gorges. Trails provide views of the Bay of Fundy and the chance to see rare birds. The towering cliffs at Cape Enrage offer the best view of the area.

LEFT: Greenock Church, St Andrews.
BELOW: Hopewell Rocks.

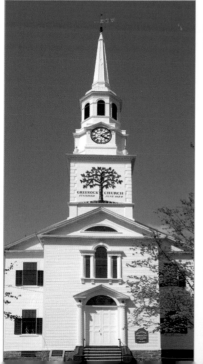

pot Rocks," which is what these peculiar formations look like at low tide, when you can explore the tidal pools surrounding them.

Beyond the Fundy coast is the city of **Moncton** ㉓, an old railroad town, called the "hub of the Maritimes." It was first settled by Middle Europeans, but following the era of deportation and the influx of Acadians into what is now New Brunswick, it became known as the unofficial capital of Acadia. The Université de Moncton is the only French university in New Brunswick. Moncton is also a good place to observe the phenomenon of the Fundy tides.

Sackville ㉔ is a tiny town that resembles an English village. It is the home of Sackville Harness Limited, which has the distinction of being the only place on the continent where horse collars are still made by hand. Sackville is also a university town. The first degree given to a woman in the British Empire was handed out by the town's Mount Allison University in 1875.

Nearby Fort Beauséjour is where the French and English last battled in this region. Today, there is little echo of its past, but a rather magnificent panoramic view of the surrounding area.

The Acadian coast

The coastal region of New Brunswick, north of Moncton, is known as the "Acadian coast." Washed by the warm tides of the Northumberland Strait, it is primarily to this region that the Acadians returned following the deportation. In Bayfield, at the foot of Confederation Bridge, the **Cape Jourimain Nature Centre** (mid-May–mid-Oct daily; charge) on Jourimain Island offers lovely coastal views, a historic lighthouse, an interpretation center, walking trails, and excellent birdwatching opportunities. Further up the coast, they say that Shediac has the warmest saltwater north of Virginia. It also bills itself as the lobster capital of the world.

Tiny Acadian fishing villages are strung along the coast. **Bouctouche** is particularly well known for its oysters, and for the Irving Eco-Center; La dune de Bouctouche, which introduces visitors to the ecosystem of one of the last

BELOW: Grande Anse lighthouse, near Baie des Chaleurs. **RIGHT:** fishing in the mist.

great sand dunes on North America's northeastern coast. The **Kouchibouguac National Park**  ❷❺, 100km (62 miles) north of Moncton, has preserved miles of deserted but fine sand beaches. It is a pleasant drive out to Point Escuminac, a place that has never forgotten its distinction as the site of the province's worst fishing disaster. A powerful monument to the men who lost their lives here in 1959, carved by New Brunswick artist Claude Roussel, stands with its back to the sea, as a constant reminder of this tragedy.

Farther north along the coast is the city of **Miramichi** ❷❻, a recent amalgamation of Chatham and Newcastle, early lumber towns that have preserved some British culture.

This area is famous for its ballads and folklore, as well as for its illustrious native sons. Chatham's once-busy shipyards have now been replaced by port facilities for exporting local wood products. Newcastle was the boyhood home of Lord Beaverbrook, who was exceedingly generous in his bequests to this town.

Acadian flags, a French tricolor with a yellow star in the upper part of the blue stripe, become increasingly visible as you continue northward. Shippagan is a typical fishing village, home of the exceptionally fine **New Brunswick Aquarium and Marine Center** (early May–end Sept daily; charge) devoted to the world of fishing in the Gulf of St Lawrence. A ferry will transport you to the delightfully deserted beaches of Miscou Island.

Caraquet ❷❼, 20km (12 miles) west of Shippagan, is the most prosperous town on the Acadian coast and a cultural center for the region. Le Festival Acadien each August draws celebrants from up and down the coast and includes the traditional blessing of the fleet. The town also has one of the largest commercial fishing fleets in New Brunswick and the only provincial fisheries school. There are boat builders and fish markets on the wharf. Caraquet's **Village Historique**

Acadien (June–mid-Sept daily; charge) has re-created an Acadian settlement reflecting the century from 1780 to 1880, a time of re-establishment here following the deportation. It is nestled near the marshland *levées* constructed by early Acadian settlers.

Off the coast are the waters of Baie des Chaleurs, literally "Bay of Warmth." Named by Cartier in 1534, the bay is notorious for a phantom ship, which has been sighted along the coast from Bathurst to Campbellton. Some people believe it to be the ghost of a French ship lost in battle, while others suggest there must be a more scientific explanation.

Dalhousie and **Campbellton** ❷❽ at the western end of the Chaleur Bay, were settled by Scots, Irish, and Acadians, and a fine-tuned ear is needed to place the accents. Campbellton rests at the foot of Sugarloaf Mountain; it is a center for salmon fishing and winter sports, and a gateway to Québec.

Beyond, to the south and east, lie the Atlantic provinces: Nova Scotia, Newfoundland and Labrador, and Prince Edward Island. ❏

BELOW: Hotel Paulin, Caraquet, is a fine example of Acadian architecture.

NOVA SCOTIA

This Maritime province, where French, Loyalist, and Scottish cultures predominate, has a rich seafaring past. Its rugged coast and sheltered inlets were home to pirates and shipbuilders alike

The name of Nova Scotia brings to mind a vision of craggy highlands, echoing with the sound of bagpipes. But before Highlanders fled to "New Scotland," there were Mi'kmaq, French, British, and Loyalists from the American colonies. All have left a stamp on this province. Today 77 percent of Nova Scotians are of British descent and 10 percent of French (Acadian) extraction. Nova Scotia also has the largest black population in Canada.

Nova Scotians are as close to the sea as they are to the past – inextricably bound to it by their nature, by economics, and by geography. Part of the province, Cape Breton, is an island; and the mainland is attached to Canada by the Isthmus of Chignecto.

Appropriately, the shape of the province resembles a lobster, with no point more than 56km (35 miles) from the sea. People are drawn to Nova Scotia for its overwhelming friendliness, exemplified by the traditional Gaelic greeting *Cead mile failte* – 100,000 welcomes.

Out of the past

The original inhabitants of Nova Scotia, the Mi'kmaq, still walk this land and fish these waters, though their numbers are greatly reduced.

It is thought possible that Norsemen visited here around AD 1000, and some evidence of this has been substantiated. Centuries later, John Cabot, exploring under the English flag, touched upon northern Cape Breton

Island. And French and Portuguese fishermen caught and cured fish here in the 16th century.

The French called this land Acadie. It encompassed what is now Nova Scotia, New Brunswick, Prince Edward Island, and Maine. They settled along the Bay of Fundy and on the marshy land surrounding the Annapolis River, developing what is still the most fertile land in Nova Scotia.

A sense of Maritime pride and tradition still runs strong in Nova Scotia, but great prosperity largely abandoned

Main attractions
HISTORIC PROPERTIES, HALIFAX
MARITIME MUSEUM OF THE ATLANTIC, HALIFAX
PIER 21
PEGGY'S COVE
LUNENBURG
PORT ROYAL
GRAND-PRÉ NATIONAL HISTORIC SITE
CABOT TRAIL
CAPE BRETON MINERS' MUSEUM
FORTRESS OF LOUISBOURG

LEFT: buoys in Nova Scotia.
BELOW: the Old Town Clock, Halifax.

Skilled sea raiders, the Mi'kmaq were the province's first masters of wooden boats. Their canoes were adapted for use by the early explorers and fur traders.

the province with the advent of the 20th century. Over the years, central Canada has often looked upon the area as a liability because of the financial aid it receives from the federal government.

Long before the St Lawrence became the foremost river of commerce, with the creation of the St Lawrence Seaway in 1959, the area's importance as a transportation channel had been greatly diminished. Steam-powered, steel-hulled vessels rendered the wooden sailing ships obsolete, and killed off an all-important industry and economic base. Coal mining later supplanted shipbuilding economically, only to falter after World War II.

But the province also has other natural endowments to fall back on: forestry is a significant provider of jobs; there are abundant freshwater and saltwater fishing grounds; and the rich productive land of the Annapolis Valley, once so highly prized by the Acadians. And then there is tourism, which is a long-standing tradition here and a major contributor to the economy of the region.

Twin cities

The first and second largest Nova Scotian cities respectively, **Halifax**, the provincial capital, and **Dartmouth** ❶ sit on opposite sides of one of the world's great harbors, connected by two suspension bridges. Magnificent **Halifax Harbor** is one of the world's largest natural harbors, as well as being free of ice year round. The Mi'kmaq called it *chebucto*, meaning "big harbor." It has long been a bustling international port and naval base.

As the commercial and educational center of Atlantic Canada, Halifax is unquestionably the more dominant and favored of the twins, yet Dartmouth is not without its charms. Though known for its industry, they call it the "City of Lakes" for its 25 sparkling bodies of water.

This allows Dartmouthians to enjoy freshwater fishing and canoeing all through the summer without leaving the city, and lake-top skating parties in the winter. Dartmouth was founded in 1750 (a year after Halifax), when British troops from across the harbor came on woodcutting expeditions. It was to

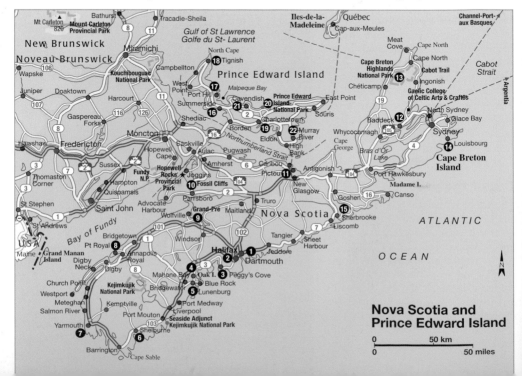

Nova Scotia and Prince Edward Island

develop largely in response to Halifax's needs, and as early as 1752 it began operating a ferry between the two settlements. The boats continue to ply the harbor, in what is the oldest saltwater ferry service in North America.

Quakers from Nantucket Island settled here between 1785 and 1792 following the American Revolution. They made Dartmouth the headquarters of a whaling company whose operations were centered at what is now the **Dartmouth Shipyards**. They also left behind a number of homes. These simple structures, with their front doors placed off-center, were built to endure; a stroll down Ochterloney Street shows several, including the historic **Quaker House**, probably the oldest house in Dartmouth (June–Aug Tue–Sun 10am–1pm and 2–5pm; contribution).

On Dartmouth's Main Street, the **Black Cultural Centre for Nova Scotia** (June–Aug Tue–Fri 9am–5pm, Sat 10am–3pm, Sept–May Tue–Fri 9am–5pm; charge) offers a powerful yet little-known perspective on the region's blacks, who first arrived in Nova Scotia in the late 1700s.

The twin waterfronts of Halifax and Dartmouth have undergone a significant transformation, as have waterfronts across Canada. Halifax's restoration and redevelopment have been the most dramatic.

In the mid-1960s the people of **Halifax ❷** took it upon themselves to transform their city's gray image. The waterfront area now known as **Historic Properties** was saved from demolition and is now Canada's oldest-surviving group of waterfront warehouses. Tourists can shop, dine, and explore in this cobblestoned area, which externally appears as it did in the 19th century when privateers used it to cache their goods. Nearby, off Lower Water Street, are the more recently restored **Brewery Market** and the Maritime Museum of the Atlantic. Alexander Keith, the onetime mayor of Nova Scotia, built his brewery in 1820 and its courtyards and arched tunnels are filled once again with spirit. Amid the variety of enterprises is the **Halifax Farmers' Market** (Sat 7am–1pm), which operates year round.

The **Maritime Museum of the Atlantic** (May–Oct daily, Nov–Apr

In Dartmouth, the Evergreen Historic House on Newcastle Street was the home of the folklorist and author, Dr Helen Creighton, author of "Bluenose Ghosts."

BELOW: al fresco dining in Halifax.

TIP

Halifax is known as the "city of trees." It has eight parks, plus galleries, museums, shopping centers, and restored waterfronts. Explore on foot, or by boat or rickshaw.

Tue–Sun; charge) not only features a magnificent view of the harbor, but a huge hydrographic ship, the *CSS Acadia*. Now moored behind the museum, the *Acadia* once plied the frigid waters of the Arctic and North Atlantic while charting northern coastlines.

Heading south along the waterfront you come to **Pier 21** (May–Nov daily, Dec–Mar Tue–Sat, Apr Mon–Sat; charge), the portal for the 1 million immigrants who entered Canada from 1928 to 1971. Pier 21 documents their experiences through interactive displays.

Just to the west of the waterfront is Halifax's business district. Amid the office towers and hotels is the **World Trade and Convention Centre**. Easily spotted by its huge weathervane depicting the schooner *Bluenose*, it plays host to shows, conventions, and live concerts. North on Prince Street beside the Old Montreal Trust Building is where 14 newspapers used to be published. The eight pre-Confederation buildings, where the likes of Charles Dickens and Oscar Wilde are said to have stayed, have been incorpo-

rated into an attractive complex called **Founders Square**.

Halifax was founded in 1749 not only because of its great harbor, but as a fortress to counter the French installation at Louisbourg. On a hill overlooking downtown Halifax is the **Citadel** (Nov–early May grounds only, early May–Oct daily; charge). The current star-shaped 19th-century structure is the fourth to occupy this pedestal. It no longer serves as a military installation, but as a National Historic Park, housing the expansive collection of the **Army Museum** (early May–Oct daily; admission included with Citadel), while affording a spectacular view of Downtown and the waterfront. This is the best vantage point from which to see the **Town Clock**. With its four clockfaces and belfry to ring the hours, Haligonians (residents of Halifax) need not wear wristwatches. Its construction was ordered by Prince Edward, Duke of Kent, a stickler for punctuality.

Two churches not to be missed are **St Mary's Basilica**, topped by the world's tallest polished granite spire, and **St Paul's Anglican Church** (1750) on

BELOW: all smiles at the Royal Nova Scotia International Tattoo. **RIGHT:** St Mary's Basilica.

Grand Parade, the oldest Protestant church in Canada. The Grand Parade also serves as an open-air venue for Maritime artists. Nearby on Hollis Street is **Province House** (July–Aug daily, Sept–June Mon–Fri; free), Canada's oldest-standing legislative building. Charles Dickens referred to it as "a gem of Georgian architecture."

At the foot of the citadel are the **Public Gardens**. Established in 1867, these are the oldest Victorian formal gardens in North America. Near the gardens on Summer Street is the **Museum of Natural History** (June–mid-Oct daily, mid-Oct–May Tue–Sun; charge), headquarters of a province-wide system incorporating 24 sites. The collection here is devoted to the natural and social history of Nova Scotia, particularly Mi'kmaq artifacts, some dating back 11,000 years.

Going back to the waterfront, at the southern tip of the peninsula that Halifax occupies, is **Point Pleasant Park**. The federal government rents this piece of greenery to the city for one shilling a year under the terms of a 999-year lease. **The Prince of Wales' Martello Tower** (July–Labor Day daily; free) was raised here in 1796 and still stands, the first in a series of these circular stone sentinels to be constructed along the coastal regions of North America and the British Isles. The park, a favorite with joggers, hikers, swimmers, picnickers, and ship-watchers, is said to be the only place on the continent where Scottish heather grows wild (from seeds shaken from the mattresses of British soldiers). At the other end of Halifax stands **Fort Needham** park, in memory of the **Halifax Explosion** in 1917 *(see page 228)*.

The South Shore

The rugged and idiosyncratic Atlantic coastline, southwest from Halifax, is known as the **South Shore** and promoted by the tourist bureau as the "Lighthouse Route." It is an accurate appellation, yet despite these sentinels of the night, this beautiful, mysterious, and punishing coastline is no stranger to shipwrecks. Nor are its people strangers to the wrath and bounty of the sea.

The circuitous South Shore, with all its bays, coves, inlets, and islands, was

BELOW: a lonely beacon at Peggy's Cove.

A wooden house on stilts at Peggy's Cove.

a favorite of pirates and privateers. At **Indian Harbor** and **Peggy's Cove ❸**, 45km (28 miles) from Halifax, fishing villages nestling among and atop the granite outcroppings are treasures of a different sort. The latter has become a semi-official showcase for the province and is said to be the most photographed fishing village in the world. Yet it has not been robbed of its simplicity and authenticity. There is some quandary over the name Peggy's Cove. Some believe it to be a diminutive of St Margaret's Bay, while others believe it was named after the sole survivor of a shipwreck, who subsequently married one of the local men.

The late William E. de Garthe (1907–83), a marine artist who resided here, apparently sided with the latter theory. Taking a decade to complete, he carved the images of 32 local fishermen, their wives, and their children, in a 30-meter (100ft) face of granite rock located behind his house, which became known as the "Fisherman's Monument." De Garthe also included the image of the young woman of the shipwreck legend. The **Lighthouse**,

BELOW: Halifax harbor at night.

combined with post office, is a landmark that draws many to Peggy's Cove. Sadly, the tragedy of a Swissair jetliner that plunged into the ocean off Peggy's Cove in the summer of 1998, with 229 people on board, is a memory that the locals – who played a heroic role in the rescue and salvage operations – will be living with for years to come.

St Margaret's Bay, named by Samuel de Champlain in 1631, is known for its fine sand beaches and summer cottages. It is followed by the notorious **Mahone Bay ❹**, with its 365 islands. This was once the realm of pirates, and its name was probably derived from the French *mahonne*, a low-lying craft used by these sea raiders. Other names echo that era, such as **Sacrifice Island** and **Murderer's Point**, but **Oak Island** is the most intriguing. Long the site of treasure hunts, it is said that Captain Kidd buried another part of his treasure here. The island was once densely covered by large oaks and, according to local legend, the mystery of the buried treasure will not be solved until all the oaks have died and seven

The Halifax Explosion

During World War 1, Halifax harbor was constantly crowded with wartime shipping. The city's population was swollen with troops, as well as those who came to benefit from copious work. On December 6 1917, a catastrophic explosion shook Halifax, causing enormous loss of life. A French munitions ship, the *Mont Blanc*, loaded with a cargo of ammunition and explosives, including TNT, collided with a Norwegian relief ship, the *Imo*, in Halifax harbor. As the ships burst into flames, people came rushing down to the waterfront to watch. Suddenly the *Mont Blanc* exploded. Two thousand men, women, and children lost their lives in an instant, many thousands more were injured, and a large area of northern Halifax was destroyed. Windows were shattered as far away as Truro, 100km (60 miles) from the city. It is said to have been the largest manmade blast prior to the bombing of Hiroshima in 1945.

Halifax picked up the pieces and symbolically placed a sculpture containing remnants of metal from the *Mont Blanc* – some discovered several kilometers away – in front of the Halifax North Memorial Library as a monument to those who lost their lives.

The event features beside the Titanic in an exhibition of Nova Scotia's seafaring past at the Maritime Museum of the Atlantic, Water and Prince Streets (May–Oct daily, Nov–Apr Tue–Sun; charge).

lives have been lost. (Six persons have so far lost their lives and only a few trees remain standing.)

Home of the *Bluenose*

"A Snug Harbor since 1753." That's what they say about **Lunenburg** ❺, one of Canada's most important fishing ports. Nowhere in Canada are the traditions of the sea more palpable – carried on by sailors, fishermen, and shipbuilders. The renowned schooner *Bluenose*, the "Queen of the North Atlantic," winner of four international schooner races, was built here in 1921.

A symbol of pride for the people of Lunenburg, she was ultimately lost off the coast of Haiti in 1946. The shipyards of this city later made the ship used in the film *Mutiny on the Bounty*; it was sailed to Tahiti by a Nova Scotian crew. This inspired the creation of *Bluenose II*, a replica of the original, built by the same shipwrights, which is open to visitors when in port.

On the waterfront, the **Fisheries Museum of the Atlantic** (May–Oct daily; charge) will give you a vivid sense of the history of sailing and fishing along Nova Scotia's coasts. Old Town Lunenburg has dozens of beautifully maintained historic buildings dating back to 1760. Many have been converted into attractive inns, restaurants, shops, and galleries. Summer is lively with the Lunenburg Craft Festival in July; and in August, the Lunenburg Folk Harbour Festival, the Nova Scotia Folk Art Festival, and the Nova Scotia Fisheries Exhibition.

Across the harbor, walk over the cliffs to The Ovens. These caves were the scene of a mini goldrush in 1861, when New Englanders poured into the area to pan nuggets from the shale on the beach. A museum contains some of their tools and a few bits of gold.

Caribbean trading port

Quiet now, **Port Medway** was a major port in the late 19th century, engaged in a brisk Caribbean trade: fish and

Lunenburg Academy, an outstanding landmark, is now a public school.

BELOW:
International Dory Races at Lunenburg.

Windsurfing at Lawrencetown Beach, Halifax.

lumber in return for rum and molasses. Things are still bustling in **Liverpool**, 142km (88 miles) west of Halifax, which is built on the banks of the Mersey River like its English counterpart. Privateering figures prominently in the city's history, and this heritage is celebrated each July during "Privateer Days." Of particular interest here is the **Perkins House Museum** (June–mid-Oct daily; charge) built in 1767. Perkins kept a diary that chronicled life in colonial Liverpool, and his home is a showcase for the same.

West along the coast is **Port Mouton**, a pleasant fishing village named by Sieur de Monts and his party in 1604 when one of their sheep was lost overboard here. Tiny **Port Joli** is a bird sanctuary, a favorite spot of Canadian geese in autumn and winter.

Shelburne ➏ lies 67km (41 miles) west of Liverpool. A treasure trove of 18th-century history, it's referred to as "The Loyalist Town," for it was settled by 16,000 United Empire Loyalists from America between 1783 and 1785. It became an instant boom town – bigger than not only Halifax, but also

Montréal. The population dropped abruptly after 1787 with the termination of government support and by the 1820s fewer than 300 people called this home. Shelburne's **Ross Thomson House** (June–mid-Oct daily; charge), built in 1784, is a Loyalist home and store – thought to be the only surviving 18th-century store in Nova Scotia. It now functions as a provincial museum, fully stocked and decorated to reflect the 1780s.

The only surviving New England-style meeting house in Nova Scotia (*c.*1765) is in nearby **Barrington**, with a 19th-century woolen mill. The town was settled by the French and called *Le Passage* until it was destroyed by New Englanders, and its people deported to Boston. In 1760, colonists from Cape Cod and Nantucket came here, making it one of the oldest outposts of settlers from New England.

Edging north toward the **Bay of Fundy** brings you to **Yarmouth ➐**. As the terminus of ferry services from the US, this is the start of many a Canadian journey. During the golden age of sail this was one of the world's great ports.

The French Shore

The **French Shore**, home of Nova Scotia's largest Acadian population, is synonymous with the municipality of **Clare**, midway between Yarmouth and Digby, which locals are fond of saying rivals Toronto's Yonge Street as the largest main street in the world, for it consists of 27 villages, more than half of which sit along the main thoroughfare. Many Acadians returned to this area following the deportation to start anew, some on foot through the wilderness. In **Meteghan**, 40km (25 miles) north of Yarmouth, a short path takes hikers in **Smuggler Cove Provincial Park** down to a secluded beach with a natural cave, purported to have been a cache for contraband rum during the days of Prohibition in the United States.

Most Acadian villages are dominated by their church, and in **Church Point** (*Pointe d'Eglise*) this is particularly true. **St Mary's Church**, built early in the 20th century, is the tallest and largest wooden church in North America. Its 56-meter (185ft) spire, swayed by bay breezes, is stabilized by 36 tonnes (40 tons) of ballast. This landmark sits on the campus of the **Université Sainte-Anne**, the only French university in the province. As a center for Acadian culture, the institution hosts the **Festival Acadien de Clare** for the first two weeks of August.

East of St Mary's Bay, at the southern tip of the Annapolis Basin and overlooking Digby Gut, is **Digby**. The town has a long maritime history and was named for the commander of a ship that carried Loyalists here from New England in 1783 (among them, the great-grandfather of inventor Thomas Edison). This is home of the renowned **Digby Scallop Fleet** (the world's largest), which is celebrated each August during the Digby Scallop Days Festival.

The Annapolis Valley

Champlain wrote of the Annapolis Basin: "We entered one of the most beautiful ports which I had seen on these coasts." His compatriot Marc Lescarbot considered it "a thing so marvelous to see I wonder how so fair a place did remain desert." Although orchards and other farmlands have replaced the

At Port Joli in 1750 an American crew captured by natives were given the option of standing barefoot in a fire or jumping into the sea; they jumped and drowned.

BELOW: apple blossom in the Annapolis Valley.

TIP

For unsurpassed views of St Mary's Bay on the northwest coast, a hiking trail heads out along the cliff-tops between Cape St Mary and Bear Cove.

primeval forest along the Annapolis Basin and River, this completely transformed region is still beautiful to behold.

Built in the 1780s, **Old St Edward's Loyalist Church** in **Clementsport** is situated high on a hill within an ancient cemetery. It was one of the province's earliest museums, showing off not only its own architectural integrity, but a fine collection of Loyalist artifacts. Its elevated setting also provides one of the best vantage points from which to appreciate the Annapolis Basin.

On the other side of the basin is **Port Royal ❽**, 10km (6 miles) from Annapolis Royal, with its reconstructed **Habitation** (mid-May–mid-Oct daily; charge), the settlement built by Sieur de Monts and Samuel de Champlain in 1605. It is a place that witnessed many firsts: the first permanent North American settlement north of Florida; the first Roman Catholic Mass celebrated in Canada; the first Canadian social club (Champlain introduced the Order of Good Cheer as an antidote to the prospect of another dismal winter); and the first Canadian dramatic production

(*Le Théâtre de Neptune* orchestrated by lawyer and writer Marc Lescarbot in 1606). Burned by the English in 1613, its reconstruction in 1939, after years of research, was one of the first great successes of Canada's historic preservation movement.

The Annapolis Valley, sheltered by the North and South Mountains and extensively diked by Acadian settlers, is an agriculturally and scenically gifted area, known particularly for its apples. In spring the scent of apple blossoms lingers in the air, and the **Apple Blossom Festival** is celebrated.

Though settled primarily by Planters and Loyalists following the deportation, the valley pays homage to Acadians – nowhere more poignantly than in **Grand Pré ❾**, the village immortalized by Longfellow in *Evangeline*. Grand Pré was the most important Acadian settlement in Nova Scotia before the deportation. Longfellow's *Evangeline – A Tale of Acadie* (1847) describes the separation of a young couple during the deportation and the subsequent search by the woman for her lover.

At **Grand-Pré National Historic**

BELOW: Joggins Fossil Cliffs on the Bay of Fundy.

The Joggins Fossil Cliffs

During the "Coal Age" 300 million years ago, Joggins was covered by lush forests that ultimately created the coal deposits that gave this period of history its name.

Today, embedded within some 15km (9 miles) of cliff face along the Bay of Fundy, is the world's most complete fossil record of life at that time, including the earliest reptiles entombed within once hollow trees. The first true reptile, *Hylonomus lyelli* – the ancestor of all dinosaurs that would rule the earth 100 millions years later – was discovered here by Canadian-born scientist Sir William Dawson. With the Bay of Fundy's extreme tides rising and falling 15 meters (47ft) twice daily, new fossils are constantly exposed, and a new crop of fossils is revealed every three of four years.

Site (mid-May–mid-Oct daily; charge), a simple stone church contains many artifacts relating to Acadian culture. Outside the church stands a statue of Longfellow's tragic heroine.

Southeast of Grand Pré, where the Avon and St Croix rivers converge, is the town of **Windsor**. Anyone fond of expressions such as "raining cats and dogs," "quick as a wink," and "an ounce of prevention is worth a pound of cure," should visit Windsor's **Haliburton House** (*c.*1839). Now a museum, it was once the home of judge, humorist, and author Thomas Chandler Haliburton who created *Sam Slick*, the fictional Yankee peddler who spouted his witticisms on his travels through Nova Scotia (June–mid-Oct daily; charge).

Chignecto Isthmus

The northern aspect of mainland Nova Scotia is washed by the Bay of Fundy, with the highest tides in the world; and, on the other side of the Chignecto Isthmus, by the Northumberland Strait. Whereas some bizarre natural phenomena occur only once in a lifetime, the Fundy tides put on their show twice daily, with a repertoire that varies according to the location. **Burntcoat Head**, on the **Minas Basin**, is the point at which Canada's highest tides have been recorded – a difference of 17 meters (54ft) between low and high.

Perhaps this atmosphere of extremity inspired William D. Lawrence to construct Canada's largest wooden-hulled ship in nearby **Maitland**, 20km (12 miles) west of Truro. His namesake, a fully rigged sailing vessel, was launched in 1874 and was a technical and financial success.

Lawrence's stately home is now a museum containing artifacts and memorabilia relating to ships and shipbuilding, including a model of the record-breaking *William D. Lawrence*.

Truro was originally settled by Acadians (they called it Cobequid), and later by people from Northern Ireland and New Hampshire. It is a good place to observe the tidal bore, or "wall of water," in which the incoming Fundy tide rushes into the Salmon River at the rate of 0.3 meters (1ft) a minute. East across the isthmus is a region washed by the Northumberland Strait, strung with

TIP

Showing the evolution of gardens from the Acadian era, the 7-hectare (17-acre) Annapolis Royal Historic Gardens are magnificent. Daily May–Oct; charge.

BELOW: Longfellow's heroine, Evangeline, at Grand Pré.

BELOW: Cape Breton at sunset. **BELOW RIGHT:** clusters of wild lupins are a common sight.

beaches and often echoing with the sound of bagpipes. It is said that more clans are represented in Nova Scotia than in Scotland and a good number of them can be found right here. To the west of Truro, the 300-million-year-old fossils at Joggins **Fossil Cliffs** ❿ have been designated a World Heritage Site by Unesco. (Visitor Center and guided tours late Apr–Oct daily; charge).

Pictou ⓫, 76km (47 miles) east of Truro, is the "Birthplace of New Scotland," where the first Scottish Highlanders landed here, aboard the *Hector* in 1773. This fine harbor saw many subsequent waves of Scottish immigration. Today it is a center for shipbuilding and fishing. Each July brings the **Pictou Lobster Carnival**.

Like Pictou, **Antigonish**, 74km (46 miles) southeast, took its name from the Mi'kmaq and later became characterized by the culture of Highland Scots. The annual **Highland Games** draw competitors from far and wide every July, in what is the oldest such spectacle in North America. With Scottish music, dance, and sports, they also feature the ancient caber toss.

Cape Breton Island

Alexander Graham Bell once wrote: "I have traveled around the globe. I have seen the Canadian and American Rockies, the Andes and the Alps, and the highlands of Scotland; but for simple beauty, Cape Breton outrivals them all." Bell's words have not gone unheeded; **Cape Breton Island** is the most popular tourist destination in Nova Scotia. Ironically, the island is also the most economically depressed region in a province less affluent than much of the rest of Canada, due in some part to the decline in coal mining.

Cape Breton has always been a place apart – occupied by the French longer than the rest of Nova Scotia (they called it *Ile Royale*) and a separate province until 1820. The **Canso Causeway**, an umbilical cord to the "Mainland," was not constructed until 1955.

The Cabot Trail, which is named after the explorer John Cabot, is a 298km (185-mile) loop which rollercoasts around the northern part of Cape Breton. This road is popularly thought of as one of the most spectacular drives to be found in North America, wind-

ing through lush river valleys, past (and often clinging to bluffs high above) a rugged and dramatically beautiful coastline, through dense forest lands, and over mountains.

It was once a series of death-defying footpaths and, later, equally treacherous trails. By 1891, a narrow wagon trail forged its way circuitously over Cape Smoky, featuring a sheer rock cliff off one side and a 366-meter (1,200ft) plunge to the sea off the other. Automobiles began taking their chances here in 1908; one of these early motorists' tricks was to tie a spruce tree behind the car to prevent it running away downhill. The trail still has its hair-raising stretches and most people drive it in a clockwise direction, clinging to the inside of the road.

Alexander Graham Bell, himself born in Scotland, built a summer house in **Baddeck ⑫**, the official beginning and terminus of the Cabot Trail, and spent his last 35 years here. As a teacher of the deaf, he directed Helen Keller's education and undertook research that led to the invention of the telephone. **The Alexander Graham Bell National Historic Park** (May–Oct daily, Nov–Apr by appointment, tel: 902-295-2069; charge), through photographs and exhibits, is a monument to Bell – the teacher, inventor, and humanitarian. The Cabot Trail, traveling clockwise beyond Baddeck, traces the **Margaree River**, renowned for its beauty and an abundance of trout and salmon.

The stretch of Gulf of St Lawrence coastline from the Margaree to the Cape Breton Highlands National Park is dotted with Acadian fishing villages, inhabited by descendants of the mainland French who came here at the time of the deportation.

Just as the Acadian language has retained its 17th-century flavor, the culture of the people here has remained relatively undiluted. Acadian flags fly in the sea breeze, and a church steeple signifies the next community. Such is the case with **Chéticamp**, the biggest town in these parts. **Cape Breton Highlands National Park ⑬** begins a few miles north of Chéticamp, extending from the Gulf to the Atlantic and bordered on three sides by the Cabot Trail. This magnificent wilderness

Pugwash, 50km (30 miles) east of Amherst, is a Scottish center. It hosts the annual Gathering of the Clans every July, and the town's street signs are in Gaelic.

BELOW: a moose, loose in Cape Breton Park.

preserve is a paradise for hikers, swimmers, campers, golfers, and other lovers of the great outdoors.

The trail reaches its northernmost point at **Cape North**, and from here another road heads farther north to the fishing village of **Bay St Lawrence**. En route, at the base of **Sugarloaf Mountain**, is the site where Cabot is believed to have landed in 1497. This event is re-enacted each June 24.

At the eastern exit from the park are the **Ingonish**, a group of communities that have long been a great attraction for visitors. Just beyond Ingonish Harbor is Cape Smoky, its head in the clouds, rising 366 meters (1,200ft) above the sea. Tourists can ski its slopes in winter while looking out upon the Atlantic. In summer, a ride on the chairlift to the top of Cape Smoky provides a breathtaking view (weather permitting) of this rugged, misty isle.

The stretch from Cape Smoky to Baddeck is known as the **Gaelic Coast**. Skirting the coast of St Ann's Bay will take travelers to **Gaelic College of Celtic Arts and Crafts**. As the only institution of its type in North America, it serves as a vibrant memorial to the Highland Scottish who settled here, and has been nurtured by their descendants. In early August the clans are well represented as they gather for the annual **Gaelic Mod**, a seven-day festival of Celtic culture. While on campus, visit the **Great Hall of the Clans** (mid-June–Sept daily; charge). It tells the story of the Great Migration from the highlands, while interactive displays focus on the music, dance, song, stories, and crafts of Nova Scotia Gaels.

Coal and steel country

Jumping off the Cabot Trail into what is called **Industrial Cape Breton** becomes an introduction to a world of smokestacks and steel mills. Coal was once king in this area. Today the Nova Scotia government still uses coal for the majority of its electrically generated stations.

Cape Breton Miners' Museum in **Glace Bay** has developed into one of Nova Scotia's finest museums (June–Oct daily, Nov–May Mon–Fri, with underground tours by appointment only; charge). Artifacts and photo-

graphs chronicle the history of coal mining in this town and commemorate the men who risked their lives working in the depths; but the highlight of any visit here is the mine tour. Salty, veteran miners bring visitors down into the **Ocean Deeps Colliery** (carved from under the ocean floor), and tell stories of pain, death, pride, hard work, low wages, and camaraderie.

Coal has been mined in the vicinity of Glace Bay since the 18th century when soldiers from nearby Louisbourg were assigned this duty.

The last French stronghold

Passing by the sentries into **Fortress of Louisbourg** ⓮ (May–Oct daily; charge) is like stepping back in time to the summer of 1744. Fortress Louisbourg was the last great military, commercial, and governmental stronghold of the French in the region that was once Acadia, but by 1758 it was in ruins. The site remained untouched until two centuries later when reconstruction began, in what has been termed the most ambitious project of its kind ever undertaken in Canada.

From the costumed staff (performing roles of fishermen, merchants, and soldiers) trained in 18th-century deportment, to the authenticity of the structures and their furnishings, Louisbourg never fails to impress. You will need a full day to do it justice.

A center for scuba diving is **Louisbourg Harbor**, and the waters off the southern coast of Cape Breton are known as fertile ground for "wreck-hunting" – the legacy of centuries of maritime activity.

Off the south shore, just before reaching mainland Nova Scotia, is **Isle Madame**, reached by a small bridge across the Lennox Passage. A scenic loop meanders through Acadian fishing villages. Of particular note is **LeNoir Forge Museum** (May–Sept daily 10am–6pm; contribution) in Arichat, a restored stone blacksmith shop with working forge, in what is the oldest building on the island (1793). At Little Anse, a trail leads to **Cap Rouge** at land's end. From here you can look out upon **Green Island** with its lighthouse, one of the last remaining manned beacons in the province.

The Cape Breton Highlands National Park encompasses an exceptional landscape of mountains and coastline with 25 hiking trails. Enquire locally about whale-watching excursions.

BELOW: drummers beat it out at Fortress Louisburg.

The sawmill at Sherbrooke.

RIGHT:
sea kayaking in
Nova Scotia.
BELOW: another day
in Sherbrooke
Village.

The eastern shore

The eastern shore of Nova Scotia, between Cape Breton and the Twin Cities, is characterized by its unspoiled beauty, an abundance and variety of fishing opportunities, and its traditional personality. Locals maintain that things have changed little over the years.

Closer than all other mainland communities to the great Atlantic fishing banks, **Canso** has developed into a center for fishing and fish processing. Its harbor has witnessed the history of this region, from the early European fishermen and traders to the British fleet that made its rendezvous here before the final assault on Louisbourg.

Along the banks of St Mary's River is the village of **Sherbrooke** ⑮, 80km (50 miles) west of Canso. It was a French fur-trading post in the 17th century, but the first permanent settlers came here in 1800 attracted by the tall timber and the river, then as now, filled with salmon. Sixty-one years later something happened to change the face of this town for all time – they discovered gold. The boom, referred to as "Sherbrooke's Golden Age," lasted only 20 years.

Sherbrooke became quiet again, left alone except for seasonal visits by salmon fishermen, until the 1970s when a restoration project was established. The heart of town is now almost entirely restored to the period from 1860–pre-World War I, and certain streets have been closed to traffic to create **Sherbrooke Village**.

It's inhabited by people in costume going about their daily business, so visitors can walk through 21st-century Sherbrooke and happen upon a town steeped in another era.

In use since the 1870s, **The Blacksmith Shop** produces items used in the restoration and sold in the Emporium, as does **Sherbrooke Village Pottery**. Most fascinating of all is the jail, built in 1862 and used for 100 years. Not a jail really, but an ordinary 19th-century home inhabited by a jailor, his family, and the offenders.

Continuing for 85km (52 miles) west along the coastal road brings visitors to **Tangier**, home of an enterprise known to gourmets and gourmands the world over – J. Willy Krauch and Sons. Krauch, now joined by his sons, has spent the better part of his life smoking Atlantic salmon, mackerel, and eel, using the Danish system of wood-smoking.

A farther 30km (18 miles) west at **Jeddore Oyster Pond** is the **Fisherman's Life Museum** (June–mid-Oct daily; charge). The museum is the modest homestead of Ervin and Ethelda Myers and their 13 daughters, restored to reflect the period after the turn of the 20th century. ❑

WHALE-WATCHING IN COASTAL WATERS

For the Inuit, whaling meant survival; for the Europeans it was big business. Today whales live under the watchful eyes of scientists and tourists

ROUTE DES BALEINES

While Christopher Columbus and Jacques Cartier were still recounting their New World discoveries, Basque whalers were quietly making fortunes on the Canadian coast. Their Red Bay, Labrador, whaling station employed 1,000 men, and refined up to two million liters of valuable oil each season. At the same time, unknown to the Basques, Inuit were catching whales in the Arctic Ocean far to the west, and the Nootka people were hunting off Canada's west coast. Other European and later American whalers joined the Basques, expanding their hunts to the edges of the known world on each of Canada's three coasts. They would pursue the whale in a small boat, thrust their harpoon into the mammal, and let out a line. The frenzied whale would take the boat on what became known as a "Nantucket sleigh ride" until, exhausted, it would fall victim to its hunters. Then its carcass would be towed ashore for stripping.

When the 19th century brought steamships, and harpoon guns to shoot a missile that exploded inside the animal, whale stocks went into decline.

Whaling Gives Way to Whale-Watching

By the onset of World War I, profitable whaling had ceased in the Canadian Arctic, but it continued along the British Columbian and Newfoundland coasts with the introduction of factory ships for processing. The International Whaling Commission began controlling catches in the late 1940s, but stocks off Canada's coasts diminished at a dramatic rate. Commercial whaling was ended by the government in 1972. Today only the Inuit are allowed to take whales, for their own consumption.

ABOVE: Canada's coastal waters provide a habitat for various species of whales: bowhead and white whales are found around Baffin Bay, while orcas (below) and gray whales can be seen off British Columbia.

RIGHT: Inuit were the most skilled at finding a use for almost every part of the whale. They ate the skin, blubber, and flesh, used the bones for weapons and the oil for light and heat.

ABOVE: a reconstructed whale bone roof frame near Resolute, Nunavut.

WHERE TO SPOT A WHALE

NEWFOUNDLAND'S east-coast ports, including those in Trinity and Bonavista bays, date back to the heyday of whaling. Today operators combine whale-watching with sighting bald eagles and other rare bird species. A bonus here is a close-up look at spectacular icebergs as they drift south.

Further to the south, the BAY OF FUNDY has krill-rich waters stirred by enormous tides. These attract families of huge right whales, so called by whalers who found them valuable and easy to catch. The most popular spot for viewing is New Brunswick's Grand Manan Island, where expeditions are run by marine biologists.

At the confluence of Québec's Saguenay and St Lawrence rivers, whales are readily seen from the shore and on guided expeditions. Several species here include a permanent colony of small white beluga whales, the only such group found outside the Arctic.

Churchill, on MANITOBA'S Arctic Coast, also includes belugas among its whale species. In addition to the traditional excursions, visitors here can go scuba diving among the whales.

On BRITISH COLUMBIA'S coast, excursions leave from Vancouver and Victoria and many smaller ports. Gray whales, which migrate each spring down the west coast of Vancouver Island, are best seen between mid-March and early April.

BELOW: whale bones scattered on the beach, near the mouth of the Firth river in the Yukon.

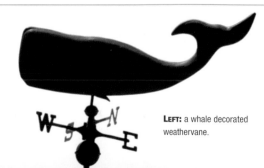

LEFT: a whale decorated weathervane.

PRINCE EDWARD ISLAND

The birthplace of the Canadian Confederation and the setting for L.M. Montgomery's novel Anne of Green Gables, Prince Edward Island is the tiniest province in a land of vast horizons

Prince Edward Island (P.E.I.) rests in the Gulf of St Lawrence, cut off from the mainland by the Northumberland Strait. Less rugged than its fellow Atlantic Provinces, P.E.I.'s quaintness seems untouched by the modern world and it has a gentle, rural atmosphere. Agriculturally, the land is well-groomed and cultivated. Some go so far as to describe the island as two beaches divided by potato fields. The importance of potatoes cannot be overestimated; they are the pre-eminent crop. Tourism is second in economic importance. There are close to 140,000 inhabitants on the island, most of them the descendants of early French, Scottish, English, and Irish settlers.

P.E.I. is an island begging to be explored. Since 1997 it has been joined to the mainland by the Confederation Bridge, an imposing 13km (8-mile) structure between Borden and Cape Jourimain, New Brunswick. There is also a ferry service between Wood Islands and Caribou, Nova Scotia.

Abegweit

According to Mi'kmaq legend, the Great Spirit molded brick-red clay into "the most beautiful place on earth" and gently placed it in the Gulf of St Lawrence. He presented it to his people and they came here in summer to camp and to fish nearly 2,000 years ago. They called it *Abegweit*, "land cradled on the waves." Today the Mi'kmaq

account for less than one percent of the population of the island.

The first European to covet the island was Jacques Cartier, who claimed it for France in 1534. He considered it "the fairest land 'tis possible to see," yet **Ile-St-Jean**, as the French affectionately named it, had no permanent settlement until 1719 at **Port La Joye**. It became the breadbasket for the French stronghold at Louisbourg and the island still serves a similar function for the region as the "Garden of the Gulf."

Main attractions

NORTH CAPE COASTAL DRIVE
GREEN PARK PROVINCIAL PARK
CHARLOTTETOWN FESTIVAL
BLUE HERON DRIVE
P.E.I. NATIONAL PARK
GREEN GABLES HOUSE
POINTS EAST COASTAL DRIVE
ORWELL CORNER HISTORIC VILLAGE
BASIN HEAD FISHERIES MUSEUM

LEFT: Shipwreck Point Lighthouse.
BELOW: catch of the day.

Lobster traps are stacked on the quay-side at Malpeque harbour at the start of the lobster fishing season.

The west: North Cape Coastal Drive

P.E.I. is geographically separated into three parts: traveling from west to east – **Prince**, **Queens**, and **Kings**. The westernmost region is less developed than the other two in terms of tourism, but it is no less attractive.

North Cape Coastal Drive meanders around a deeply indented coastline; past sandstone cliffs and sun-bleached dunes; and through tiny villages, many of them ringing with the sounds of Acadian French. (Almost 5 percent of P.E.I.'s population is French-speaking.)

The route begins and ends in **Summerside ⑯**, the second largest of only two cities in P.E.I. (its capital, Charlottetown, is the largest). Located on **Bedeque Bay**, the town was presumably named for being on the warmer or "sunny-side" of P.E.I. Once a center for shipbuilding, the waterfront is now crowded with vessels loading up with potatoes. One highlight of Summerside's calendar comes in mid-July with eight days of gustatory merriment known as the Lobster Carnival.

BELOW: a farmhouse in Summerside.

On a musical note, the one-of-a-kind College of Piping and Celtic Performing Arts of Canada offers high-energy performances of Celtic music and dance during July and August.

The spires of **St John the Baptist Church**, one of the island's loveliest churches, announce one's arrival in **Miscouche**, 10km (6 miles) west. It was in this town that the National Acadian Convention decided to adopt the red, white and blue Acadian flag in 1884. Today, this banner can be seen throughout French-speaking regions of Atlantic Canada. Miscouche is also home of **Le Musée Acadien** (July–Aug daily 9.30am–5pm, Sept–June Mon–Fri 9.30am–5pm, Sun 1–4pm; charge), whose collection of antique tools, household items, religious artifacts, photographs, and documents aims to preserve the culture of these early settlers.

Oyster center

Five kilometers (3 miles) north of Miscouche is **Malpeque Bay**, where the world-renowned Malpeque oysters were first discovered. The Tyne Valley Oyster Festival celebrates these bivalves annually in August. Malpeque Bay is also known for its fine sand beaches and for having been a great center for shipbuilding in the 19th century, a part of the island heritage commemorated at **Green Park Provincial Park** in **Port Hill ⑰** to the west of the bay. Green Park is the former estate of shipbuilding magnate James Yeo, Jr, which today includes his restored home, Yeo House (c.1865), a shipbuilding museum and a re-created 19th-century shipyard (June–mid-Sept daily, closed rest of year; charge).

Beyond Port Hill is a causeway leading to **Lennox Island**, and the largest community of Mi'kmaq in P.E.I. Lennox Island's Indian Art and Craft of North America specializes in the sale of beaded and silver jewelry, clay pottery, wood carvings, woven baskets, and ceremonial headdresses made by Indians from many different nations.

The **Cape Kildare** area, 45km (28 miles) north of Port Hill, is where Jacques Cartier dropped anchor in 1534, thereby "discovering" the island. Inland 12km (7 miles) to the north is **Tignish** ⓲, a community founded in 1799 by a group of Acadians who were later joined by two Irishmen. Both cultures are still well represented and, typically, the church is the focal point of the community. The **Church of St Simon and St Jude** has a fine pipe organ, which is played at recitals during July and August (times advertised locally).

The northernmost tip of P.E.I., **North Cape**, is a continually eroding point, so much so that the lighthouse and the road that encircles it have been moved inland several times. Its strategic location prompted development of the **Atlantic Wind Test Site**, a national facility for the testing and evaluation of wind generators, where visitors are welcome.

South from North Cape, along the Northumberland shore, tourists are likely to see Irish moss drying by the road or perhaps, following a storm, being gathered and hauled by horse-drawn carriages and pick-up trucks along the beach. The area around Miminegash is particularly known for the harvesting of this commercially viable seaweed. Sightings of a "ghost ship," full-rigged and aflame, are frequently reported between **Camp-bellton** and **Burton** on this shore. Legends abound here, from Mi'kmaq lore to tales of Captain Kidd's buried treasure at **West Point**.

Inland from West Point is **O'Leary**, in the center of one of P.E.I.'s richest and largest potato-producing areas, home of the **Potato Museum** (part of the **O'Leary Museum**) and host to the annual Potato Blossom Festival (July).

Tracing **Egmont Bay**, approaching the Summerside area, is the Région Acadienne – punctuated by the villages **Abram-Village**, **Cap-Egmont** and **Mont-Carmel**. There are some excellent opportunities to experience Acadian culture and *joie de vivre* during the summer season, including *l'exposition agricole et le festival acadien* in early September. The latter both include agricultural competitions,

When the British Deportation Order of 1755 forced Acadians into exile, about 30 families remained in hiding on P.E.I. – the ancestors of many local Acadians.

BELOW:
harvesting Irish moss on Cavendish beach.

step dancing, fiddling, lobster suppers, the Blessing of the Fleet, and more. Abram-Village is also a center for crafts (particularly quilts and rugs), which are demonstrated and sold at the local Handcraft Co-operative.

The seaside community of Cap-Egmont has a rather unusual attraction – **The Bottle House**. A recycling project (undertaken in retirement) of the first magnitude; Edouard T. Arsenault built his glass houses and chapel from bottles (the first called for 12,000 of them). After a "long winter cleaning bottles," the former fisherman and carpenter began work in 1980, lovingly laboring over the project until his death four years later. Arsenault's typically Acadian spirit, a mixture of creative energy and humor, shines through the walls.

The island's capital city

Not the least of **Charlottetown**'s ⑲ considerable charms is that it is still predominantly wooden (structurally, but decidedly not in demeanor). It is the center of all things for P.E.I. – government, commerce, and culture –

though it seems more like an elegant small town, complete with a town crier and gaslights. Historically, Charlottetown is best known for being the "Cradle of the Confederation." The 1864 meeting, which led to the formation of the Dominion of Canada three years later, was held in **Province House** (June–mid-Oct daily, mid-Oct–end May Mon–Fri; small charge), the province's first public building. Ironically, P.E.I. was at first hesitant to join Canada, and it did not enter the Confederation until 1873. This neoclassical stone structure is now a National Historic Site and the chamber where the Fathers of Confederation met has been restored, though it still houses the legislature.

Next door is the **Confederation Centre of the Arts**. Established to commemorate the centennial of the main event, the center showcases the talents of Canadian artists, year round. Each province contributed 15 cents for each of its citizens to help to finance construction. It includes gallery and theater spaces and is host each summer to the **Charlottetown Festival**.

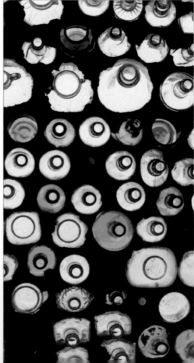

Running from mid-June until mid-September, it is Canada's best-known music and theater festival. One of the loveliest parts of town is **Rochford Square**, its beautiful shade trees the legacy of Arbor Day 1884. Adjacent to the square is **St Peter's Anglican Church** (1869) with a notable attachment, **All Souls' Chapel**, created in 1888 as a memorial to one of the cathedral's first clergymen. It was a labor of love for William Harris, who designed it, and for his brother Robert, who created luminous wall paintings. Harris specified that island materials be used, from the rich, red sandstone exterior to the wood and stone used for interior carvings – a testament to the spirit of both brothers, and to the skill of island craftspeople.

The center: Blue Heron Drive

The central region of Prince Edward Island (P.E.I.) is traced by the route known as **Blue Heron Drive**, which comes full circle at Charlottetown. It is distinguished by fine beaches – white sand along the Gulf shore and red sand along the Northumberland shore – colorful fishing villages, *Anne of Green Gables*-related attractions (an Island sub-industry), and community lobster suppers. Every summer night throughout P.E.I.'s small towns and districts, amazing feasts are organized and prepared by local women. Held either in churches or big halls, as many as 400 to 500 people are fed. For a reasonable price travelers can experience some of the best home-made food and lobster dishes they will ever taste.

Most of **Queens County's gulf coast** belongs to **P.E.I. National Park** ⑳, 24km (15 miles) northwest of Charlottetown, with some of the finest beaches in eastern Canada (year round; charge). The Victorian mansion of Dalvay-by-the-Sea, now a hotel, near the eastern entrance to the park, was built in 1896 by the oil magnate Alexander Macdonald.

Rustico Island, part of the national park, is the summer home of a protected colony of great blue herons, the possessors of 2-meter (6ft) wing spans, while **North Rustico** is a traditional fishing village. You can purchase

TIP

Stretching 45km (25 miles) along the island's northern coastline, P.E.I. National Park offers 14 scenic hiking trails, ranging from 0.7km to 10km (½ to 6 miles) in length, all designated as either easy or moderate.

BELOW: red sand dunes at Cavendish.

A resident mariner of Prince Edward Island.

BELOW: freshly ploughed field.
RIGHT: animal rights activists on the ice floes near the Gulf of St Lawrence.

seafood practically off the boats here, pass the time talking with locals, or go out on a tuna charter. In late July, the Rendez-vous Rustico festival offers three days of traditional and contemporary Acadian music.

Green Gables House

Still within P.E.I. National Park, 10km (6 miles) west of the Rusticos, is **Cavendish ㉑**, the center of *Anne of Green Gables* country. Visitors come from far and wide to see the settings described by Lucy Maud Montgomery in her book about an orphan girl, published in 1908, and other works of fiction, as well as to explore landmarks in the author's life. The lovely **Green Gables House** itself, on Highway 6, has undergone restoration following a fire in 1997. The **L.M. Montgomery Birthplace** (mid-May–mid-Oct daily) can be found in **New London**, 15km (9 miles) southwest. A brochure sets the stage by stating: "As you walk through the rooms of the Birthplace, you will thrill to the realization, that it was in this house that Lucy Maud first saw the light of day."

Victoria (its residents like to call it Victoria-by-the-Sea), 30km (18 miles) southwest of Charlottetown facing the Northumberland Strait, is an English-flavored town, which is both an active fishing port and a center for antiques. From early July to mid-September, theater performances take place at the restored **Victoria Playhouse**. The Provincial Park, which is edged by red sand, is a good place to have a picnic.

The east: Points East Coastal Drive

The easternmost piece of P.E.I., most of it corresponding to Kings County, is encircled by the **Points East Coastal Drive**. This is the longest of the three routes. In the **Orwell Corner Historic Village** (late May–June Mon–Fri 9am–5pm, July–early Sept daily 9.30am–5.30pm, early Sept–Oct Sun–Thur 9am–5pm; charge), 30km (19 miles) east of Charlottetown, the atmosphere of a late 19th-century rural crossroads community has been re-created. Most of the early settlers here were Scottish and in summer the sounds of the Highlands can be enjoyed at a weekly

ceilidh (pronounced kay-lee). Beside the village, the Sir Andrew Macphail Homestead (mid-June–mid-Oct Wed–Sun; donation) reflects the life and times of a prominent Islander at the turn of the 20th century.

In 1803 a Scotsman by the name of Lord Selkirk financed the immigration of three shiploads of Highlanders to P.E.I., and the "Selkirk Pioneers" settled in **Eldon**, 13km (8 miles) south of Orwell. Over time, the settlement became the **Lord Selkirk Provincial Park**. In late July/early August, it is the site of the annual P.E.I. Highland Games & Festival, hosted by the Caledonian Club of Prince Edward Island.

Sculptors and seals

At **Wood Islands**, a boarding point for the Nova Scotia ferry, the museum at the **Wood Islands Lighthouse** (early June–early Sept daily; charge) offers a spectacular 360-degree view and is an interpretive museum with themed displays including the way of life for lighthouse keepers, rum-running during Prohibition, and phantom ships.

Eighteen kilometers (11 miles) beyond Wood Islands is **Murray River** ㉒. This lovely town was once an activity center for shipbuilding, but today wood is worked on a much smaller scale. **Murray Bay** is the home of a large natural seal colony. These sleek creatures can be best observed from the **Seal Cove Campground** in **Murray Harbor North**, cavorting in the sun on their offshore sandbar.

Approaching the easternmost tip of P.E.I. is the **Bay Fortune Area**, washed by a string of legends. There is talk of the early 19th-century murder by a tenant of landlord Edward Abell at **Abell's Cape**, of buried treasures along the sandstone cliffs, and of actor Charles Flockton, who in the late 19th century bought the cape and spent each summer here with his comedy company. American playwright Elmer Harris was inspired to feature nearby **Souris** as the setting for his book *Johnny Belinda* (based on the local

legend of a deaf and mute girl). Today Souris is an embarkation point for passengers heading for the nearby Iles de la Madeleine.

Basin Head, 12km (7 miles) east of Souris, is home of the **Fisheries Museum** (mid-June–Sept daily; charge). The museum is located beside a particularly beautiful stretch of dunes, where the sand "sings" as you walk. Rounding **East Point** (called *Kespe-menagek*, "the end of the Island," by the Mi'kmaq), brings one to **North Lake**, the "Tuna Fishing Capital of the World." Tourists flock here in pursuit of the giant bluefin tuna – regarded as the ultimate in sportfishing.

Heading back to Charlottetown one realizes that in 2,000 years little has changed. The Mi'kmaq were right in calling P.E.I. *Abegweit*. The island is indeed a land cradled by waves. The Gulf Coast provides endless water activities for travelers, from fishing and boating to swimming and digging a clam dinner out of the brick-red sand beaches. Inland, the flat, quaint terrain provides a perfect route for adventurous trekkers and cyclists. ❑

Souris was apparently named after three plagues of mice between 1720 and 1738 literally ate early French settlers out of house and home.

BELOW: a memorial to WWI soldiers in Charlottetown.

NEWFOUNDLAND AND LABRADOR

While settlements are sparse and many areas are only accessible by boat or light plane, the province's craggy coastline, mountains, lakes, and rich history appeal to visitors worldwide

Newfoundland's mountains are not as high as the Rockies and are much less accessible. There are no theme parks or world-class art galleries. Tourist facilities, while adequate, are rarely luxurious. Yet Newfoundland's remoteness has cultivated the most individualistic part of North America. Imagine a land mass three times the area of New Brunswick, Nova Scotia, and Prince Edward Island combined, then remember that the rugged terrain is home to less than four people per square mile. A third of the total population live around St John's on the east coast, while the rest live in smaller inland communities, or in coastal towns and villages, known as "outports." English is the most common language spoken and 96 percent of the people were born here. Jokes about Newfies can be heard across the country, but Newfoundlanders have their own brand of humor, calling Newfoundland simply "The Rock."

The first explorers

To understand Newfoundland, one must understand some of its history. The **Grand Banks** are the fishing grounds southeast of Newfoundland that have been worked by European fishermen since the 15th century. Giovanni Caboto from Italy (also known as John Cabot) sighted this coast in 1497 and claimed the land for the English king, Henry VII, who had financed his voyage. Henry, who had hoped the

expedition would find gold, gave him £10 and had to be content with fish. Cabot reported that the cod were so numerous that "they would fill a basket lowered over the side." The Spanish, Portuguese, and French who also fished in the area, salted their catch to preserve it for the trip home. But the English, who lacked a source of cheap salt, had to dry their cod, and to do this the fleets needed to go ashore.

Britain originally did not want a colony and actively discouraged settlement. In fact it was illegal for any-

Main attractions
MARBLE MOUNTAIN
GROS MORNE NATIONAL PARK
TERRA NOVA NATIONAL PARK
L'ANSE-AUX-MEADOWS
  NATIONAL HISTORIC SITE
CAPE SPEAR NATIONAL
  HISTORIC PARK
SIGNAL HILL NATIONAL
  HISTORIC SITE
THE ROOMS
BATTLE HARBOUR

LEFT:
Newfoundland
Caribou Memorial.
BELOW: Trinity Bay.

First-time visitors are invited to taste screech, the local brew, at a "screeching-in" ceremony held in town halls. A scroll is issued as proof of passage.

one to winter in Newfoundland. The "Masterless Men" were the first European settlers after the Vikings to come to Canada. They were sailors who jumped ship, preferring life in one of Newfoundland's many natural harbors to life aboard. Their independence and spirit of survival are still very much a part of Newfoundlanders' character today.

The Viking settlements ("Vinland") of the early 11th century did not survive, perhaps because of climate change or a vitamin deficiency causing a weakening of the bones. Stories of Vinland have indicated that the first child born in the Americas of European origin was Snorri Torfinnsson. When Christopher Columbus visited Iceland in the 1480s, before his "discovery" of the New World in 1492, he probably would have heard the stories of the Vikings' Newfoundland voyages. The site of Vinland is at L'Anse-aux-Meadows at the northern tip of the Great Northern Peninsula.

Oral tradition

Since St John's is closer to Ireland than to Toronto, its language is not surpris-

ing. It is a unique blend of dialects from England's West Country and southwest Ireland, brought over by the original settlers and left largely unchanged by the passing centuries. It is the closest dialect in the modern world to Shakespearean English and the only place where many words and expressions that were common in the 17th century still survive.

A tradition preserved in Newfoundland is storytelling. The oral form of handing down stories from generation to generation is still alive. Times are changing but not all Newfoundlanders will change with them. Guglielmo Marconi was dubbed an "irrepressible dandy" when he came to Newfoundland to receive the first transatlantic wireless message in 1901. The "old days" are described as the times when "most people could neither read nor write, but my, how they could talk!" Modern times differ only in that people can now read and write as well.

In fact, Newfoundland is Canada's most recent province. Confederation (union) with Canada was, and sometimes still is, one of the liveliest topics for discussion in Newfoundland. It did not take place until 1949 and was a hard-won victory for the federalists.

Modern life

Until well into the 20th century the majority of Newfoundlanders lived along the coasts making a difficult living from the sea. Cod, which was the foundation of Newfoundland's economy, has virtually disappeared from the waters off Canada's east coast. As a result, cod fishing is now highly restricted – as Fisheries Department scientists insist it is the only way the cod stocks will return to healthy levels. Nevertheless, it is still available at supermarkets and fish-and-chip stores.

Sealing, however, remains an annual ritual, and almost all Newfoundland fishermen continue to be proud of their humane killing methods and adherence to quotas. In 2009, the federal government set seal quotas at

BELOW: a print of Newfoundland fishermen from *Le Petit Journal*, 1892.

280,000, a far cry from back in the 19th century, when the annual quota was around half a million.

In the last 50 years, the importance of forestry in Newfoundland has declined. However, a huge nickel deposit discovered in Labrador in the 1990s is now being mined, and three offshore oil developments – Hibernia, Terra Nova, and White Rose – discovered off the coast, rival those in the North Sea. As well, hydroelectricity produced at Labrador's Churchill Falls is now a major contributor to the province's economic health. Tourism is a relatively recent phenomenon in Newfoundland. The prevailing attitude is still that visitors should "take us as they find us." However, there are plenty of B&Bs throughout the province – and also two lighthouses – where tourists can sleep and enjoy home-cooking in Newfoundland homes.

Screech, found in many households and taverns, is the dark rum drink for which Newfoundland is famous, and has been popular since salt fish was first shipped to the West Indies and exchanged for rum. It is rather like the Newfoundland character – more interesting than it is refined. While Screech is still popular, so are iceberg vodka and various berry-based wines, which are also made here. For the seafood lover, Newfoundland homes are the ideal venue. Fish is served as often and in as much variety as one could wish: halibut, crab, Atlantic salmon, cod, lobster, and much more.

Exploring the province

The independent traveler will need a car. There are bus services to virtually all locations but the farther off the beaten path, the more infrequent the service. There are still many locations that are best reached or only accessible by boat. The main road in Newfoundland is the **Trans-Canada Highway**, which runs through Newfoundland on an indirect path between **Channel-Port-aux-Basques ❶** in the west (terminus for the ferry from North Sydney, Nova Scotia), to St John's in the east. It's 905km (562 miles) long and is the lifeline of the province. Right off the Trans-Canada Highway, 200km (137 miles) northeast of Channel-Port-aux-

Gros Morne means "great bluff." Here you can wade along sandy beaches or set off on a four-day hike into the wilderness across the glacier-carved landscape.

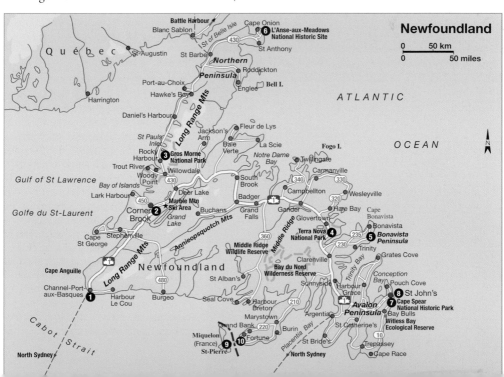

TIP

Whales can often be seen in the waters off Cape Spear in spring and summer – ask a park ranger where to look. This is also a good place to see icebergs.

Basques, **Corner Brook ②** is the scenic business center for Newfoundland's west coast.

The national parks are a source of pride for Newfoundlanders and a source of delight for the visitor. On the west coast is mountainous **Gros Morne National Park ③**. Its fjords are best seen by boat from **Western Brook Pond**: here you have the chance of seeing seals, caribou, and moose. **Terra Nova National Park ④** on the east, is a piece of typical Newfoundland fishing coast. Here there is boating, fishing, and moonlight cruises on beautiful **Clode Sound**. Inland in the park there is good camping and hiking, and the water in the lakes is warm enough to swim.

East of the park lies the **Bonavista Peninsula ⑤**. This region attracted worldwide attention in 1997 when, in a re-enactment of Cabot's voyage 500 years earlier, a replica of his boat, the *Matthew*, sailed from Bristol, England, and landed amid great ceremony at Cape Bonavista.

Visitors can get a feel for life on this isolated cape at the **Cape Bonavista**

Lighthouse, restored to the 1870s period (mid-May–mid-Oct daily), and the **Ryan Premises National Historic Site** (mid-May–mid-Oct daily; charge).

At the most northerly tip of Newfoundland, **L'Anse-aux-Meadows National Historic Site ⑥** (June–Sept daily; charge) is also worth a visit. Dwellings from an 11th-century Viking settlement have been reconstructed and Norse artifacts found on site are displayed at the Visitor Center.

Cape Spear National Historic Park ⑦ is the most easterly point of both Newfoundland and the continent. Take a boat tour to see and listen to a school of whales. Even the shortest boat ride off the coast will remind you of the power of the sea.

Sport fishing opportunities are as many and as varied as the Newfoundland coast and all the rivers and lakes inland. Fishing lakes are known as "ponds." Salmon, arctic char, and northern pike are the favored catches.

St John's

The capital of Newfoundland and Labrador, **St John's ⑧**, sited on the northeast

BELOW: over 7,000 moose have made their home in Gros Morne National Park.

Corner Brook

The second largest city in Newfoundland, Corner Brook lies 40km (25 miles) inland on the salmon-rich Humber River – which winds through the lovely Humber Valley to the Bay of Islands on Newfoundland's west coast. First charted by Captain James Cook in 1767, Corner Brook is surrounded by water and the rugged Long Range Mountains. An outdoor enthusiast's idea of paradise, there is all manner of recreation virtually year-round. Marble Mountain is Atlantic Canada's largest ski resort, where skiers and snowboarders can take advantage of the vertical drop of 518 meters (1,700ft), 37 runs, five lifts and an average annual snowfall of close to 5 meters (16ft). Zipline tours soar across the scenic Marble Mountain Gorge, right above Steady Brook Falls, in every season.

of the Avalon peninsula, is one of the oldest cities in North America. Its streets were originally cowpaths wandering up from the harbor. **Government House** has a moat of sorts – in fact, a cost-effective method in the 19th century when the mansion was built, to allow light through the basement windows.

Signal Hill National Historic Site (mid-May–mid-Oct daily, mid-Oct–mid-May Mon–Fri; charge) must be seen: more events of historical importance have taken place on this site than in most other provinces. It was here that the first transatlantic wireless message was received by Marconi. Signal Hill was the site in 1762 of the last battle of the Seven Years' War. Visitors can still see fortifications ranging from the Napoleonic Wars to World War II. Despite its historic significance, Signal Hill got its name originally from the practice of putting up flags to let people know of ships in the harbor. Views from here of Downtown, the harbor, and down the coast to Cape Spear are extraordinarily good.

The best way to get a sense of St John's is to walk down Water Street,

the oldest street on the continent. When Newfoundland joined Canada in 1949 most of the province lived in poverty, but Newfoundland had more millionaires (they were known as "Water Street Men") per capita than anywhere in North America.

The Rooms on Bonaventure Avenue (June–mid-Oct daily, mid-Oct–May Tue–Sun; charge) house the provincial museum, the provincial art gallery, and the provincial archives. Perched high above downtown St John's, the striking building is based on the buildings and shoreline structures found in outport Newfoundland and Labrador.

The museum recounts the human history of the island, and how nature interwove with the lives of the peoples who lived here from 9,000 years ago to 1730. Five fires devastated St John's in the 19th century. One of the few buildings to escape was the clapboard

Tourists climb aboard for a nautical trip round the bay.

BELOW: Signal Hill, St John's.
RIGHT: getting to grips with Viking boat building at L'Anse-aux-Meadows National Historic Site.

BELOW: oil well drilling pipes in storage. **RIGHT:** championship concentration for Newfoundland curling skip, Brad Gushue.

Commissariat House, King's Bridge Road, now restored to reflect the 1830s. **Quidi Vidi Village**, 3km (2 miles) north of Signal Hill, has the typical "pocket" harbor of an outport.

Outpost of France

Not only is Newfoundland closer to Ireland than Toronto but it is also closer to France than to Nova Scotia. At least it's closer to a part of France. Just off the end of the Burin Peninsula on Newfoundland's southern coast are the islands of **St Pierre and Miquelon** ❾. They are the remnants of France's once-great empire in North America. The islands can be reached by a passenger-only ferry from **Fortune** ❿ or by air, and a passport is usually required. It truly is a taste of Europe, with narrow streets and European cars. With a population of 6,000, St Pierre and Miquelon send a *député* to the French Parliament and a member to the Senate.

Journey to Labrador

For the truly adventurous, Labrador beckons, just 17km (10 miles) across

the Strait of Belle Isle from northern Newfoundland. Subject to the weather, ferries make the short crossing from **St Barbe** to **Blanc Sablon** on the Labrador-Québec border. From here, Route 510 connects a string of coastal settlements including the fishing village of **L'Anse-au-Clair**, founded by the French in the early 18th century; **L'Anse-Amour**, where aboriginals are known to have lived 9,000 years ago; **Red Bay**, site of a Basque whaling station (*c.*1550); and **Cartwright**, 400km (248 miles) from the Québec-Labrador border. Only the first 80km (50 miles) of Route 510 are paved. On an island about an hour's ferry ride from Mary's Harbour, **Battle Harbour** (www.battle harbour.com) is possibly the province's best-preserved traditional outport, and was declared a national historic district in the mid-1990s.

Changing times

Newfoundland's first day as a Canadian province was April 1 1949. In the last 40 years, the changes in Newfoundland and Labrador have been profound, and show no signs of slowing. Between 1954 and 1972 more than 27,000 people from more than 220 isolated outport communities were resettled in larger centers. However, some 700 outports are still home to many tough and tenacious Newfoundlanders. The impact of the multi-million dollar oil projects off the east coast of St John's has been huge. In ten years it has transformed from a quiet capital to a booming oil port. Countless new restaurants offer cuisine from around the world, and trendy boutiques have replaced the traditional Water Street merchants. Nightlife ranges from dinner theaters and pubs to CD launch parties and live music.

In many ways, Newfoundland and Labrador is the most unusual province, in many other ways it is the most typical. It is a land of beauty and of hardships, and a place where even the short-term visitor may gain memories to last a lifetime. ❏

THE WEST

From Manitoba to the Pacific Coast, western Canada
offers a rich diversity of landscapes and cultures

A fter a century of off-handed treatment from Ontario and
Québec, over the past thirty years, the West has emerged
as a powerful presence in Canada. Rich in minerals, oil,
and natural gas, Manitoba, Saskatchewan, and, even more so,
Alberta, are now economic forces to be reckoned with.

Sometimes referred to as Canada's "Garden of Eden," British
Columbia, Canada's most westerly province, enjoys the most
temperate climate. It encompasses the splendid and irascible
Rocky Mountains, as well as a twisted coastline with fjords as
spectacular as those in Norway.

The West section opens with an exploration of Vancouver, Canada's
third largest city and its window on the Pacific. The following section
on British Columbia begins with a description of the early years after

the arrival of European explorers. Modern B.C. is
encountered first in Victoria, the province's capital
city. After a stroll through its streets, readers are given
a glimpse of its massive wilderness. The province is
rich with parks and hiking trails that will appeal to
all levels of skill.

The next chapters take the reader to Canada's Prairie provinces: Alberta, Saskatchewan, and Manitoba.
These three provinces provide wonderful contrasts
between mountains, wide open prairie, and the more than 200,000 lakes
in this part of the country. Alberta begins the search for the "prairie
existence" and demonstrates its diversity by journey-
ing up into Canada's vast playground: the Rocky
Mountains. Banff's splendid beauty contrasts with
the exciting city-life of Edmonton and Calgary. Saskatchewan is explored through its rich history and
its proud and prolific cultural features. Manitoba,
concluding the section, provides an experience of
the prairie itself: wide open spaces, no longer shaded
by forests, rolling on to a distant horizon. ❏

PRECEDING PAGES: galloping through the Rockies. **LEFT:** Merritt, the country music
capital of Canada. **ABOVE:** Canada Place, Vancouver; taking a break in Riding
Mountain National Park, Manitoba; having fun at the Calgary Stampede.

VANCOUVER

Sited between the Pacific Ocean and the Rocky Mountains, this green and vibrant city combines a diverse heritage with a thriving arts, cultural, entertainments, and sports scene

The mainland city of **Vancouver** is more than the West Coast's shining star. It is invariably selected as one of the top cities in the world for quality of life.

Evidence of prosperity can be seen in the elegance of its luxury hotels Downtown, including two built to coincide with The Expo '86 world's fair, the Canadian Pacific Waterfront Hotel and the Pan-Pacific Hotel Vancouver, the latter adjoining **Canada Place Ⓐ**. Canada Place, built as the Canada pavilion for the fair, is meant to approximate a cruise ship leaving port – comparisons to the Sydney Opera House (it has five large sails for a roof) are apparent. This edifice is also the main cruise ship terminal for the trip to Alaska, so it is frequently an image that rests in the mind of visitors.

If Canada Place is the first sight, **Stanley Park Ⓑ**, is the first stop for the rest of the senses. This 405-hectare (1,000-acre) thumb of forest jutting into the Burrard Inlet is home to Douglas fir, cedar, and hemlock. This evergreen oasis was dedicated in 1889 in the name of a governor general, Lord Stanley, the same Stanley whose name stands for supremacy in professional hockey: the Stanley Cup.

Stanley Park has a 10km (6-mile) perimeter sea wall that offers a panoramic view of the water and the city skyline, and entertains visitors with every type of vessel, from kayak to sailboat to yacht to cargo ship. Cruise ships plying the Pacific West Coast north to Alaska dock regularly in the harbor from May through September. Vancouver is Canada's foremost West Coast port, shipping bulk tonnage such as coal, grain, sulfur, potash, liquid chemicals, and fuel oil. Additionally, it is the general container cargo port for inbound goods to the west. A steady parade of cargo vessels and cruise ships, plus recreational boaters, makes for fascinating viewing.

One of the highlights in the park is the **Vancouver Aquarium Marine Science Center** (daily, including all

Main attractions
CANADA PLACE
STANLEY PARK
MUSEUM OF ANTHROPOLOGY
TELUS WORLD OF SCIENCE
VANCOUVER ART GALLERY
CHINATOWN
GASTOWN
WHISTLER VILLAGE

PRECEDING PAGES: Convention Center. **LEFT:** Downtown from Stanley Park. **BELOW:** Queen Elizabeth Park.

TIP

For some of the best views of the harbor, city, and mountains, take a 15-minute ride on a seabus plying the waters between Downtown and North Vancouver.

holidays; charge). The aquarium holds more than 70,000 creatures, including docile beluga whales and gregarious dolphins, but it is the tanks holding nurse sharks that devour huge pieces of meat in the blink of an eye that draw the biggest crowds. The focus of this aquarium is definitely on research and education, so it's a great spot to learn and be entertained at the same time.

Vancouver's list of museums of history and fine art is extensive. Leading these on the campus of the University of British Columbia is the **Museum of Anthropology ⓒ** (mid-May–mid-Oct daily, Sept–Apr Tue–Sun; charge), which contains an outstanding collection of totem poles, including a full-size replica of a West Coast native village complete with long houses. There are also significant artifacts from the South Pacific, as well as many other parts of the world. Contemporary works by living First Nations artists demonstrate how the art and culture is being kept alive. The small museum shop has an excellent selection of pieces – and their authenticity is certain. Located between the university and Downtown, is the **Van-**couver Museum ⓓ (July–Aug daily, Sept–June Tue–Sun; charge), Canada's largest civic collection, which traces the history of the city, from the first settlement by native peoples through to the arrival of European settlers and the modern history of the city.

Also here on the grounds of the city museum is the **H.R. MacMillan Space Center** (July–Aug daily, Sept–June Tue–Sun; charge), a planetarium, observatory, motion simulator, and theater. In addition to conventional constellation showings, there are also laser-light music shows featuring the likes of Coldplay, Radiohead, and Pink Floyd. Close by is the **Vancouver Maritime Museum** (mid-May–Aug daily, Sept–mid-May Tue–Sun; charge) preserving the RCMP Arctic-exploring schooner, the *St Roch*. This hardy little ship made two passages of the ice-laden Northwest Passage and established Canada's supremacy over the region.

Hugely popular with kids is **Telus World of Science ⓔ** at the waterfront Expo '86 site. The ultimate hands-on experience, the dome, has everything from exploding pickles (charged with

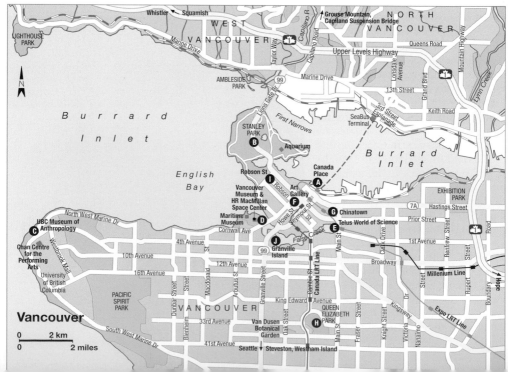

80,000 volts), to the interior of a beaver lodge (daily; charge). There is also an **OMNIMAX Theatre**, with the second-largest screen of its kind in the world.

On the corner of Robson and Howe streets is the **Vancouver Art Gallery ⑤** (daily; charge), which has an impressive collection of the works of both Canadian and international artists. It is home to a superb collection of paintings by Emily Carr, a world-renowned British Columbia-born artist who painted the skies, forests, and native cultures of the area in the first three decades of the 20th century.

The theater season runs from September to June and offers every kind of performance. The **Orpheum** on Smithe Street, a completely refurbished movie theater built in 1927, is home to the Vancouver Symphony Orchestra, while traditional theater and opera can be found at the **Queen Elizabeth Theatre** on Cambie Street. The **Chan Centre for the Performing Arts**, renowned for its acoustics, is surrounded by gardens on the idyllic UBC campus.

Entertaining and comedic plays are performed at the **Arts Club** on Granville Island, and outdoor Shakespearean theater is presented all summer long at **Bard on the Beach**, near the Vancouver museum.

It's true that Vancouver gets a lot of rain – the annual rainfall is 111cm (42 inches) – so it's natural that indoor attractions are also popular. But the rain and mild climate create the best in parks and gardens in Canada.

The **Dr Sun Yat-Sen Classical Chinese Garden** (May–Oct daily, Nov–Apr Tue–Sun; charge) in **Chinatown ⑥** is the first such garden to be built outside China, and includes special river rocks, pavilions, and covered walkways, most of which were imported from China. More conventional gardens include **Van Dusen Botanical Garden** (daily; charge) and **Queen Elizabeth Park ⑪**, the latter boasting a rose garden, quarry-pit garden, conservatory, tennis courts, and miniature golf circuit.

Neighborhood life

Like all great cities, Vancouver offers a variety of fascinating neighborhoods. These are the places where people and buildings are not just anonymous cogs in some swirling commercial mass, but where they take on a character of their own, and live out a culture unique to their block or avenue. Vancouver has several distinctive neighborhoods that give it this kind of life .

The stores along **Robson Street ①**, are a far cry from the schnitzel houses and small European delicatessens that reflected the European immigrants who came to Vancouver after the war. By the late 1970s, the street that was frequently called Robsonstrasse was heading for a transformation. The high-rises of the downtown business core and the apartment blocks of the West End met along Robson Street and entrepreneurs responded with more shopping and better restaurants. The street now offers exceptional dining and great window shopping. From Aritzia to Zara, with three Starbucks occupying three of the corners at Thurlow Street, Robson is the city's busiest shopping street, which

The Orpheum Theatre began as a vaudeville house in 1927, hosting the likes of Charlie Chaplin, the Marx Brothers, and Rudy Vallee.

BELOW: there are many exotic species of birds at the Bloedel Conservatory in Queen Elizabeth Park.

Capilano Suspension Bridge in North Vancouver is a sight not to be missed. This 140-meter (450ft) undulating steel cable bridge crosses a dramatic canyon.

means it is also one of the best people-watching places. In early August, the streets are closed so that more than 500,000 people can watch and participate in the Pride Parade.

The **Granville Island Public Market**  (daily) is more than just a food market located in the middle of the city. The fresh food market offers scores of small producers of everything from artisanal chocolates to wild mushrooms and seaweeds, with an emphasis on locally grown and created products.

Another urban food mecca is **Chinatown**, close to the downtown core, but a world apart. It's one of the largest Chinatowns in North America, vying for size with San Francisco and New York. While it offers a diversity of shopping for everything from cooking supplies to furniture, the main attraction is food. Dim sum restaurants provide the neophyte a great opportunity to point and choose. Small dishes of delicacies come hot out of the kitchen and waiters wander through the restaurant offering them to patrons. The waiters keep a running tally of the dishes selected and the final bill is generally far less

than expected. The Asian community is well-established here: the first wave of Chinese immigrants helped to keep the gold rush going when white frontiersmen had lost interest and left for home, and a second wave was in large part responsible for the construction of the Canadian Pacific Railway.

Successive waves of immigrants from most European countries after World War II, followed by more recent arrivals from India, Pakistan, Hong Kong, Taiwan, China, Korea, Viet Nam, and other Asian countries has created a truly cosmopolitan city. While English is still the dominant language, more than 70 languages are actively spoken in Vancouver, including Mandarin, Cantonese, Punjabi, Tagalog, and German.

Across Burrard Inlet, on the north shore of Vancouver, the **Grouse Mountain** skyride (daily; charge) offers a panoramic city view and, in winter, skiing. On the way, the **Capilano Suspension Bridge** (daily; charge) is more than a suspension bridge; it also offers a First Nations' Cultural Center, complete with demonstrations of traditional weaving, beadwork, and carving.

BELOW: pick your own fruit at Granville Island fresh food market.

Whistler

Whistler has evolved from a gondola and a few t-bars serving local die-hard skiers to the top ski resort in North America. While partly due to the careful creation of a European-style village, the real reason is the spectacular mountains that have been developed to yield their best. Two separate mountains, Whistler and Blackcomb, share accommodation and entertainment.

There are activities all year long to keep both avid adventurers and those less accustomed to outdoor activity more than satisfied.

Exceptional food and drink rewards a day of hiking, skiing or braving the Zipline, a series of ten individual steel cables strung across 2,400 meters (8,100ft) of forest, interspersed with suspension bridges and viewing platforms.

North of Vancouver

About 100km (62 miles) north of Vancouver is **Whistler Village,** co-host of the 2010 Winter Olympics (with Vancouver). Whistler is an international destination, with the two mountains of Whistler and Blackcomb vying for honors as skiers' preferred slopes. Mountain biking and hiking trails make it almost as popular in summer as winter.

North of Whistler 32km (20 miles), a pleasant half-hour walk along the Green River leads to **Nairn Falls.** Although not particularly high, its powerful tumble is loud and very impressive.

South of Vancouver

Now a neighborhood with a small-town feel, the fishing village of **Steveston** has a dark side to its history. In 1887 a single Japanese fisherman came to this tiny town for the salmon season. Just 40 years later there were 3,000 Japanese here, mostly fishermen. However, government bureaucrats placed quotas on the number of fishing permits allowed to Japanese immigrants.

All Japanese communities along the coast were dealt a more severe blow when the government began forcibly evacuating Japanese families from coastal areas during World War II. Virtually the entire village of Steveston was evacuated, and all their boats and fishing equipment was confiscated. Many people were interned in camps in Northern Ontario and central Alberta. Freed after the war, many returned to Steveston.

Today Steveston is a great place to browse in the shops and wander down to the wharves where the day's catch of salmon, tuna, snapper, prawns, crab, and herring is sold right off the boat.

The **George C. Reifel Waterfowl Refuge** (daily; charge) on **Westham Island** at the mouth of the Fraser River supports the largest wintering population of waterfowl in Canada. The 340-hectare (850-acre) habitat and estuarine marsh serves as a sanctuary to more than 240 species of birds.

In November, vast flocks of migrating snow geese stop here on their route from their Arctic breeding grounds to the Sacramento River Valley in California. Even mid-summer, close to 50 species can be spotted. ❑

TIP

Westham Island, site of the Reifel bird sanctuary, is also a great spot for picking up fresh fruits, vegetables, honey, and even award-winning fruit wines.

BELOW: Whistler Village, the top resort in B.C.'s Coastal Mountains.

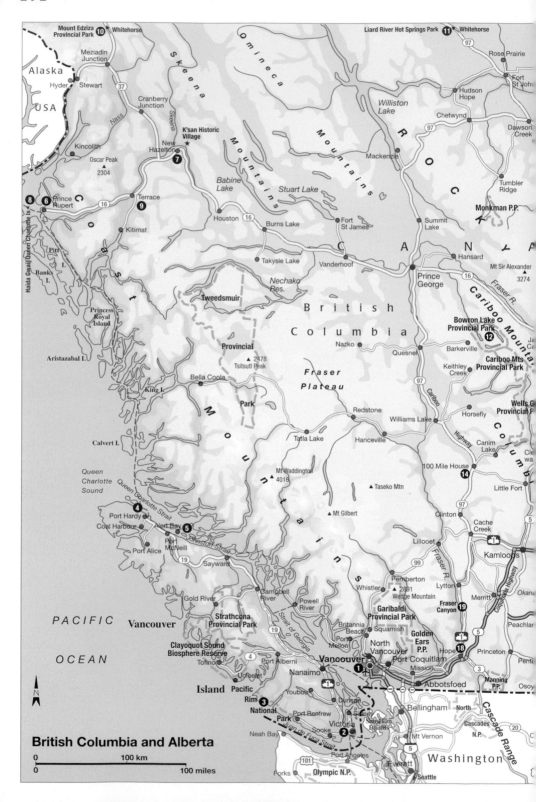

Mount Edziza Provincial Park ❿ Whitehorse
Meziadin Junction
Hyder Stewart
Alaska
USA
37
Cranberry Junction
Kincolith
New Hazelton ❼
Oscar Peak 2304
K'san Historic Village ★
❽ ❻ Prince Rupert
Terrace
❾
Kitimat
Houston 16
Burns Lake
Takysie Lake
Vanderhoof
Pitt I.
Banks I.
Babine Lake
Stuart Lake
Fort St James
Summit Lake
Nechako Res.
Princess Royal Island
Aristazabal I.
Tweedsmuir
Provincial
▲ 2478 Tsitsutl Peak
Bella Coola
King I.
Calvert I.
Park
Fraser Plateau
Nazko
Quesnel
Redstone
Williams Lake
Tatla Lake
Hanceville
Queen Charlotte Sound
Queen Charlotte Strait
▲ Mt Waddington 4016
▲ Taseko Mtn
▲ Mt Gilbert
Port Hardy
Coal Harbour Alert Bay ❺
Port McNeill
Port Alice
Sayward
19
Gold River
Campbell River
Powell River
Strathcona Provincial Park
Vancouver
PACIFIC
OCEAN
Clayoquot Sound Biosphere Reserve
Tofino
Ucluelet
Port Alberni
4
Island
Pacific
Rim
National
Park
Nanaimo
Youbou
Duncan
Port Renfrew
Sooke
Neah Bay
Victoria ❷
Olympic N.P.
Forks
Liard River Hot Springs Park ⓫ Whitehorse
97
Rose Prairie
Fort St John
Hudson Hope
Chetwynd
97
Dawson Creek
Williston Lake
Mackenzie
Tumbler Ridge
Monkman P.P.
Hansard
Mt Sir Alexander 3274
Prince George
16
Cariboo Mountains
Bowron Lake Provincial Park ⓬
Barkerville
Keithley Creek
Cariboo Mts Provincial Park
Horsefly
Wells G Provincial F
Canim Lake
100 Mile House
⓮
Little Fort
Clinton
Cache Creek
1
Lillooet
99
Fraser R.
Kamloops
Whistler
Pemberton
▲ 2891 Wedge Mountain
Lytton
Merritt
Fraser Canyon ⓲
Peachlar
Garibaldi Provincial Park
Britannia Beach
Squamish
Port Mellon
North Vancouver
Golden Ears P.P.
1
18
Hope
Princeton
Vancouver ❶
Port Coquitlam
Mission
Abbotsford
Manning P.P.
3
Osoy
Bellingham
North
Cascades
N.P.
20
Mt Vernon
5
Washington
Everett
Seattle
Port Angeles
101
Strait of Georgia
Johnstone Strait
Juan de Fuca Strait

British Columbia and Alberta

0   100 km
0   100 miles

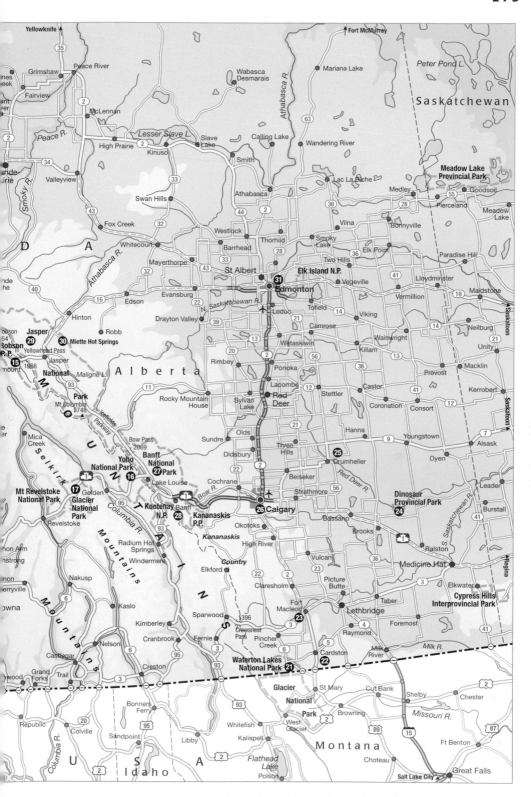

BRITISH COLUMBIA

People are drawn to the overwhelming natural beauty of British Columbia – its rocky coastline and thick forests, teeming mountains, mild temperatures – and to its relaxed lifestyle

Almost half the people who live in British Columbia (B.C.) were born somewhere else. The area has attracted health enthusiasts, die-hard hippies and vegetarians, monarchists, trade unionists, and profit-oriented business people. With its diverse interests and great beauty, the 4.2 million residents can't be wrong about B.C.'s appeal. Nor can the millions of visitors who come to explore **Vancouver ❶** and the surrounding province each year.

The natural beauty and the hospitable climate prompted many First Nations peoples to settle all along the Pacific coast. Each community developed its own unique and complex lifestyle based on the assured harvest of the annual salmon runs, and the abundance of forest products. They developed intricate trading relationships with both coastal neighbors and inland nations.

Today, pride of culture and history is increasing among First Nations communities across the province, as they work to overcome some of the legacies of the prohibition of their culture and the wholesale shipment of their children to residential schools.

For West Coast First Nations, first contact with Europeans came in 1778, when Captain Cook claimed the land for Britain. Over the next century, explorers mapped the interior of the area, exploring its rugged canyons and raging rivers. Simon Fraser, of Scottish descent, but born in New York during the American Revolution (1776–1862), made the exploration of the northwest his life's work, whilst working for the North West Company. He established the Fraser River as an important fur-trading route.

Fur trading in the 19th century was big business, and the competition for control of this new market marks the early history of British Columbia. The North West Company was chartered by the British Government specifically to develop the resources of the northwest.

Main attractions

VICTORIA
GULF ISLANDS
PACIFIC RIM NATIONAL PARK
LIARD RIVER HOT SPRINGS PARK
BOWRON LAKE PROVINCIAL PARK
WELLS GRAY PROVINCIAL PARK
OKANAGAN VALLEY

PRECEDING PAGES: cattle ranch, Quilchena. **LEFT:** a giant logger. **BELOW:** enjoying the view.

Victoria, garden city and capital of British Columbia, was founded in 1843 as a trading post on Vancouver Island by the Hudson's Bay Company.

BELOW: the harbor at Victoria.

The company had to fight for trade routes and profits with the Hudson's Bay Company, an older "eastern" company that already had a monopoly on Canadian trade with Europe.

The Nor'west, as the company became called, established an inland trading post, Fort George, which is now the city of Prince George. The Hudson's Bay Company, being the larger of the two enterprises and seeing the value of the fur trade as well as the future of lumber and mining, bought out Nor'west in 1821 and maintained virtual monopoly control over the area until 1858.

The 49th Parallel

In the 19th century, the fur trade along the Columbia River was carried out by a combination of French Canadians and Americans, although the American population grew faster than the British. The desire of the southerners to control the river trade became increasingly clear. The American battle

cry "Fifty-Four-Forty or Fight!" (referring to the latitude that marked the northern boundary of the territory) prompted the British to build Fort Victoria in 1843.

The territory was finally divided in two at the 49th parallel. This handed most of the Columbia River, and the best fur-trading territory, over to the United States.

The British Loyalists needed to find an "all British route" inland to the fur trapping territory. In 1856 James Douglas, a bear-like man with political skill, called for Vancouver Island's 774 European immigrants (half of whom were under the age of 20) to elect their first legislature. Two years later Queen Victoria named the region British Columbia and made Douglas the first governor.

Gold and its aftermath

In April 1856, gold was discovered in the North Thompson River, just above Kamloops. A survey team subsequently reported that there was gold in B.C. and the rush, in often perilous conditions, was on.

As the mainland developed, the city of Victoria suffered from an economic hangover. Its glory days were over, and the bust that followed the gold rush left Vancouver Island economically dependent on the rest of the colony. New industry was needed to diversify the island's economy and to provide jobs for the thousands of men who didn't make their fortunes in the gold fields of the Cariboo along the upper Fraser River.

Remember, gold was not the first wealth offered by the rich land, it had simply replaced furs. Looking around, the European settlers on Vancouver Island looked at the vast forests and saw the future in lumber. The Alberni Sawmill, the first sawmill west of the Rockies in Canada, was built on the west coast of Vancouver Island, on land casually appropriated from the native people. The tension this created was exacerbated by the hierarchy of labor created by the sawmill: "whites" were paid 25 cents an hour to log and work the mill, while "Asians and Indians" were paid a mere 15 cents.

This was not the glorious future imagined by the gold-rushers of 1858.

The river beds had been panned out, and working in a sawmill or a gold mine was similar to the factory work they had abandoned to come here: low-wage labor and difficult to get.

The independent spirit of the colony came into harsh conflict with the economic reality of its need for the outside world. With the promise to build a Canadian Pacific Railway, which would link the young city of Vancouver with the rest of Canada, British Columbia became a Canadian province in 1871. It took another 14 years to deliver on the promise, with the completion of the railway. Today, with natural resources subject to currency shifts and other factors influencing commodities, British Columbians have had to diversify away from the lumber and mining industries. While forestry is still important, many mills have closed permanently, leaving rural areas to shift efforts to tourism and other service industries.

While tourism is generally more environmentally sound, the development of infrastructure has been slow in some areas. It's a province in transition, with a cosmopolitan population

Not only gold, but timber attracted the Europeans. George Vancouver described the land in the 1860s, "Well covered with trees of large growth principally… pine."

LEFT: stacked logs at Merritt lumberyard.
BELOW: a Canadian Pacific locomotive travels through the Rockies.

that sees its future in attracting visitors to enjoy its diverse offerings.

Victoria

Just as the history of British Columbia begins in **Victoria ②**, the capital is still the "first" city in the province for many tourists. Victoria, a city with the mildest climate in Canada, is located on the southern tip of Vancouver Island approximately 56km (35 miles) from the city of Vancouver, reached by navigating past the lush Gulf Islands. The most common access is via BC Ferries, large car ferries that travel to the outskirts of Victoria from the major terminal south of Vancouver called Tsawwassen. It is also accessible from Seattle by passenger ferry. Although this proximity to its southern US neighbor should imply shared characteristics, Victoria is not only thoroughly Canadian, it is more British than most other places in Canada. Some would say it is more British than Britain.

The **Parliament Buildings ⓐ** (late May–Labor Day daily, Sept–mid-May Mon–Fri; free) make an excellent place to begin a tour of this province. Built in 1897, it was erected by someone with a playful sense of what might best evoke merry old England. There is a bit of London's St Paul's Cathedral in the huge central dome topped by a gilded statue of Captain George Vancouver. The neo-Romanesque arched entrance recalls London's Natural History Museum, and the smaller domed turrets suggest an Englishman's castle. The fairytale effect is enhanced at night when thousands of light bulbs outline the building.

But if the political rhetoric there proves tiresome, instant relief can be found by joining people who still celebrate the British monarchy in style at **The Fairmont Empress ⑧**. Named after Queen Victoria, Empress of India, the hotel was designed by English-born Francis Rattenbury and completed in 1908 at a cost of $750,000. It has been renovated numerous times, most recently in 2008, when the renovation of its famous tea room alone cost close to $1 million. The 477 rooms are being refurbished on an ongoing basis, always in keeping with the stature of

BELOW:
the Parliament Buildings, Victoria.

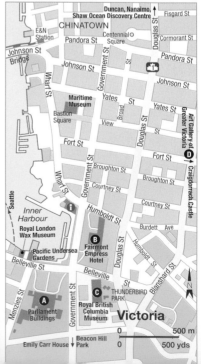

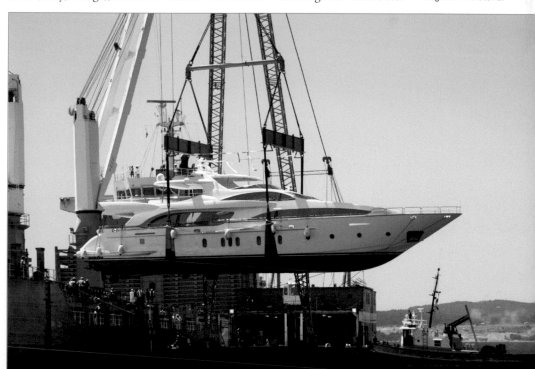

the building. Afternoon tea is a major tourist attraction, drawing over 100,000 people a year.

In between these two Victorian edifices sits the **Royal British Columbia Museum ⊙** (daily; charge) with its exceptional First Peoples gallery depicting life both before and after the arrival of Europeans. Its Modern History exhibit spans 200 years of fur-trading, the gold rush, farming, and the influx of immigrants from all over the world. There are also displays covering the natural history of the province and the impact of environmental changes.

History buffs will appreciate **Emily Carr House** (June–Aug daily, May and Sept Tue–Sat, closed Oct–Apr; charge), the artist's childhood abode; **Craigdarroch Castle** (daily; charge), the mansion of a ruthless coal baron; and, a bit further afield, **Fort Rodd Hill** and **Fisgard Lighthouse** (daily; charge), a park with a military history and sweeping ocean views across the mighty Pacific.

Near the Parliament Buildings, children may enjoy **Pacific Undersea Gardens** (daily; charge), a look at Victoria underwater, and the **Royal London Wax Museum** (daily; charge), with characters from history frozen in time.

Perhaps more exciting is the **Shaw Ocean Discovery Centre** (daily 10am–4pm; charge) located near the Swartz Bay ferry terminal in Sidney, a new aquarium focused entirely on the astonishingly diverse marine life of the surrounding waters.

The city has several fine art collections – notably the **Art Gallery of Greater Victoria ⊙** on Moss Street (daily; charge) and the **Maltwood Art Museum** (Mon–Fri; free) on the campus of the **University of Victoria**. The equivalent of Vancouver's Stanley Park, **Beacon Hill Park**, east of Douglas Street and south of Downtown, offers tranquil visits to see the swans after a busy day of shopping along **Government Street**. North of the city, en route to the ferry terminal, the century-old **Butchart Gardens** (daily; charge) offers a world-renowned quarry garden in a 22-hectare (55-acre) display of seasonal splendors.

Without a doubt, the greatest of the island's offerings are outdoors.

TIP

The Swartz Bay ferry terminal is close to Sidney, a perfectly charming seaside spot for coffee and a visit to the new Shaw Ocean Discovery Centre.

BELOW: a luxury yacht arrives by freighter in Victoria.

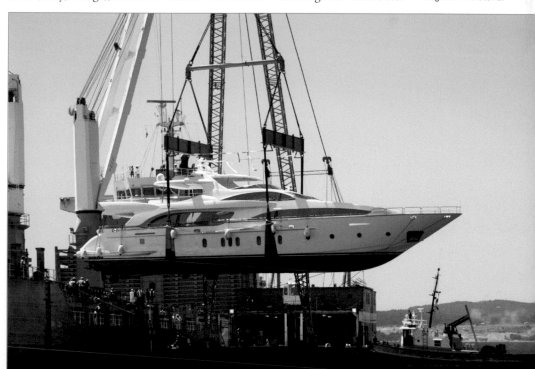

TIP

The best time to sail north from Port Hardy to Prince Rupert along the Inside Passage is in summer, when the ferry makes the 15-hour trip in daylight.

In fact, the whole province is a vast fisherman's paradise – saltwater and freshwater fishing, game fishing, and, for those more interested in the results than the process, just plain good eating. Salmon reigns supreme, but trout, tuna, and also halibut provide great challenges for sport fishing. Regulations are enforced, so it is essential to obtain proper licenses and understand the rules.

Hitting the trail

A trip to **Barkley Sound** on the west coast of Vancouver Island offers top-notch fishing, and the scenery of the **Pacific Rim National Park ❸** (year-round, fully operational mid-Mar–mid-Oct; charge). Here is an excellent view of the Pacific Coast in all its glory: rocky islands, sea lions playing in the crashing surf, harbor seals hiding in the coves, and sea birds hovering above. The area also holds a wealth of backpacking opportunities. The **Broken Group Islands**, off the southwest coast of Vancouver Island, are accessible by boat, and **Long Beach** has hiking trails and sunsets into the endless

Pacific. While the 75km (46-mile) **West Coast Trail** (May–Sept; reservations to hike are mandatory) is the serious hiker's dream, it is suitable for experts only – it is defined by steep hills, narrow muddy paths, nearly impenetrable forests, and stretches along the beach that can only be traversed at low tide. The trail offers spectacular views of gray whales, sea lions, seals, rock formations, two lighthouses, and good spots for surf-casting.

More civilized backpacking and hiking is available in any of British Columbia's numerous provincial parks. They offer excellent views, trails, and invigorating exercise, as well as a closeness to nature that can make every tree seem like a unique experience in color.

Between Vancouver Island and Vancouver, the stunning **Gulf Islands** offer unique communities, known for their laid-back lifestyles and sometimes eccentric inhabitants. The islands share the same climate as Victoria, offering up rugged forested coastlines that appeal to sailors and kayakers alike. The larger islands have regularly scheduled ferry service. It's a good idea to

BELOW: backpacking through Monkman Provincial Park.
RIGHT: fishing on the Fraser River.

make reservations for all ferries around weekends during summer.

The best way to see the coast in all its lush-green mountainous glory is to take the trip on the **Prince Rupert Ferry**. Once the only way to get from Victoria to Prince Rupert or Alaska, the B.C. Inside Passage route ferry still makes the 15-hour journey, leaving from **Port Hardy ❹** at the northern tip of Vancouver Island (reservations required). On the way to Port Hardy stop at **Port McNeill**, 350km (217 miles) north of Victoria, and take the short ferry to **Alert Bay ❺** for a chance to see important art forms of the northwest in the right context: totem poles and masks. Alert Bay is a Kwakwaka'wakw village that dates back more than 8,000 years, and one of the the best places to see totem poles, including the world's tallest (56 meters/173ft). The masks and other pieces on display at the **U'mista Cultural Centre** (Mon–Fri; charge) tell the heartbreaking story of the prohibition of potlatch, the traditional gathering outlawed by government in 1884, labeling it "immoral" and "heathen". Potlatch went underground, but

in 1921, the activity was captured and goods confiscated. Some masks and other pieces were sold, while some were sent off to museums. After the law restricting potlatch was finally deleted in 1951, efforts began to recover the pieces, which by then were dispersed as far away as England. Most of the collection has been returned and it now represents a focal point of a people proud of their heritage who are committed to preserving it.

From **Prince Rupert ❻** it is possible to visit a number of other sites where native carving is practiced including 'Ksan, (year round; charge for guided tour) near **New Hazelton ❼**, where the Gitxsan people work at a full-size model of a traditional native village. Another ferry to the **Queen Charlotte Islands ❽** (7 hours) – also know as Haida Gwaii or Islands of the People– will take travelers to see the highly regarded work of the Haida at **Skidegate**, and the beaches at **Sandspit** where legend says the raven *Ne-kil-stlas* landed and discovered a cockle shell that contained the first people – the origin of the human race.

There are more than 250 different First Nations Bands in British Columbia. Some have signed treaties, while scores more are in various stages of negotiation.

BELOW: surfing at sunset at Tofino.

Long Beach

Some of the most spectacular scenery in British Columbia lies along the west coast of Vancouver Island. The towns of Tofino and Ucluelet effectively bookend Long Beach, where brave souls in wet suits surf and children build sandcastles. In winter, stormwatching tourists keep hotels and restaurants busy along this tourist-driven area.

To the north, the Clayoquot Sound was recognized by the United Nations in 2000 as a World Biosphere Reserve, a refuge for thousands of grey whales and hundreds of thousands of shorebirds that migrate along the Pacific coast. The people of the Nuu-Chah-Nulth First Nations, protectors of the lands that have been inhabited for at least 5,000 years, are also amazing artists, creating spectacular carved masks and bentwood boxes.

Northern lake country

Heading inland from Prince Rupert the amount of open land becomes overwhelming. The choice of direction is limited by the distinct lack of roads. Aside from the main East/West Highway (the Yellowhead Highway 16), most are unpaved and only one-and-a-half lanes wide, designed for logging rather than for tourism.

One of the longest and most beautiful roads north is Highway 37 from **Terrace** ❾, more than twelve hours of driving before intersecting the Alaska Highway near **Watson Lake**, Yukon. It offers numerous side trips, including **Mount Edziza Provincial Park** ❿ (on foot, horseback or chartered plane only) and the town of **Stewart**. From Stewart one can cross over to **Hyder**, Alaska. The road to Stewart passes through the Cambria snowfield and offers spectacular views of **Bear Glacier**.

In terms of wildlife, everything from moose and caribou to the bald eagle and the white Kermode or "spirit" bear can be seen here. The lakes to the south have rainbow-, lake-, and brook-trout, and the delicious Dolly Varden – a member of the char family, not as heavy as salmon, but meatier than trout. Farther north in the **Peace River Area** the fishing action turns to the arctic grayling and the northern pike.

One wonderful stop in the northeast corner of the province is the remote **Liard River Hot Springs Park** ⓫ (year-round; charge) at Mile 493 of the Alaska Highway. The springs are naturally heated, slightly sulphurous pools of water, surrounded by orchids and tropical vines as thick as the northern forests just a few yards away. The water is over 43°C (110°F) and has created a microclimate. It is so relaxing and almost impossible to get up the steps out of the water. The pools are only open May 1–August 1, as bear activity in late summer gives way to icy and slippery conditions on the boardwalks that lead to the pools.

Cariboo Gold Rush route

South of **Prince George**, through **Quesnel** and south all the way to **Cache Creek**, travelers can trace the history of the gold rush. The **Cariboo Highway** now follows roughly the

The Gold Rush Trail

The forested plateau of the Cariboo, lying north of Lillooet, between the Coast Mountains and the Cariboo Mountains, may not be the most scenically spectacular region of British Columbia, but its rich history more than compensates the visitor.

Gold was discovered in the area in the late 1850s, but it was in 1862 that Billy Barker, a Cornish sailor, struck the vast quantities at Williams Creek that sparked the Cariboo Gold Rush. Boom towns such as Barkerville appeared within months and a 640km (400-mile) supply road was constructed in a remarkable feat of engineering along the inhospitable Fraser River canyon from Yale in the south. At its peak, some 10,000 people lived in Barkerville, not only fortune-seeking gold prospectors, but also every kind of support service, from saloon to general store, from church to post office. But within 10 years the gold deposits were exhausted.

Today Highway 97 and Highway 26 follow the route of the original Cariboo Highway to Barkerville, restored as a living museum with all the atmosphere of a gold-rush town (mid-May–Labor Day daily 8.30am–8pm, Oct–Apr 8.30am–4.30pm; charge). Among the original buildings there are stores, saloons, and hotels; from May to September, there are in-depth tours of the town and activities for all ages.

same route as the old Cariboo Wagon Road. Ironically, the completion of the road, as well as the exhaustion of easily panned gold, helped to end the frontier phase of the gold rush and made way for more organized shaft-mining operations. While gold continued to be mined in quantity until the 1870s, the romance was gone.

The fact that the rush is over should not discourage tourists from trying their hand at panning for wealth at historic **Barkerville**, (year-round; May–Sept only, charge) a reconstructed gold-rush ghost town with dance hall girls and plenty of western fun. Two days' panning should generate enough "dust" to buy a newspaper back in Vancouver. Visitors may prefer to hike along the streams that have beds of raw jade stone, although the green stone might not be as impressive as the gold. Nearby **Bowron Lake Provincial Park ⑫** (year-round, camping mid-May–end Sept; charge) offers a famous collection of interlocking lakes for canoe enthusiasts. The circuit takes 6–10 days, depending on skill level. The park is a wildlife sanctuary, and it's not unusual to see deer, moose, bears, and caribou. The forest cover is mainly white spruce and alpine fir.

Campgrounds abound in the many provincial parks in this area. One of the largest is the **Wells Gray Provincial Park ⑬** (year-round, camping May–Oct; charge). It has all the beauty that the rest of B.C. has shown, along with old homesteads abandoned by families that did not survive the 19th-century frontier days. There are five major lakes here as well as a multitude of waterfalls and rapids.

This is also cowboy country, where most of the province's cattle industry is located. Here travelers are able to see modern-day cowboys, in addition to helping the area to celebrate the old glories with rodeos and horseback riding. The hub of much of this summer activity is **100 Mile House ⑭**, which started as a stagecoach rest stop during the gold rush. One of the original Barnard Express stagecoaches is on display at the north end of town. Winter activities include snowmobiling, dog sledding, ice-fishing, and cross country skiing.

In July, Williams Lake, 15km (9 miles) northwest of 100 Mile House, stages one of the biggest rodeos in Canada – second only to the Calgary Stampede.

BELOW: testing the limits at Whistler.

Four hours by car east from Vancouver is the Okanagan, famous for fruit and wine. Here you can wind-surf or waterski on the warm waters of Lake Osoyoos.

BELOW: a softer kind of gold dots the mountain slopes. **RIGHT:** St John the Divine church and museum at Yale, north of Hope.

Continuing south and west, all roads begin to lead to Vancouver, but there is still plenty to see in the areas that border the US. For example, while Banff and Jasper in Alberta are more famous, there is no denying the beauty of the **British Columbia Rockies**, and the parks that preserve it are well worth visiting: **Mount Robson Provincial Park ⑮** contains the highest point in the Canadian Rockies, while **Yoho ⑯** and **Glacier ⑰ National Parks** have camping, skiing, and views of snow-fields. Highway 1 north from **Hope ⑱** to **Cache Creek** travels along the Fraser and Thompson rivers. The faster Coquihalla Highway is appealing, but the old road through the **Fraser Canyon ⑲** gives visitors some idea of the challenges facing the both the first explorers like Simon Fraser, as well as the miners and prospectors.

Land of fruit and wines

About five hours east of Vancouver by car, the geography begins to change. The rainfall is less frequent, there are arid hills and even sagebrush. This is Canada's best-known fruit belt – the Okanagan Valley. Water from **Okanagan Lake ⑳** is used for irrigation and, combined with long hot sunny days, creates a lush garden. Apples, peaches, plums, grapes, cherries, apricots, and pears all grow here in abundance. The area is also known for its sandy beaches and lakes. Some favorite spots for travelers are **Penticton** between Lake Okanagan and Lake Skaha, and **Kelowna**. Kelowna is the marketing center for the Okanagan fruit belt and is famous for its **International Regatta** held in July.

The valley is a destination for wine lovers, who compare the wines and the valley to Napa Valley of the 1980s, full of potential and excitement. More than 50 wineries propose tastings and sales of their pleasing dry whites and dry reds along with some more refined wines from the nobler European varieties: Pinot Noir, Cabernet Sauvignon and Riesling. Among the wineries you can visit are Calona and Cedar Creek in Kelowna, Mission Hill in West Bank, and Gray Monk at Okanagan Centre.

The particular appeal to this area is the abundance of lakes warm enough to play in all summer long, a short distance from the mountains that offer great skiing in winter.

Down in the southeast corner of the province, **Nelson** grew up as supply town to the gold miners. Nelson has more than 300 heritage buildings, which is probably one reason why the town has served as a backdrop to several feature films.

It's a small town that seems to live in a time warp, but a good one – with great food and a focus on lifestyle, culture, and the outdoors, the people who live here seem to have everything – and they know what a good life they have.

The whole province seems to offer up beautiful routes just to drive along. Highway 3, the "Crowsnest Highway," offers spectacular views for those not in a hurry – most of the road is two lanes, so a slow-moving camper can hold up the traffic. ❏

FLORA AND FAUNA OF THE UNTAMED WEST

Stretching from the 49th parallel to the North Pole, western Canada provides diverse habitats for a rich array of plants and wildlife

Western Canada is blessed with a multitude of different environments. The north has tundra and some of the continent's loftiest mountains, while the south includes prairie grasslands, thousands of lakes, and mountain ranges. It even has the northern tip of the central American desert, and yet a few hundred kilometers away you can find lush temperate rainforest. Given this huge assembly of habitats, western Canada's flora ranges from lichens clinging to permanently frozen rocks through varieties of cacti and lush ferns to such exotica as rhododendrons, azaleas, and wild orchids. Perhaps most striking are the fir trees and aspens which make up forests stretching to the horizon.

Traditional Emblems

In spring, Canada bursts into color with a host of wildflowers. An indication of the variety is seen in the floral emblems of the territories and provinces. Yukon is depicted by the brilliant pink fireweed, while the Northwest Territories has pretty mountain avens. The western dogwood is British Columbia's floral representative, Alberta has the wild rose, Saskatchewan the prairie lily, and Manitoba the prairie crocus. Among its fauna, beavers are traditionally recognized as Canada's emblem because their valuable pelts were a major stimulus to early exploration. The dams and intricate lodges they build in ponds and lakes are particularly visible.

ABOVE: hunting and disease have seriously depleted the bison, and those that remain in Canada can be found in the grasslands.

RIGHT: Douglas Firs, the forest giants of the West Coast, can grow as tall as 90 meters (295ft).

LEFT: the bald eagle, symbol of the United States, is common along Canada's Pacific coastline. Today the eagle is a protected species.

RUNNING WILD IN CANADA'S PARKS

The national and provincial parks of Canada provide natural habitats for many species. For spectacular beauty, rich in wildlife, few areas in the world can match the Yukon's Kluane National Park, with its herds of caribou, Dall sheep, wild goats, and the rare blue bear.

While black bears are found all over Canada, grizzlies are confined to the forests and wetlands of the West. Many are regular campground visitors, so it's wise to heed the rangers' warnings – even baby bears should be considered dangerous, since they are bound to have a very big mom lurking nearby.

White-tailed deer, with Bambi-like spotted fawns, are commonplace in the parks. So are the huge, prehistoric-looking moose, readily spotted in the swamplands. In the Rocky Mountains' parks there are elk, wild goats and mountain sheep, coyotes, and wolf.

The largest population of bison is in Wood Buffalo National Park on the Northwest Territories/Alberta border. Some 4,000 free-roaming wood bison live here, as do white pelicans, rare whooping cranes, eagles, and wolves but, since this park is the size of Switzerland, you will need a guide to help locate them for you.

ABOVE: above the timberline in the Rockies, and across Arctic Canada, a wide variety of plants, especially alpine fireweed, survive freezing winters to burst into bloom in the summer months.

LEFT: Inuits lead safaris across the Arctic in search of polar bears in Oct–Nov.

RIGHT: caribou are known as *tuktu*, or *tuktuk*, by the Inuit who depended on them for food, clothing, tools, and weapons.

ALBERTA

From the soaring peaks of the Rockies to the wide open prairies, snowcapped national parks to arid dinosaur trails, modern cities to small towns, Alberta is a province of dramatic contrasts

I f a province could walk, Alberta would swagger just a bit, chest out, chin up, eyes fixed firmly on the future. And why not? It has the best of the west: fertile farmland; oil, gas, and coal in abundance; exciting cities like Calgary and Edmonton; and the incomparable blue Canadian Rockies for a playground. Albertans exuberantly inform the rest of the country about the virtues of their province, and their pride sounds to some like flat-out American bragging. The petroleum industry, which fueled Alberta's tremendous economic growth in the 1970s, was founded mostly by American companies that parachuted some of their brightest and sometimes brashest from Texas oil country. Their can-do spirit, essential in a business that rewards risktakers, seems to have rubbed off on everyone else.

Oil-rich Alberta

Rancher John Lineham didn't risk much when he sank a well in 1902 among the oil-seepage pools along the Akamina Parkway in the southwest corner of the province. The Kutenai, First Nations people in the area, had been using the oil for centuries as a balm to heal wounds. Lineham's well, the first in western Canada, produced 300 barrels a day until the flow ebbed after four years. The site of **Discovery Well** is prominently marked in **Waterton Lakes National Park ㉑**, 250km (155 miles) south of Calgary.

The park's landscape changes abruptly from rolling grasslands to snowcapped peaks chiseled by Ice Age glaciers. Boat tours on the lakes pass outstanding glacier-carved formations, including hanging valleys high up mountain walls. A hiking trail winds through **Red Rock Canyon**, streaked with the red, purple, green, and yellow of mineral deposits; another path leads to **Cameron Lake**, a blue gem set in a bowl-shaped valley.

Canada's first Mormon temple, a pristine white marble edifice finished

Main attractions
THE ROCKY MOUNTAINS
ALBERTA BADLANDS
CALGARY
BANFF NATIONAL PARK
JASPER NATIONAL PARK
EDMONTON

PRECEDING PAGES: Vermillion Lakes, Banff National Park. **BELOW:** pumping for oil.

The rich fossil beds of Dinosaur Provincial Park conceal the remains of 35 species of dinosaurs from 75 million years ago. Visit the Field Station (daily).

in 1913, gleams in the prairie sun at **Cardston ㉒**, 45km (28 miles) east of the park. Born here was Fay Wray, the 1930s movie star who slumped in King Kong's gorilla hands. It was founded by Charles Ora Card, a son-in-law of Brigham Young. Visitors can tour the grounds and Card's 1887 cabin. The Mormons emigrated from Utah in 1887. They developed Canada's first major irrigation project soon after their arrival, digging 96km (60 miles) of canals out from the St Mary River, and growing bumper crops of vegetables.

Less desirable American immigrants were the traders who came up from Montana in the 1870s to swap furs and buffalo hides with the local native population for a shot of rotgut whiskey. **Fort Macleod ㉓**, 60km (37 miles) north of Cardston, was built in 1874 and manned with North West Mounted Police (precursors to the Royal Canadian Mounted Police) who halted the trade. The fort museum tells about daily life around the post; interpretative guides dressed in 1870s police uniforms parade on horseback (May–Aug daily; charge).

Lethbridge, some 75km (46 miles) northeast of Cardston is home to the first and most notorious of the whiskey forts the Mounties put out of business, **Fort Whoop-up** (July–Aug daily, Apr–May and Oct Wed–Sun, June and Sept Tue–Sun, Nov–Mar Sat–Sun only; charge). Nearby, the last major battle between First Nations (the Cree and Blackfoot Nations) in Canada is commemorated at **Indian Battle Park**. Locals claim Lethbridge gets 2,400 hours of sunshine a year, making it one of Canada's sunniest cities. The town's role in a dark chapter of the country's history is brightened by the **Nikka Yuko Japanese Garden** (mid-May–early Oct daily; charge), a serene oasis of water, rocks, and willows. The garden was built by the city in 1967 for Canada's centenary, inspired by the contributions of the Japanese Canadians who were interned here during World War II and stayed on to make it their home.

Prehistoric finds

The **Alberta Badlands**, once part of a subtropical swamp that sheltered a vast

BELOW: fossilized remains at Dinosaur Provincial Park. **RIGHT:** Calgary City Hall.

array of prehistoric life, contain one of the world's finest repositories of dinosaur fossils. The most spectacular badlands are preserved along the Red Deer River in **Dinosaur Provincial Park** ㉔, 175km (108 miles) east of Calgary, selected as one of Unesco's World Heritage Sites in 1979. From a lookout near the park entrance, visitors can survey 7,000 hectares (18,000 acres) of this gnarled sandstone landscape with its weirdly eroded formations. A circular 5km (3-mile) drive with side trips on foot leads to dinosaur bones preserved where they were found. Other areas of the park are accessible on organized bus tours and hikes (May–Oct; reservations tel: 403-378-4344).

The town of **Drumheller** ㉕, 138km (86 miles) northeast of Calgary, lies deep within the badlands, which drop abruptly here below the lip of the prairie. The sheer unexpectedness of the scene shocks the eye and delights the imagination. A 48km (30-mile) circular drive called the **Dinosaur Trail** takes motorists from the impressive **Royal Tyrrell Museum of Paleontology** (mid-May–Aug 31 daily, Sept–mid-May Tue–Sun; charge), 6km (4 miles) northwest of Drumheller, containing one of the best collections of dinosaur fossils in the world, up to the rim of the mile-wide valley. Highlights of the trip are the lookout at **Horsethief Canyon** and the **Bleriot Ferry**, one of the last cable ferries in the province.

Calgary

The city of **Calgary** ㉖ feels different than any other Canadian city. First and foremost, it is a boom and bust town, its roller coaster ride over the past 40 years closely linked to the price of oil. Suburbs sprawl in all directions, and in boom times, the city lavishly creates public structures such as the Jack Singer performing arts center, home of the Calgary Philharmonic; and the 17,000-seat **Saddledome**, Calgary's premier sports arena. The arena was built for the hockey and skating competitions of the 1988 Winter Olympics, but it is now better known as the home base for the Calgary Flames hockey team.

When oil prices plummet, Calgarians tighten their belts and demonstrate that pioneer spirit that saw their forefathers

BELOW: Calgary Stampeders in action.

Head-Smashed-In

Alberta is home to five of the fourteen Unesco world heritage sites in Canada, each showcasing fascinating geology and geography. One of these sites falls into the category of "cultural" heritage – Head-Smashed-In Buffalo Jump, near **Fort Macleod**.

It's a unique opportunity to understand how the Blackfoot and other First Nations lived for close to 6,000 years, herding buffalo past hundreds of stone cairns that guided them into a narrow valley and over a steep cliff to their death, then stripping the carcasses, using every part of the animals. Skeletal remains at the base of the cliff several meters thick tell the story of a way of life. An estimated 80 million buffalo roamed the North American plains at the time of the arrival of European explorers.

The town of Banff is named after Banffshire in Scotland, the birthplace of two of the financiers of the Canadian Pacific Railway.

through the depression. There is an eternal optimism that seems to come with the southern Alberta territory – a firm belief that things will turn around. So far, they have and, with each economic recovery, the city seems to jump higher and faster than other Canadian cities, attracting ambitious people with a love of action and excitement.

Part of the price for this rapid growth is downtown congestion. The light rail "C trains" help, and pedestrians have the advantage of elevated promenades. Most of the downtown core is connected by "Plus 15s" – skyways 5 meters (15ft) over the traffic that link office towers, shopping complexes and hotels. At an elevated indoor park called **Devonian Gardens**, office workers on their lunch-break brown-bag it on benches scattered amid waterfalls, ponds, and greenery. There is also a five-block pedestrian mall along Stephen Avenue, a civilized thoroughfare of two-story buildings and street-level shops, with benches to sit on and wandering musicians to provide entertainment. It also has convenient entrances to some of the higher-end shopping in the city.

Rodeo days

The slicker the city gets, the more it seems to revel in the down home fun of the Calgary Stampede, the world's largest rodeo, with $2 million in prize money. For 10 days in early July residents of Canada's number-one cowtown don Stetson hats and cowboy boots and let loose at flapjack breakfasts, square dancing, and parades. Beer flows freely and a party atmosphere pervades the whole city. Long-time residents generally leave town, but it's a great place to get caught up in the romance of the rodeo. The most thrilling and popular event on the **Exhibition Grounds** is chuck-wagon racing.

Pioneer days are also relived at **Heritage Park Historical Village**, on Heritage Drive, a first-rate collection of reconstructed buildings and authentic structures gathered from all over the province (mid-May–Labor Day daily, Sept–mid-Oct Sat–Sun and holidays; charge). A vintage steam train tours the site, and a replica paddlewheeler plies the **Glenmore Reservoir**.

Delve further into the past at the **Glenbow Museum**, which displays

BELOW: Moraine Lake, Banff National Park.

the best collections of prairie-dwelling First Nations peoples' artifacts in the world (daily; charge). Other sections of the museum show what the early lives of settlers were like and how oil exploration and cattle ranching fostered the strong survival instinct that pervades the Alberta approach to life.

If Calgary's hectic pace becomes overwhelming, a visit to the zoo will put things back in perspective. The zoo spans **St George's Island** in the Bow River and a huge swath of land on the north side of the river. There is a comfortable transition from the present to the past, with life-size reproductions of dinosaurs occupying their own piece of the park, adjacent to the Canadian Wilds exhibit, which boasts endangered species like the whooping crane, along with the ever-popular bears, bison, and moose.

Travelers heading for the mountains can get a taste of the Alpine adventure to come by ascending the 190-meter (626ft) high **Calgary Tower** (daily; charge). Below the new glass floor is the sprawling city, and, to the west, the serrated ridge of the **Rockies**, much of which is protected by national and provincial parks. One such area is **Kananaskis Provincial Park**, a 45-minute drive southwest of Calgary, containing foothills, mountains, ice-caps, and sparkling lakes. Dirt-bike trails thread its forests, fishermen try their luck in dozens of prime trout streams, and downhill skiers challenge the slopes at **Nakiska**. One of the best ways to enjoy the Kananaskis is to stay at a guest ranch, where greenhorns work up mountain-size appetites on trail rides or hiking trips and then satisfy themselves with hearty, home-cooked fare, including large portions of Alberta beef.

Jewel of the Rockies

Crown jewel of the Rockies, **Banff National Park** ㉗ has some of the continent's finest mountain scenery within its confines along the eastern flank of the Continental Divide. The park was founded more than a century ago as

Canada's first national preserve to protect hot springs just outside the present-day town of **Banff** ㉘ to the southeast.

The restored **Cave and Basin Hot Springs Centennial Center** on Cave Avenue, Banff, features a natural cave pool fed by a hot spring. The center's museum (daily; charge) traces the history of the Canadian parks, and the geology of the area. Visitors can take a dip in the sulphurous waters at **Upper Hot Springs**, Mountain Avenue, where the average temperature of the mineral water feeding the outdoor public pool is 47°C (116°F) in the winter, 27°C (81°F) in the summer. The bathhouse has been restored to its early 1930s glory (daily; charge).

A gondola ride up **Sulphur Mountain**, 3km (2 miles) from Banff (daily; charge), ends at a summit cafeteria where mountain sheep are often seen snuffling for snacks. Here, a boardwalk trail leads to the restored 1903 weather observatory. In winter, **Mount Norquay**, 8km (5 miles) out of town, also affords panoramas of encircling

The Saddledome and Calgary Tower.

BELOW: elk, white-tailed deer and woodland caribou all inhabit Banff National Park.

TIP

Take a rubber-tired SnoCoach along the Athabasca Glacier, 105km (65 miles) south of Jasper (Apr–Sept 9am–5pm, Oct 10am–4.30pm; buses depart every 15–30 minutes).

peaks from the top of its ski lifts. Other world-class ski resorts include Lake Louise and Sunshine, a little further from Calgary, but offering great variety of terrain.

Jutting above the trees are the granite spires of **The Fairmont Banff Springs Hotel**, a massive 768-room Victorian edifice built in 1888, styled after a Scottish baronial castle. Sunday brunch is a popular outing.

Banff has all the flavor of an Alpine town. In summer, its sidewalks are crowded. Strollers browse in the dozens of gift shops or munch on delights in the Cascade Plaza. In winter, après-ski life abounds. Stores stay open late and there is a wide variety of restaurants.

To escape the crowds, wander the grounds of the **Banff Center**, a world-class conservatory of fine arts, music, and drama. In this Salzburg of the Rockies, the summerlong Banff Arts Festival showcases opera, dance, cabaret, musical theater, and jazz.

Glacier country

BELOW:
Mistaya Canyon.

Lake Louise, 90km (56 miles) north of Banff, a jade gem set against the back-drop of Victoria Glacier, is one of the Rockies' most photographed spots. A Scottish piper wanders among the flowers and pines in the grounds of **The Fairmont Château Lake Louise**; the echo of his skirling resounds from surrounding peaks. Romantics rent canoes and sigh as they paddle around the edge of the lake. The more ambitious hike the moderately difficult trail (7km/4½ miles round-trip) to **Lake Agnes** to a teahouse perched near the top of a waterfall.

The junction of Highways 93 and 11, 76km (47 miles) north of Lake Louise, is the starting point of the **Icefields Parkway**, one of the world's great mountain drives. The beauty of Lake Louise is challenged within 40km (25 miles) by **Peyto Lake**, set in the **Mistaya River Valley**. A platform at the end of a half-mile trail off the parking lot affords unobstructed views of the deep, turquoise-colored lake, 240 meters (800ft) below.

The parkway continues north in the valley of the Mistaya (Cree for "grizzly"), then follows the braided channels of the North Saskatchewan River to the Rockies' apex: the **Columbia Icefield**, at 326 sq km (126 sq miles) the biggest ice cap in the range. This "mother of rivers" feeds three systems: the Columbia, the Athabasca, and the Saskatchewan. **Athabasca Glacier**, one of dozens that flow from Columbia's bowl of ice, extends almost to the Parkway.

Here, the Parkway enters **Jasper National Park ㉙**, the largest and most northerly in the Rockies. Take the scenic alternate route, 93A, along the west bank of the Athabasca River to Athabasca Falls, which thunder over a 30-meter (100ft) high ledge and hurtle through a narrow canyon. A self-guiding trail along the gorge provides close-ups of the violent beauty of the powerful cataract.

Another highlight along the way is **Mount Edith Cavell**, a snow-covered dome of rock rising sheer from **Angel Glacier**. Fur traders in the early

1800s called this the "mountain of the great crossing;" in World War I it was renamed after a heroic British nurse who was executed for helping Allied troops. A hiking trail climbs into alpine meadows spangled with colorful wildflowers; another path wanders across the boulder-strewn outwash of the glacier.

The town of **Jasper**, smaller and quieter than Banff, is the starting point for dozens of scenic hiking trails, bicycle routes, and driving tours. The Jasper Tramway (end Apr–mid-Oct, weather permitting; charge), 4km (2½ miles) south of the town, whisks sightseers close to the stony summit of **The Whistlers**, a 2,464-meter (8,084ft) peak. From its summit, looking 77km (48 miles) northwest into British Columbia, on a clear day you can glimpse the solitary tip of the highest peak in the Rockies, Mount Robson (3,954 meters/12,972ft).

Jasper's answer to the Banff Springs Hotel is the more rustic **Fairmont Jasper Park Lodge**, a hotel with an additional cluster of 50 chalets along **Lac Beauvert**. Room service comes on a bicycle, bears have been known to commandeer the lawns, and a moose once took over a pond on the golf course. And, yes, there is a piper. He performs at a sunset flag-lowering ceremony.

The **Maligne Valley Drive** offers spectacular views of **Maligne Canyon**, 11km (7 miles) east of Jasper, where the river plunges into a steep-walled limestone gorge; **Medicine Lake**, 16km (10 miles) southeast, drained by a vast underground river system; and **Maligne Lake**, a further 10km (6 miles) on, which can be explored by boat in summer and is a cross-country ski center in winter.

En route to Edmonton, take a sidetrip to the **Miette Hot Springs** ㉚, 60km (37 miles) north of Jasper, the hottest in the Rockies. The waters are cooled to 40°C (104°F) before being fed into a huge swimming pool (May–mid-Oct; charge; swimsuits, towels, lockers available for rent).

Travelers reluctantly leave the Rockies behind as they head east through the parklands and forests of northern Alberta. Hearty fare like Russian borscht and Ukrainian cabbage rolls from the Homesteader's Kitchen at the **Stony Plain Multicultural Center** (daily; by donation), 20km (12 miles) west of Edmonton, may take the edge off the disappointment. On Saturdays, don't miss the farmers' market for a sample of other regional food.

Edmonton

Provincial capital and Canada's most northerly metropolis, **Edmonton** ㉛ is noted for its scenic river valley and numerous arts festivals. The **West Edmonton Mall** is the largest in North America, with an astounding 800 stores, restaurants, fast-food outlets, and a massive indoor amusement park; the **Citadel Theatre** houses five separate venues all under a single roof; the **Telus World of Science** (daily; charge) houses Canada's largest planetarium and the western world's largest Zeiss-Jenastar projector.

Oil deals are made at the head offices

Yellowhead Highway 16, heading northeast from Jasper, follows the route of the fur traders. Viewpoints offer dramatic glimpses of the terrain they endured.

BELOW: the Muttart Conservatory, Edmonton.

in Calgary; the actual work of turning black gold into commodities such as gasoline and diesel occurs in Edmonton. The city flexes its industrial muscle along **Refinery Row**, a glittering galaxy of tubes, giant storage tanks, and gas flares that light up the night sky like a scene from a science-fiction movie.

But Edmonton is no blue-collar town. In fact, it seems more sophisticated in some ways than its southern rival, where the backyard mountains attract lots of outdoors types more interested in backpacking than Bach. Seat of provincial government and home of the **University of Alberta**, Edmonton has opera and classical ballet companies, a symphony orchestra, and several professional theater groups. Why, crystal chandeliers even adorn a couple of its rapid transit stations!

Summer celebrations

All this refinement is inclined to be overshadowed in late July during **Capital EX**, a 10-day revival of the Klondike Gold Rush. The city's vast **Northlands Park** is lit up by midway lights and

nightly fireworks, rocked by the sounds of the country's best bands, and clouded with the dusty haze of the chuckwagon and thoroughbred races. It is followed by Heritage Days in August, an ethnic festival celebrating more than 80 cultures with music, dance, and, above all, food. From Afghani shami kabobs to Gweru (chicken stew) from Zimbabwe, visitors buy tickets to sample delicacies from all parts of the world.

An outdoor museum beside the river, **Fort Edmonton Park** is perhaps a clearer window on the past (mid-May–late Sept daily; charge). Thirty-five buildings along three small-town streets recapture the flavor of three separate eras: 1846, 1885, and 1920. Old Strathcona, the city's original commercial district, preserves along its narrow streets early structures such as the **Old Firehall**, **Strathcona Hotel**, and **Klondike Cinema**. This is also the site of the **International Fringe Theater Festival**, North America's oldest and largest fringe festival, attracting performers from all over North America and Europe every August for 10 days. The streets echo with mime, music, puppet shows, and plays.

An impressive urban greenbelt preserves riverbank along the North Saskatchewan River, where you can hike, cycle, picnic, and ride horseback on more than 100km (62 miles) of trails. Guides at a nature center near Fort Edmonton conduct walks in all seasons. Four glass pyramids nestled in the valley house the **Muttart Conservatory**, a showcase of plants from the tropics to the deserts of the world (daily; charge).

The valley is also the site of a man-made wonder that expresses Alberta's exuberant spirit. As his contribution to the province's 75th anniversary celebrations back in 1980, artist Peter Lewis installed a series of water pipes along the top of the **High Level Bridge**. Now, on civic holidays in summer, a tap is turned somewhere and the bridge becomes a spectacular waterfall higher than Niagara Falls. ❑

Rodeos: an Alberta passion

Almost any summer or autumn weekend you'll find a rodeo somewhere in Alberta's cattle country.

Rodeos, big or small, will give you a day of excitement and fun along with a generous slice of western Canadian culture. In fairgrounds across the province, locals urge neighbors on as they compete at broncobusting, steer-wrestling and calf-roping, while big city stadiums attract professional rodeo riders from all over North America competing for valuable purses.

Originating in 16th-century Mexico, rodeos continue to demonstrate cowboy skills. For example, the broncobuster riding the wild horse must adapt to its bucking gait, while keeping his spurs above the animal's shoulders and without touching it with his hands.

The niceties of bullriding may be lost on the average tenderfoot tourist, but still it is one of the most exciting rodeo events. With only one hand on the single halter, a contestant has to ride the back of a huge Brahma bull for eight seconds. Then, after the inevitable fall, he escapes the enraged animal's flailing horns and hooves in his race for safety. The rider's sole protection is a team of fleet-footed rodeo clowns who run interference across the bull's path. To the crowd's delight they must sometimes take refuge in barrels strategically placed around the arena.

Tension gives way to hilarity in the wild cow-milking contest, in which participants are required to get at least some milk into their pails. Calf-roping calls for yet a different set of skills, including excellent horsemanship. Speed is everything here as the rider lassoes his sturdy calf, then dismounts and ties its legs. All the while the horse keeps the lasso rope taut, positioning the calf for branding.

These are just some traditional features of Alberta's rodeos. For pure drama, the larger events add chuck-wagon races. They hark back to an era when cowboys slept in bedrolls under a prairie sky and depended on these primitive mobile kitchens for meals.

On Saturday afternoons they would race their wagons home, and the last driver to reach home bought the first round in the town saloon. Now, with prizes as high as $150,000, modern races are held in heats of four competing wagons, each drawn by four horses with its own team of outriders. Each outfit must race around a figure-of-eight course, then dash to the finish line, where the iron stove is unloaded and a wood fire coaxed into flame. In view of the number of horses involved on a tricky course, accidents are commonplace.

The rodeo circuit spans all four western provinces, with events every weekend from mid-April through mid-October. They culminate with the Canadian Finals Rodeo held every November in Edmonton, pitting the country's top cowboys against the top-ranking bucking bulls and horses, the finale of a summer-long quest to be recognized as the best.

For "The Greatest Show on Earth," plan to attend the annual Calgary Exhibition and Stampede, which dates from 1912. Street parades, fireworks, pancake breakfasts cooked and served on city sidewalks, agricultural exhibitions, and funfairs are all part of the big show. During stampede week most locals and visitors go about their business dressed in western clothes. If that seems a bit ambitious, you should at least buy a ten-gallon hat. It's part of the rodeo tradition.

See Travel Tips for more on the Calgary Exhibition and Stampede.   ❏

RIGHT: Bareback, Bull Riding, Barrel Racing, Saddle Bronc, it's all at the Calgary Stampede.

SASKATCHEWAN

Canada's Old Northwest lies at the very heart of Saskatchewan, a province of highlands, plains, deserts, and lakes, once home to gangsters, gunrunners, and fur traders

Ahush falls over the crowd as the solemn jurors return to the courtroom with their verdict. They pass the dock where the defendant, Louis Riel, kneels in prayer. Riel has been charged with high treason for leading the Métis people in rebellion against the Crown. Riel rises to meet his fate. The clerk of the court asks the foreman if the jury members are agreed upon their verdict. "How say you: is the prisoner guilty or not guilty?"

"Guilty."

The foreman asks the judge for leniency, but the judge passes his sentence: Riel will hang. This scene from *The Trial of Louis Riel*, a play by John Coulter, is re-enacted every July at the Shumiatcher Theater at the MacKenzie Art Gallery, Regina. Each time the jury finds Riel guilty beyond a shadow of doubt.

Traitor to some, hero to others, Louis Riel twice tried to defend the rights of his people, the mixed-blood offspring of aboriginal women and French fur-traders. In 1869 he established a provisional Métis government in Manitoba, an ill-fated experiment in self-determination that ended when the Canadian militia put down the insurrection. Riel fled to Montana where he lived quietly as a school teacher.

Métis uprising

In 1884 federal agents began surveying Métis lands in the Saskatchewan River Valley in preparation for the coming of white settlers. Métis leaders again called on Riel, who returned to Canada to lead a ragtag army against the Canadian militia. The Métis' brief uprising ended in defeat at Batoche on May 15, 1885. Riel was tried in Regina, and was hanged later that year.

Saskatchewan has a hard time with heroes, especially with Riel, a fiery, French-speaking Catholic who once called himself "Prophet, Infallible Pontiff and Priest King." That sort of talk delayed his acceptance as an authentic folk hero for about 80 years; this

Main attractions
REGINA
QU'APPELLE RIVER VALLEY
MOOSE MOUNTAIN PROVINCIAL PARK
CYPRESS HILL INTERPROVINCIAL PARK
T. REX DISCOVERY CENTRE
SASKATOON
BATTLEFORD NATIONAL HISTORIC PARK

LEFT: an early morning dip.
BELOW: Louis Riel, leader of the Métis.

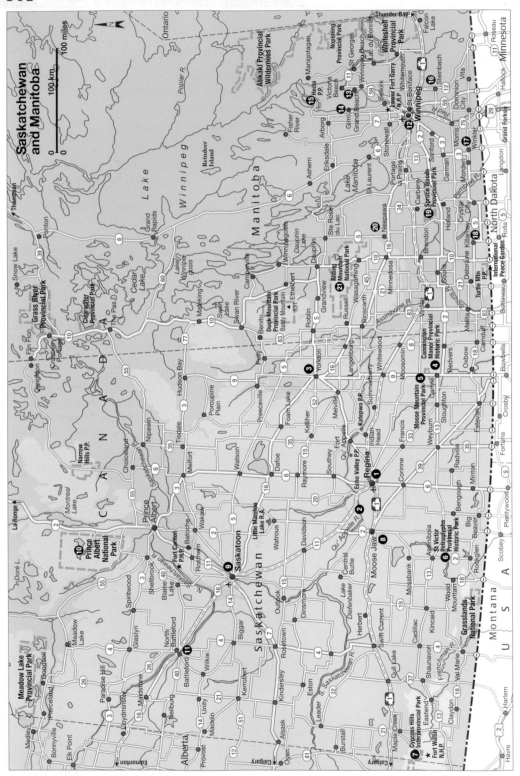

Saskatchewan and Manitoba

province demands humility, even from its hockey stars.

Saskatchewan's indifference to Riel has been due in part to another tragedy that looms larger in prairie hearts and minds: 10 lost years called the Great Depression, when hail, grasshoppers, and drought destroyed millions of acres of wheat, leaving the prairie provinces destitute. The inaction of government nurtured a cautious people skeptical about the pronouncements of politicians.

The 1930s will color provincial perceptions as long as anyone who lived through the era is alive. But the experience also produced sturdy self-reliance. Take Regina, for example, provincial capital and Queen City of the Plains. Its less-than-regal setting prompted Sir John A. Macdonald, Canada's first prime minister, to remark in 1886: "If you had a little more wood, and a little more water, I think the prospect would be improved."

The making of Regina

When **Regina ❶** was named capital of the newly-formed province of Saskatch-ewan in 1905, city leaders took Macdonald's suggestion of "more wood" to heart. They dammed muddy Wascana Creek to create a small lake, erected the Legislative Building, planted trees, laid out formal gardens, and splashed it all with fountains, including one from London's Trafalgar Square.

The result was **Wascana Center** (May–Oct; free), still an oasis of woods and water. Cyclists and joggers circle the lake, picnickers take a ferry out to shady **Willow Island** (mid-May–Labor Day Mon–Fri noon–4pm; charge), and bird-lovers feed the Canada geese at the waterfowl sanctuary.

You can also admire the Egyptian sculpture in the **University of Regina's** art gallery, or visit the **Saskatchewan Science Center** (daily; charge), featuring the human body, astronomy, and geology. The **Royal Saskatchewan Museum** (daily; donations requested), one of the finest natural history museums in Canada, offers an excellent introduction to the province's flora and fauna. Its First Nations Gallery traces 10,000 years of aboriginal history and culture.

Regina's 40-float Buffalo Days Parade in early August heralds a week of horse racing, rodeo riding, agricultural and livestock shows, and plenty of free entertainment.

BELOW: the Royal Canadian Mounted Police on parade.

The Mounties

Once headquarters for the North West Mounted Police (1882–1920), Regina is home to Canada's training academy for the Royal Canadian Mounted Police (RCMP). The history of the Mounties is central to Saskatchewan. In 1874 a detachment of North West Mounted Police was sent from Manitoba to establish law and order in the northwest, where the illegal trade in whiskey, guns, and fur was growing apace. Today the inter-provincial highway has been named the Red Coat Trail after their epic 1,300km (800 miles) trek west on horseback. They set up posts across the province, many of which have been restored and are open to visitors, including Fort Walsh in the Cypress Hills and Fort Battleford to the north.

The RCMP Heritage Centre (daily; charge) in Regina houses displays which trace the history of the force, from the early days of establishing law and order on the frontier to its modern role in solving crime through technology. Prized artifacts include the handcuffs worn by the rebel, Louis Riel, and the crucifix he carried to his execution on a site just outside the museum (daily; charge). In summer, the Sunset-Retreat ceremony includes a troop drill display in the famous scarlet tunic, military music, the lowering of the Canadian flag, and the March Past (July–Aug 15 Tue 6.45pm; free).

Grasslands National Park is a perfect spot to view the wide open landscapes of the prairies.

Wide and open prairies

To the northeast of Regina the **Qu'Appelle River Valley ❷** is a welcome change from the Queen City in topography and tempo. Carved by glacial meltwaters, this verdant furrow in the brown prairie divides the flat and open plains to the south and rolling parkland to the north. The valley is best appreciated from Highway 56 where it flanks the **Fishing Lakes** – four broadenings in the Qu'Appelle River. **Echo Valley** and **Katepwa** provincial parks offer camping, fishing, swimming, and nature trails that wind through wooded ravines.

Eastern spires crown many churches northeast of the Qu'Appelle, testifying to the predominance of Ukrainian settlers. In **Yorkton ❸**, a stroll through the **Western Development Museum** (Apr–

Dec daily, Jan–Mar Tue–Sun; charge) reveals household scenes of early settlers. A colorful Ukrainian pioneer kitchen, brightened with ceramic tiles and embroideries, contrasts with an austere English parlor. In the summer, the museum sponsors the Threshermen's Show, with wagon rides, threshing competitions, and square dancing.

British eccentricity

Eccentricity is a traditional English export, and few were more flamboyant than the aristocrats who tried to re-create a corner of their sceptered isle on the bald prairie at **Cannington Manor ❹** (mid-May–Labor Day Wed–Mon; charge), now an historic park 200km (125 miles) southeast of Regina. Here, in 1882, Captain Edward Pierce established a manorial village, where blue bloods bred racehorses, played rugby and cricket, and hired immigrants to do the farming. When the railroad bypassed Cannington, the settlement became a ghost town. Still standing are the **Maltby** and **Hewlett** houses, a carpenter's shop, and **All Saints Church**. Beside the log

BELOW: a grain elevator stands out in the distance. **RIGHT:** plenty to shout about.

church is the grave of Captain Pierce, far from his beloved England. **Moose Mountain Provincial Park 5**, 27km (17 miles) northwest, is a favorite with bird-watchers who scan the skies for turkey vultures, teal, ducks, and dozens of other species.

The Badlands

At the turn of the century the **Big Muddy Badlands** south of Regina sheltered a community every bit as strange as Cannington Manor. Law enforcement was finally established in the American territory of Montana to the south, so outlaws such as Bloody Knife and the Pigeon Toed Kid moved their base of operations north to the empty badlands, hiding out in caves between cattle rustling raids on Montana ranches. The rock formations depict 65 million years of history, glaciers advancing and retreating, carving rocky pleateaus and riverbeds.

St Victor Petroglyphs Provincial Historic Park 6, 150km (93 miles) southwest of Regina, tells a bit of the human history at a weirdly eroded sandstone outcrop, where prehistoric peoples carved dozens of designs in the soft rock. The outcrop also affords a panorama of chessboard crops, alkali lakes, escarpments, and brightly painted grain elevators, those "cathedrals of the plains" which give prairie towns their distinctive (and often only) skylines. South-central Saskatchewan is the province's predominantly French-speaking region but English is spoken just as readily.

Wood Mountain, 50km (30 miles) southwest of St Victor, briefly became a refuge to Sitting Bull and his band of Sioux after the Battle of Little Big Horn in 1876. The barracks and mess hall of a Mountie post established to watch over the Sioux have been re-created in the **Wood Mountain Post Historic Park** (June–July daily, Aug Thur–Mon; donation requested).

Cypress Hills Interprovincial Park 7, on the southwest border with Alberta, is situated in one of the few parts of Western Canada left uncovered by Ice Age glaciers. The hills rise like a long, green wedge near **Eastend** and extend west into Alberta. This oasis of coniferous forests, cool valleys, and

Grasslands National Park, on the border with the US, is a good site to view prairie wildlife, including black-tailed prairie dogs and endangered burrowing owls.

BELOW: horseback riding by the South Saskatchewan River.

Little Manitou Lake, 120km (70 miles) to the southeast of Saskatoon, was known by the Natives as "place of healing waters." It is now a well-established spa.

rounded buttes has long been a refuge for travelers from the hot and dusty plains. Campgrounds, cabins, tennis, golf, and skiing are all available at **Loch Leven**.

There is history here, too, at **Fort Walsh** (mid-May–Labor Day daily; charge), built by the North West Mounted Police in 1875 to bring order to the region, controlling the whiskey traders and horse thieves. They tried to manage the influx of Lakota refugees from the Great Sioux War of 1877–78. From 1878–82 it served as the headquarters of the North West Mounted Police. The re-created fort shelters the officers' quarters, commissioner's residence, and other buildings.

It's worth making a quick detour into Eastend to visit the **T. Rex Discovery Centre** (daily; charge), a state of the art facility housing the area's astounding fossil finds – including a complete Tyrannosaurus rex skeleton. There are tours throughout the day and a visit to an active quarry may be possible.

Fifty km (30 miles) north of Cypress Hills, the "Old Cow Town" of **Maple Creek** drowses beneath its canopy of cottonwoods. Capital of bone-dry ranchland, Maple Creek is about as Old West as Saskatchewan gets.

Heading back towards Regina, sheltered in a broad valley 312km (194 miles) east on Highway 1, **Moose Jaw** ❽ is a quiet city with a lively past. In the 1920s bootleggers and brothels flourished along **River Street**, and Chicago gangsters cooled their heels here. In the city's historic center, **Temple Gardens Mineral Spa** has a natural geo-thermal mineral water pool. And beneath the city, visitors experience the **Tunnels of Moose Jaw** (daily; charge), in which bootlegging tales are brought to life on interactive tours. Moose Jaw's **Western Development Museum** (daily; charge) emphasizes early transportation.

Saskatoon's temperance days

Bootleggers never darkened the streets of **Saskatoon** ❾, founded in 1884 as a temperance colony, a legacy that endures only in the sign for **Temperance Avenue**. One of the city's most defining features is the **North**

Saskatchewan River, which flows between high, wooded banks protected from development by parks. The summer cruise boat *Saskatoon Princess* passes riverside landmarks such as the turreted **Bessborough Hotel**, the **Mendel Art Gallery and Conservatory**, and the graystone buildings of the **University of Saskatchewan**. The university gives Saskatoon a cultural and cosmopolitan cachet. Five theater groups and a symphony orchestra perform here, and restaurants can be found that border on the bohemian.

Six weeks each summer, from early July to mid-August, sold-out audiences fill riverside tents during **Shakespeare on the Saskatchewan**. The ensemble has worked closely for more than 20 years, their innovative productions making Shakespeare's plays as pertinent to today's audiences as they ever were. The Persephone Theater in the new River Landing location offers national and international repertoire year round.

Historic sites

On the northern edge of Saskatoon the **Wanuskewin Heritage Park** (pronounced Wah-nus-kay-win, Cree for "peace of mind;" daily; charge) portrays 6,000 years of Northern Plains Indian culture. Here, with the help of native elders, visitors can see what life was like in a Plains Indian encampment, with cultural demonstrations and a restaurant serving authentic native cuisine.

Continuing north towards Prince Albert, a high bluff commands a mighty bend of the South Saskatchewan River where the Métis made their last stand during the Northwest Rebellion of 1885. The only remains of the Métis "capital" at **Batoche** are a simple white church, which served as Louis Riel's headquarters, and a bullet-scarred rectory. A few miles west stands palisaded **Fort Carlton** (mid-May–Labor Day; charge), once the most important fur-trade depot between the Red River and the Rockies.

Eighty km (50 miles) northeast of this battle-scarred valley is **Prince Albert**, gateway to the province's northlands, famous among fishermen for both its pristine lakes and its record-size trout.

Straddling a transition zone between parkland and boreal forest is **Prince Albert National Park ⑩**. Pines scent the air of **Waskesiu Lake**, park headquarters and an attractive year-round resort town. Sailboats and fishing boats are available at the townsite.

About 160km (100 miles) southwest of the park, **Battleford ⑪**, the former capital of the Northwest Territories, occupies a wooded setting far superior to that of its successor, Regina. The **Fort Battleford National Historic Park**, a Mountie post where Canada's last public execution took place in 1885, contains officers' quarters and residences, and other restored buildings. The fort's most poignant artifact recalls Louis Riel: the Gatling gun used in the battle of Batoche. The weapon's brass is as shiny as a century ago, when the dreams of the Métis died on a bluff above the North Saskatchewan River (mid-May–Labor Day daily; charge). ❏

TIP

In Prince Albert National Park, little-visited lakes, including Ajawaan, former home of the British naturalist, Grey Owl, can be seen at their best by canoe.

BELOW: dog sledding, the best way to get around.

MANITOBA

A traveler coming from the east through the forests of Ontario will find Manitoba bursting upon the senses with space, light, and color, with towns and cities as varied as the settlers themselves

A h, thinks the traveler, approaching Manitoba along northern Ontario's corridor of ragged trees, the prairie at last! Suddenly the land rolls on and on to a distant horizon. The sky, once confined to a gray strip above the highway, expands into a dome of deep blue.

Well, yes and no. The boreal forest is close by, blanketing the northern two-thirds of Manitoba with a lake-dotted wilderness that remains virtually unpopulated, and the sunny south refutes the old equation of prairie equals flat. West of Whiteshell Provincial Park, the land rises in stone and gravel ridges, flattens around Winnipeg, turns marshy south of Lake Manitoba, dips into the valleys of the Pembina and Assiniboine rivers, then rises again in the western uplands.

Thriving communities

The towns and cities are as varied as the land, and herein lies Manitoba's special appeal. Settlers from Europe and eastern Canada established towns with character, not just as supply centers for farmers, and proudly added their ethnic flavor: French Canadians at Ste Anne, Icelanders at Gimli, Russians at Tolstoi.

The vigor of these communities is remarkable considering the overwhelming presence of **Winnipeg** ⑫, provincial capital and home to 700,000 people, more than 60 percent of Manitoba's population.

Provincial capital

Winnipeg sometimes startles visitors with its canopy of trees contrasting visibly with the surrounding treeless prairie. There's no mistaking the junction of Portage and Main, however, reputedly the widest, windiest street corner in Canada. But downtown avenues curve with the Assiniboine and Red rivers, giving some buildings delightfully quirky angles and avoiding the West's usual rigid street grid. **The Forks**, dubbed Winnipeg's meeting place, is the site of several summer festivals.

Main attractions
WINNIPEG
GRAND BEACH
GIMLI
HECLA ISLAND
STEINBACH
KILLARNEY
SPIRIT SANDHILLS
NEEPAWA
RIDING MOUNTAIN NATIONAL PARK

LEFT: polar bear statues.
BELOW: the Winnipeg Mint.

Within the strikingly designed structure of the Winnipeg Art Gallery is the world's largest collection of contemporary Inuit art.

BELOW: the Legislative Building.

Outstanding green swathes are a feature in Assiniboine Park. Behind the pavilion is the new Lyric Outdoor Stage for performances, including the Royal Winnipeg Ballet's annual Ballet in the Park. Also in the park are the tropical **Palm House Conservatory** (daily; free), and the **Zoo** (daily; charge) with over 1,200 creatures, including polar bears.

Winnipeg is also an old city in a young land. The first Europeans to build on this site were French fur traders who constructed Fort Rouge in 1738 near the flood-prone confluence of the Red and Assiniboine rivers,

silt-laden waterways which eventually gave the city its Cree name of *Winnipi* (muddy water). After the French came those fierce fur-trade rivals, the London-based Hudson's Bay Company and the North West Company of Montréal. During the late 18th and early 19th centuries, the two companies built a series of palisaded forts within shooting distance near the Assiniboine and Red rivers.

In 1812 Scottish crofters, who had been turned out of their homes by the Highland Clearances, arrived on the scene with a few farming implements and a bull and a cow named Adam and Eve. The trip, tools, and livestock were courtesy of the Scottish humanitarian Lord Selkirk, who established farming colonies throughout North America for homeless Highlanders. But, like cattle ranchers and sheep farmers, fur traders and settlers did not mix. Conflict erupted on June 19, 1816, when Métis employees of the North West Company slaughtered 20 settlers in what became known as the Seven Oaks Incident.

Lord Selkirk heard the bad news in Montréal, and promptly marched

west with a private army. He arrested the fur traders and their Métis employees, then re-established his settlement, which eventually prospered. There are several reminders of the fur-trade era in Winnipeg. **Grant's Old Mill** (June–Aug; charge) is a working replica of the settlement's first gristmill, built in 1829 by Cuthbert Grant, leader of the Métis at the massacre.

The **Seven Oaks House** (late May–Labor Day daily; donation requested) and the **Ross House** (June–Aug Wed–Sun; free), both of which were built in the 1850s by fur traders, are museums worth visiting, as is the **Manitoba Museum** (mid-May–Labor Day daily, Sept–May Tue–Sun; charge). Its most impressive fur-trade display is a full-size replica of the *Nonsuch*, a Hudson's Bay Company vessel that in 1668 carried the very first cargo of furs from Canada to England.

The most evocative relic of this exciting era is the lone remaining gate of the last of the five forts built in the area, **Upper Fort Garry**, built by the Hudson's Bay Company in 1836, and now preserved in a quiet park in the shadow of the turreted **Fort Garry Hotel**. This hotel came from the later railway era, opened in 1913 as an elegant Grand Trunk Pacific Railway hotel for passengers breaking the long journey across the country.

Multicultural influences

The city's economic good times arrived with the completion of the Canadian-Pacific Railway in 1885 and the hundreds of thousands of immigrants who followed the ribbon of steel: Europeans fleeing persecution, British city-dwellers hungry for land, Americans who saw their own West filling up. Almost all came through Winnipeg, and enough stayed on to swell the city's population.

Each year for two weeks in August, Winnipeg remembers its rich ethnic mosaic with **Folklorama**, a festival held in some 40 informal pavilions scattered throughout the city. In the evening, church basements and school auditoriums are filled with the aromas of Polish sausage and Ukrainian cabbage rolls, and the strains of German polkas and Greek *sirtakis*,

The Manitoba Museum offers the best introduction to the province's history – including the Hudson's Bay Company Gallery, which highlights the fur trade's colorful, 300-year history.

LEFT: the Leo Mol Sculpture Garden in Assiniboine Park.
BELOW: performers at Folklorama.

Step back to the 19th century at Riel House, the family home of Louis Riel, leader of the Métis, 330 River Road, St Vital (mid-May–Labor Day daily; charge).

as each group celebrates its heritage with food, song, and dance. Today, Filipinos are Winnipeg's largest immigrant group.

Ukrainian Canadians are particularly prominent in Winnipeg. The pear-shaped domes of half-a-dozen major churches grace the skyline, and the **Oseredok Ukrainian Cultural and Educational Center** contains a museum (Mon–Sat 10am–4pm, July–Aug also Sun 1–4pm; charge) displaying such treasures as 17th-century church vestments, as well as a series of rooms decorated with the hand-carved furniture and hand-painted ceramics typically found in village homes.

East across the Red River is **St Boniface**, bastion of French culture in western Canada, where streets are *rues*, and Orthodox domes yield to the belfries of **St Boniface Basilica**, built in 1908 and partially destroyed by fire in 1968. Close by, on the site of **Fort Gibraltar** (late May–Aug 30 Wed–Sun; charge), a 1978 replica of the fort built by the North West Company in 1809 recaptures the height of the fur trade with a depiction of life at the fort in 1814. In

February, the fort is the focal point for the 40-year old **Festival du Voyageur**, a ten-day celebration of the history of the province (complete with competitions ranging from snow sculpture to beard-growing to fiddling).

Winnipeg still offers the greatest cultural diversity in the prairies. Visitors between September and May can enjoy the Manitoba Opera Company, the Winnipeg Symphony Orchestra, mainstream plays at the Manitoba Theater Center, and experimental works at the intimate MTC Warehouse Theater. And if you're really lucky, the celebrated Royal Winnipeg Ballet will be in town during your visit.

Once considered something of a dowager by the younger, upstart prairie communities such as Calgary and Edmonton, Winnipeg is turning its age into an asset with a flurry of sandblasting, wood stripping, and brass polishing. This fling with the past is centered on the historic **Exchange District**, a 15-block area which is bounded by Main and Princess Streets, and William and Notre Dame Avenues. Here, the largest concentration of commercial,

BELOW: St Boniface Basilica.
RIGHT: windmill at the Mennonite Museum, Steinbach.

early 20th-century architecture in the West has been given a new lease of life. It's an area alive with shopping, restaurants, and night life.

Visitors who want more tranquil pursuits can board the *Paddlewheel Princess* or the *Paddlewheel Queen*, and cruise north on the Red River to **Lower Fort Garry National Historic Park** (mid-May–Sept 30 daily; charge), North America's last intact stone fur-trade fort and the most impressive historic site on the prairies, restored to the 1850s era. The landscaped grounds and the riverside setting are complemented by costumed attendants demonstrating how old-timers made candles and pressed beaver pelts into 41kg (90-pound) bales for shipment back to Europe.

Lakeside retreats

Larger than Lake Ontario, vast **Lake Winnipeg** stretches north into the wilderness. Cottage communities ring its southern end: **Grand Beach** ⓭, 87km (54 miles) north of the provincial capital, **Winnipeg Beach** and **Victoria Beach**, all slightly commercialized

Paddling at Winnipeg Beach.

and crowded but blessed with long stretches of white sand where it's still possible to find seclusion.

Seventy-six kilometers (47 miles) north on the western shore, the Icelandic community of **Gimli** ⓮ remembers its past with a statue of a Viking and the **New Icelandic Heritage Museum** (daily; charge), which tells the story of the Icelandic experience in North America and explains the fishing economy established on Lake Winnipeg by the town's forebears. **Hecla Island** ⓯, 50km (30 miles) north, once a self-governing Icelandic republic, is now part of a provincial park. Sunrise bird-watching safaris, hiking and ski

BELOW: the coastline at Churchill.

trails, tennis courts, and a fine golf course are among the attractions.

The good earth

South of Winnipeg stretches flat farmland with rich, black gumbo soil of silt and clay. This land was described by the 18th-century fur trader Alexander Henry as "a kind of mortar that adheres to the foot like tar." In the middle stands **Steinbach** ⑯, whose tidy streets and freshly painted houses reflect the enduring values of the town's industrious Mennonite founders. The **Mennonite Heritage Village** (May–Sept daily, Oct–Apr Tue–Fri; charge) recalls the old ways with reconstructed thatched-roof cabins, a blacksmith's shop, and a wind-driven gristmill. Excellent borscht and spicy sausages are served at the museum restaurant.

West of the Red River and south to the American border lies the **Pembina Triangle**. Sheltered by the gentle Pembina Hills, the region has Manitoba's longest growing season and the only apple orchards between the Niagara Peninsula and the Okanagan Valley.

Seemingly every town in the region advertises the local agricultural specialty with theme fairs. Fields of sunflowers nodding in hot prairie breezes around the Mennonite community of **Altona**, 98km (61 miles) south of Winnipeg, inspired the Manitoba Sunflower Festival, held in July. Nearby **Winkler** ⑰, 24km (15 miles) west, settled by Anabaptist Hutterites, holds the Winkler Harvest Festival each August with barbecues, pancake breakfasts, and old-time sidewalk sales.

The **Pembina Valley** is steep enough at **La Rivière**, 61km (38 miles) west of Winkler, for a downhill ski run. The valley was carved by the willow-fringed Pembina River, which broadens into a chain of sparkling canoeing and fishing lakes – **Pelican**, **Lorne**, **Louise**, and **Rock**.

About 64km (40 miles) west, the attractive town of **Killarney** ⑱ has a small lake at its feet and a hill wooded with maple and oak at its back. This setting, said to be reminiscent of Kerry, Ireland, has produced Killarney's Celtic touches: a green fire engine, and Erin Park with its replica of the Blarney Stone.

BELOW: sunflowers are grown for oil in Manitoba.

The **International Peace Garden**, 32km (20 miles) southwest of Killarney, straddles the North Dakota-Manitoba border, near the geographical center of the continent. Dr Henry Moore, an ardent gardener from Toronto, tabled a modest proposal for a joint peace park in 1929 at a meeting of the Gardeners Association of North America. Three years later, his dream became a reality.

If all this cultivation creates a craving for wilderness, visit the **Spirit Sandhills** in **Spruce Woods Provincial Park** ⓳, 145km (90 miles) west of Winnipeg: grassy plains and barren sand dunes along the sinuous Assiniboine River. The sandhills were formed about 12,000 years ago when a mile-wide glacial river deposited a vast delta of sand, silt, and gravel. Ernest Thompson Seton, a naturalist-author who homesteaded near Carberry in the 1880s, made them the setting for his book, *The Trail of the Sandhill Stag*. He spent every spare moment in what came to be known as "Seton's Kingdom" observing grouse, deer, and wolves. Be sure to try the self-guiding **Spirit Hills Trail**, which winds through barren dunes inhabited by rarities like hognose snakes, spadefoot toads, and northern prairie skinks. Fifty kilometers (30 miles) west lies **Brandon**, noted for handsome public buildings and gracious private homes dating from the early 1900s.

Highway 10 leads north past fields of wheat and rye interspersed with pothole lakes that attract millions of ducks and geese during spring and fall migrations. A short detour takes you to **Neepawa** ⓴, 75km (47 miles) northeast of Brandon, where you can visit the childhood home of the acclaimed Canadian author Margaret Laurence (mid-May–Sept 30 daily; charge), before continuing north into the forests of **Riding Mountain National Park** ㉑.

Approaching the park from this direction, the usual reaction is: *Where's the mountain?* Patience will be rewarded on reaching the edge of the park, where the "mountain" rises abruptly, 450 meters (1,500ft), above a patchwork of crops: yellow rapeseed, brown squares of oats and barley, and rolling green and gold wheatfields. ❑

BELOW:
the lights of the
Aurora Borealis.

Polar Bear Capital

Getting to the polar bear capital of the world is a challenge (there are no roads in, so air and rail are the only options), but **Churchill** offers spectacular nature tourism. In May through July, over 200 species of migratory birds pass through the area.

Summer brings more than 3,000 beluga whales to the mouth of the Churchill River to feed. Polar bear tours take place in October and November. The aurora borealis are visible throughout the year, but are most spectacular in January through March. There isn't much else to do during the long winter nights, but a visit to the **Eskimo Museum** (June–Oct Mon 1–5pm, Tue–Sat 9am–noon and 1–5pm, Nov–May Mon–Sat 1–4.30pm; donation requested) will shed light on Inuit culture and its 4,000-year history.

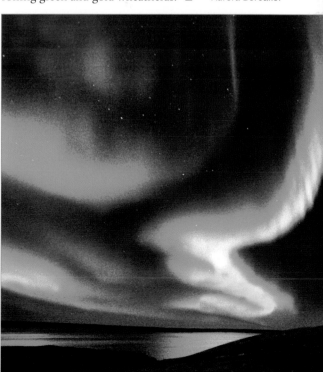

THE NORTH

The long sunny days of summer lend themselves to exploring what is perhaps Canada's last uncharted frontier

The hardest thing to understand about the Canadian North is its magnitude. Although the three territories combined are home to a scant 100,000 people, the land north of 60 degrees latitude comprises one-third of the country. It is massive, larger than India and about ten times the size of Germany. Here it genuinely *is* bitterly cold in winter, here some people *do* live in snow huts, and here dogsled racing across the frozen tundra *is* a popular form of entertainment.

Despite its formidable geography and vast distances separating remote outposts, the North is the natural habitat of the "first Canadians," the Inuit, who have survived here for thousands of years and who, in 1999, finally acquired their own territory of Nunavut.

Canada's northern hinterland is not the vacation spot for everyone, as it is difficult to get to and offers limited accommodation and often challenging weather. But for those intrigued by unusual habitats, landscapes, and wildlife, the North presents an exciting adventure. The Yukon, the Northwest Territories, and Nunavut are regions of delicately balanced ecosystems and unparalleled glacial beauty.

The Yukon is the first of Canada's three northern territories to be explored. Here, the reader can discover the significance of the gold rush for Canada's neglected North along with a description of the Yukon's varied geography and spectacular vistas.

The Northwest Territories are treated in similar fashion, although with greater emphasis on geological formations and wildlife. As Nunavut is the most recently created territory, its political evolution is touched upon, along with the diverse range of activities awaiting its visitors.

The three chapters together present a compelling picture of the radically different world looming over Canada's southern provinces. And, as the region being most drastically affected by climate change, it is the one which is evolving the fastest. ❑

PRECEDING PAGES: panning for gold at an early age in the Yukon.
LEFT: an *inukshuk* (standing stone) in the twilight.
ABOVE: musk oxen, Devon Island; delphiniums in the Yukon; an Eskimo doll.

THE YUKON

Today, tourists trace the footsteps of the gold prospectors who once made their fortunes in this northerly outpost. Glaciers, wide plateaus, and magnificent mountains characterize the Yukon

Before 1896, the northwest corner of Canada was a mountainous wilderness where few outsiders, besides the occasional whaler and fur trader, ventured. The Dene had lived here for perhaps 60,000 years, but it was terra incognita for the rest of the world. But in 1896 this forgotten land was suddenly overrun by man and beast. Gold, and lots of it, had been discovered in the Klondike.

The young Dominion of Canada had to deal with the headaches that accompany sudden wealth. If the government could not bring order (or at least a civilizing influence) to the North, it might lose millions in gold tax revenues. Therefore, the queen's ministers, in recognition of the sudden prominence of a land most only knew about from sketchy maps, decided to redraw those maps. In 1898, they roped off the northwest corner of the North-west Territories and created the Yukon Territory. What the federal officials lassoed in their haste to reassert Canadian sovereignty is a territory larger than the New England States, double the land mass of the British Isles, and two-and-a-half times the size of Texas.

This is a land of wild beauty and varied landscapes known as part of the Western Highlands. Along the eastern border of the territory there lie the **Mackenzie Mountains** that straddle the border with the Northwest Territories (N.W.T.) and gently roll up to the mouth of the **Mackenzie River**. Within

this range there are rivers carved into the rock by ancient glaciers. One such river, the **Nahanni**, contains Virginia Falls. However, unlike Ontario's great Niagara, no one has ever attempted to go over these falls in a barrel – it is twice the height, although much narrower and virtually unknown to anyone who hasn't been to the Yukon.

Mountain country

Mountains are an omnipresent sight in the Yukon. The **Selwyn Mountains** lie to the west of the Mackenzie

PRECEDING PAGES: a dog-sled team racing. **LEFT:** First Nations drummer. **BELOW:** the White Pass and Yukon Route.

mountain range and to the north are the very ancient **Ogilvie Mountains**.

The best known peaks are **St Elias** and **Mount Logan** on the province's southwest border with Alaska. Standing at 5,959 meters (19,550ft), Mount Logan is second only to Mount McKinley in Alaska as the highest mountain in North America.

Many peaks in the St Elias Range poke through glaciers that are in part sustained by the "chill factor" associated with great heights. The St Elias Range, besides offering some of the most spectacular sights in the world, also acts to block much of the moisture coming off the Pacific Ocean. It is because of this that most of the interior of the Yukon receives little precipitation. The average in **Whitehorse** ❶, capital of the Yukon, is 26cm (10 inches) a year. In the High Arctic there is less precipitation than farther south. Yet the Yukon does receive more precipitation than the N.W.T. and, because of the relatively cold temperatures and high altitudes, whatever snow falls in winter will not melt until spring. This snow helps provide excellent cross-country trails.

Plateau land

Between the mountain ranges are plateaus, the **Pelly**, the **Porcupine**, and the **Yukon**. Each plateau is named after the river that flows through it. The Yukon Plateau is the largest of the three. Although glaciers remain in Yukon Territory, much of the Yukon Plateau was untouched by the last glacial era and for this reason it is unique among geological areas in North America. Thus the Yukon River, unlike the other northern rivers that felt the effects of glaciation, flows gently through the plateau and is devoid of rapids, falls, and other such hazards that can make canoe trips a thrilling and dangerous excursion. Ice-free millennia have allowed the Yukon River to find its own path.

Within the plateau one finds mountains that have dome-like summits rising to heights of 1,800 meters (6,000ft). These domes were formed by a million years of sediment accumulating on top of the mountains. Unlike the neighboring ranges, such as the Mackenzie or St Elias that have been scoured by glaciers and left with

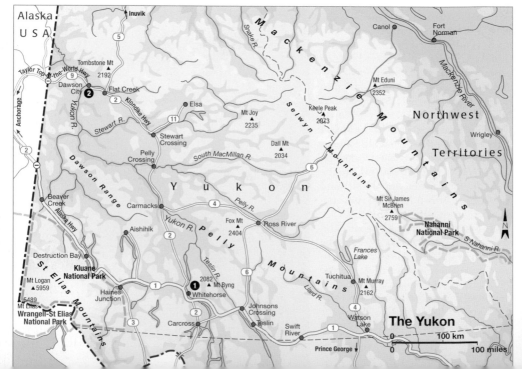

whittled-down pencil-shaped peaks, the mountains of the Yukon Plateau have few rocky outcroppings.

This plateau is a relic of another age, one that stands apart from the geological violence of the last Ice Age. For that reason, ancient mastodon and mammoth species survived far longer here. Likewise, the plateau offered shelter for the people who entered North America across the Bering Strait thousands of years ago.

Owing to the plenitude of vegetation there is an excellent food supply to support the many species of animals, including moose, caribou, Dall sheep, mountain goats, cougars, grizzly, and black bears. Within the rivers of the Yukon there are usually large runs of salmon – they hatch in the creeks and rivers that empty into the Pacific, eventually returning to spawn and die.

Golden days

There was a time when not only thousands of salmon swam through the Yukon River, but thousands of men waded into her. Unlike the salmon that are driven by biological imperative, these men were driven by the promise of the placer gold that laid buried deep in the sediment of river beds.

In contrast to the manner in which it is extracted, placer gold is created by the eternally slow process of erosion. Gradually the river flows over a rock face wearing down the quartz-bearing gold until it breaks off into pieces varying anywhere in size from that of a tennis ball to a microscopic speck.

This iridescent mineral lay complacently in Yukon river beds for thousands of years. Legend has it that an American, George Washington Carmack, and two Tagish First Nations scouts, Skookum Jim and Dawson Charlie, struck gold at **Rabbit Creek** (renamed **Bonanza**) on August 17 1896, a day that is now a territorial holiday. Within two years, the population of Dawson City had exploded to more than 40,000. Eventually, close to 80,000 men would scurry northward to seek their fortune, with the gold stories that were published in William Randolph Hearst's hyperbolic newspapers rattling in their heads. The routes that some miners chose to take were

Map opposite

TIP

To the east of Yukon, Nahanni National Park features gorges deeper than the Grand Canyon. Visit Fort Simpson to arrange tours, flights, and canoe rentals.

BELOW: gold panning on Discovery Creek.

The Yukon's Cities

Whitehorse began as a Yukon River shanty town in the late 1890s, its population ebbing and flowing with the gold rush. Its future was secured with the construction of the Alaska Highway in 1942. Visit the steamboat *SS Klondike II* (mid-May–mid-Sept; charge), one of several hundred steamwheelers that once plied the river to Dawson City. Also worth a visit is the spectacular Miles Canyon, 9km (6 miles) south.

Dawson City was the largest city in western Canada in 1898, when the gold rush brought hopeful prospectors by the tens of thousands. Some of the original theaters, bars, and brothels that entertained them remain. Start at the Front Street Visitor Reception Center, then relive the Klondike at the Dawson City Museum (mid-May–Labor Day daily; charge).

rather bizarre. A group of Edmonton businessmen, for instance, advertised a trail through the rugged interior of Alberta and British Columbia. Little did those who took this passage know that Dawson City, the center of the gold rush, lay a few thousand miles away and that this "trail" was a hoax. Of the thousands who attempted this route, many lost their lives and only a handful managed to straggle on into the Yukon.

Soapy Smith and Sam Steele

A more conventional route was to travel by steamer to Skagway, Alaska, and then onwards through either the White Pass or the Chilkoot Pass into Yukon. Although these trails were better than the Edmonton Trail, they posed many dangers: not the least of which was the other people encountered along the way. In Skagway a ne'er-do-well named "Soapy" Smith managed to gather around him a rather unscrupulous flock who fleeced many a would-be prospector of his stake long before he got to Dawson. The Wild

West made quite a revival in northern Skagway. Soapy's downfall came when a group of armed townsfolk drew him and his boys out. The gang quickly scattered; Soapy held his ground and was shot dead, but not until he had managed to mortally wound the vigilante who shot him.

The Canadian authorities looked upon both the outlaw activity and the vigilantism with disdain. The Canadian cabinet ordered that 300 North West Mounted Police be sent to the Yukon.

They were headed by a man whose name almost stereotypically symbolized not only his own character but that of his police force – Sam Steele. Steele was charged with several tasks, the first of which was to enforce and impress upon the prospectors Canadian sovereignty. More than 90 percent of those entering the Yukon were Americans. Another of Steele's responsibilities was to ensure that every man and woman entering the Yukon had enough supplies to last an entire year. Steele stationed Mounties at all mountain passes and ordered that all would-be Yukoners with less than 453kg (1,000lbs) of equipment and food be turned back. This was a sensible order: you could hope for, but not depend on, charity in the Yukon.

Carrying the requisite equipment through mountain passes 1,160 meters (3,800ft) or more in height was a Herculean task. In April of 1898, with spring well on its way, 63 people were smothered to death in an avalanche at Chilkoot Pass. Within a day the pass was reopened and people continued their grim ascent.

Boom to bust

During the early years of the gold rush in **Dawson City** ②, inflation was rampant: oranges sold for 50 cents apiece and a pint of champagne cost $40. Gold poured out of the Yukon. In 1896, $300,000-worth of gold was produced; the following year $2.5 million-worth was mined; in 1898, $10 million in gold was extracted; and by

1900, the peak year, more than $22 million-worth of gold was taken from the Yukon. Yet every boom has a bust and the Yukon's halcyon days began to fade in 1902. There was simply less gold to be had. In addition, large companies began filing claims on many "used" claims and then reworking them. In this way corporations consolidated the gold industry and displaced the traditional small-time operators. They packed up and left, many of them seeking the next new frontier.

With the exodus of the original "sourdoughs" there followed the closing of the dancehalls, gambling parlors, and drinking establishments. The freewheeling and freespirited days were over. At the height of the gold rush the Klondike region had a population of 30,000, some 16,000 of whom were in Dawson City. By 1910 there were only 1,000 inhabitants. Today, just less than 2,000 people live there, and few are prospectors.

There has been speculation that both the Yukon and Canada missed a great opportunity to develop what would have become an indigenous industry. If the small-time operator had been encouraged to stay, perhaps a tertiary industry could have sustained the remarkable culture. Interestingly, there remain roughly 200 one- or two-man placer-gold outfits who are still working the rivers of the Yukon, long after the large gold companies have left.

Mining was the backbone of the Yukon's economy. When the gold production began to slow, large zinc, lead, and silver deposits were discovered, allowing mining to continue.

The Yukon today

In recent years, tourism has played an increasingly important role in the Yukon. Naturally, Klondike nostalgia is used as a major theme. So even if the gold boom broke more than 100 years ago, today its legacy is still paying a modest dividend. In Dawson City, the former capital of the Yukon and hub of the gold rush, there stands Canada's first legalized casino. In the summer months this little gambling establishment, along with a Klondike-style dance revue, is a reminder that the Yukon was founded by hustlers, gold diggers, and dreamers, not fishermen or farmers. There are tours that will take travelers down the same rivers that paddlewheelers once traveled.

Along the riverbanks and hiking trails are the remains of the prospectors' old camps and abandoned towns; tourists to the Territory can relive the "golden days" of the Yukon's Klondike. Ironically, many in the tourist industry now wish to restrict or eliminate the activities of the modern placer-gold prospectors. Placer-gold extraction has done and can do tremendous environmental damage to riverbeds.

With all the emphasis on Yukon's faded "glory days," there is another perspective. To understand the region from a First Nations viewpoint, visit **Danoja Zho (Long Time Ago) Cultural Center** (June–Sept Mon–Sat, Oct–Apr by appointment), a community and heritage center for Tr'ondëk Hwëch'in culture. ❑

The Porcupine Caribou – an estimated 100,000 of them – migrate hundreds of miles across Alaska and the Yukon as they have done for tens of thousands of years.

BELOW: the steamer, SS *Keno*, used to transport silver, lead and zinc ore from the Mayo District to Stewart.

LIVING IN A WHITE WORLD OF SNOW

In a country where great numbers of people exist amidst a snowy white blanket for many months of the year, how do they cope with everyday life?

Snow angels practically define a Canadian childhood. You plonk yourself down on your back, flap your legs and arms up and down over the snow's soft surface, then leap up to inspect the enchanting result. This instinctive communing with nature frequently launches a lifelong affair with snow. Every winter, lakes, rivers, even back yards, are converted into ice rinks, where youngsters play hockey and their parents simply skate. Countless Canadians are addicted to outdoor activities from skiing to snowshoeing, snowmobiling, dogsledding, ice fishing, and horse-drawn sleigh rides.

Indoor Pursuits

Not all Canadians welcome snow with such enthusiasm. Fortunately winter also heralds a plethora of cultural activities, from experimental theater to symphony concerts and operatic galas, literary fests and eye-popping art exhibits. Sports fans' weekends revolve around *Hockey Night in Canada*, a long-standing Saturday-night TV fixture. January and February's gloom is often brightened by extravagant culinary and wine-tastings, and by March stores are awash with sparkling springtime fashions and Easter bunnies.

In urban centers, snow is more easily avoided. From Calgary to St John's, Canadians take refuge in networks of underground passageways where shops, restaurants, theaters, even ice rinks, offer diversions galore from the harsh reality of winter.

ABOVE: playing indoors with a traditional toy in Nanuvut.

LEFT: snowmobiles have largely replaced the dogsled teams as a means of transport across the snow. The huskies' diet of Arctic char, caribou, and seal meat enabled them to work for days on end without food when supplies were low. Today fuel supplies are flown in to remote areas.

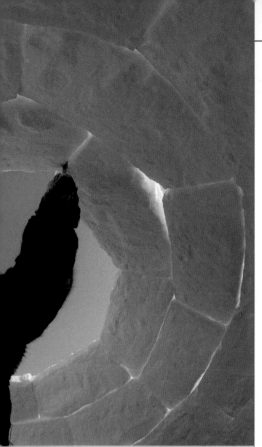

ABOVE: igloo building began in the fall, when snow was compacted into blocks. The inhabitants depended on further snow for insulation.

BELOW: Montréal's Underground City, a network of subway lines and shop filled tunnels, make it possible to live a satisfying life without stepping outside, and is a welcoming diversion to the harsh winters.

SURVIVAL IN THE FAR NORTH

Hunting and trapping have been the lifeline of Arctic communities for several thousands of years. Huskies (or *qimmiit*) were the workhorses of the Arctic, pulling wooden sleds *(qamutiit)* carrying Inuit hunters and their provisions for hundreds of miles during the fall, when extensive caribou hunts were necessary to provide sufficient food for the family. *Inukshuks*, which were slabs of rock piled high, were built to guide startled caribou into a blind where hunters waited with bows and arrows. Once the meat was removed, the skins were turned into clothing and blankets.

Winter was spent largely within their igloos, which were heated by *qulliqs* – soapstone oil lamps fueled by seal blubber. To break the monotony, storytelling, wrestling contests, throat singing, and drum dances took place in a *qaggiq*, which was a large snowhouse.

In the longer days of March, the huskies helped to locate seal breathing-holes in the ice, and the hunters then waited patiently with their harpoons for seals to emerge. Spring and summer saw the return of Arctic char, birds, and an abundance of Arctic berries. Inuit survival depended on the riches of both land and sea.

LEFT: snow tubing has taken off in a big way, and has become a favorite family activity.

RIGHT: in the Yukon, much of the land lies under a snowy blanket from October to April, providing opportunities for all kinds of outdoor pursuits.

THE NORTHWEST TERRITORIES

Far away from the pressures of urban life, the Northwest Territories conceal a sparkling landscape of mountains, rivers, and canyons. Here visitors can climb, canoe, fish, and watch wildlife

Many would picture the Northwest Territories as a flat and perennially icy slab stretching from the 60th parallel toward the North Pole, with the occasional polar bear or Inuit igloo to give some relief to this monotonous landscape. However, the landscape is anything but monotonous, and it is not one land but a multitude of lands – lands that are foreign to most people, and yet so mystical that each person who visits there is not so much a tourist as an explorer.

The Northwest Territories cover an immense area of almost 1.2 million sq km (over 450,000 sq miles). To gain some insight into how large this is, combine Spain, France, Switzerland, the Netherlands, and Belgium. The southern border stretches across Saskatchewan, Alberta, and part of British Columbia, along the 60th parallel and stretches 3,400km (2,110 miles) up to the North Pole. This means that the total landmass of the N.W.T. is larger than Texas, Oklahoma, Arkansas, and Louisiana combined, yet the area has a population of a mere 43,000.

More than half of these residents are aboriginal, some of whom have ancestors that lived on this land since the last Ice Age.

Scars of the Ice Age

Venturing north above the tree line into the tundra, where it is too cold for lush vegetation and forests to survive, the scars of thousands of centuries of geological history stand before the eyes. It was only 10,000 years ago that the last Ice Age, the Pleistocene, finally retreated from much of the area, leaving behind moraines, dry gravel beds, and drumlins.

There are also thousands upon thousands of rivers and lakes that cover more than half of the territory's landmass. Many of these lakes and rivers, particularly those in the Mackenzie Delta, were formed by glaciers creating indentations in the earth and leaving behind melted glacial ice.

Main attractions
YELLOWKNIFE
WOOD BUFFALO NATIONAL PARK
NAHANNI NATIONAL PARK
PRINCE OF WALES NORTHERN
   HERITAGE CENTER

LEFT: Inuit in caribou fur.
BELOW: salt flats, Wood Buffalo National Park.

TIP

To view the tundra and mountains north of the Arctic Circle, take the 730km (450-mile) Dempster Highway from Dawson City, Yukon, to Inuvik, N.W.T.

Rivers and lakes notwithstanding, much of the territory is classified by geographers as desert. The stereotypical picture of the Canadian North being smothered in snow is surprisingly inaccurate. In fact, the mean annual precipitation for both the eastern and western Arctic is only 30cm (12 inches), which is the equivalent of just a single Montréal snowstorm.

During the long Arctic winters, however, the sun may only appear for a few brief hours, if at all, so whatever snow does fall will not melt until spring. Temperatures in the region are legendary. At Inuvik, the territory's capital, two degrees north of the Arctic Circle, the average winter temperature drops to a perishing –31°C (–24°F) at night, while in July, its warmest month, it averages close to 20°C (68°F).

For a traveler trying to plan what clothing to pack for an adventure – which is what any trip to the Northwest Territories will be – the standard rule of lots of layers applies. The temperature may vary, but one thing does not. When summer arrives here the sun only just dips into the horizon before beginning its slow upward journey, and conditions are ideal for hiking or camping. In fact, the summer in this region is remarkably similar to that in the rest of Canada, except of course that there is more sunshine and a much lower probability of rain in the north.

Breeding grounds

While the Northwest Territories receives relatively few human visitors, it is estimated that 12 percent of North America's bird population breeds here during the spring and summer months. Close to 300 species are tracked here, with biologists looking to learn more about migratory habits. They believe that one of the main attractions to this part of North America is the relative lack of predators and, in summer, an abundant source of food.

This is a birder's paradise, as it provides the potential of seven different species of owls, a huge variety of eagles, hawks, and other raptors. Ocean birds, shore birds, and even songbirds can be spotted here, provided the right planning is undertaken. The land is so vast that it makes sense to rely on the tour

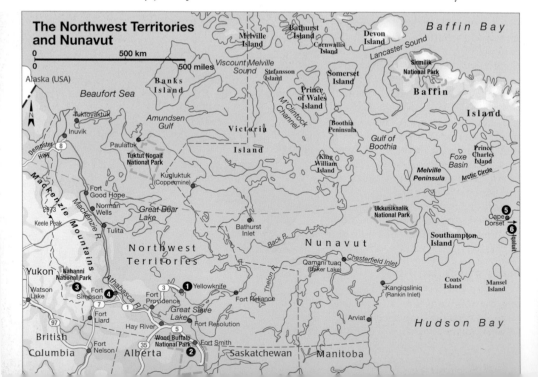

The Northwest Territories and Nunavut

operators who cater to keen birders and photographers for help with itineraries and timing.

Below the tree line, where the weather is less harsh and the trees offer protection from the elements, there are moose, beaver, marten, muskrat, red fox, timber wolf, and black bear, as well as massive herds of caribou and bison. Above the tree line are arctic wolves with white coats, as well as arctic fox, lemmings and, in the summer and fall, caribou. Along the coastline and on the islands polar bears, seals, walrus, and even lemmings can be seen. **Banks, Victoria, and Melville Islands** in the far north are inhabited by the exotic, hirsute musk ox.

Life in the tundra

Perhaps one of the most remarkable facts about survival on the tundra is the dependency of all life on soil frozen to a depth of between 30 and 300 meters (100 to 1,000ft). This ground is appropriately called permafrost. During the summer, the sun's rays are able to melt topsoil here to a depth of 24 meters (80ft). It is within this layer of

soil that small organisms, including lichen, grow. Lichen and low-lying vegetation are a main source of food for the mammals of the tundra.

In summer seasons that are too short in length for plant life to grow, all species lose members from their population. Although over many seasons, decimated species eventually recover and the natural order is maintained, this order becomes a precarious one and any external force can disrupt the fragile ecosystem. It is for this reason that the intrusion of southern development is seen as a dangerous threat.

The Canadian north is being closely examined by scientists concerned about climate change. As they observe the impact of the recent increases in temperature experienced here, they are trying to put the changes in the context of the delicate ecosystem and the countless plants and animals that have adapted themselves to survive here.

Early explorations

Since the first European explorers, the North has held a sense of mystery for all outsiders. Many believed there were

Catch sight of the Aurora Borealis, or Northern Lights, from late August through winter, when the night sky comes alive with a dazzling display of colors.

BELOW: the Northwest Territories are a birdwatcher's paradise.

A River Runner's Dream

The idyllic rivers of Canada's Northwest Territories are untamed, unpolluted, and flow through hundreds of miles of unmatched wilderness, offering some of the most wonderful and stimulating paddling experiences in the world. In boreal forest rivers including the Nahanni, the Natla-Keele, the Mountain, or the Slave, deep canyons, rapids, and spectacular plunging waterfalls prove great challenges to the paddler, whitewater canoeist, and photographer alike.

Further north, Arctic rivers also have incredible appeal, meandering their way through the expansive open tundra, where the majority of plants grow no taller than a foot (30cm/12 inches) high, and where great wildlife spectacles may include the mid-summer migrations of the caribou or grizzly bears and tundra wolves.

Yellowknife owes its existence to the discovery of gold here in 1934. Named after the copper knives of the local Indians, the city became capital of N.W.T. in 1967.

untold fortunes to be made there, so they approached it with this in mind.

The first recorded European exploration of the Arctic was undertaken by the Elizabethan, Martin Frobisher, who searched for gold and the elusive Northwest Passage in 1576. Frobisher found neither gold nor the Passage on his first or many subsequent journeys. However, he did manage to bring back to England seven hundred tons of fool's gold from Baffin Island (now part of the new territory of Nunavut).

Henry Hudson was another intrepid English explorer who set out to try his luck and find the Passage. Hudson traveled extensively in the North for several years. Not only did he fail to find the Northwest Passage but his long-suffering crew mutinied, causing havoc. Hudson, his son, and seven other explorers were set adrift in a barque in the bay that now carries Hudson's name. The nine men were never seen again. Owing to the discouraging results of expeditions undertaken by Frobisher, Hudson, and others of the era, the British Crown and other financial backers became disenchanted and

abandoned the search for a northerly route to the Orient and India.

Within Canada, fur traders were searching for routes to markets in Europe. One such entrepreneur was Alexander Mackenzie, who in 1789 followed the Mackenzie River for its entire length (4,240km/2,630 miles) in the hope that it would eventually lead to the Pacific Ocean. It led instead to the Arctic Ocean. Little did Mackenzie realize in the 18th century that he had reached an opening to a sea that covered vast and lucrative oil deposits.

Even though this area had proven to have little commercial value in the 17th and 18th centuries, there were those in England during the 19th century who looked towards the Arctic region with a mixture of wide-eyed romanticism and genuine scientific curiosity. This era in Arctic exploration was similar to the period of space exploration of the 1960s and 1970s. The British Parliament offered prizes to any person who could find the Northwest Passage and/or discover the North Pole.

Other daring explorers include William Parry, who managed to collect a

BELOW:
boats wait for the spring thaw on the Mackenzie River.

purse of £5,000 for his excursion to the far Western Arctic islands (1819–21), and John Franklin, who, in characteristic, bloody-minded British bulldog manner, risked his life a great number of times on his journeys mapping the Arctic coastline.

On his final journey in 1845, Franklin departed from England with a crew of 129 men aboard two ships; their lofty objective was to find the Northwest Passage. Unfortunately the ships were locked in the ice for two years at Victoria Strait. In 1848, search parties were sent out, and eventually over the next eight years articles of clothing, logbooks, and mementos were found strewn across the chilly coastline. Of the 129 men on the Franklin expedition not one survivor was found.

Traveling today

Today, however, travel to the Arctic is thankfully a great deal less hazardous than it was in Franklin's day. After the Franklin debacle, "outsiders" began to pay attention to the ways of the Inuit, the Dene and other First Nations peoples who had not only survived in the North for millennia, but had also developed rich cultures with strong oral traditions, passing on practical information about how to thrive in such extreme and difficult conditions.

With the arrival of the airplane in the early 1920s, the Northwest Territories became far more accessible to the outside world. Air travel is now both routine and safe in the Territories. To reach many communities, air routes have become the "real" highways for the North. The area is served by several airlines from major cities in Canada to all large communities. Once there, approximately 30 scheduled and chartered services fly between cities and remote camps.

The N.W.T. has conventional highways too, which connect the majority of the large communities, including **Yellowknife ❶**, **Hay River**, **Fort Smith**, **Inuvik**, and **Fort Simpson**, with the outside world. These highways

are all hardpacked gravel, rather than paved, so some adjustment to your driving style may be necessary. Yellowknife is also connected to Edmonton by a regular "black top" (asphalt) road.

Owing to a distinct lack of vehicular traffic, travel in the territories can indeed be a relaxing experience and a great relief to those more accustomed to aggressive city driving. Drivers will see few vehicles on the roads, and are likely to see bison, caribou or other wildlife along the way. The **Dempster Highway** places restrictions on travel during fall and spring while herds of caribou numbering in the thousands make their annual migration.

The Western Arctic

In all the territory west of **Great Slave** and **Great Bear Lake** up towards Inuvik – the Western Arctic – there are numerous equipment stores in the major communities. Below the tree line, canoe trips take place from late May to mid-September. In the tundra area most

A seaplane taxis, ready to take off.

BELOW:
a lynx on the prowl in an aspen forest.

Map on
page 332

trips take place from mid-June to mid-
August. In recent years, cross-country
skiing trips have been set up during the
spring so that tourists can witness the
spectacular migration of caribou herds
in style. Participants are flown into a
base camp, and from there they glide
onto frozen lakes and rivers to observe
the caribou migration.

Domain of the bison

In the southern region of N.W.T. there
are two spectacular national parks.
Wood Buffalo National Park ❷ is
located on either side of the Alberta–
N.W.T. border and was established in
1922 to preserve the bison. This objective has been a success and one can now
attend a "Bison Creep" to view these
creatures. Occupying an area roughly
the size of Switzerland, the national
park covers a remarkable landscape
of forests, meadows, sinkholes, and an
unusual salt plain.

The second national park, further to
the west, is located on the Yukon border. **Nahanni National Park ❸**, which
is a Unesco World Heritage Site, is in
the Deh Cho Region, also known as the

Nahanni-Ram, in the vast and remote
southwest corner of the N.W.T. The
region was once home to a mysterious
band of natives called Nahaa or Nahan-
nis. Legends of wild mountain men, a
white queen, evil spirits, lost maps, lost
gold, and headless men are myths that
prevail to this day.

Bird enthusiasts are one group that
hasn't been deterred from venturing into the Deh Cho. In addition to
seeing such exciting birds as white
pelicans, peregrine falcons, and the
threatened trumpeter swan, there are
impressive river gorges, underground
caves, and bubbling hot springs. Those
who enjoy water travel can take an
exciting trip down the South Nahanni
River, one of the wildest rivers in Canada. Access to the park is by air only,
from **Fort Simpson ❹**.

Culture in Yellowknife

Yellowknife now promotes itself as "the
diamond capital of North America,"
not only because of its proximity to
the only commercial diamond mines
on the continent, but because of the
dazzling scenery that surrounds it.
Overlooking Frame Lake is the **Prince
of Wales Northern Heritage Center**
(June–Aug daily 10.30am–5.30pm,
Sept–May Mon–Fri 10.30am–5pm,
and weekend afternoons; free), which
houses excellent histories and artifacts
of the Inuit, Dene, and Métis.

A unique experience

The Northwest Territories is a land different from anywhere else on the globe
because so much of it is completely
untouched by civilization. Here, the
traveler sees first and foremost the land
and how the plants and animals here
have adapted to their environment. The
impact of humans on this land has been
minimal, allowing its delicate balance
to survive. The impressive mountains,
the barren grounds, the stunted forests,
the over-arching skies, the thousands of
freshwater lakes, and rivers of this vast
land combine to create a unique and
humbling experience. ❑

BELOW: a frosty
musk ox.
RIGHT: spectacular
Hood River.

NUNAVUT

Nunavut – Canada's most recently established territory and home to more than half of the country's Inuit population – is a vast terrain of barren ground, plateaus, and mountains, and a hauntingly beautiful retreat

Main attractions
CAPE DORSET
IQALUIT
AUYUITTUQ NATIONAL PARK RESERVE
INUIT HERITAGE CENTER, BAKER LAKE

BELOW: mask, Cape Dorset culture.

The Eastern Arctic, including much of the Archipelago and the terrain east of Great Slave Lake, remained a hidden world until the age of the airplane. It became the new territory of Nunavut – which means "our land" in Inuktitut – on April 1 1999 when the Northwest Territories were split into two. Approximately 85 percent of Nunavut's population is Inuit and it had been vying for independence since 1973, fueled by the desire for a self-governed territory with firm control over its own future. The Nunavut Land Claim Settlement, proclaimed in July 1993, is now regarded as a global benchmark in aboriginal matters and includes title to nearly 356,000 sq km (138,000 sq miles), mineral rights, a share of federal royalties on oil, gas, and mineral development on Crown lands, and the right of first refusal on sport and commercial development of Nunavut's renewal resources.

The Great Outdoors

Canada's newest territory is also its largest, occupying about 20 percent of the country's landmass, almost entirely above the timberline and spread across three time zones. Nunavut extends from the eastern shores of Baffin and Ellesmere Islands, west to the plateaus and cliffs of the Arctic Coast on the Coronation Gulf, and north to the High Arctic Islands and the North Pole. It is home to various outpost settlements and 28 communities, the largest of which is the capital, Iqaluit, with a population of around 6,500 citizens.

Although neither cheap nor easily accessible, the delights of Nunavut's great outdoors still draw those who can afford the time and money to visit. As there are virtually no roads in Nunavut, other than a 21km (13-mile) stretch between Arctic Bay and Nanisivik, travel by air, snowmobile or dogsled are the only options. The challenging weather conditions also mean frequent delays and changed itineraries. The rewards of visiting this isolated land are infinite.

Most tourists come during the two-to-three-month summer, when temperatures average 12°C (54°F). Nonetheless, some seasoned adventurers brave the frigid Arctic winter, when the mercury plummets to –46°C (–51°F), to accompany a traditional Inuit seal hunt or view the spectacular Northern Lights under winter's perpetually dark skies.

Irrefutably, Nunavut's main draw is the outdoors. Outfitters arrange packages from building igloos to polar-bear watching, dogsledding, and encounters with narwhals (one-tusked whales at one time believed to be cousins to the mythical unicorn).

Baffin Island

Baffin Island is home to roughly a quarter of Canada's Inuit population and some of the oldest northern communities in the world. **Cape Dorset ❺**, on the southwest coast, is the home of modern Inuit art, the understated simplicity of which expresses the harmonic Inuit vision of Arctic life. Inuit art has been attracting international attention since it was first developed commercially in the 1950s, and it continues to do so today. Examples are on display and for sale at the **West Baffin Eskimo Co-op** (tel: 867-897-8827). For action-lovers, Cape Dorset also offers hiking, dogsledding, and cross-country skiing tours. **Iqaluit ❻** (formerly known as Frobisher Bay), on the southeast coast, is the capital of Nunavut and another Baffin Island community rich in Inuit heritage. The glaciers on Baffin Island are another source of inspiration. The **Penney Ice Cap** is 5,700 sq km (2,200 sq miles) of ice and snow. To view this glacier high up in the mountains of **Auyuittuq National Park Reserve** is to revisit the Ice Age. Sections of Baffin Island's east coast, where there are fjords and spectacular cliffs that rise to a height of 2,100 meters (7,000ft), higher than the walls of the Grand Canyon, also offer a taste of the Ice Age. Tours by snowmobile or dogsled to the floe-edge offer a fabulous way to experience Baffin Island's wildlife.

Summer is spectacular on the Arctic coast, when drifts of minute tundra flowers carpet the ground. The lure of abundant wildlife and an historic Inuit settlement make Bathurst Inlet a magnet for naturalists, birdwatchers, photographers, botanists, and archeologists alike.

Baker Lake

Situated on the shores of **Baker Lake** (its Inuit name – *Qamani'tuaq* – means "huge widening of the river") is the small community of Baker Lake, which lies at the heart of the Keewatin barrenlands and is the geographical center of Canada. This is another popular base for delving into Arctic history and Inuit culture. Baker Lake is known for its soapstone carvings and exquisite prints. Northeast of here is the Thelon River, first explored by Europeans in 1893, when two brothers, James and Joseph Tyrell, descended the Thelon on behalf of the Geological Survey of Canada. The area has long been occupied by Inuit, whose art and heritage is well documented in the **Inuit Heritage Center** (tel: 867-793-2598) in Baker Lake. ❑

Nunavut seems designed for the nature photographer with its estimated 500,000 caribou, 60,000 musk ox, and hundreds of millions of birds – more than 40 different species.

BELOW: young Inuit on Baffin Island.

※INSIGHT GUIDES TRAVEL TIPS

CANADA

TRANSPORTATION

GETTING THERE AND GETTING AROUND

GETTING THERE

By Air

Many people choose to fly into Canada, then continue their trip by bus, train, plane, or rented car. Most major cities have direct air connections with US cities. Many international airlines connect Toronto, Montréal, and Vancouver with all parts of North and South America, Europe, and Asia. There are more limited services between Europe and Edmonton, Calgary, Halifax, and St John's, Newfoundland. Air Canada and several regional carriers including WestJet connect with extensive feeder routes operated by associated airlines.

Private plane pilots are required to file a trans-border flight plan prior to

Airlines

Air Canada
Tel: UK 0871-220-3220
Canada and US toll-free 1-888-247-2262
www.aircanada.ca
Air Canada Jazz
Tel: toll-free 1-888-247-2262
www.flyjazz.ca
Air Transat
Tel: toll-free 1-866-847-1112
www.airtransat.ca
First Air, Airline of the North
Tel: 613-688-2635
toll-free 1-800-267-1247
www.firstair.ca
Westjet Airlines
Tel: 403-250-5839
toll-free 1-800-538-5696
www.westjet.com

departure, and to land at a Canadian Customs port of entry. Full aircraft and personal documentation is required.

Airport Charges

A number of airports across Canada levy an Airport Improvement Fee (AIF) to all visitors departing from the airport. These fees are generally added to the ticket price, so there is no additional fee payable on departure.

By Sea

There are car-ferry services between Maine and Nova Scotia, and between Washington State and British Columbia. Many cruise lines sailing from the US call at ports on the Atlantic and Pacific coasts, and there are also a few cruises in Arctic waters. Many yachtsmen sail to favorite Canadian cruising grounds on the coasts and within the Great Lakes, but in summer dock space can be tight. US and other foreign yachts are required to clear Canadian Customs at a designated port of entry.

By Road

From the US, visiting Canada by car is simply a matter of driving to the border then passing through customs and immigration.

The major bus company with routes into Western and Central Canada is Greyhound (US) and its associated companies. Some routes end at a city just over the border, where you can subsequently transfer to a Canadian carrier, but there are also special packages from certain US cities (including Boston, New York, Chicago, and San Francisco)

to Vancouver, Winnipeg, Toronto, Montréal, and other destinations in Canada. Greyhound offers a 7-day, 15-day, 30-day, or 60-day International Canada Travel Pass, which can be used in the country. Greyhound Lines of Canada have packages for use solely in Canada. Voyageur Colonial Lines, which runs buses in Ontario and Québec, also offers package discounts. These options are often honored by regional and provincial bus lines. For further details, contact Greyhound Canada on 1-800-661-8787, www.greyhound.ca.

By Rail

Amtrak offers two direct passenger train routes into Canada: Seattle to Vancouver; Washington, and New York to Montréal. VIA Rail has similar services from New York to Toronto via Niagara Falls; and from Chicago to Sarnia, London, and Toronto. VIA Rail offers group, family, and senior-citizen's discounts, as well as flat-rate "Canrail" passes. Both first-class and coach accommodations are available, each with dining cars.

For further information, telephone the nearest train station or contact:
VIA Rail,
3 Place Ville Marie, Ste 500, Montréal, PQ H3B 2C9
Tel: 514-871 6000
Or you can call the following toll-free numbers: 1-888-842-7245 (from anywhere in Canada); 514-989-2626 (from Montréal); 416-366-8411 (from Toronto).
www.viarail.ca
To call **Amtrak** in the US dial 1-800-USA-RAIL; in Canada dial 1-800-872-7245; or visit
www.amtrak.com

GETTING AROUND

For travelers who know where they want to go to in Canada, there are a number of different transportation options available.

By Air

Domestic air services are preferable, both for traveling long distances and for accessing any particularly remote areas, since driving can be very time-consuming. (A straightforward drive between Toronto and Montréal will take five hours.) While Air Canada is the main carrier, a number of smaller no-frills and discount airlines emerged after the collapse of Canadian Airlines. Some have not survived the fierce cut and thrust of Canada's passenger airline industry, but the survivors both compete with Air Canada on the most-traveled routes, and offer services to smaller, less accessible communities.

Air Canada
Tel: 1-888-247-2262
www.aircanada.com
Air Transat
Tel: 1-866-847-1112
www.airtransat.com
First Air
Tel: 613-688-2635/1-800-267-1247
www.firstair.ca
WestJet
Tel: 1-800-538-5696
www.westjet.com
Zoom Airlines
Tel: 613-235-9666/1-866-359-9666
www.flyzoom.com

By Rail

Railways are good for both short and long distances, although trains take five days to travel the 6,360km (3,950 miles) from Halifax in the east to Vancouver in the west. VIA Rail, which is Canada's major passenger train service, offers a range of cost-saving package discounts and travel passes. Ontario and British Columbia also operate some passenger rail services. For further information on bus and train routes, prices, and timetables contact:

Brewster Transportation
Box 1140, 100 Gopher St, Banff,
AB TIL IJ3
Tel: 403-762-6700/1-877-791-5500
www.brewster.ca
Bus service through Calgary and the Canadian Rockies.
Greyhound Canada
877 Greyhound Way SW, Calgary,
AB T3C 3V8
Tel: 1-800-661-8747
www.greyhound.ca
Rocky Mountaineer Railtours
1st Floor, 1150 Station St,
Vancouver, BC V6A 2X7
Tel: 604-606-7245/1-800-665-7245
www.rockymountaineer.com
Their two-day journey is billed as "the most spectacular train trip in the world."
VIA Rail Canada
3 place Ville Marie, Ste 500,
Montréal, PQ H3B 2C9
Tel: 514-871-6000/1-888-842-7245
www.viarail.ca

By Road

Buses

Buses are inexpensive and especially good for shorter distances or for getting to small towns not serviced by rail or air. Canada's major bus lines – Greyhound Canada and Voyageur Colonial – offer a number of travel passes and packages.

Driving

If general touring is on the agenda, it is usually straightforward to hire a car. Foreign drivers' licenses are valid in Canada, and accident liability insurance is required. Driving is on the right and conventions are similar to those in the US. Highway speed limits are usually 100kph (60mph), but speed limits, seat-belt regulations, and other laws differ slightly from province to province. Provincial regulations are usually summarized in tourist literature and on many official road maps.

The Canadian Automobile Association, a federation of nine automotive clubs across Canada, is a good source for information, maps, and driving regulations. Members of European automobile associations can contact any of the nine clubs through the CAA's main website: www.caa.ca.

If you are traveling from the US check with your insurer before you depart to make sure it covers you during your stay in Canada. Be aware that most of Canada requires that you carry at least $200,000 in liability insurance.

Gasoline prices range from around 80 cents to $1.10 per liter (there are

Steam Trains

Canada is a beautiful country and it is possible to make your journey part of, or the main focus of, your vacation. With the railway playing such a vital role in Canada's development, it is not, perhaps, surprising that there are some terrific steam train rides to be enjoyed across the country.

On the Québec side of the Ottawa River, the **Hull–Chelsea–Wakefield Steam Train** is one of Canada's last remaining authentic steam-powered trains, carrying passengers from the city of Gatineau along the shores of the Gatineau River and up to the village of Wakefield, in the Gatineau hills. It's a lovely way to enjoy the beauty and history of Western Québec. For more information

tel: 819-778-7246/1-800-871-7246, www.steamtrain.ca.

In Ontario, the **Agawa Canyon Tour Train** offers a spectacular excursion, some 180km (114 miles) north from Sault Ste. Marie, over towering trestle bridges, alongside pristine northern lakes and rivers, and through the granite rock formations and mixed forests of the Canadian Shield to the Agawa Canyon. It is especially popular during the fall, when advance reservations are an absolute necessity. For more information tel: 705-946-7300/1-800-242-9287, www.agawacanyontourtrain.com.

In Manitoba, **Prairie Dog Central Railway** (tel: 204-832-5259; www.pdcrailway.com), running

on weekends during the summer and before Christmas (the Santa Express),takes passengers from the big city – Winnipeg – to rural Manitoba, visiting country markets in Grosse Isle and Warren, where the track terminates. The fully restored vintage rail coaches were built between 1901–13 and the engine from 1882.

The 11km (7-mile) round trip on **The Spirit of Kamloops**, offered by the Kamloops Heritage Railway (tel: 250-374-2141; www.kamrail.com), travels through spectacular scenery. Operating Friday through Sunday, July and August, passengers have the option of riding in a custom-designed open-air "Hayrack" car or reliving the past in a 1930s heritage coach.

TRANSPORTATION · ACCOMMODATIONS · EATING OUT · ACTIVITIES · A – Z · LANGUAGE

Rules of the Road

Besides remembering to drive on the right, there are few other safety considerations to keep in mind. As some traffic rules vary from province to province, ask your car rental company if you have any queries of this nature.

While Canada has an extensive and modern system of highways, most of which are well numbered and clearly marked, at times it is very helpful to know your north from south and your east from west. Speed limits are posted in kilometers per hour (kph) and they vary from 30 to 50kph (19–31mph) in built-up areas to between 80 and 100kph (50–62mph) on highways.

To improve highway safety, some Canadian provinces and territories require vehicles to be driven with headlights on for extended periods after dawn and before sunset. The headlights of most newer vehicles turn on automatically once the engine is started.

In all Canadian provinces except Québec, you may turn right at a red traffic light after coming to a full stop and making sure that the way is clear before you do so.

School buses display flashing lights for around 150 meters (500ft) before stopping and 30 meters (100ft) after leaving a stop; drivers may only pass the bus at this time with caution. If the bus has stopped and is flashing its red lights, other drivers must stop behind that bus. Remember that pedestrians have right-of-way at all intersections without stoplights and crosswalks.

3.8 liters in a US gallon and 4.5 liters in a Canadian imperial gallon).

Car Rentals

Several international car rental companies have offices throughout Canada and rentals can be easily arranged before arriving in the country.

Call the following firms, toll-free, for information:

Avis
Tel: 1-800-331-1212 in Canada and the US
www.avis.com
Budget
Tel: 1-800-527-0700 in Canada and the US; 0870-156 5656 in the UK
www.budget.com
Discount Car and Truck Rentals
Tel: 1-800-263-2355 in Canada and the US
www.discountcar.com
Hertz
Tel: 1-800-263-0600 in Canada and the US
www.hertz.com
National
Tel: 1-800-837-0032 in Canada and the US; 0870-400 4560 in the UK
www.nationalcar.ca
Thrifty
Tel: 1-800-847-4389 in Canada and the US
www.thrifty.com

Motor Homes

If you plan to rent a camper/recreational vehicle (RV) in July and August you should book 3–4 months in advance.
Canadream Campers
2508–24th Ave NE, Calgary,

AB T1Y 6R8
Tel: 403-291-1000
(Also in Vancouver, Whitehorse, and Toronto.)
www.canadream.com
Cruise Canada
2980 26th Ave, Calgary AB T1Y 6R7
Tel: 1-800-671-8042
(Also in Vancouver, Toronto, and Montréal.)
www.cruisecanada.com

Car Ferries

There are numerous car ferries all over Canada which cross lakes and rivers large and small. Of the large ferries, the most notable are those operated by BC Ferries along the British Columbia coast, and Marine Atlantic's between Nova Scotia and Newfoundland and New Brunswick.

Province by Province

Alberta

By Air Calgary and Edmonton international airports are served by a number of airlines from elsewhere in Canada and from the US, Europe, and Asia, principally Air Canada, WestJet, Delta, Northwest, American, and United.

By Rail VIA Rail (tel: 1-888-842-7245; www.viarail.ca) has thrice-weekly services to Edmonton and Jasper (a six and a half hour ride) on its transcontinental route.

Rocky Mountaineer (tel: 1-877-460-3200 Canada/USA, 00-800-0606-7372 UK and New Zealand, 00-11-800-0606-7372 Australia/604-606-7245; www.rockymountaineer.com) operates a seasonal two-day sightseeing service from Calgary to Vancouver, with an overnight stop at Kamloops B.C. so patrons can enjoy the spectacular sightseeing that spans the 1,000km (625 mile) journey.

By Bus Greyhound Bus Lines (tel: 1-800-661-8747; www.greyhound.ca), which has its Canadian headquarters in Calgary, and Red Arrow Motorcoach (tel: 1-800-232-1958; www.redarrow.ca) provide access to almost every Alberta community, while Brewster Transportation & Tours (tel: 1-800-760-6934; www.brewster.ca) provides major bus services to the parks and other tourist locations.

By Car Trans-Canada Highway No. 1 runs west to southeast across Alberta, through Calgary. Highway 2 passes through Calgary on its way from the US border to Edmonton and points north. The major car rental companies are all represented, as well as a number of camper/RV rental agencies. Taxis are readily available in Calgary, Edmonton, Banff, and Jasper.

Calgary (403)

Calgary Transit (tel: 262-1000; www.calgarytransit.com) operates bus #57 from the airport to Downtown and light rail transit (LRT or the C-Train). City bus tours can be arranged through the tourist information center at the Calgary Tower on Center Street, or through most hotels.
Taxi: Yellow Cab (tel: 974-1111).

Edmonton (780)

Edmonton Transit (tel: 442-5311; www.edmonton.ca/transportation) operates city buses and an efficient LRT line.
Airport Transfer: Skyshuttle (tel: 465-8515).
Taxi: Yellow Cab (tel: 462-3456).

British Columbia

By Air Vancouver International Airport, located just south of the city in Richmond, is western Canada's major air hub. It is served by major North American, European, and Asian airlines, including Air Canada, WestJet, AirTransat American, British Airways, Continental, Delta, Horizon, Northwest, and United . Many smaller airlines and charters also serve northern B.C. and the Yukon.
Airport Transfer Vancouver Airporter Service (tel: 1-800-668-3141; www.yvrairporter.com) and Quick Shuttle (tel: 1-800-665-2122) from Seattle. For fast inexpensive public transport, see Translink comments below under Vancouver.
By Sea There are numerous ships and services between Victoria,

Vancouver, and other points along the coast. Of note is the "Inside Passage" as far as Prince Rupert (from Port Hardy at the north end of Vancouver Island): a scenic, day-long cruise through deep fjords and narrow channels. Booking is mandatory, and can be done online at www.bcferries. com). Contact Tourism BC (tel: 1-800-663-6000) for further information.

By Rail VIA Rail (tel: 1-888-842-7245; www.viarail.ca) operates passenger services connecting Prince Rupert with Alberta and the rest of Canada. It also has a four and a half hour service between Victoria and Courtenay half way up Vancouver Island. Amtrak (tel: 1-800-872-7245; www.amtrakcascades. com) offers services from Seattle and points further south. In addition to its trips from Calgary, Rocky Mountaineer offers regularly scheduled services to Whistler.

By Bus Greyhound Lines of Canada (tel: 1-800-661-8747; www.greyhound. ca) offers services throughout British Columbia. Pacific Coach Lines (tel: 1-800-661-1725) run from Vancouver to Victoria every two hours. Tourism BC (www.hellobc.com) provides details of several other regional bus services.

By Car Interstate 5 in Washington becomes Highway 99 at the US border 48km (30 miles) south of Vancouver. Vancouver is a 3-hour drive from Seattle. Highway 1, the Trans-Canada Highway, enters Vancouver from the east as does Highway 3, the Crowsnest Highway, which crosses southern B.C. From Alaska and the Yukon, the Alaska and Klondike Highways provide rugged routes into the province.

Vancouver (604)

Translink (tel: 953-3333; www.translink) provides a mass-transit system for the whole region, with a rapid transit LRT service, buses and trolleys, and Seabus harbor ferries to North Vancouver. The 15-minute Seabus ride is an inexpensive way to get a great tour of the Vancouver harbor, with a public market and plenty of restaurants in the area around the North Vancouver terminal. Among others, Gray Line (tel: 1-800-667-0882), offer bus tours of Vancouver and environs, including Capilano Canyon and Grouse Mountain, and as far as Whistler. There are also numerous companies offering harbor cruises, some with deluxe buffet dinners.

By Taxi Yellow Cabs (tel: 681-1111) and Blacktop (tel: 683-4567).

Victoria (250)

BC Transit (tel: 382-6161; www. bctransit.com/regions/vic) provides bus services throughout Greater Victoria. A number of tour companies, including Gray Line (tel: 1-800-663-8390; www.graylinewest.com), offer several bus tours, some on British-built double-decker buses. For slower, more romantic sightseeing, hire a horse-drawn carriage on Belleville Street, near the Royal British Columbia Museum.

By Taxi Blue Bird Cabs (tel: 382-1111) and Empress Taxi (tel: 381-4432).

By Boat and Ferry Black Ball Transport (tel: 386-2202; www. cohoferry.com) operates car ferries daily between Victoria and Port Angeles, Washington in the US. Victoria Clipper (tel: 206-448-5000/1-800-888-2535; www.clippervacations.com) operates a daily passenger-only service between Victoria and Seattle. Washington State Ferries (tel: 206-464-6400; www.wsdot.wa.gov/ferries) travels daily between Sidney, north of Victoria and Anacortes, Washington.

BC Ferries (tel: 1-888-223-3779; www.bcferries.com).

Manitoba (204)

By Air Winnipeg International Airport is served principally by Air Canada, WestJet, and Northwest Airlines. There are also a number of regional and charter carriers.

By Rail Winnipeg's Main Street Station is on VIA Rail's trans-continental passenger service and is the terminus of the line to Churchill for polar bear viewing in winter (tel: 1-888-842-7245; www.viarail.ca). Greyhound Bus Lines (tel: 1-800-661-8747; www.greyhound.ca) serves scores of small towns across the province – the Winnipeg terminal is located at 487 Portage Ave.

By Car A reliable network of good paved roads extends across the southern part of the province and north to Thompson and Flin Flon. Several large car rental companies have offices in Winnipeg, both at the airport and Downtown.

Winnipeg (204)

Winnipeg Transit System (tel: 986-5700; www.winnipegtransit.com) has an efficient bus system.

New Brunswick (506)

By Air Air Canada (tel: 1-888-247-2262) offers daily flights into the major airports at Moncton, Saint John, and Fredericton, with connections via associated airlines to smaller communities.

By Sea For ferry services connecting Blacks Harbor to Grand Manan Island call Coastal Transport (tel: 662-3724). For ferries between Deer Island and Campobello, call East Coast Ferries on 1-877-747-2159.

By Rail VIA Rail passenger services between Halifax and Montréal follow two routes in New Brunswick: three times a week via McAdam, Saint John, Sussex, and Moncton; and three times a week via Campbellton, Bathurst, Newcastle, Moncton, and Sackville. For details call 1-888-842-7245 or check www.viarail.ca.

By Bus Greyhound and Voyageur offer routes into New Brunswick and transfers to the province-wide service provided by Acadian Bus Lines (tel: 1-800-567-5151).

By Car New Brunswick has excellent highways. Since the 1980s the

BELOW: cruise ships are an excellent way to view Canada's scenic coastline.

province has undertaken an ambitious freeway construction program, the focal point of which is the Fredericton–Moncton highway. The 12.9km (8-mile) Confederation Bridge, a toll facility, joins Prince Edward Island and Cape Jourimain, New Brunswick. A shuttle bus operates on demand.

Newfoundland and Labrador (709)

By Air Air Canada and WestJet operate regular air services to Newfoundland and Labrador. Air Labrador also offers services through St Anthony to many points in Labrador. Provincial Airlines offers services to the French island of St Pierre. Air Transat and Skyservice offer seasonal services to Newfoundland through Toronto and Halifax.
By Sea The large ferries of Marine Atlantic cross up to four times a day in summer from North Sydney, Nova Scotia, to Channel-Port-aux-Basques (6-hour journey) and Argentia, Newfoundland (18-hour journey). Marine Atlantic also operates freight/passenger services from St Antony and Lewisport to the Labrador Coast.

In addition, a ferry service operates between St Barbe and Blanc Sablon, on the border with Labrador. There are a number of coastal ferries that carry a few passengers. For more information on these services contact Newfoundland and Labrador Tourism (tel: 729-0862/1-800-563-6353).
By Rail A 10-hour trip from Sept Iles, Québec to Emeril, Labrador (approximately 45 minutes drive from Labrador City) is provided through Tshiuetin Rail Transportation Inc. (Sept Iles, QC, tel: 1-866-962-0988).
By Bus DRL Coachlines connects the Port-aux-Basques ferry docks with St John's, a distance of some 905km

(562 miles). Tel: 263-2171 in St John's or 1-888-263-1854.
By Car The major car rental agencies are represented at St John's and Deer Lake. Major highways are paved, though a few secondary roads are gravel surfaced. The 80km (50-mile) stretch between the Blanc-Sablon ferry dock and Red Bay, Labrador, is paved, but Labrador highways are otherwise largely gravel surfaced. Some car rental agencies have rules and regulations regarding travel along unpaved roads and may require you to rent a larger vehicle.

St John's

The city's Metrobus system (tel: 722-9400) is efficient and inexpensive.
By Taxi It is often difficult to hail taxis on the street, so the best bet is to find one at a downtown hotel or to call Bugden's Taxi (tel: 726-4400).

Northwest Territories

By Air Getting around this huge region is possible only by using a network of regional airlines. Centers of operation include Yellowknife, Inuvik, Hay River, and Fort Smith. Air Canada, WestJet, and the main regional carrier, First Air (tel: 1-800-267-1247; www.firstair.ca), all fly into Yellowknife from Edmonton. From Yellowknife you can travel elsewhere in the Northwest Territories and to the Yukon by First Air and Canadian North (tel: 1-800-661-1505 in Canada, internationally 1-867-873-4484; www.cdn-north.com). Buffalo Airways (tel: 1-867-873-6112; www.buffaloairways.com) flies six days a week from Yellowknife to Hay River.

Numerous charter companies located in Yellowknife airport serve most northern destinations west of Hudson Bay.
By Bus Greyhound Bus Lines (tel: 1-800-661-8747; www.greyhound.ca)

Area Codes

Telephone area codes are given in brackets after the place name.

offer services between Edmonton and Yellowknife.
By Car The territory has three highways, all hard-packed gravel. The Dempster Hwy stretches from Dawson City, Yukon to Inuvik on the Arctic Ocean. The Mackenzie Hwy runs between Edmonton and Yellowknife. The Liard Hwy runs from the Alaska Hwy near Fort Nelson, B.C. to Fort Liard, close to Nahanni National Park, and connects with the Mackenzie Hwy to Yellowknife.

For special precautions about driving in the north, see the Yukon Getting Around section (page 347). Note that highways here become impassable during the spring thaw, and autumn freeze-up (usually May and November). Call 867-873-7799 for ferry schedules and the latest road information. Should visitors need to rent a vehicle, several agencies are available, but it is wise to reserve as far in advance as possible.

Nova Scotia (902)

The Check In Nova Scotia Reservation Service (tel: 1-800-565-0000; www.checkinnovascotia.com) offers information on transportation, including car rentals, as well as on campgrounds, tours and most accommodations in Nova Scotia.
By Air Air Canada (tel: 1-888-247-2262) connects Halifax and Sydney with the rest of Canada as well as the eastern US. Other carriers providing services to Nova Scotia include American Airlines, Delta Airlines, United Airlines, WestJet, and Northwest Airlines.

BELOW: getting around Toronto at night.

By Sea A number of car-ferry services are available, ranging from 1- to 6-hour voyages to a more luxurious overnight special with cabins and entertainment.

For travel from Bar Harbor and Portland, Maine to Yarmouth, from Wood Island, P.E.I. to Caribou, and from Saint John, N.B. to Digby, contact Bay Ferries (tel: 1-888-249-7245; www.nfl-bay.com). For travel from Port-aux-Basques, NFL to North Sydney, contact Marine Atlantic (tel: 1-800-341-7981).

By Rail VIA Rail provides services from Montréal to Halifax via Amherst and Truro. For schedules and fares call 1-888-842-7245.

By Bus Acadian Lines Ltd operates daily throughout Nova Scotia (tel: 1-800-567-5151), as does DRL Coachlines (tel: 1-888-738-8091; www.drlgroup.com). Cabana Tours of Halifax (tel: 444-3350) is one of a number of tour companies that offer seasonal bus tours of the province.

By Car Nova Scotia highways are generally in very good condition. Four travelways converge in Halifax: the Marine Drive, Evangeline Trail, Glooscap Trail, and Lighthouse Route. Cars can be rented in downtown Halifax, Yarmouth, or Sydney, and at the two airports. Recreational vehicles can be hired out using the province's accommodations reservation system (tel: 1-800-565-0000).

Halifax
Metro Transit (tel: 902-490-4000) operates a bus system in the Halifax/ Dartmouth area. The system's pedestrian ferry service between Halifax and Dartmouth is a truly delightful way to see the Halifax waterfront. Drivers will find that parking in downtown Halifax on business days can be difficult or expensive.

A number of tour companies, including Acadian Lines (tel: 1-800-567-5151), offer bus tours from the major hotels. However, the city is compact enough to explore on foot, either with a conducted group or on a self-guided tour, both of which are available from Tourism Halifax in the Old City Hall on Barrington Street. Taxis in Halifax are fairly inexpensive and easy to catch, as there are many cab stands.

For **Airport Transfer** to and from hotels in the metro area contact Airporter (tel: 873-2091).

Nunavut (867)
By Air Air Inuit (tel: 514-636-9445/1-800-361-5933), Calm Air (tel:

1-800-839-2256), Canadian North (tel: 1-800-661-1505; www.cdn-north.com), First Air (tel: 1-800-267-1247; www.firstair.ca) have scheduled flights. There are also numerous charter air services available across Nunavut, using twin- or single-engine propeller aircraft. Helicopter charter services are also available, as they are sometime more appropriate for the distance and terrain.

By Road As there is no road connecting Nunavut to the south, and only one 21km (13-mile) stretch of road within the territory, which connects the communities of Arctic Bay and the mining town of Nanisivik, travel by bus or car is not an option.

Ontario
By Air Lester Pearson International Airport, just 30 minutes northwest of Toronto, is served by nearly all the major Canadian airlines as well as international carriers. Useful numbers are as follows:
Air Canada (tel: 1-888-247-2262).
American Airlines (tel: 1-800-433-7300).
Continental Airlines (tel: 1-800-784-4444).
Delta Airlines (tel: 1-800-221-1212).
Airport Express (tel: 905-564-3232/1-800-387-6787) provides a bus service every 20 minutes from all three terminals to several downtown hotels (journey time of 40 minutes). The service operates between 4.45am and 12.30am.

Ottawa's MacDonald Cartier Airport (tel: 613-248-2000) is located 15 minutes south of the city. Ottawa Airport Shuttle provides a service between downtown hotels and the airport every 30 minutes, from 5am–12.35am.

Many of the province's northern hunting/fishing resort camps can be reached only by air. Usually, the price of a chartered air fare is included in a package deal. Ask Ontario Travel *(see page 397)* for its *Ontario Northern Trip Planner*.

By Rail Toronto's famous Union Station on Front Street is the city's main rail terminus, with direct access to the subway as well. VIA Rail (tel: 1-888-842-7245) can whisk you across Canada, including to and from US connections in Windsor and Niagara Falls. VIA Rail serves Ottawa from Toronto and Montréal. The Ottawa station is located at 200 Tremblay Rd, near the Queensway.

By Bus Toronto's bus terminal is located at 610 Bay Street, close to City Hall and the Eaton Centre. The major two carriers are Greyhound

ABOVE: driving in Tremblant, Québec.

Lines of Canada (tel: 1-800-661-8747), which provides services throughout the province and Coach Canada (tel: 1-800-461-7661), which provides services along the Highway 401 corridor, between Windsor, Toronto, and Montréal.

By Car The speed limit on Ontario highways is 100kph (60mph), unless otherwise posted. Remember that adults and children weighing over 40lb must wear seat belts. In Ontario, drivers are allowed to turn right on a red traffic light, as long as traffic conditions make it safe to do so. Ontario's road network is among the best maintained in North America, so your car should leave the province in as good shape as it came. Unless, of course, you travel the dirt and gravel sideroads of northern Ontario, in which case a post-vacation underbody flush will be appropriate. See the Getting Around introduction for toll-free car rental numbers (page 344).

Toronto (416 and 647)
Toronto features an excellent mass-transit system, including clean, efficient, and safe subways, with connections to punctual buses and trolley buses. For information call the Toronto Transit Commission (TTC; tel: 416-393-4636). Route maps are often available at hotels.

Taxis are easily hailed on the street. Otherwise call Diamond (tel: 416-366-6868), Metro Cab (tel: 416-504-8294), or Beck Taxi (tel: 416-751-5555).

As in any large city, driving in Toronto can enervate the most patient of drivers, especially at rush hours. Parking, naturally, is expensive, although less so in municipal lots marked with a large, green "P". When a streetcar comes to a halt, stop behind it so that its passengers can exit through the right lane to the

(see page 397)

ABOVE: take your pick of canoe or kayak.

sidewalk. Whenever possible, it's more pleasant to walk or take the subway.

Ferries (tel: 416-392-8193) leave for Centre Island daily every 30 minutes from the foot of Bay Street.

Gray Line Sightseeing (tel: 1-800-594-3310) runs several daytime excursions, which often include extended stops at the CN Tower, Royal Ontario Museum, or Casa Loma. Moreover, Gray Line offers pleasant, meandering bus tours to Niagara Falls.

To enjoy a harbor cruise call Toronto Harbour Tours (tel: 416-868-0400) or wander through the Harbourfront area, where smaller outfits and privately owned yachts run tour cruises.

Ottawa (613)
Ottawa is served by OC Transpo (tel: 613-741-4390). For tours of Ottawa contact Gray Line Tours (tel: 1-800-594-3310. For taxis call Blue Line (tel: 238-1111).

Prince Edward Island (902)
By Air Air Canada (tel: 1-888-247-2262) and some of the smaller airlines fly into Charlottetown daily from numerous Canadian cities. Delta Air Lines and Northwest Airlines offer direct seasonal services from Boston, New York, and Detroit.

By Sea During the summer, Northumberland Ferries (tel: 1-877-635-7245) leave hourly from Caribou, N.S., to Wood Islands, P.E.I., a 75-minute trip. The ferries are almost always crowded. Early morning and evening sailings have the shortest wait.

By Bus Greyhound, under the auspices of Acadian Bus Lines, provides services to the island. For information call 1-800-567-5151. There are few local bus services, but there are several taxi companies such as City Cab (tel: 892-6567) and Co-op Taxi (tel: 628-8200).

Abegweit Sightseeing Tours (tel: 894-9966) is one company that runs tours of Charlottetown, the North Shore beaches, and other island attractions.

By Car Confederation Bridge is a toll bridge that permits driving to the island from Cape Tormentine. N.B: The island speed limit is 90kph (55mph). See Getting Around introduction (page 344) for toll-free rental car numbers.

By Bicycle Cyclists adore P.E.I.'s rural lanes. Rent a bike by the day or week from one of a number of agencies. MacQueen's Bike Shop and Travel, 430 Queen St in Charlottetown (tel: 368-2453/1-800-969-2822, www.macqueens.com) will design a customized itinerary, arrange accommodations, and provide all equipment – even an emergency road service.

Québec
By Air Montréal-Pierre Elliott Trudeau International Airport (tel: 514-394-7377/1-800-465-1213) is located on the outskirts of the city. It serves domestic, US, and international flights. Montréal-Mirabel International Airport (tel: 514-394-7377/1-800-465-1213), some distance northeast of Montréal, handles mainly charter

and cargo flights. All major Canadian airlines and numerous international carriers fly into Montréal, including Air Canada (tel: 1-888-247-2262).

Visitors piloting private aircraft should check first with Transport Canada in Ottawa.

By Rail Contact VIA Rail (tel: 1-888-842-7245, or visit www.viarail.ca).

By Bus Greyhound provides services throughout Québec (tel: 514-844-4040/1-800-661-8747).

By Ferry Many ferries offer year-round or seasonal services on the St Lawrence and other major rivers. The CTMA ferry service (tel: 1-888-986-3278, www.ctma.ca) travels between the Iles-de-la-Madeleine and Prince Edward Island, while a passenger/cargo ship, the Relais Nordik (tel: 1-800-463-0680; www.relaisnordik.com), connects Lower North Shore between Havre-St-Pierre, Iles d'Anticosti and Blanc-Sablon. Places on this ship should be reserved in advance in peak season.

Hitchhiking

Hitchhiking is permitted in most of Canada, except on high-volume highways where stopping for passengers constitutes a danger. It is prohibited in certain municipalities, so prospective hitchhikers should check with tourist boards about local regulations.

By Car Perhaps the best way to travel Québec is by automobile, which gives you the flexibility to explore, and the freedom to stop and sample the local cuisine and to meander through the exceptional provincial parks. While good maps are available from most service stations, bear in mind that north of the major population areas the roads are often unpaved and sometimes even impassable in winter. The speed limit on autoroutes is 100kph (60mph), and drivers and all passengers must wear seat belts. Turning right on a red light is permitted throughout the province except in Montréal, where it is strictly prohibited unless there is an additional green arrow.

Montréal (514)
The City Transit System, STMC (tel: 786-4636), services the city with buses and its excellent Metro. You can use a bus transfer for admission to the subway and vice versa. If you drive, try to make overnight parking arrangements in advance

with a hotel. Be prepared to pay $20 a day to park around the city. Taxis abound in Montréal. The base rate is around $4. For car rentals try:
Avis (tel: 800-879-2847)
Hertz (tel: 800-654-3131)
Budget (tel: 800-268-8900)

Québec City (418)
In the old city, walking is by far the easiest and most convenient way to get around. Woe to those who drive: parking is scarce and expensive (check with your hotel). You can avoid traffic snarls by renting a bicycle from Cyclo Services (tel: 692-4052).

Saskatchewan (306)
By Air Saskatchewan's two principal airports, situated in Regina and Saskatoon, are served by the following airlines: Air Canada, (tel: 1-888-247-2262; www.aircanada.com), WestJet (tel: 1-888-937-8538; www.westjet.com), and Northwest Airlines (tel: 1-800-441-1818; www.nwa.com). There are also a number of regional and charter carriers offering flights across the area.
By Rail Saskatoon is on VIA Rail's transcontinental service, with bus links to Regina. For information call VIA Rail (tel: 1-888-842-7245; www.viarail.ca).
By Bus The Saskatchewan Transportation Co. (tel: 1-800-663-7181; www.stcbus.com), and Greyhound Bus Lines (tel: 1-800-661-8747; www.greyhound.ca) serve the province from the Regina terminal at 1717 Saskatchewan Drive, and the Saskatoon station at 50 23rd Street.
By Car The speed limit in Saskatchewan is 100kph (60mph). Free maps can be obtained from Tourism Saskatchewan or from any other travel bureau in the province. Avis, Budget, National, and Thrifty car rental agencies all have depots at both airports as well as Downtown. (*See Getting Around introduction, page 344, for toll-free numbers.*)

Regina and Saskatoon (306)
Regina Transit (tel: 777-7433) runs several bus routes through the city and to the airport. In Regina, taxis are readily available Downtown; otherwise, Capital Cab (tel: 781-7777) is a popular choice to call for a pick-up. Saskatoon Transit System (tel: 975-3100) provides a regular bus service. Taxis are available in Saskatoon, or call United (tel: 652-2222).

The Yukon
By Air Air Canada (tel: 1-888-247-2262; www.aircanada.com) runs direct flights to Whitehorse from Vancouver and Calgary. Air North (tel: 1-800-661-0407; www.flyairnorth.com) offers services to Fairbanks, Alaska, and First Air (tel: 1-800-267-1247; www.firstair.ca) offers flights to Yellowknife, then connecting flights across most northern airports.
By Sea Most visitors arrive in the Yukon aboard cruise ships as part of a package tour. Independent travelers will find that Skagway, the Alaskan port close to three hours' drive from Whitehorse, is served by Alaska Ferries (http://ferryalaska.com).
By Rail There's a seasonal sightseeing rail service between Skagway and Lake Bennett, about halfway to Whitehorse, with connecting buses to complete the journey. For details contact White Pass and Yukon Railway (tel: 1-800-343-7373; www.wpyr.com).

By Bus Greyhound Bus Lines (tel: 1-800-661-8747; www.greyhound.ca) travels from Edmonton to Whitehorse, and Alaska Highways through Yukon. Regional bus lines service the interior and connect with Alaska.
By Car Among the national car rental agencies Budget and Alamo are represented in Whitehorse and there are also a number of local car and RV rental companies.
The speed limit is 90kph (55mph). Yukon roads are well maintained and most major highways are paved. The Alaska Highway runs from Dawson Creek, B.C., through Whitehorse and Haines Junction, the Yukon, and on into Alaska. The Klondike Highway commences in Skagway and cuts north from Whitehorse to Dawson. There it splits into the Dempster Highway, which runs due north to Inuvik, the Northwest Territories, and the Top of the World Highway, which drops west into Alaska.
Although these are open year round, travel is recommended only between mid-May and mid-September. Any trek should be planned and undertaken with great care, following these recommendations:
• Headlights must remain on at all times.
• When journeying between October and April, make sure that the vehicle is properly winterized.
• Before starting, ensure that the vehicle is in good working order. Bring at least two spare tires and plenty of water.
• Refuel frequently.
By Taxi for bookings in Whitehorse, call the Yellow Cab at 668-4811.

BELOW: a seaplane departs from in front of the Fairmont Empress Hotel in Victoria, B.C.

TRANSPORTATION

ACCOMMODATIONS

EATING OUT

ACTIVITIES

A – Z

LANGUAGE

A CCOMMODATIONS

HOTELS, YOUTH HOSTELS, BED AND BREAKFAST

Canadian accommodations are similar to those in the US in the range of choices available, but some lodgings in Canada are more personalized and service-orientated. Reservations are essential in the busy summer months. Hotels generally will hold a room until 6pm, but if you plan to arrive later, notify the establishment in advance. If you have not reserved, begin looking for accommodations early in the afternoon, particularly during the summer when most establishments (especially those along highways) fill up quickly. Almost all hotels, motels, and resorts accept major credit cards, but it's a good idea to check in advance, especially if you travel in remote areas. More and more hotels

Hostelling

Budget travelers interested in hostelling can write to:
Backpackers Hostels Canada
Auberges Backpackers Canada, Longhouse Village, RR 13, Thunder Bay, ON P7B 5E4
Tel: 807-983-2042/1-888-920-0044
www.backpackers.ca
Hostelling International
Ontario E, 205 Catherine St, Ste 400, Ottawa, ON K2P 1C3
Tel: 613-237-7884
www.hihostels.ca
Hostelling International – Great Lakes
76 Church St, Toronto, ON M5C 2G1, tel: 1-877-848-8737; Kingston, tel: 613-531-8237; Niagara Falls, tel: 1-888-749-0058; Thunder Bay, tel: 807-475-6381.

are completely smoke-free, so if you require a smoking room, make sure to ask. Bed-and-breakfasts and hostels are becoming increasingly popular. Generally cheaper and more friendly, they are located throughout the country. Another place to stay is in one of Canada's 2,000 campgrounds, most of which accommodate recreational vehicles as well as tents.

Although the rates quoted are for the lowest current rack rate at the time of going to press, ask about special packages and promotions when making a reservation. The prices indicated are based on double occupancy.

Prairie Farms

Farm vacations are a great way to get a true sense of the prairies. Lasting from one day to a week or more, they offer a wide enough variety of different activities to suit almost any taste.

Manitoba Farm Vacations

For further information write to Manitoba Country Vacations Association, Jim Irwin, Box 11, Lake Audy, MB RDJ 020
Tel: 204-848-2265/1-866-517-9501
www.countryvacations.mb.ca.
If you prefer to have a similar kind of hospitality but in a more urban setting, try Bed and Breakfast of Manitoba at www.bedandbreakfast.mb.ca.

Alberta's Guest Ranches

Alberta's "country vacation" program provides the chance to experience life on an Albertan farm or ranch. Like other packages of this sort, it's fun,

inexpensive and, if you choose, hard work. Unlike other programs, you can select from a list of accommodations ranging from large cattle ranches to small family farms. www.albertacountry vacation.com.

Québec Farm Vacations

The Fédération des Agricotours du Québec and the Québec Ministry of Agriculture co-sponsor an inexpensive B&B farm vacation program which offers several possibilities. It's an interesting alternative for campers. Fédération des Agricotours du Québec, 4545 ave Pierre de-Coubertin, C.P. 1000, Succursale M, Montréal, PQ H1V 3R2, tel: 514-252-3138
They publish a useful bilingual book, *Inns and Bed & Breakfasts in Québec*, which can be purchased through the website at www.agricotours.qc.ca or at most Canadian bookstores.

Saskatchewan Farm Vacations

There are farm vacations and then there are Saskatchewan farm vacations. Time and again, travelers return home with glowing accounts of their stay on a Saskatchewan farm: the hearty home cooking, the fresh air, even sharing the chores, are often raved about. Camping on a farm can be arranged. Vacation farms are listed along with B&Bs in Tourism Saskatchewan's annual *Accommodation, Resort & Campground Guide*. For further information, write to Saskatchewan Bed and Breakfast Association, which includes many farms among its members, at Box 694, Lumsden, SK S0G 3C0, tel: 306-731-2646, www.bbsask.ca.

ACCOMMODATIONS LISTINGS

ALBERTA

Bed and breakfasts are a popular alternative to hotels, with prices generally in the inexpensive to medium range. In smaller communities, they are generally a better choice. The Alberta Bed and Breakfast Association, www.bbalberta.com, is a no-fee reservation service that represents B&Bs throughout Alberta. All members have been inspected and approved by the association.

For detailed information on Alberta's campgrounds, request a copy of the *Alberta Campground Guide* from Travel Alberta *(see page 396)*. With five national parks, more than 300 provincial parks and recreation areas, and over 600 privately or municipally owned campgrounds, there is a great choice. All have been inspected and approved by Travel Alberta. It's advisable to book ahead.

Travel Alberta also distributes a guide to other types of accommodations, a sampling of which is given below.

Banff (403)

Banff Alpine Center
801 Hidden Ridge Way
Tel: 762-4123/1-866-762-4122
A mix of dormitory and private rooms for the budget-conscious traveler, with on-site pub. **$**
Banff International Hotel
333 Banff Ave
Tel: 762-5666/1-800-665-5666
www.banffinternational.com
New hotel within walking distance of downtown Banff. Provides a complimentary downtown shuttle in the evening. **$$$**
Fairmont Banff Springs Hotel
405 Spray Ave
Tel: 762-2211/1-800-441-1414

www.fairmont.com/banffsprings
This resort is a town unto itself. Its famous golf course is as scenic as it is challenging. **$$$**
Irwin's Mountain Inn
429 Banff Ave
Tel: 762-4566/1-800-661-1721
www.irwinsmountaininn.com
One km (½ mile) from the town center. Some suites suitable for light self-catering. **$$**
Tunnel Mountain Resort
502 Tunnel Mountain Rd
Tel: 762-4515/1-800-661-1859
www.tunnelmountain.com
2.5km (1½ miles) from downtown Banff. 95 chalets and suites. Chalets designed for family accommodations; each comes with full kitchen. **$$–$$$**

Calgary (403)

Calgary International Hostel
520–7th Ave SE
Tel: 269-8239
www.hihostels.ca/alberta
Single rooms or dormitories, some rooms with bath. **$**
Fairmont Palliser Hotel
133–9th Ave SW
Tel: 262-1234/1-800-441-1414
www.fairmont.com/calgary
Everything about this 1914 Edwardian hotel is done on a grand scale, including the rooms. Deluxe suites are available. **$$–$$$**
Holiday Inn Macleod Trail
4206 Macleod Trail
Tel: 287-2700/1-866-554-0162
www.holidayinn.com
All rooms are non-smoking. Convenient location. **$$–$$$**
Hotel Arts
119–12th Ave SW
Tel: 403-266-4611/1-800-661-9378
www.hotelarts.ca
A recently revamped, boutique-style hotel located in midtown Calgary, with 175 stylish rooms and suites. **$$–$$$**

International Hotel Suites Calgary
220–4th Ave SW
Tel: 265-9600/1-800-661-8627
www.internationalhotel.ca
Centrally located high-rise all-suite hotel features almost 250 gorgeous suites. Good value for families. **$$–$$$**
Kensington Inn
1126 Memorial Drive NW
Tel: 228-4442
www.kensingtonriversideinn.com
Small friendly Inn located in trendy Kensington. **$$$**
University of Calgary Housing
3456–24th Ave NW
Tel: 220-3203
www.ucalgary.ca/hotelandconference
Summer accommodations in student dormitories and hotel rooms all year round on this sprawling campus. **$–$$**
The Westin Calgary
320–4th Ave SW
Tel: 266-1611/1-800-228-3000
www.westin.com
Very large luxury smoke-free hotel located in the financial district; caters to the business set. **$$–$$$**

Drumheller (403)

Best Western Jurassic Inn
1103 Hwy 9 S
Tel: 823-7700/1-888-823-3466
www.bestwesternalberta.com
Spacious rooms with fridges and microwave ovens, all smoke-free. Fitness center and hot tub. **$$**

Edmonton (780)

Alberta Place Suite Hotel
10049–103 St
Tel: 423-1565/1-800-661-3982
www.albertaplace.com
Comfortable suites come with kitchenettes. **$$**
Delta Edmonton Centre Suite Hotel
10222–102 St
Tel: 429-3900/1-800-661-6655
www.deltahotels.com
A unique city-center hotel,

part of the City Center West shopping mall. **$$–$$$**
Fairmont Hotel Macdonald
10065–100 St
Tel: 424-5181/1-800-441-1414
www.fairmont.com/macdonald
Beautifully restored heritage hotel. **$$–$$$**
Hostelling International – Edmonton Hostel
10647–81st Ave
Tel: 988-6836/1-866-762-4122
An attractively refurbished convent in the lively Old Strathcona neighborhood. Mix of dormitories and doubles. **$**
Union Bank Inn
10053 Jasper Ave
Tel: 423-3600/1-888-423-3601
www.unionbankinn.com
Small, attractive inn with 34 individually designed rooms. **$$–$$$**

Jasper (780)

Fairmont Jasper Park Lodge
Old Lodge Rd
Tel: 852-3301/1-866-540-4454
www.jasperparklodge.com
Elite resort, with golf course and many amenities; perhaps the most beautiful of its kind in the Rockies. **$$$**
Jasper Inn & Suites
98 Geikie St
Tel: 852-4461/1-800-661-1933
www.bestwesternjasperinn.com

PRICE CATEGORIES

Price categories are for a double room with breakfast:
$ = under $100
$$ = $100–200
$$$ = over $200

Smoke-free condominium-style hotel accommodations suitable for self-catering holidays. **$$$**
Pine Bungalows
2km (1 mile) east of Jasper Townsite
Tel: 852-3491
www.pinebungalows.com
Open May–mid-Oct. Cabins, many with fireplaces, beside the Athabasca River. Groceries, laundry, shop. **$$**
Wapiti Campground
5km (3 miles) south of Jasper on Hwy 93

Tel: 852-6176/1-877-737-3783
Reserve online: www.pccamping.ca
362 sites, 40 equipped with power. Open year round.

Lake Louise (403)

Fairmont Château Lake Louise
111 Lake Louise Dr
Tel: 522-3511/1-866-540-4413
www.fairmont.com/lakelouise
This famous, chateau-like resort complex in the Rockies, set next to the

turquoise lake, offers all the luxury amenities. **$$$**
Lake Louise Inn
210 Village Rd
Tel: 522-3791/1-800-661-9237
www.lakelouiseinn.com
Large estate offering a choice of smoke-free rooms, kitchen apartments or inn-style accommodations. Some deluxe, others moderately priced. **$$–$$$**
Mountaineer Lodge
101 Village Rd, 3km (2 miles) from Lake Louise
Tel: 522-3844

www.mountaineerlodge.com
Open mid-May–mid-Oct. One- and two-bedroom apartments, some with mountain views. Whirlpool and steam room available. **$$–$$$**
Paradise Lodge and Bungalows
105 Lake Louise Dr
Tel: 522-3595
www.paradiselodge.com
Rustic cabins and suites, just a short drive from the lake. Closed in winter. **$$–$$$**

BRITISH COLUMBIA

Tourism BC publishes several useful guides, including the *British Columbia Insider's Guide* that lists accredited motels, hotels, B&Bs, resort accommodations, and camp-grounds in the province. Printed or electronic versions can be ordered either at www.hellobc.com or by calling tel: 1-800-HELLO BC.
    Western Bed and Breakfast Innkeepers Association (www.wcbbia.com) has more than 170 inspected members situated in B.C. and Alberta.

100 Mile House (250)

The Hills Health and Guest Ranch
Hwy 97, 108 Mile Ranch (13km/8 miles north of 100 Mile House)
Tel: 791-5225/1-800-668-2233
www.spabc.com
Lodge with 21 rooms or individual chalets. **$$–$$$**

Fairmont Hot Springs (250)

Fairmont Hot Springs Resort
5225 Fairmont Resort Rd (on Hwys 93 and 95)
Tel: 345-6000/1-800-663-4979
www.fairmonthotsprings.com
Year-round resort lodge and cabins; great for skiing and golfing. **$$–$$$**

Kelowna (250)

The Cove Lakeside Resort
4205 Gellatly Rd
Tel: 1-877-762-2683
www.covelakeside.com
Suites with full kitchens, plus an excellent dining room for special occasions. **$$–$$$**
Manteo Beach Club & Resort
3762 Lakeshore Rd
Tel: 860-1031/1-800-445-5255
www.manteo.com
Year-round resort complex

on the shores of Okanagan Lake. **$$–$$$**

Penticton (250)

Best Western Inn at Penticton
3180 Skaha Lake Rd
Tel: 493-0311/1-800-780-7234
www.bestwesternbc.com
Three blocks to the beach, modern hotel with outdoor pool and amenities. **$$**

Prince George (250)

Coast Inn of the North
770 Brunswick St
Tel: 563-0121/1-800-716-6199
Modern hotel close to center of town. Indoor pool. **$$**
Connaught Motor Inn
1550 Victoria St
Tel: 562-4441/1-800-663-6620
Comfortable motel, with indoor pool, hot tub, and sauna. **$**
Four Points by Sheraton Prince George
1790 Hwy 97 S
Tel: 564-7100
www.starwoodhotels.com
New hotel with all the amenities, great value. **$$**
Ramada Hotel Downtown
444 George St
Tel: 563-0055/1-800-830-8833
www.ramadaprincegeorge.com
Downtown hotel with all facilities. **$–$$**

Prince Rupert (250)

Coast Prince Rupert Hotel
118 6th St
Tel: 624-6711/1-800-716-6199

www.coasthotels.com
Pleasant, comfortable lodgings with views over the harbor. **$$**
Totem Lodge Motel
1335 Park Ave
Tel: 624-6761/1-800-550-0178
www.totemlodge.com
Pleasant modest motel near ferry docks. **$**

Revelstoke (250)

The Peaks Lodge
Hwy 1, 4.5km (3 miles) west of Revelstoke
Tel: 837-2176/1-800-668-0330
www.peakslodge.com
Alpine-style lodge in mountain setting; some units with kitchen. Outdoor hot tub. **$**

Quesnel (250)

Billy Barker Casino Hotel
308 McLean St
Tel: 992-5533/1-888-992-4255
www.billybarkercasino.com
Downtown location with antique-styled rooms. **$–$$**
Cascade Inn
383 St-Laurent Ave
Tel: 992-5575/1-800-663-1581
Quiet downtown location with many facilities. **$**

BELOW: a friendly welcome at the Pan Pacific Hotel.

Vancouver (604)

Best Western Chateau Granville
1100 Granville St
Tel: 604-669-7070
www.chateaugranville.com
Close to Yaletown, large rooms. **$–$$**

The Fairmont Hotel Vancouver
900 W Georgia St
Tel: 684-3131/1-800-441-1414
www.fairmont.com/hotelvancouver
Spacious, old-fashioned rooms with graceful touches in heritage building. **$$$**

The Fairmont Waterfront
900 Canada Place Way
Tel: 691-1991/1-800-441-1414
www.fairmont.com/waterfront
Modern glass tower with tremendous views. **$$$**

Four Seasons Hotel
791 W Georgia St
Tel: 689-9333/1-800-819-5053
www.fourseasons.com/vancouver
This mid-town hotel is one of Vancouver's most luxurious. Attached to Pacific Center Mall. **$$$**

Granville Island Hotel
1253 Johnston St
Tel: 683-7373/1-800-663-1840
www.granvilleislandhotel.com
An elegant hotel in a spectacular setting amid the action of Granville Island. **$$–$$$**

Howard Johnson Hotel Downtown
1176 Granville St
Tel: 688-8701/1-800-359-6689
Centrally located, renovated hotel, close to Stanley Park. **$–$$**

Hyatt Regency
Royal Centre, 655 Burrard St
Tel: 683-1234/1-800-233-1234
www.vancouver.hyatt.com
Recently renovated luxury rooms in superb downtown location. **$$$**

Pan Pacific Vancouver
300–999 Canada Place
Tel: 662-8111/1-877-324-4856
www.vancouver.panpacific.com
Luxurious waterfront hotel with views over the harbor and Stanley Park. **$$$**

Sylvia Hotel
1154 Gilford St
Tel: 681-9321
www.sylviahotel.com
Attractive old hotel overlooking English Bay, adjacent to Stanley Park.

Surprising grandeur for the price, hence very popular, especially during the summer. **$–$$**

UBC Conference Centre
5961 Student Union Blvd
Tel: 822-1010
www.ubcconferences.com/accommodations
Single and twin units on University of B.C. campus offering cheap rooms year round. Access to campus facilities. **$–$$**

Wedgewood Hotel
845 Hornby St
Tel: 689-7777/1-800-663-0666
www.wedgewoodhotel.com
Charming boutique hotel with antique-style furnishings and a European ambience, in the heart of Vancouver. **$$$**

Westin Bayshore
1601 Bayshore Dr
Tel: 682-3377/1-800-937-8461
www.westinbayshore.com
Airy rooms overlooking Coal Harbor and Stanley Park. Resort ambience. **$$$**

YWCA Hotel/Residence
733 Beatty St
Tel: 895-5830/1-800-663-1424
www.ywcahotel.com
Near B.C. Place Stadium. Comfortable rooms; accommodations suitable for singles, couples, and families. **$–$$**

Victoria (250)

Abigail's Hotel
906 McClure St
Tel: 388-5363/1-866-347-5054
www.abigailshotel.com
A centrally located smoke-free boutique hotel. **$$–$$$**

Bedford Regency Hotel
1140 Government St
Tel: 384-6835/1-800-665-6500
www.bedfordregency.com
Small, heritage hotel close to Bastion Square. **$–$$**

Château Victoria Hotel
740 Burdett Ave
Tel: 382-4221/1-800-663-5891
www.chateauvictoria.com
Pleasant, large rooms and central location. **$–$$**

The Fairmont Empress
721 Government St
Tel: 384-8111/1-800-441-1414
www.fairmont.com/empress
Heritage hotel. Subtly decorated rooms, with

ABOVE: Whistler's resort is also popular during the summer.

impeccable service for the discriminating traveler. **$$$**

Harbour Towers Hotel & Suites
345 Québec St
Tel: 385-2405/1-800-663-5896
www.harbourtowers.com
Large rooms and suites, each with a view of the city or its inner harbor. **$–$$$**

The Magnolia Hotel & Spa
623 Courtney St
Tel: 381-0999/1-877-624-6654
www.magnoliahotel.com
Elegant small hotel with attentive service and great location. **$$–$$$**

Whistler (604)

Delta Whistler Village Suites
4308 Main St
Tel: 905-3987/1-888-890-3222
www.deltahotels.com
Resort hotel favored by skiers; lower rates during summer months. **$$–$$$**

Durlacher Hof Alpine Country Inn
7055 Nesters Rd
Tel: 932-1924/1-877-932-1924
www.durlacherhof.com
Austrian hospitality in authentic pine pension. Mountain views. **$$**

The Fairmont Château Whistler
4599 Château Blvd
Tel: 938-8000/1-800-441-1414
www.fairmont.com/whistler
All that one expects of Fairmont Hotels, in a resort setting close to Whistler village and the ski-lifts. **$$$**

Four Seasons Resort Whistler
4591 Blackcomb Way
Tel: 935-3400/1 888-935-2460
www.fourseasons.com/whistler
Luxurious mountainside resort with easy access to Whistler-Blackcomb mountains. **$$$**

Hostelling International Whistler
5678 Alta Lake Rd
Tel: 932-5492/1-866-762-4122
www.hihostels.ca/whistler
Rustic lodge on shore of Alta Lake, with shared and private rooms for budget travelers. **$**

PRICE CATEGORIES

Price categories are for a double room with breakfast:
$ = under $100
$$ = $100–200
$$$ = over $200

MANITOBA

Winnipeg offers a variety of lodgings, from old and grand to slick and modern. Ask about weekend packages. In Manitoba's small towns, accommodations tend to be modest, both in decor and price. Take the opportunity to stay off the beaten path at a more remote resort – luxurious or basic, your choice – to experience the real Manitoba. Travel Manitoba will provide its annual *Accommodations and Campground Guide* (a complete list of places to stay in the province, including campgrounds) on request from www.travelmanitoba.com. In fact, they will send an entire package of materials, in English or French.

Brandon (204)

The Royal Oak Inn
3130 Victoria Ave
Tel: 728-5775/1-800-852-2709
www.royaloakinn.com
Best in town, with pool, sauna, good lounge, and dining room. **$$**

Flin Flon (204)

Victoria Inn North
160 Hwy 10–A North
Tel: 687-7555/1-877-707-7555
www.vicinn.com/flinflon
Modern hotel with pool and other facilities. **$$**

Portage la Prairie (204)

Days Inn
No. 1 Hwy & Yellowquill Trail
Tel: 857-9791/1-800-329-7466
www.daysinn.com
Pleasant motor hotel with popular dining room. **$**

Winnipeg (204)

Best Western Charterhouse
330 York Ave
Tel: 942-0101/1-800-780-7234
www.bwcharterhouse.com
Good location Downtown; large rooms, restaurant, outdoor pool. **$$**

Delta Winnipeg
350 St Mary Ave
Tel: 942-0551/1-800-311-4990
www.deltahotels.com
A first-class hotel connected to the Winnipeg Convention Center, with all facilities and attractive rooms, most with balconies. **$$–$$$**

The Fairmont Winnipeg
2 Lombard Place
Tel: 957-1350/1-800-257-7544
www.fairmont.com/winnipeg
Large luxury hotel, with all facilities and an excellent dining room. **$$–$$$**

The Fort Garry Hotel
222 Broadway
Tel: 942-8251/1-800-665-8088
www.fortgarryhotel.com
Elegant rooms set in a late 19th-century French-style château. **$$–$$$**

Guest House International Hostel
168 Maryland St
Tel: 772-1272/1-800-743-4423

www.backpackerswinnipeg.com
Semi-private and private rooms in a restored Victorian home in a quiet area of Winnipeg. **$**

Ivey House International Hostel
210 Maryland St
Tel: 772-3022/1-866-762-4122
www.hihostels.com
Restaurant and pub on site. **$**

Winnipeg Downtown Holiday Inn
360 Colony St
Tel: 786-7011/1-877-863-4780
www.holidayinn.com
Recently renovated hotel in a convenient location. **$$**

NEW BRUNSWICK

Tourism New Brunswick will provide assistance with reservations for accommodations throughout the province at each of its six Provincial Visitor Information Centres. These are in: Woodstock (tel: 506-325-4427), St Stephen (tel: 506-466-7390), Aulac (tel: 506-364-4090), Campbellton (tel: 506-789-2367), Saint-Jacques (tel: 506-735-2747), and Cape Jourimain (tel: 506-538-2133). Information on accommodations, including campgrounds, is also available at www.tourismnewbrunswick.ca.

Bathurst (506)

L'Auberge de la Vallée
1810 Vallée Lourdes Dr
Tel: 549-4100
www.aubergedelavallee.ca
In the center of Bathurst, the inn has 10 bedrooms, a fine dining room and spa facilities, including an indoor salt water swimming pool. **$$**

Campbellton (506)

Maison McKenzie
31 Andrew St
Tel: 753-3133/1-800-477-9122
www.bbcanada.com/4384.html
A lovely six-room B&B overlooking the water that offers a traditional Restigouche breakfast and seasonal kayak tours. **$**

Campobello (506)

Lupine Lodge
Tel: 752-2555/1-888-912-8880
www.lupinelodge.com
Open late June–mid-Oct. A maritime lodging and dining experience. **$$**

Owen House
Tel: 752-2977
www.owenhouse.ca
Historic oceanfront house with antiques and fireplaces. Convenient for golf, whale watching, and hiking. Some shared bathrooms. **$$**

Edmundston (506)

Auberge Les Jardins
60 Principal St, St Jacques
Tel: 739-5514/1-800-630-8011
www.auberge-lesjardins-inn.com
A comfortable and modern resort in a woodland setting. **$$**

Fredericton (506)

Carriage House Inn
230 University Ave
Tel: 452-9924/1-800-267-6068
www.carriagehouse-inn.net
Built for the city's mayor in 1865; next to The Green. Furnished with art and antiques, and take breakfast in the ballroom. **$$**

Delta Fredericton
225 Woodstock Rd
Tel: 457-7000/1-888-462-8800
www.deltahotels.com
Modern luxury hotel overlooking the St John River. Convenient for Downtown, with indoor and outdoor swimming pools. **$$–$$$**

Crowne Plaza Fredericton Beaverbrook Hotel
659 Queen St
Tel: 1-800-561-7666
www.cpfredericton.com
Close to the majestic St John River, walking trails, and historical sites. Three dining choices. **$$**

Grand Manan (506)

Shorecrest Lodge
North Head
Tel: 662-3216
www.shorecrestlodge.com
Open mid-May–mid-Oct, an attractive country inn with gourmet restaurant and lovely ocean view from the verandah. **$–$$**

The Inn at Whale Cove
26 Whale Cove Cottage Rd
Tel: 662-3181
www.holidayjunction.com/whalecove
A rustic inn with ocean views, built in 1816; five cottages are also available for weekly rentals. **$$**

Moncton (506)

Auberge Wild Rose Inn
17 Baseline Rd
Tel: 383-9751/1-888-389-7673
www.wildroseinn.com
Colonial country inn overlooking lakeside golf course. **$$–$$$**

Delta Beauséjour
750 Main St
Tel: 854-4344/1-888-351-7666
www.deltahotels.com
Moncton's finest hotel. **$$**

St Andrews (506)

The Fairmont Algonquin
184 Adolphus
Tel: 529-8823/1-866-540-4403
www.fairmont.com
Luxury resort hotel in the old style, with numerous recreations from golf to croquet. **$$–$$$**

Kingsbrae Arms
219 King St
Tel: 529-1897
www.kingsbrae.com
Surrounded by large gardens, this historic country house has marvelous views over St Andrews. **$$$**

Rossmount Inn
Hwy 127
Tel: 529-3351
www.rossmountinn.com
Victorian-style inn on historic Rossmount Estate overlooking Passamaquoddy Bay. Hiking, spa, pool, and driving range. **$$**

Treadwell Inn
129 Water St
Tel: 529-1011/1-888-529-1011
www.treadwellinn.com
Open May–Oct. Waterside property built *circa* 1820. Views of Passamaquoddy Bay. Furnished with antiques. **$$$**

Saint John (506)

Fort Howe Hotel and Convention Centre
10 Portland St
Tel: 657-7320/1-800-943-0033
www.forthowehotel.com
Great location overlooking city and harbor, and an indoor heated pool. **$**

Homeport Historic Bed & Breakfast Inn
80 Douglas Ave
Tel: 672-7255/1-888-678-7678
www.homeport.nb.ca
A beautifully restored mansion, built in the 1860s, with commanding views over the Bay of Fundy and the historic city of Saint John. **$**

Inn on the Cove
1371 Sand Cove Rd
Tel: 672-7799/1-877-257-8080
www.innonthecove.com
Overlooks Bay of Fundy, Irving Nature Park, and Digby ferry. Best Heritage Inn Award. Spa offers mineral mud wraps and hot stone massge. **$–$$$**

Hilton Saint John
One Market Square
Tel: 693-8484/1-800-445-8667
www.hilton.com
Luxury hotel overlooking harbor. Indoor pool and 2 restaurants. **$$$**

NEWFOUNDLAND AND LABRADOR

Finding good lodgings in Newfoundland and Labrador is not difficult and, although few small-town hotels and motels provide all modern conveniences, travelers almost always find the rooms comfortable and the owners hospitable. There are also many bed and breakfast establishments which provide excellent opportunities to meet the locals. As the town of St John's becomes increasingly cosmopolitan, so do its hotels, which are generally more modern and more expensive than those located in Newfoundland's interior. The Department of Tourism, Culture & Recreation publishes an excellent Travel Guide which includes detailed lists of campgrounds. It can be ordered at www.newfoundland labrador.com or at tel: 1-800-563-6353.

Note that lodgings carry a 12 percent provincial tax and 7 percent federal Goods and Services Tax.

Channel-Port-aux-Basques (709)

St Christopher's Hotel
146 Caribou Rd
Tel: 695-3500/1-800-563-4779
www.stchrishotel.com
A panoramic harbor view, and a warm introduction to Newfoundland. **$–$$**

L'Anse au Clair (709)

Northern Light Inn
58 Main St
Tel: 931-2332/1-800-563-3188
www.northernlightinn.com
A comfortable base for exploring the Labrador Straits; large restaurant, laundry, close to ferry. **$$**

Port Rexton (709)

Fishers' Loft Inn
Mill Rd
Tel: 1-877-464-3240
www.fishersloft.com
On the Bonavista Peninsula, one of the province's best inns, with gorgeous views overlooking the harbor. **$$–$$$**

St John's (709)

The Battery Hotel and Conference Centre
100 Signal Hill
Tel: 576-0040/1-800-563-8181
www.batteryhotel.com
On historic site with lovely views of the harbor and city. All modern amenities. **$–$$$**

Sheraton Hotel Newfoundland
115 Cavendish Square
Tel: 726-4980
www.starwoodhotels.com
Hotel in traditional style, considered one of the city's best downtown hotels, overlooking the harbor. **$$–$$$**

Everton House
23 Kings Bridge Rd
Tel: 754-1326/1-866-754-1326
www.evertonhouse.com
An elegant heritage home with whirlpool tubs and spacious rooms. **$$**

The Roses Bed and Breakfast
9 Military Rd
Tel: 726-3336/1-877-767-3722
www.therosesbandb.com
One of a number of superior

B&Bs situated close to the Sheraton Hotel Newfoundland. Charming rooms in a restored heritage home **$**

Trinity Bight (709)

Peace Cove Inn
Tel: 464-3738/1-866-464-3738
www.peacecoveinn.ca
On the Bonavista Peninsula, an original sea captain's home by the sea offers all modern amenities. **$–$$**

PRICE CATEGORIES

Price categories are for a double room with breakfast:
$ = under $100
$$ = $100–200
$$$ = over $200

TRANSPORTATION ACCOMMODATIONS EATING OUT ACTIVITIES A – Z LANGUAGE

THE NORTHWEST TERRITORIES

Nearly every community has at least one inn or hotel, often an Inuit co-operative. Most have dining rooms or kitchenette facilities, and meals are occasionally included in the overnight price. The amenities will vary: private bathrooms, radios and even TVs are not uncommon; however, room service is rare, bellhops unheard of. Expect to pay $80–250 for a double. Although there is no sales tax on lodgings here, the federal 5 percent Goods and Services Tax is payable. Summer reservations should be made the previous spring.

For a complete accommodations listing contact NWT Tourism. Tel: 1-800-661-0788/1-867-873-7000; www.explorenwt.com. Ask for its latest Explorers' Guide which includes hotels, B&Bs, and campgrounds.

Fort Smith (867)

Pelican Rapids Inn
152 McDougal Rd
Tel: 872-2789
Small modern hotel. $$

Hay River (867)

Ptarmigan Inn
10J Gagnier St
Tel: 874-6781/1-800-661-0842
www.ptarmiganinn.com
Comfortable rooms and suites. Good facilities for leisure and business travelers. $$

Inuvik (867)

Capital Suites
198 Mackenzie Rd
Tel: 678-6300/1-877-669-9444
www.capitalsuites.ca
A brand new property, a block from Downtown, a wide range of well-equipped suites. $$

Yellowknife (867)

Back Bay Boat Bed & Breakfast
3530 Ingraham Dr
Tel: 873-4080/1-867-873-4080
Email: info@backbayboat.com
Spacious home on the Back Bay of Great Slave Lake, in the city's Old Town. $
Château Nova
4401–50th Ave

Tel: 873-9700/1-877-839-1236
www.chateaunova.com
New downtown hotel infused with Northern spirit, with 80 rooms and suites. $$
The Explorer Hotel
4825 49th Ave
Tel: 873-3531/1-800-661-0892
www.explorerhotel.ca
Modern urban hotel with restaurant and other facilities. $$

NOVA SCOTIA

Tourism Nova Scotia (see page 397) publishes an annual Doer's and Dreamer's Complete Guide, which contains listings of lodgings and campsites in the province. Any of Nova Scotia's 70 visitor information centers will reserve accommodations, or call toll-free 1-800-565-0000. For information on hostels in Nova Scotia check the Hostelling International website at www.hihostels.ca or call 902-422-3863.

Baddeck (902)

The resort town of Baddeck is the starting point for the world-famous Cabot Trail.
Inverary Resort
368 Hwy 205/Shore Rd
Tel: 295-3500/1-800-565-5660
www.capebretonresorts.com
On the waterfront of Bras d'Or Lake, with an excellent dining room, pool, and private beach. $$–$$$
Telegraph House & Cottages
479 Chebucto St
Tel: 295-1100/1-888-263-9840
www.baddeck.com/telegraph
A Victorian house (circa 1861) that has become a Cape Breton favorite. $–$$

Cheticamp (902)

Parkview Motel
Route 19, 5km (3 miles) north of town
Tel: 224-3232/1-877-224-3232
www.parkviewresort.com
Lovely location on banks of Cheticamp River, at entrance to Cape Breton Highlands National Park. $

Grand Pré (902)

Evangeline Inn and Motel
11668 Hwy 1
Tel: 542-2703/1-888-542-2703
www.evangeline.ns.ca
Historic house with five rooms. Set in rock gardens and waterfalls. $

Halifax (902)

Garden Inn
1263 South Park St
Tel: 492-8577/1-877-414-8577
www.gardeninn.ns.ca
An 1875 heritage home close to Downtown, restored and full of antiques. $$
Halifax Waverley Inn
1266 Barrington St
Tel: 423-9346/1-800-565-9346
www.waverleyinn.com

A relaxed, Victorian-era inn where Oscar Wilde once stayed, pleasantly located in a quiet neighborhood. $$
Halliburton House Inn
5184 Morris St
Tel: 420-0658/1-888-512-3344
www.halliburton.ns.ca
A heritage property (1820) with a courtyard garden and an acclaimed restaurant. $$
Prince George Hotel
1725 Market St
Tel: 425-1986/1-800-565-1567
www.princegeorgehotel.com
An elegant hotel and chic restaurant, connected by an underground walkway to the World Trade and Convention Center. $$$

Ingonish Beach (902)

Keltic Lodge
Middle Head Peninsula
Tel: 285-2880/1-800-565-0444
www.kelticlodge.ca
Spectacular cliff-top location, a short distance from the Cabot Trail. Renowned for golfing and whale-watching. $$–$$$

Liverpool (902)

Whitepoint Beach Resort

Tel: 421-1569/1-800-565-5068
www.whitepoint.com
A luxurious beachfront resort on the South Shore with rooms and cottages, and good facilities. $$

Lunenburg (902)

Kaulbach House Historic Inn
75 Pelham St
Tel: 634-8818/1-800-568-8818
www.kaulbachhouse.com
Gracious Victorian house near the waterfront. $$

Shelburne (902)

The Cooper's Inn
36 Dock St
Tel: 875-4656/1-800-688-2011
www.thecoopersinn.com
An 18th-century house on historic Dock Street. Good food in relaxed setting. $$

NUNAVUT

Consult Nunavut Tourism's website, at www.nunavut tourism.com for detailed information and to order a free CD containing a complete list of hotels, wilderness lodges, tour operators, and suggested activities.

Cambridge Bay (867)

Elu Lodge
Tel: 1-800-663-9832
www.elulodge.com
This lodge offers comfortable accommodation, beautifully located on the shores of Elu Inlet, next to Mount Elu and the mouth of the Itibiak River, surrounded by pristine wilderness. 3–7-day packages including airfare from Cambridge Bay. **$$$**

Cape Dorset (867)

Dorset Suites
PO Box 4
Tel: 867-897-8806
www.dorsetsuites.com
6 1-bedroom suites, an executive suite plus 3 separate 2 or 3 bedroom houses with full kitchens, all in a contemporary design. A variety of eco-culture trips are on offer. **$$**

Kingnait Inn
PO Box 89
Tel: 897-8863
17 rooms, 8 with private bath; laundry facilities available; and payphone. **$$**

Iqaluit (867)

Discovery Lodge Hotel
PO Box 387
Tel: 979-4433
www.discoverylodge.com
Centrally located and long established hotel, offering conference facilities for more than 100 people. **$$$**

Frobisher Inn
PO Box 4209
Tel: 979-2222/1-877-422-9422
www.frobisherinn.com
A 95-room hotel frequented by tourists and visiting dignitaries alike. Comfortable rooms and conference facilities. They even cater to anglers by freezing their catch. **$$$**

Victoria Island (867)

High Arctic Lodge
Tel: 250-497-2000/1-800-661-3880
www.higharctic.com
Open early July–mid-Aug, the lodge and individual cabins are 480km (300 miles) north of the Arctic Circle. Weeklong fishing packages. **$$$** including airfare from Cambridge Bay.

ONTARIO

Ontario Travel *(see page 397)* provides details of accommodations in the *Ontario Discovery Guide*, which lists over 4,000 hotels, motels, resorts, and fly-in camps. It's worth enquiring about weekend packages – many hotels discount their rooms up to 50 percent if visitors stay on Friday and Saturday nights.

Try to book summertime resort accommodations at least a month in advance. Resorts of Ontario represent over 200 lakeside resort properties providing waterfront accommodations in lodges. For more information and brochures contact Resorts of Ontario, PO Box 2148, 29 Albert St N, Orillia, ON L3V 5J9, tel: 705-325-9115/1-800-363-7227, www.resortsofontario.com

Algonquin Park (705)

Arowhon Pines
Little Joe Lake
Tel: 633-5661 (summer)/416-483-4393 (winter)/1-866-633-5661
www.arowhonpines.ca
Legendary lodge and cottages. Canoeing, swimming, hiking, and other outdoor facilities are available. A member of the Relais & Château chain of superior lodgings. **$$$**

Bracebridge (705)

Clevelands House
1040 Juddhaven Rd, Minett
Tel: 765-3171/1-888-567-1177
www.clevelandshouse.com
Historic lodge on Lake Rosseau, with modern amenities; full summertime facilities, including tennis, golf, and water sports. **$$$**

Kingston (613)

Hochelaga Inn
24 Sydenham St S
Tel: 549-5534/1-877-933-9433
www.hochelagainn.com
A B&B in a lovely old home close to Downtown. **$$**

Holiday Inn
2 Princess St
Tel: 549-8400/1-800-465-4329
www.hikingstonwaterfront.com
Central waterfront location, with a rooftop garden restaurant, and indoor and outdoor pools. **$$**

Kitchener-Waterloo (519)

Hillcrest House
73 George St
Tel: 744-3534
www.hillcresthouse.ca
An elegant, Italianate B&B with 3 private suites, in a quiet neighborhood in the center of Waterloo. **$$**

Niagara Falls (905)

Rates vary wildly with the season, but are highest from late June to late September, especially weekends.

Crowne Plaza Fallsview
5685 Falls Ave
Tel: 374-4447/1-800-263-7135
www.niagarafallshotels.com/crowne
Very popular hotel next to the casino, with three-quarters of the rooms overlooking the Falls. **$$**

Old Stone Inn
5425 Robinson St
Tel: 357-1234/1-800-263-6208
www.oldstoneinn.on.ca
A century-old, former flour mill converted into a charming boutique hotel. **$$$**

Fallsview Plaza Hotel
6455 Fallsview Blvd
Tel: 357-5200/1-888-238-9176
www.fallsviewhotel.com
Walking distance to the Falls, and connected by a glass walkway to the Fallsview Casino. **$$**

Travelodge Clifton Hill
4943 Clifton Hill
Tel: 357-2200
www.falls.com
In the heart of the action, close to the Falls and Casino Niagara; outdoor heated pool. **$$**

PRICE CATEGORIES

Price categories are for a double room with breakfast:
$ = under $100
$$ = $100–200
$$$ = over $200

ABOVE: the jetty at Clevelands House, Bracebridge.

Niagara-on-the-Lake (905)

Niagara-on-the-Lake Bed & Breakfast Association
Tel: 468-0123/1-866-855-0123
www.bba.notl.on.ca
Oban Inn
160 Front St
Tel: 468-2165/1-866-359-6226
www.obaninn.ca
Historic inn – the town's first – overlooking Lake Ontario and Canada's oldest golf course. **$$$**
Prince of Wales Hotel
6 Picton St
Tel: 468-3246/1-888-669-5566
www.vintage-hotels.com
Replete with the grandeur one expects in Niagara-on-the-Lake. Indoor recreational facilities include spa, excellent dining, and a cozy lounge. **$$$**
White Oaks Conference Resort & Spa
253 Taylor Rd SS4
Tel: 688-2550/1-800-263-5766
www.whiteoaksresort.com
Niagara-on-the-Lake's largest resort yet an intimate ambiance, with golf, spa treatments, fitness center, and racquet club. **$$$**

Ottawa (613)

ARC The Hotel
140 Slater St
Tel: 238-2888/1-800-699-2516
www.arcthehotel.com
One of Ottawa's stylish designer hotels, in the heart of Downtown. **$$$**
The Bostonian
341 MacLaren St
Tel: 594-5757/1-866-320-4567
www.thebostonian.ca
A luxury studio and one-bedroom suite hotel in historic Somerset West. **$$$**
Capital Hill Hotel
88 Albert St
Tel: 235-1413/1-800-463-7705
www.capitalhill.com
Family-run lodgings of rooms and suites, within walking distance of Parliament Hill. **$$**
Carleton University
Tour and Conference Center,
261 Stormont House,
Carleton University
Tel: 520-5611/520-5609 (after May 7)
www2.carleton.ca/housing/conference-services/guest-accomodations/
For cheap, summertime lodgings in Ottawa. **$**
Crown Plaza Hotel Ottawa
101 Lyon St
Tel: 237-3600/1-800-2CROWNE
www.cpottawa.com
Renovated, high-rise hotel, with all the amenities and a rooftop lounge. **$$**
Delta Ottawa Hotel & Suites
361 Queen St
Tel: 238-6000/1-888-890-3222
www.deltahotels.com
Beautiful rooms and a health club complete with a 35 meter (115ft) indoor water slide. **$$**
Fairmont Château Laurier
1 Rideau St
Tel: 241-1414/1-866-540-4410
www.fairmont.com
An Ottawa landmark renowned for grandeur befitting its château-style appearance. Spacious rooms. **$$$**

Benner's Bed & Breakfast
541 Besserer St
Tel: 789-8320/1-877-891-5485
www.bennersbnb.com
Located in a leafy residential neighborhood within walking distance of downtown attractions. **$–$$**
Hostelling International Ottawa
75 Nicholas St
Tel: 235-2595/1-866-299-1478
www.hihostels.ca
In what was formerly the Carleton County Jail (1862–1972), this is an excellent downtown location for budget accommodations. **$**
Lord Elgin
100 Elgin St
Tel: 235-3333/1-800-267-4298
www.lordelginhotel.ca
A regal atmosphere; smallish yet modern rooms. Near Parliament Hill and across from the National Arts Centre. Great value. **$$**
Novotel Ottawa Hotel
33 Nicholas St
Tel: 230-3033/1-800-668-6835
www.novotelottawa.com
Comfortable hotel, well located beside the Rideau Centre. **$$$**

Port Carling (705)

Delta Sherwood Inn
1090 Sherwood Rd
Tel: 765-3131/1-888-890-3222
www.deltahotels.com
In the heart of Muskoka, on the edge of tiny Lake Joseph. Surrounded by towering pines, the postcard-perfect views and romantic setting are as "old cottage country" as it gets in Ontario. A very luxurious base for outdoor adventures. **$$$**

Port Severn (705)

Christie's Mill Inn & Spa
263 Port Severn Rd N, Box 125
Tel: 538-2354/1-800-465-9966
www.christiesmill.com
A relaxing, European-style lakefront resort in Georgian Bay. **$$**

Stratford (519)

Check with the Theater Box Office (see page 373 for address) about B&B

accommodations during the festival.
Albert Street Inn
23 Albert St
Tel: 272-2581/1-866-572-2581
www.albertstinn.com
Spacious rooms in comfortable B&B. **$$**
River Garden House
53 William St
Tel: 271-1403/1-877-771-1403
www.rivergardenhouse.com
An elegant B&B overlooking the river. **$$**
The River Garden Inn
10 Romeo St N
Tel: 271-4650/1-800-741-2135
www.therivergardeninn.com
An expansive, newly renovated hotel with an indoor pool. Reservations essential during the festival. **$$**

Sudbury (705)

The Parker House Inn
259 Elm St
Tel: 674-2442/1-888-250-4453
www.parkerhouseinns.com
A casually elegant estate home in the heart of the city. **$–$$**
Travelway Inn
1200 Paris St
Tel: 522-1122/1-800-461-4883
www.travelwayinnsudbury.com
Spacious rooms, all with a view, and a minute's walk from Sudbury's biggest attraction, Science North. **$$**

Toronto (416)

Between an open-ended tourist season and a large convention market, there is constant demand for Toronto hotel rooms. There are accommodations to match every budget, and the standards are high. Tourism Toronto and the Greater Toronto Hotel Association offer a free year-round reservations service. Tel: 203-2500.
Cosmopolitan Toronto Centre Hotel and Spa
8 Colborne St
Tel: 1-800-958-3488
www.cosmotoronto.com
A contemporary boutique hotel in the Financial District, with a zen-like ambience. **$$$**

Delta Chelsea
33 Gerrard St W (between Yonge and Bay)
Tel: 595-1975/1-800-CHELSEA
www.deltahotels.com
Large hotel with upscale accommodations in convenient downtown location. Good programs for children. **$$**

Drake Hotel
1150 Queen St W
Tel: 531-5042/1-866-DRAKETO
www.thedrakehotel.ca
Amid trendy shops and art galleries in edgy West Queen West, epitomizes bohemian luxury. **$$–$$$**

Fairmont Royal York
100 Front St W
Tel: 368-2511/1-866-540-4489
www.fairmont.com/royalyork
A Toronto landmark in the heart of Downtown, right across from Union Station. **$$$**

Four Seasons Hotel
21 Avenue Rd
Tel: 964-0411/1-800-819-5053
www.fourseasons.com/toronto
Understated elegance, jet-set clientele; spacious rooms with nice views. **$$$**

Hotel Le Germain
30 Mercer St
Tel: 345-9500/1-866-345-9501
www.germaintoronto.com
A sleek boutique hotel in the heart of the Entertainment District. **$$$**

Le Meridien King Edward
37 King St E
Tel: 863-9700/1-800-543-4300
www.lemeridien-kingedward.com
An old Toronto favorite. Marble columns punctuate the lobby; the spacious rooms are gracefully decorated. **$$–$$$**

Madison Manor Boutique Hotel
20 Madison Ave
Tel: 922-5579/1-877-561-7048
www.madisonavenuepub.com
An elegant inn in the Annex that is frequented by visiting academics and includes an extremely popular pub. **$$**

Park Hyatt Hotel
4 Avenue Rd (at Bloor)
Tel: 925-1234/1-888-591-1234
www.parktoronto.hyatt.com
Located in trendy Yorkville; its Roof Lounge is favored by the city's literati. **$$$**

Renaissance Toronto Hotel Downtown
1 Blue Jays Way
Tel: 341-7100/1-800-237-1512
www.renaissancetoronto.com
Literally part of the Rogers Centre, it's the world's only sports-and-entertainment hotel. A dream for baseball fans. **$$$**

Sheraton Centre Toronto Hotel
123 Queen St W
(opposite City Hall)
Tel: 361-1000/1-800-325-3535
www.sheraton.com
Almost 1,400 rooms; walking distance to most downtown attractions; atop underground shopping, restaurants, and movie theaters. **$$–$$$**

Sutton Place Hotel
955 Bay St
Tel: 924-9221/1-866-378-8866
www.toronto.suttonplace.com
Elegant, low-key hotel, rising 17 stories above Bay Street. Intended to resemble the grand hotels of Europe, and a favorite with showbiz types. Rooms have nice touches. **$$$**

Westin Harbour Castle
1 Harbour Square
Tel: 869-1600/1-800-937-8461
www.westin.com/harbourcastle
Plush decor throughout. All rooms in the two towers offer a sparkling view of the harbor, especially the Lighthouse Restaurant on the 37th floor. **$$$**

Windsor (519)

The Windsor Inn On The River
3857 Riverside Dr E
Tel: 945-2110/1-866-635-0055
www.windsorinnontheriver.com
An elegant bed-and-breakfast with unobstructed views of the Detroit River and Belle Isle. **$$**

Hilton Windsor
277 Riverside Dr W
Tel: 973-5555/1-800-445-8667
www.hilton.com
Deluxe hotel overlooking the Detroit River. **$$$**

PRINCE EDWARD ISLAND

P.E.I.'s hotels, motels, and resorts fill fast in the summer, so reservations should be secured as far in advance as possible. Write or call Tourism P.E.I. *(see Tourist Offices section, page 397)* for their annual *Visitors Guide* or for help in making reservations. Once you are on the island, any visitors information center can help to arrange accommodations in hotels, motels, campgrounds, and resort lodgings, as well as organize stays at farm, tourist, and vacation homes. For about $60 a day per person, visitors share meals, activities, and sometimes farmwork with their hosts. Those who have experienced this often claim this is the best (and cheapest) way to get to know P.E.I. and its inhabitants.

Private and provincial campgrounds are scattered throughout Prince Edward Island. The fees range from $15–25 a night, depending on the services available. Note that camping anywhere other than on a designated campground is illegal.

Cavendish (902)

Kindred Spirits Country Inn and Cottages
Route 6, Memory Lane
Tel: 1-800-461-1755
www.kindredspirits.ca
An antique-filled inn close to Green Gables House and Golf Course. Open mid-May–late Oct. **$$**

Charlottetown (902)

Delta Prince Edward
18 Queen St
Tel: 566-2222/1-888-890-3222
www.deltahotels.com
Luxury waterfront hotel with views over the harbor and Old Charlottetown. **$$–$$$**

Bed of Roses by the Sea B&B
185 Queen Elizabeth Dr
Tel: 892-0185/1-866-892-0009
www.bedofrosesbythesea.com
A waterfront bed and breakfast – with fireplaces, whirlpools, and a cathedral glass roof – that promises breathtaking sunsets, yoga, massage, and wellness retreats year-round. **$$–$$$**

The Rodd Charlottetown
75 Kent St
Tel: 894-7371/1-800-565-7633
www.rodd-hotels.ca
Old-fashioned elegance with renovated rooms and facilities. **$$**

Grand Tracadie (902)

Dalvay-By-The-Sea
Tel: 672-2048/1-888-366-2955
www.dalvaybythesea.com
Luxury resort of Victorian inn and cottages, inside P.E.I. National Park. **$$$**

Souris (902)

A Place To Stay Inn
Tel: 687-4626/1-800-655-STAY
http://peislandconnections.com/stayinn
A relaxed inn and hostel, close to some of P.E.I.'s best beaches and the Iles de la Madeleine ferry, with lovely views of the countryside and the harbor. **$**

PRICE CATEGORIES

Price categories are for a double room with breakfast:
$ = under $100
$$ = $100–200
$$$ = over $200

Summerside (902)

Clark's Sunny Isle Motel
720 Water St E
Tel: 436-5665/1-877-682-6824.
www.sunnyislemotel.com
Within a 20-acre garden,
comfortable rooms at low
prices. **$**
Lakeview Loyalist Resort
195 Harbour Dr

Tel: 436-3333/1-877-355-3500
www.lakeviewhotels.com
A traditional inn overlooking
Summerside harbor with an
indoor pool, sauna,
exercise room, and bike
rental. **$$**
**Quality Inn Garden of the
Gulf**
618 Water St E
Tel: 436-2295/1-800-265-5551

www.qualityinnpei.com
Summerside's fanciest
hotel features pool and
beachfront swimming,
restaurant, and dinner
theater. **$$**
Silver Fox Inn
61 Granville St
Tel: 436-1664/1-800-565-4033
www.silverfoxinn.net
Elegant B&B in lovely 19th-

century villa; 6 rooms
furnished with antiques;
cozy tea room. **$$**

Wood Islands (902)

Meadow Lodge Motel
Tel: 962-2022/1-800-461-2022
www.peisland.com/meadowlodge
Country lodgings close to
ferry; restaurant nearby. **$**

Québec

Book lodgings as far in
advance as possible. Large
hotels often offer discounts
at weekends, but resort
areas will be crowded and
therefore more expensive. If
you reserve rooms with two
double beds, your child can
usually stay free; if need be,
you can rent extra roll-away
beds at a low extra cost.

Most hotels in Montréal
fall in the expensive to
deluxe range, especially
those downtown. Yet a full
range of accommodations is
available, and most hotels
have excellent restaurants.

Although a wide variety of
accommodations can be
found within the old city,
Québec is renowned for its
grand old hotels and
modest, European-style
guest homes. Visitors
looking for larger or more
modern lodgings may have
to stay in the new city.

The hotel association
Hôtellerie Champêtre-
Québec Resorts & Country
Inns offers charming
country inns in beautiful
locations. Tel: 514-861-
4024/1-800-861-4024.
www.hotelleriechampetre.com.
Montréal and Québec
use the European system of
accommodations in
residents' homes. Tourism
Québec publishes an
excellent *Accommodations
Guide* that includes B&Bs,
tourist residences (for five
or fewer guests), youth
hostels, educational
institutions, and resort
villages.

Baie St-Paul (418)

**Le Gîte Nature et
Pinceaux**
33 Rue de Nordet
Tel: 435-2366
www.natureetpinceaux.qc.ca

A tranquil setting just
outside Baie St-Paul,
overlooking the St
Lawrence. **$$**

Magog (819)

**Auberge L'Etoile-sur-le-
Lac**
1200 Rue Principale Ouest
Tel: 843-6521/1-800-567-2727
www.etoile-sur-le-lac.com
Great location on Lake
Memphremagog. Minutes
from Mont Orford for hiking
and skiing. **$$**

Mont Tremblant (819)

Château Beauvallon
6385, Montée Ryan
Tel: 681-6611/1-888-681-6611
www.chateaubeauvallon.com
One of the area's many
small, cozy, New England-
style resorts. Ask about their
ski packages. **$$$**

Hôtel Quintessence
3004 chemin de la Chapelle
Tel: 425-3400/
1-866-425-3400
www.hotelquintessence.com
A luxury boutique hotel on
the banks of Lac Tremblant.
$$$
Tremblant
Tel: 514-876-7273/
1-888-738-1777
www.tremblant.com
Largest year-round resort
in Eastern Canada
offering a wide range
of accommodations.
$$–$$$

Below: the picturesque resort of Mont Tremblant.

Montréal (514)

Auberge de la Fontaine
1301 rue Rachel Est
Tel: 597-0166/1-800-597-0597
www.aubergedelafontaine.com
Beside Parc Lafontaine in Plateau Mont-Royal neighborhood. **$$**

Fairmont The Queen Elizabeth
900 René-Lévesque Ouest
Tel: 861-3511/1-866-540-4483
www.fairmont.com
Dependable comfort in prime location. **$$–$$$**

Hilton Montréal Bonaventure
900 de la Gauchetière Ouest
Tel: 878-2332/1-800-445-8667
www.hiltonmontreal.com
Central location, first-class facilities and service, and gloriously peaceful rooftop garden. **$$$**

Hotel Gault
449 Rue Sainte-Hélène
Tel: 904-1616/1-866-904-1616
www.hotelgault.com
In Old Montréal, a marvellous conversion offers 30 ultra modern loft-style rooms. **$$–$$$**

Hôtel Le Germain
2050 rue Mansfield
Tel: 849-2050/1-877-333-2050
www.hotelgermain.com
A chic boutique-hotel in a former office building, trendily located in downtown Montréal. **$$$**

Hôtel Nelligan
106 rue St-Paul Ouest
Tel: 788-2040/1-877-788-2040
www.hotelnelligan.com
Beautifully restored stone-and-brick building, dating to 1830s, in heart of Old Montréal, with 63 comfortable and spacious rooms and a superb restaurant, Verses. **$$$**

McGill University Residences
3425 rue University
Tel: 398-5200
www.mcgill.ca/residences/summer
Central budget accommodations available during the summer. **$**

Ritz Carlton Montréal
1228 rue Sherbrooke Ouest
Tel: 842-4212/1-800-363-0366
www.ritzmontreal.com
In the heart of the Golden Square Mile, the Ritz caters to an élite clientele. **$$$**

North Hatley (819)

Auberge La Rose des Vents
312 chemin de la Rivière
Tel: 842-4530
www.rosedesvents.qc.ca/rosea.htm
In the center of this charming village, overlooking Lac Massawipi and the river, the inn has 12 guest rooms, a bar, and a small dining room. **$$**

Manoir Hovey
575 chemin Hovey
Tel: 842-2421/1-800-661-2421
www.manoirhovey.com
An impressive lakeside mansion inspired by George Washington's Mount Vernon. Cozy English country-style decor; excellent dining. **$$$**

Orford (819)

Auberge de la Tour
1837 chemin Alfred-Desrochers
Tel: 868-0763/1-877-668-0763
www.auberge-de-la-tour.com
A neo-colonial home on the edge of Mont Orford Provincial Park and its ski hills. Cozy bedrooms, lovely terrace, and heated swimming pool. **$**

Percé (418)

Hôtel-Motel Rocher Percé
111 Route 132 Ouest, CP 34
Tel: 1-888-467-3723
www.hotelperce.com
A modest but pleasant establishment, across from Percé Rock, with direct beach access at low tide. It has one of the Gaspé's most beautiful views, and is a convenient base for visiting Forillon National Park. **$**

Hôtel La Normandie
221 Route 132 Ouest, CP 129
Tel: 782-2112/1-800-463-0820
www.normandieperce.com
A beachside property facing Bonaventure Island and Percé Rock, with a pleasant restaurant and a gym. **$$**

Québec City (418)

Auberge de la Place d'Armes
24 rue Ste-Anne
Tel: 694-9485/1-866-333-9485
www.quebecweb.com/placedarme

ABOVE: browsing the streets of Québec City.

Simple but elegant rooms; excellent locale near city hall. **$$**

Centre International de Séjour de Québec
19 rue Ste-Ursule
Tel: 694-0755/1-866-694-0950
www.hihostels.ca/Quebec
Sizable youth hostel featuring B&B lodgings. **$**

Fairmont Le Château Frontenac
1 rue des Carrières
Tel: 692-3861/1-866-540-4460
www.fairmont.com
600-room castle set atop a cliff overlooking the St Lawrence River – worth seeing even if one doesn't stay overnight. **$$$**

Hôtel Château Bellevue
16 rue de la Porte
Tel: 692-2573/1-800-463-2617
www.vieux-quebec.com
Within the old city; antique facade conceals ultra-modern accommodations. Free parking. **$–$$$**

Hôtel Château Laurier
1220 place George V Ouest
Tel: 522-8108/1-800-463-4453
www.vieuxquebec.com
On the Plains of Abraham, a perfect location for Winter Carnival. **$$**

Hôtel Clarendon
57 rue Ste-Anne
Tel: 266-2165/1-877-778-8977
www.quebecweb.com/clarendon/introang.asp

The city's oldest hotel. Centrally located and good value. **$$–$$$**

Hotel 71
71 rue Saint-Pierre
Tel: 692-1171/1-888-692-1171
www.hotel71.ca
In Le Vieux-Port, a designer-boutique hotel within a neo-classical building, formerly the National Bank's first head office. **$$$**

Hôtel Manoir Victoria
44 côte du Palais
Tel: 692-1030/1-800-463-6283
www.manoir-victoria.com
Renovated hotel in heart of Old Québec, with European ambience. **$$–$$$**

Québec Hilton
1100 blvd René-Lévesque Est
Tel: 647-2411/1-800-445-8667
www.hilton.com
Massively renovated, with spacious rooms; children can sometimes stay free. **$$$**

Ste-Adèle (450)

Hôtel Le Chantecler
1474 chemin Chantecler

PRICE CATEGORIES

Price categories are for a double room with breakfast:
$ = under $100
$$ = $100–200
$$$ = over $200

Tel: 1-888-916-1616
www.lechantecler.com
Popular lakeside resort,
with combination of modern
and rustic accommo-
dations; wide range of
summer and winter
activities on and beyond the
resort. **$$**

Auberge de la Tour du Lac
173 chemin Tour du Lac
Tel: 326-4202/1-800-622-1735
www.aubergedelatourdulac.com
25km (15 miles) north of
Ste-Adèle, a charming hotel

set in lovely grounds on Lac
des Sables. Public rooms
are furnished with antiques;
guest rooms are spacious.
$$

Val David (819)

Auberge Le Rouet

1288 rue Lavoie
Tel: 322-3221/1-800-537-6838
www.aubergelerouet.com
12km (7 miles) north of
Ste-Adèle, a lovely inn
combines the relaxed
ambience of a log cabin
with warm French-
Canadian hospitality. **$–$$**

SASKATCHEWAN

Moose Jaw (306)

**Temple Gardens Mineral
Spa Hotel/Resort**
24 Fairford St E
Tel: 694-5055/1-800-718-7727
www.templegardens.sk.ca
In heart of historic district,
with a geo-thermal mineral
spa. Full facilities. **$$–$$$**

Regina (306)

Delta Regina
1919 Saskatchewan Dr
Tel: 525-5255/1-877-814-7706
www.deltahotels.com
A modern tower in the
heart of Downtown,
connected by skywalk to
Casino Regina. **$$$**
**Radisson Plaza
Hotel Saskatchewan**
2125 Victoria Ave

Tel: 522-7691/1-800-333-3333
www.hotelsask.com
Elegantly restored heritage
hotel, with modern
accoutrements. **$$$**
**Regina Inn Hotel &
Conference Centre**
1975 Broad St
Tel: 525-6767/1-800-667-8162
www.reginainn.com
Good rooms and suites.
Piano bar, dinner theater,
restaurant. **$$**
**Wingate by Wyndham
Regina**
1700 Broad St
Tel: 584-7400
Convenient location, near
shopping mall. **$$**

Saskatoon (306)

Delta Bessborough
601 Spadina Cres E

Tel: 244-5521/1-888-890-3222
www.deltahotels.com
Elegant riverside château-
style hotel. Recreational
facilities, bars, and
restaurants. **$$–$$$**
Park Town Hotel
924 Spadina Cres E
Tel: 244-5564/1-800-667-3999
www.parktownhotel.com
Centrally located, a modern
smoke-free hotel with nice
views of the South
Saskatchewan River. **$$**
Saskatoon Inn
2002 Airport Dr
Tel: 242-1440/1-800-667-8789
www.saskatooninn.com
Modern hotel with pool,
restaurant, children's
activities. Situated close to
the airport. **$$**
Sheraton Cavalier
612 Spadina Cres E

Tel: 652-6770/1-866-716-8101
www.sheratoncavalier.com
Luxury downtown smoke-
free hotel; skytop lounge. **$$**

Prince Albert (306)

Comfort Inn
3863 2nd Ave W
Tel: 763-4466
www.choicehotels.ca
Clean, comfortable rooms.
$$

THE YUKON

The Yukon offers a good
variety of lodgings. Make
reservations early in the
year for the crowded
summer months,
particularly July. Tourism
Yukon – http://travelyukon.com
– provides a complete list
of accommodations in its
*Official Vacation Guide (see
Tourist Offices section,
page 398).*

Dawson City (867)

Dawson City River Hostel
Tel: 993-6823 (summer only)
www.yukonhostels.com
Open mid-May–Oct 1,
depending on ferry service.
Beside Yukon River, across
from Dawson City, with
rustic accommodations
that offer some of the best

city views. Only a few
minutes' walk from the
ferry landing in West
Dawson. **$**
**Westmark Inn Dawson
City**
Fifth & Harper sts
Tel: 993-5542/1-800-544-0970
www.westmarkhotels.com/dawsoncity
Prestigious chain hotel.
Downtown area, good dining
room, also Klondike
barbecue. **$$**

Whitehorse (867)

Hawkins House B&B
303 Hawkins St
Tel: 668-7638
Luxurious Victorian home,
converted to a B&B. **$$**
River View Hotel
102 Wood St
Tel: 667-7801

www.riverviewhotel.ca
Centrally located
accommodation. Rooms
overlook Yukon River. **$$**
Westmark Klondike Inn
2288 2nd Ave
Tel: 668-4747/1-800-544-0970
www.westmarkhotels.com/klondike
Modern hotel with great
view of the mountains.
Cocktail lounge and dining
room on the premises. **$$**
The Yukon Inn Hotel
4220 4th Ave
Tel: 667-2527/1-800-661-0454
www.yukoninn.com
Modern, spacious rooms,
lounges, dining room, hair
salon. **$$**

Campgrounds

Numerous campgrounds,
many with modern facilities,

dot Yukon highways. Bring
a tent or bring or rent a
camper or trailer. Contact
Tourism Yukon for more
details *(see page 398).*

PRICE CATEGORIES

Price categories are for
a double room with
breakfast:
$ = under $100
$$ = $100–200
$$$ = over $200

E ATING OUT

RECOMMENDED RESTAURANTS, CAFÉS AND BARS

Where to Eat

Canada's culinary history is like a recipe made up of many ingredients, with each province having its own specialties. The Atlantic waters of the Maritimes dish up excellent seafood, while Québec's French roots, combined with the native ways of eating, have created a unique cuisine. Ontario is known for its vegetables, fruits, and wines; the Prairies produce wheat and choice beef; British Columbia is synonymous with salmon; and the north with Arctic char.

Dining out in Canada's cities is every bit as sophisticated and varied as in any of the world's major cities. For the more casual eater, fast-food restaurants, diners, and coffee shops, some open 24 hours, dot the landscape. Provincial sales tax (except in Alberta and the three northern territories) and the national 5 percent Goods and Services Tax apply to eating out.

Drinking Notes

Canada is traditionally a beer-drinking nation, and fine beer is brewed locally where microbreweries produce lagers, ales, pilsners, and bock. Imports from Europe, Australia, and Mexico are also popular. Canadian wines, mostly from Ontario and British Columbia, represent great value and have also won international acclaim, although many restaurants still tend toward French, Italian, and Californian wines. Liquor laws vary from province to province, and sales are heavily regulated. In most provinces, alcohol can only be purchased in government stores and some special stores. In Québec, alcohol can also be purchased in privately owned convenience stores called *dépanneurs* (check the Yellow Pages). Most restaurants are licensed to serve alcohol, but it's best to check first. The legal age for drinking is 18 or 19, depending on the province.

RESTAURANT LISTINGS

ALBERTA

Alberta is cowboy country in the midst of fertile famland, producing some of the best grain-fed beef in North America. Not surprisingly, it's a steak-lover's paradise. French, Italian, Continental, and Asian cuisine are also well represented.

Banff (403)

Balkan Restaurant
120 Banff Ave
Tel: 762-3454
www. banffbalkan.ca
Casual, classic Greek fare.
$-$$
Caramba! Restaurante
337 Banff Ave

Tel: 762-3667
A fun, laid-back atmosphere with open kitchen. Mediterranean-based dishes plus B.C. seafood, Alberta beef, and Asian specialties. **$-$$**
Giorgio's Trattoria
219 Banff Ave
Tel: 762-5114
www.giorgiosbanff
Italian decor and menu. Pizza prepared in a wood-fired oven. **$$**
Le Beaujolais
Banff Ave and Buffalo St
www.lebeaujolaisbanff.com
Tel: 762-2712
French four-star restaurant in a pleasant setting. **$$$**

Calgary (403)

Cafe Metro
7400 Macleod Trail S
Tel: 255-6537
Whimsical murals on the walls, smoked meat, poutine, bagels, latkes, pizzas, and burgers on the menu. **$**
Capo
#4, 1420 9 Ave SE
Tel: 264 2276
www.caporestaurant.ca
Creative and meticulously prepared Italian located in an intimate contemporary room. **$$$**
El Sombrero Restaurante
520–17th Ave SW
Tel: 228-0332

A "cheap and cheerful" restaurant with substantial Mexican fare. **$$**
Galaxie Diner
1413 11th St SW
Tel: 228-0001
www.galaxiediner.com
Great diner for breakfasts and lunches. **$**
Globefish Sushi & Izakaya
332 14 St NW
Tel: 521-0222

PRICE CATEGORIES

Price categories are for a meal for one, excluding alcohol, taxes, and tip:
$ = under $25
$$ = $25–50
$$$ = over $50

Creative rolls, one of Calgary's best sources for sushi. **$$**
Newport Grill
747 Lake Bonavista Dr SE
Tel: 271-6711
www.newportgrill.com
Lakeside patio, floor-to-ceiling windows. Continental health menu. Children's menu. **$$**
River Café
On Prince's Island
Tel: 261-7670
www.river-cafe.com
Romantic location with well crafted local cuisine. **$$$**
Spiros
Corner of 33rd St and 17th Ave SW

Tel: 685-4444
www.spirospizza.ca
Great family-run Greek restaurant that never disappoints. Famous for its pizza. **$–$$**

Edmonton (780)

Bistro Praha Gourmet Cafe
10168–100A St
Tel: 424-4218
Sober decor, heavy furnishings, antique lamps. Central European theme and menu. **$$**
Blue Plate Diner
10145–104 St
Tel: 429-0740

www.blueplatediner.ca
In the heart of the Warehouse District, an unpretentious restaurant decorated with paintings by local artists. Gluten-free, vegetarian, and vegan options, along with plenty of meat and seafood. **$$**
Cafe Select
10018–106th St
Tel: 423-0419
Low-light elegance. Superb beef and lamb, sinful desserts. **$$$**
The Crêperie
10220–103rd St
Tel: 420-6656
www.thecreperie.com

French-style stuffed crêpes served in an intimate candle-lit environment. **$$**
Dadeo Diner & Bar
10548a Whyte Ave Edmonton
Tel: 780-433-0930
www.dadeo.ca
Delicious New Orleans inspired diner located on happening Whyte Ave near the University. **$**
Jack's Grill
5842–111th St
Tel: 434-1113
www.jacksgrill.ca
An innovative menu with a thoughtful wine list. Save room for home-made bread pudding. **$$$**

BRITISH COLUMBIA

British Columbians take justifiable pride in the bounty of their province. Restaurants compete to offer the freshest food with the most unusual combinations of cuisines. Fusion cuisine ensures that the same menu may include sushi, clam chowder, fettuccine, rack of lamb, and a pork loin in calvados. The lush Okanagan Valley produces varied tree fruits, along with world-class wines.

Vancouver takes its culinary inspiration from all corners of the world, with a focus on fresh and local,

Don't be surprised to hear your server recite the provenance of each ingredient. The result is that this food-obsessed city is overflowing with acclaimed chefs and some of the best restaurants in the country.

Kelowna (250)

Bouchons Bistro
1180 Sunset Dr
Tel: 763-6595
www.bouchonsbistro.com
A classic French bistro, with a wine list that gives equal billing to French and BC wines. **$$–$$$**

BELOW: a Vancouver-style twist on the traditional breakfast.

Old Vines Restaurant and Wine Bar at Quail's Gate
3303 Boucherie Rd
Tel: 769-2500
Not only superb food, but also beautiful setting overlooking the vineyards and lake. **$$$**

Penticton (250)

Theo's
687 Main St
Tel: 492-4019
www.eatsquid.com
Great food, friendly staff, extensive well-priced wine list. **$**

Prince George (250)

Ric's Grill
547 George St
Tel: 614-9096
Lots of choices for kids and adults alike. **$$**

Vancouver (604)

Diva at the Met
Metropolitan Hotel, 645 Howe St
Tel: 602-7788
Flawless execution of seasonal menu with focus on local products and a spectacular wine cellar. **$$$**
Go Fish
1505 W 1st Ave
Tel: 730-5040
Outdoor cafe serving fresh fish and shellfish. Don't be put off by the line-up, people come back for a reason. **$**

Hapa Izakaya
1479 Robson St
Tel: 689-4272
www.hapaizakaya.com
Japanese tapas with a West coast flare, second location in Kitsilano. **$–$$**
Le Crocodile
909 Burrard St
Tel: 669-4298
Alsatian menu and consistently impeccable service. **$$$**
Le Gavroche
1616 Alberni St
Tel: 685-3924
French cuisine in an intimate setting, astonishing wine list. **$$$**
O'Doul's
1300 Robson St
Tel: 661 1400
www.odoulsrestaurant.com
West coast dining with live jazz every night. **$$–$$$**
Provence
1177 Marinaside Cres
Tel: 681-4144
www.provencevancouver.com
Mediterranean cuisine all day long. Or, order a picnic to go, and take the active West Coast approach to life. **$$$**
Rtl – regional tasting lounge
1130 Mainland St
Tel: 638-1550
www.r.tl
Share small plates of house-smoked duck, ouzo-flamed prawns, and house-made gnocchi in an elegant dining room with good

friends – classic Yaletown trendy. **$$–$$$**
Vij's
1480 11th Ave W
Tel: 736-6664
www.vijs.ca
Exceptional Indian food with an obsession for flavors – lamb popsicles plus plenty of great vegetarian choices. **$$–$$$**

Victoria (250)

Aura Restaurant & Patio
Inn at Laurel Point, 680 Montréal St

Tel: 386-8721
Exceptional menu in a prime waterfront location, lunch very affordable, dinner a worthwhile treat. **$$–$$$**
The Bengal Lounge
Empress Hotel, 721 Government St
Tel: 389-2727
Colonial life at its best, complete with curry buffet, plus full west coast menu. Tasteful elegance. **$$–$$$**
Rebar
50 Bastion Square
Tel: 361-9223
www.rebarmodernfood.com

A funky vegetarian restaurant. Drinks range from the juice bar's selection to regional wines and microbrewed beers. **$**
Sooke Harbour House
1528 Whiffen Spit Rd, Sooke
Tel: 642-3421
www.sookeharbourhouse.com
40km (25 miles) out of town but worth the journey for fresh local seafood and an extensive wine list. **$$$**
Spinnakers Brew Pub and Restaurant
308 Catherine St

Tel: 386-2739
West Coast pub-style restaurant, overlooking Inner Harbour. In-house brews. **$–$$**

Whistler (604)

Ciao-Thyme Bistro
#2-4573 Chateau Blvd
Tel: 932-7051
www.ciaothymebistro.com
Open from 8am to 10pm, organic ingredients and great value, oh, and delicious yam fries. **$$**

MANITOBA (204)

Selkirk whitefish and Winnipeg gold-eye are delicacies in a region that's dominated by beef. Along with the other Prairie Provinces, Manitoba's significant Ukrainian population contributes pierogies (ravioli-like crescent-shaped pockets of cheese, cabbage, or potato), cabbage rolls, and spicy sausages to the local cuisine.

Flin Flon

Kelsey Dining Room, Victoria Inn
160 Hwy. #10-A North
Tel: 687-7555
Steak house in hotel, good

variety for breakfast and lunch as well. **$$**

Portage la Prairie

Bill's Sticky Fingers
210 Saskatchewan Ave E
Tel: 857-9999
Home-style cuisine, with children's menu. **$**

Winnipeg

Bistro Dansk
63 Sherbrook St
Tel: 775-5662
Central European cooking at reasonable prices. **$$**
Cafe Carlo
243 Lilac St

Tel: 477-5544
www.cafecarlo.com
A sophisticated, pan-ethnic menu, with everything made from scratch, and a casual ambience. **$$**
Earl's
Multiple locations including
191 Main St
Tel: 989-0103
A reliable chain across Western Canada offering consistent meals and upbeat atmosphere. **$–$$**
Ivory Restaurant
200 Main St
Tel: 944-1600
Indian restaurant in the city's financial district serving delicately spiced

Moghul cuisine as well as offering take-out. **$$**
Restaurant Dubrovnik
390 Assiniboine Ave
Tel: 944-0594
http://restaurantdubrovnik.com
French cuisine, almost a Winnipeg tradition, located in renovated brick townhouse. **$$$**
Sydney's At The Forks
215 – 1 Forks Market Rd
Tel: 942-6075
www.sydneysattheforks.com
Within a historic building, Sydney's fresh, creative menu embraces Asian, French, and Italian influences. Strong wine list. **$$$**

NEW BRUNSWICK (506)

Lobster, Atlantic salmon, oysters, and clams are plentiful here, but this province is particularly known for fiddlehead greens, the shoots of an edible fern. This delicacy is usually served steamed.

Campobello Island

Family Fisheries
Wilson's Beach

PRICE CATEGORIES

Price categories are for a meal for one, excluding alcohol, taxes, and tip:
$ = under $25
$$ = $25–50
$$$ = over $50

Tel: 752-2470
Very popular family restaurant and take-out, specializing in fresh fish. **$**

Fredericton

Brew-Bakers Cafe-Bistro Bar & Grill
546 King St
Tel: 459-0067
Lively joint, said to have the best wood-fired pizza in Atlantic Canada. **$**
Bruno's Seafood and Chophouse
Delta Fredericton,
225 Woodstock Rd
Tel: 451-7935
Popular restaurant overlooking the St John

River. Serves International cuisine. **$$**
Chez Riz
366 Queen St
Tel: 454-9996
Popular for its stylish decor and flavorful East Indian dishes. **$**
The Palate
462 Queen St
Tel: 450-7911
Casual fine dining, creative food in a cozy setting. **$$**

Moncton

Le Château à Pape
2 Steadman St
Tel: 855-7273
Occupies an old house overlooking a tidal inlet. An

Acadian-accented menu with an extensive wine list. **$$**
Ossie's Lunch
125 Glebe Rd, Bethel, N.B.
Tel: 755-2758
Ten minutes from downtown Moncton, this snackbar is an essential stop for seafood lovers. **$**
The Windjammer Dining Room
Delta Beauséjour, 750 Main St
Tel: 877-7137
Traditional dishes, extensive wine list, formal decor. **$$$**

Robertville

Auberge Les Amis de la Nature
2112 Cormier Rd

Tel: 783-4797/1-800-327-9999
Between Bathurst and
Campbellton, this country
restaurant has an extensive
menu. Many of the
vegetables are grown in its
own organic gardens. **$$**

Sackville

Marshlands Inn
55 Bridge St
Tel: 536-0170
Historic country inn with a
guest book that reads like a
chunk of Canadian history.
Interesting seafood
concoctions and excellent
desserts. **$$**

Saint John

Billy's Seafood Company
49–51 Charlotte St, City Market
Tel: 672-FISH/1-888-933-3474
Fresh seafood in a relaxed
environment. Extensive
menu. **$$**
Infusion Tearoom
41 Charlotte St

Tel: 693-8327
Within City Market, this café
offers an extensive range of
teas, delicious homemade
lunches, and afternoon
teas. **$**
Inn on the Cove
1371 Sand Cove Rd
Tel: 672-7799/877-257-8080
Within a historic inn, intimate
fireside suppers are served
in the Tide's Table, over-
looking the Bay of Fundy. **$$**
Lemongrass
42 Princess St
Tel: 657-8424
Superb Thai fare back-
dropped by minimalist
decor. **$$**
San Martello Dining Room
Dufferin Inn, 357 Dufferin Row
Tel: 642-2822
Located in a comfortable old
house, this dining room is
considered by many to be
the best in the province. The
specialty is fresh local lamb.
$$$
Taco Pica
96 Germain St

Tel: 633-8492
Serves mainly Guatemalan
cuisine, with a few Mexican
dishes, and a flamenco
guitarist plays every
weekend. **$**

Shediac

The Green House on Main
406A Main St
Tel: 533-7097
Fresh, creative, and healthy
dishes served in a century-
old house. **$$**
**Lighthouse Restaurant
and Beverage Room**
342 Main St
Tel: 532-6010
Located in the Centreville
Mall, and popular for its
Acadian cuisine. **$**

St Andrews

Europa
48 King St W
Tel: 529-3818
Within a remodeled dance
hall, this genial restaurant

dishes up huge servings of
excellent food from an
expansive menu. **$$**
The Gables
143 Water St
Tel: 529-3440
Casual, contemporary fare
beside the waterfront. Its
three-level rear deck is
pleasantly shaded by a
chestnut tree. **$$**
Rossmount Inn
4599 Highway 127
Tel: 529-3351
Renowned throughout
Atlantic Canada and beyond
for its creative, market fresh
cuisine, including the daily
catch from local fishermen
and organic vegetables and
herbs. Reservations highly
recommended. **$$$**
The Windsor House
132 Water St
Tel: 529-3330
In a 1798 sea-captain's
home, classic French
cuisine is served, using
freshly baked and locally
grown produce. **$$$**

NEWFOUNDLAND AND LABRADOR

Fishing has always been the
main industry here,
especially cod, which is
cooked in many ways, from
fish and chips to gratin. The
island is famous for local
specialties with unusual
names like brewis (cod),
scrunchions and "seal
flipper pie."
    Outside St John's, the
most reliable dining is
usually in hotel dining rooms
and motel coffee shops. As
a general rule, expect the
service to be cheerful, but
on the slow side.

St John's (709)

Bianca's
171 Water St
Tel: 726-9016
Bulgarian owner-chef
makes every dish a
distinctively exotic creation.
Open kitchen, large wine
selection, and even a room
for cigar smokers. **$$**
The Cabot Club
Sheraton Hotel Newfoundland,
115 Cavendish Sq
Tel: 726-4977
St John's finest. Fine harbor
view. **$$$**

Duck Street Bistro
252 Duckworth St
Tel: 753-0400
Specializes in creative
home-made meals from fish
cakes to crêpes, and an
excellent atmosphere. **$$**
Hungry Fisherman
The Murray Premises, 5 Beck's Cove
Tel: 726-5791
Fresh seafood in a historic
setting. **$$**
The Sprout
364 Duckworth St
Tel: 579-5485
Well-priced fresh vegetarian
cuisine with a twist. **$**

The Vault
291 Water St
Tel: 738-5200
Delicious and creative
dishes served in the
basement of an old bank,
with the vault serving as its
well-stocked wine cellar. **$$**
**Velma's Restaurant &
Lounge**
264 Water St
Tel: 576-2264
Renowned for downhome
goodness, its offerings
include cod tongues with
scrunchions (small cubes of
pork fried golden brown). **$**

THE NORTHWEST TERRITORIES

Food is flown into the
Northwest Territories and,
because of this, much of it is
frozen or packaged. The
traditional Inuit and Dene
(Northern Indian) ways of
eating have largely been lost,
but Arctic char – similar to
salmon but with a softer
taste – is a regional delicacy.

Inuvik (867)

Tonimoes
Mackenzie Hotel,
185 Mackenzie Rd
Tel: 777-2861
Hotel restaurant, with
lounge, breakfast, brunch
and Friday night prime rib.
$$$

Yellowknife (867)

**Fuego International
Restaurant**
4915 50th St
Tel: 873-3750
www.fuegointernational.ca
Extensive menu, both
northern and international
cuisine. good wine list. **$$$**

The Wildcat Cafe
3904 Wiley Rd
Tel: 873-4004
Open summer only. Dating
from the 1930s, it preserves
the frontier atmosphere in a
log house where strangers
share tables. Menu includes
caribou and locally caught
whitefish. **$$**

NOVA SCOTIA (902)

Clam chowder, lobster, Digby scallops, and Lunenberg sausage are part of Nova Scotia's menu, particularly the clam chowder which Nova Scotians will good-humoredly insist is superior to that of New England, their neighbor to the south. Here you'll also find delicious baked fruit puddings of Acadian origin.

A 13 percent harmonized sales tax (combining provincial sales tax and the national Goods and Services Tax) is charged in restaurants, where prices are still 20 percent higher than in southern Canada.

Ingonish Beach

Keltic Lodge
Middle Head Peninsula
Tel: 285-2880/1-800-565-0444
This famous hotel's Purple

Thistle dining room is thought to serve the best fare on Cape Breton Island, and also the most expensive. Fabulous coastal views. **$$$**

Halifax

Hotel dining rooms are popular, but the following are representative of independent restaurants and cafés:
Cheelin
Brewery Market,
1496 Lower Market St
Tel: 422-2252
A family-run restaurant offering almost 100 innovative Chinese dishes that are constantly changing. A great favorite with locals. **$$**
Chives Bistro
1537 Barrington St
Tel: 420-9626
Fresh local produce

prepared and presented imaginatively. Ever-changing seasonal menu. **$$**
De Maurizio
In Old Brewery complex,
1496 Lower Water St
Tel: 423-0859
Excellent northern Italian menu. Extensive wine list. Booking recommended. **$$$**
Five Fishermen
1740 Argyle St
Tel: 422-4421
A good seafood restaurant in an historic building and one of the city's most extensive wine cellars. **$$**
Onyx
5680 Spring Garden Rd
Tel: 428-5680
One of the city's most chic restaurants, featuring Asian-inspired global dishes influenced by French cuisine. **$$$**
Opa
1565 Argyle St

Tel: 492-7999
A large and sunny Greek restaurant built around an inner courtyard. Excellent food and a cheerful ambience. **$$$**

Shelburne

Charlotte Lane Café
13 Charlotte Lane
Tel: 875-3314
Local produce, both seafood and vegetables, a strong feature, but Asian, Cajun, and Italian grace the menu as well. **$$**

Yarmouth

Old World Bakery and Deli
232 Main St
Tel: 742-2181
Offers fresh breads and muffins right out of a wood oven, as well as local smoked fish and delicious fish chowder. **$**

NUNAVUT

Food is very expensive. Generally, visitors to Nunavut eat at their hotel, or the tour outfitters provide their meals.

Iqaluit (867)

The Granite Room
Discovery Lodge Hotel
www.discoverylodge.com

Tel: 979-4433
The best place to eat in Iqaluit, with fresh fish, meat, and vegetables flown in especially, year-round.

Particularly good for smoked Arctic char and caribou. Advance reservations necessary. **$$$**

ONTARIO

In the last few decades, the province has progressed from a meat-and-potatoes heritage to a vibrant food

culture. It is rich in cornfields, fruit orchards, vineyards producing prize-winning wines, a flourishing

BELOW: Canadian seafood comes in many guises.

cheese-making industry (Ontario cheddar is famous), and game-bird farms.

Thanks to massive immigration, Toronto has turned into a foodies' paradise, not just in its restaurants, numbering up to 5,000 at any given time, but also in its gourmet stores and countless ethnic markets.

Kingston (613)

Aroma
248 Ontario St
Tel: 541-0330
This resto-wine bar offers large entrees and tasting plates, mouth-watering homemade desserts, and

50 wines by the glass. **$$**
Chez Piggy
68 Princess St
Tel: 549-7673
Inventive food including excellent soups. Set in former livery stable and courtyard at rear. **$$**

Kitchener/Waterloo (519)

Twenty King
45 King St W

PRICE CATEGORIES

Price categories are for a meal for one, excluding alcohol, taxes, and tip:
$ = under $25
$$ = $25–50
$$$ = over $50

Tel: 745-8939
Spacious digs in an old bank building, with a menu ranging from Cajun to Moroccan to South American. Excels in appetizers and sweets. **$$$**

Niagara-on-the-Lake (905)

Epicurean
84 Queen St
Tel: 468-3408
Bistro-style menu with generous helpings and low prices. Best deal for lunch. **$**

Hillebrand Winery Restaurant
1249 Niagara Stone Rd
Tel: 468-7123/1-800-582-8412
Overlooking vineyards, with excellent soups, locally grown fruits and vegetables, and tasty entrées; home-made ice cream and local farmhouse cheeses. **$$$**

Ristorante Giardino
The Gate House, 142 Queen St
Tel: 468-3263
Located in a luxurious hotel, with northern Italian food and a splendid wine list in elegant, modern surroundings. **$$$**

Niagara Falls (905)

Carpaccio
6840 Lundy's Lane
Tel: 371-2063

A stylish airy restaurant away from "the strip," serving commendable Italian fare, accompanied by fine wines from the Niagara Peninsula and Italy. **$$$**

Ottawa (613)

ARC Lounge and Restaurant
140 Slater St
Tel: 238-2888
This pocket-sized dining room of a designer hotel has sleek white-on-white decor, a small, innovative menu, and exceptionally fine food. **$$$**

Black Cat Bistro
428 Preston St
Tel: 569-9998
Constantly changing menu, offering New American cuisine – using lots of local ingredients. Reservations recommended. **$$$**

Blue Cactus
2 Byward Market
Tel: 241 7061
Award-winning margaritas and sizzling fajitas combine with cool decor for a taste of the American Southwest. **$$**

Kinki
41 York St
Tel: 789-7559
Contemporary Japanese decor and dishes, with a mouth-watering selection of sushi and other delights. **$$**

Le Cafe
National Arts Centre, 53 Elgin St
Tel: 594-5127
Lovely setting beside Rideau Canal. Focuses on Canadian produce and wines. **$$$**

Murray Street
110 Murray St
Tel: 562-7244
A charcuterie bar that serves the best local meats – including elk salami – and cheeses, along with a reasonably priced wine selection. **$$**

Nate's Deli
316 Rideau St
Tel: 789-9191
An Ottawa landmark; specializes in smoked meat. **$**

Savana Cafe
431 Gilmour St
Tel: 233-9159
Delicious combinations, inspired by the flavors and spices of the Caribbean and Southeast Asia, in a friendly setting. **$$**

Wellington Gastropub
1325 Wellington St
Tel: 729-1315
Fresh, local, and organic ingredients used in the creation of imaginative dishes; both the trout and pork are sublime. **$$**

Picton (613)

Harvest
106 Bridge St

Tel: 476-6763
Count on a gastronomic feast – much of it created from locally grown and produced ingredients. Many Prince Edward County vintages on the wine list. **$$**

Stratford (519)

The Church Restaurant and Belfry
70 Brunswick St
Tel: 273-3424
Superb dining in what was a huge church, complete with altar and organ. Unequaled lamb, veal, trout, and lobster. Upstairs in the Belfry, the cooking is more casual, the prices lower. **$$$**

The Old Prune
151 Albert St
Tel: 271-5052
Delicious food with prix fixe menu for dinner. **$$$**

Rundles
9 Coburg St
Tel: 271-6442
Located by Victoria Lake, serving excellent food in a contemporary setting. **$$$**

The Sun Room
55 George St W
Tel: 273-0331
Hugely popular for its innovative cooking and moderate prices. Book ahead if you're planning a pre-theater dinner. **$$**

Thunder Bay (807)

Bistro One
555 Dunlop St
Tel: 622-2478
A much-acclaimed restaurant, with a wide range of imaginatively prepared North American cuisine. **$$**

Toronto (416)

Allen's Restaurant Bar
143 Danforth Ave (at Broadview)
Tel: 463-3086
A well-loved neighborhood watering-hole. Irish food with global influences. **$**

Amadeu's
184 Augusta Ave
Tel: 591-1245
Popular Portuguese seafood restaurant in heart of Kensington Market. **$$**

BELOW: taking a break in stylish surroundings.

Boulevard Cafe
161 Harbord St
Tel: 961-7676
A longtime Annex fixture, with Peruvian decor and cuisine. Extensive wine list, largely from South America and Spain. Heated outdoor terrace. **$$**

Bright Pearl Seafood Restaurant
346 Spadina Ave, 2nd Floor
Tel: 979-3988
A large and bustling spot for excellent dim sum at lunch. They even have a "dim sum for beginners" flyer to help you choose. Tasty Cantonese dishes served at a more leisurely pace in the evening. **$**

Bymark
Toronto-Dominion Tower
66 Wellington St W
Tel: 777-1144
Where powerbrokers lunch. Beautifully prepared and presented food, and where anything made with chocolate is especially fine. **$$$**

Canoe
66 Wellington St W
Tel: 364-0054
Fantastic views over-looking Lake Ontario and Downtown from the 54th floor. Canadian is the theme of both decor and food. **$$$**

George
111 Queen St E
Tel: 863-6006
Part of the Verity Club for Women, but open to the public, George's tapas-style menu features an enticing range of dishes at surprisingly affordable prices. **$$**

Delux
92 Ossington Ave
Tel: 537-0134
One of the newer additions to increasingly trendy West Queen West, offering tasty Cuban-influenced French bistro-style dishes and friendly service in unexpectedly intimate surroundings. Leave room for dessert... specifically the decadent chocolate chip cookies baked to order and served hot. **$$**

Grappa
797 College St
Tel: 535-3337
An unpretentious restaurant in the heart of Little Italy, with a superb and reasonably priced wine list. **$$**

Jacques' Bistro du Parc
126A Cumberland St
Tel: 961-1893
California-style cuisine with a Québec flavor served in attractive but narrow, second-floor walk-up space. **$$**

Lai Wah Heen
Metropolitan Hotel, 108 Chestnut St
Tel: 977-9899
Luxurious Chinese restaurant with formal service. Many come for dim sum at noon. **$$$**

Lee
603 King St W
Tel: 504-7867
Foodies come to snack on superstar chef Susur Lee's "smaller" and cheaper dishes. Funky decor includes pink plexi-glass tables and giant budgerigars. **$$$**

Le Paradis
166 Bedford Rd
Tel: 921-0995
Popular neighborhood bistro, with solid French cuisine. **$$**

Mt. Everest Restaurant
469 Bloor St W
Tel: 964-8849
Cheap, flavorful Northern Indian and Nepalese cuisine with live sitar on Mondays and Wednesdays. **$**

North 44°
2537 Yonge St
Tel: 487-4897
The newly-renovated modern digs and relaxed environment provide the perfect backdrop to enjoy gourmet cuisine, with wines to match. **$$$**

Pangaea
1221 Bay St
Tel: 920-2323
An elegant restaurant renowned for its creative offerings, combining international flavours with fresh local ingredients and an excellent wine list. **$$$**

Queen Mother Cafe
208 Queen St W
Tel: 598-4719
Combination of Thai and vegetarian. No connection to royalty, but fun. **$$**

Quigley's
2232 Queen St E
Tel: 699-9998
This Beaches institution, with a wide three-level patio around a lovely old maple tree, serves superior pub fare, a good selection of beers, and specially imported wines. **$**

Rodney's Oyster House
469 King St W
Tel: 363-8105
Toronto's first and long-time oyster bar maintains high standards... and a sense of fun. Fish and other seafood dishes are all cooked with flair. **$$$**

Southern Accent
595 Markham St
Tel: 536-3211
Excellent Creole-Cajun vittles served in a renovated two-story Victorian house. **$$**

PRINCE EDWARD ISLAND (902)

Prince Edward Island is best known for its delicious high-quality potatoes, with Malpeque oysters coming in a close second. Both are prized by the whole country.

Charlottetown

Claddagh Oyster House
131 Sydney St
Tel: 892-9661
A seafood restaurant in an historic building in Olde Charlottetown. Also serves steaks and chicken. **$$$**

Lot 30
151 Kent St
Tel: 629-3030
The best of the Island's produce, including fish and meat, beautifully served. A four-course tasting menu offered. **$$**

Off Broadway
125 Sydney St
Tel: 566-4620
Steak and seafood in a cozy setting; the 42nd Street Lounge upstairs is perfect for an aperitif or digestif. **$$**

The Pilot House
70 Grafton St
Tel: 894-4800
Located in a beautiful heritage building. An extensive pub menu features fresh seafood, as well as tender prime rib and steaks. **$$**

Summerside

Flex Mussels
Spinnaker's Landing, 2 Lower Water St
Tel: 569-0200
Twenty-three varieties of the freshest Island mussels are served, all prepared to order and sold by the pound. Open seasonally, early June–mid-Dec. **$**

Lobster Suppers

Civic groups sponsor traditional "Lobster Suppers" throughout Prince Edward Island during July and August. Expect to pay $20–25 per person for the evening, but they're usually "all-you-can-eat" dinners. Here are some of the most popular ones:

New Glasgow Lobster Suppers
#604 Route 258, New Glasgow
Tel: 964-2870

St Ann's Church Lobster Suppers
Route 224, in Hope River
Tel: 621-0635

St Margaret's Lobster Suppers
Tel: 687-3105

PRICE CATEGORIES

Price categories are for a meal for one, excluding alcohol, taxes, and tip:
$ = under $25
$$ = $25–50
$$$ = over $50

Québec

Québec's French heritage includes a passion for good food and wine, and it's taken seriously whether it's in a gourmet restaurant or a modest bistro. French cuisine dominates but restaurants also offer habitant cooking, a home-grown French provincial cuisine, such as the typical tourtière, game-and-potato pie, pea soup, and maple syrup desserts that takes advantage of the fresh herbs, vegetables, fish, rabbit, lamb, and other meats found in abundance in the province.

Québec is the world's largest maple syrup producer, and both the syrup and maple sugar candy are available everywhere.

Québec City is a gastronome's paradise, and even fast food is a cut above the average. Service and atmosphere are very important, so only the best restaurants survive. Modest restaurants also reflect this dedication to excellence.

More ethnically inclined than Québec City, Montréal rivals New York for its delicatessen fare: Montréal smoked meat is famous, and its bagels are reputed to be the best. French and international cuisine are very well represented in its more than 5,000 restaurants, bistros, and brasseries.

Baie St Paul (418)

Le Mouton Noir
43 rue Ste-Anne
Tel: 240-3030
Most of the produce from Québec, from wild-boar sausages to Charlevoix snails, is on the menu. **$$**

Hull (819)

Laurier sur Montcalm
199 rue Montcalm
Tel: 775-5030
One of the best restaurants in the Ottawa area, housed in an old railway station. Innovative cooking. Reservations a must. **$$$**

Ile d'Orleans (418)

Le Moulin de St-Laurent
754 chemin Royal, St-Laurent
Tel: 418-829-3888/1-888-629-3888
Traditional Québécois cuisine is served in a converted flourmill dating back to 1720. A fine restaurant. **$$**

Montréal (514)

Au Pied de Cochon
536 rue Duluth Est
Tel: 281-1114
Hugely acclaimed for very generous portions of fresh seafood, meat – including bison and venison in season – and fowl, all prepared to perfection.
Beauty's
93 avenue du Mont-Royal Ouest
Tel: 849-8883
A family-run, retro diner on the Plateau, producing all-day breakfasts for 60 years.
Cluny
257 rue Prince
Tel: 866-1213
A cafeteria and self-described "Art-Bar" in Old Montréal that serves overstuffed sandwiches filled with fresher than fresh ingredients. **$**
L'Express
3927 rue St-Denis
Tel: 845-5333
The essence of Montréal dining, with marble tabletops, a long narrow bar, and great, unpretentious French bistro food. **$$**
Laloux
250 ave des Pins
Tel: 287-9127
Gay Nineties decor and wonderful French food. Try the foie gras, regardless of cost. **$$**
Reuben's Deli
1116 Ste-Catherine Ouest
Tel: 866-1029
The smoked meat sandwiches are delicious and the sleek ambience is a welcome change to fluorescent diner lights. **$**

Les Filles du Roy

Hostellerie Pierre du Calvert
405 rue Bonsecours
Tel: 282-1725
French-Canadian food in a 17th-century Québec setting. Reservations advised. **$$$**
Jardin Nelson
407 place Jacques-Cartier
Tel: 861-5731
A romantic courtyard restaurant, known for delicious crêpes and nightly jazz. **$$**
Toqué
900 place Jean-Paul Riopelle
Tel: 499-2084
One of the city's – perhaps Canada's – top restaurants. Chef/patron Normand Laprise's goal is to showcase Québec produce. **$$$**

Percé (418)

La Maison du Pêcheur
155 place du Quai (Percé)
Tel: 782-5331
Seafood lovers' delight located right on the pier, with a great view of the harbor (June–mid-Oct). **$$$**

Québec City (418)

Apsara
71 rue d'Auteuil
Tel: 694-0232
The place to go for Vietnamese, Cambodian, and Thai fare. **$$**
Aux Anciens Canadiens
34 rue St-Louis
Tel: 692-1627

Price Categories

Price categories are for a meal for one, excluding alcohol, taxes, and tip:
$ = under $25
$$ = $25–50
$$$ = over $50

BELOW: a typically relaxed dining experience.

Housed in one of the oldest houses in Québec, this hugely popular restaurant serves large helpings of delicious Québécois fare. **$$**

La Marie Clarisse
12 Petit-Champlain
Tel: 692-0857
One of the city's best seafood restaurants, in the Lower Town. **$$$**

Laurie Raphaël
117 rue Dalhousie
Tel: 692-4555
A bright, airy restaurant in the Old Port, its menu

devoted to regional ingredients. **$$$**

Le Cosmos Café
575 Grande-Allée Est
Tel: 640-0606
A funky café popular for breakfast, lunch, and dinner; open late. **$**

Le Commensal
860 St-Jean
Tel: 647-3733
Outside the walls, this popular vegetarian restaurant is packed, seven days a week. **$**

Le St-Amour

48 rue Ste-Ursule
Tel: 694-0667
French cooking in romantic setting, and one of the world's best wine-lists. **$$$**

Toast
17 Sault-au-Matelot
Tel: 692-1334
A gastronomic adventure in an intimate setting; try to leave room for dessert. **$$$**

Voodoo Grill
575 Grande-Allée
Tel: 647-2000
An attractive selection of fusion dishes served in a

sultry African-themed room (complete with roving tom-tom players.) **$$**

St-Jovite (819)

A 10-minute drive from Mont-Tremblant

Le Cheval de Jade
688 rue de St-Jovite
Tel: 425-5233
With seafood imported from France for the bouillabaisse, the restaurant aims to serve the best fish in the Laurentians. **$$$**

SASKATCHEWAN

Canada's wheat grows here, so not surprisingly grain-fed beef and grain-fed fowl such as partridge and duck are extremely good. The Saskatoon berry, similar to the blueberry, makes a wonderful accompaniment to game, as well as pies and crumbles for dessert.

Regina (306)

Cathedral Village Free House
2062 Albert St
Tel: 359-1661
www.thefreehouse.com
Pub food with a twist – jerk or tandoori chicken, nachos

or pizza, lots of beer and live music. **$–$$**

The Diplomat Steak House
2032 Broad St
Tel: 359-3366
www.thediplomatsteakhouse.com/
Large menu, great wine list, big city pricing. **$$$**

Mediterranean Grill
2589 Quance St E
Tel: 757-1666
http://mbistro.sasktelwebhosting.com
Fish a specialty, but lots of other choices. Good wine list. **$$–$$$**

Saskatoon (306)

It is said that Saskatoon's Broadway Avenue has more

good, small restaurants than any other single Canadian street.

Boomtown Cafe
Western Development Museum, 2610 Lorne Ave S
Tel: 931-1910
www.wdm.ca
1910 decor. Home cooking à la Saskatchewan. No license. **$**

Calories Bakery & Restaurant
721 Broadway Ave
Tel: 665-7991
www.caloriesrestaurants.com
Famed locally for its customer loyalty, with a carefully selected eclectic menu in a French-style

bistro. **$$**

Gotta Hava Java
112 Second Ave N
Tel: 665-3336
A healthy menu with a good selection of wraps and muffins. Home-made soups and the best coffee in town.

Sushiro
737B Broadway Ave
Tel: 665-5557
www.sushiro.com
A stylish location for enjoying an excellent choice of sushi. **$–$$**

Taj Mahal
1013 Broadway Ave
Tel: 978-2227
A family-run restaurant, with superb masala dishes. **$**

THE YUKON

Food in the Yukon is expensive. Arctic grayling, salmon, and moose steak add some interest to what is otherwise a prosaic Canadian menu of hamburgers and pizzas. Outside Whitehorse, your best bet is usually a hotel or resort dining room.

Whitehorse (867)

Alpine Bakery
411 Alexander St
Tel: 668-6871
Wholesome baking and cooking with organic ingredients. Also specializes in packing food for major expeditions. **$**

The Cellar Steakhouse and Wine Bar
Edgewater Hotel,
101 Main St
www.edgewaterhotelwhitehorse.com
Tel: 667-2572
Serves excellent steaks, lobster, halibut, and king crab. Good wine list. **$$$**

Chocolate Claim Bakery and Cafe
305 Strickland St
Tel: 667-2202
www.chocolateclaim.com
European-style coffee bar. Soups, salads, desserts. **$**

Klondike Rib & Salmon BBQ
2116 2nd Ave
Tel: 667-7554

The oldest building in Whitehorse is the setting for musk ox, caribou, and bison specialties. **$$–$$$**

Sam 'n' Andy's Tex Mex Bar
506 Main St
Tel: 668-6994
Mexican bar and grill, with outdoor patio. **$$**

BELOW: an imaginative take on a Canadian specialty

TRANSPORT

ACCOMMODATION

EATING OUT

ACTIVITIES

A – Z

LANGUAGE

A CTIVITIES

THE ARTS, NIGHTLIFE, FESTIVALS, SHOPPING, SPORTS, AND CHILDREN'S ACTIVITIES

THE ARTS

Theaters and the Performing Arts

Alberta

Banff (403)

Banff Centre for Fine Arts, 107 Tunnel Mountain Drive, tel: 762-6100/1-800-884-7574; www.banff centre.ca. This center is an internationally renowned performing arts complex. Its two theaters offer dance, drama, movies, and concerts. The Banff Arts Festival in August highlights the summer season. The periodical, *Banff*, is widely distributed throughout the area.

Calgary (403)

To find out what's on in Calgary's increasingly sophisticated performing arts scene check local newspapers or visitor information sources.

EPCOR Centre for Performing Arts, 205 8th Ave SE, tel: 294-7455; www.epcorcentre.org. A unique facility which houses one of the most acoustically perfect halls, Jack Singer Concert Hall. The complex is also the home of the Calgary Philharmonic and Theatre Calgary.

Southern Alberta Jubilee Auditorium, 1415–14 Ave NW, tel: 297-8000; www.jubileeauditorium.com/southern. Calgary's cultural centerpiece, this hall houses the Calgary Opera and the Alberta Ballet Company.

Pumphouse Theatre, 2140 Pumphouse Ave SW, tel: 263-0079; www.pumphousetheatre.ca. A variety of performing arts groups can be found in this converted municipal pumphouse.

Edmonton (780)

Citadel Theatre, 9828–101A Ave, tel: 425-1820/1-888-425-1820; www.citadeltheatre.com. The city's largest theater complex.

Northern Alberta Jubilee Auditorium, 11455–87 Ave, tel: 427-2760; www.jubileeauditorium.com/northern. This facility houses the Alberta Ballet and the Edmonton Opera.

The Winspear Centre, 99 St and 102 Ave, tel: 428-1414/1-800-563-5081; www.winspearcentre.com. Home of the Edmonton Symphony Orchestra.

British Columbia

Vancouver (604)

From summer evenings dominated by Shakespeare outdoors against a scenic backdrop, to its robust music scene and art galleries, Vancouver is a happening place. Telephone the Arts Hotline at 684-ARTS, or visit www.ticketstonight.ca.

Arts Club Theatre, 1585 Johnson St, Granville Island, tel: 687-1644; www.artsclub.com. Features modern Canadian drama, both light and serious, on its two stages.

Bard on the Beach, Vanier Park, tel: 739-0559; www.bardonthebeach.org. Shakespeare performed under big tents every day from May to September.

Chan Centre for the Performing Arts, 6265 Crescent Rd, UBC Campus, tel: 822-9197; www.chancentre.com. Features recitals in a theater surrounded by gardens, and a panoramic view.

Orpheum Theatre, 601 Smithe St, tel: 665-3050. This theater in the grand style is the permanent home to the Vancouver Symphony Orchestra.

Queen Elizabeth Theatre, 600 Block, Hamilton St, tel: 665-3050. This spacious theater hosts concerts, dramas, musicals, and other major cultural events.

Vancouver East Cultural Centre, 1895 Venables St, tel: 254-9578; www.theclutch.com. Wide variety of cutting-edge events.

Victoria (250)

The Belfry, 1291 Gladstone Ave, tel: 385-6815; www.belfry.bc.ca. Professional comedy and music hall shows.

McPherson Playhouse, 3 Centennial Square, tel: 386-6121; www.rmts.bc.ca. This restored old theater is the focus of Vancouver Island's regional and professional presentations in musical comedy, opera, and drama.

The Royal Theatre, 805 Broughton St, tel: 386-6121; www.rmts.bc.ca. Home of the Victoria Symphony Orchestra. Presents classical and pop music as well as theatrical performances.

Manitoba

Winnipeg (204)

Consult the *Winnipeg Sun* or the *Winnipeg Free Press* for information and a complete listing of performing arts events.

Centennial Concert Hall, within the Centennial Center at 555 Main St, tel: 780-3333; www.mbccc.ca. The major focus of Winnipeg's cultural scene. Aside from the Manitoba Museum, the Centennial Center houses:

The Royal Winnipeg Ballet, 380 Graham Ave, tel: 956-2792/1-800-667-4792; www.rwb.org. Canada's first ballet company is over 30 years old and features world-renowned performers. It performs at home in October, December, March, and May.

Manitoba Opera, 380 Graham Ave, tel: 942-7479; www.manitobaopera.mb.ca. Presents three operas and one recital from November through April.

The Winnipeg Symphony Orchestra, 101–555 Main St, tel: 949-3999; www.wso.mb.ca. This highly prestigious orchestra offers classical, contemporary, and popular orchestral music from September through May.

Manitoba Theatre Centre Mainstage, 174 Market Ave, tel: 942-6537/1-877-446-4500; www.mtc.mb.ca. From October through May, the center presents a series of classics, comedies, and modern productions. MTC's second stage, the Warehouse, offers more experimental theater.

In the heart of St-Boniface's French district, **Le Centre Culturel Franco-Manitobain**, 340 blvd Provencher, tel: 233-8972, ext. 424; www.ccfm.mb.ca, offers productions by Le Cercle Molière (Canada's oldest continuously active theater group) as well as choral and dance groups.

New Brunswick

Fredericton (506)

The Playhouse, 686 Queen St, tel: 458-8344, www.theplayhouse.nb.ca. Houses Theatre New Brunswick, www.tnb.nb.ca, the province's premier theatrical company.

Newfoundland and Labrador

St John's (709)

St John's Arts and Culture Centre, 95 Allandale Rd, tel: 729-3650/729-3900, http://stjohns.artsandculturecentre.ca. This is the province's cultural center and, in addition to hosting formal theater, symphony orchestra, and jazz concerts, it houses a library.

The Rooms, 9 Bonaventure Ave, tel: 757-8000, www.therooms.ca. Newfoundland and Labrador's newest public cultural space, it houses the Provincial Museum, the Provincial Art Gallery, and the Provincial Archives under one roof.

Nova Scotia

Halifax (902)

In the summertime, look for free concerts and shows on the streets of the Historic Properties district. Daily local newspapers will give details of what's going on at these and other locations.

Neptune Theatre, 1593 Argyle St, tel: 429-7070/1-800-565-7345; www.neptunetheatre.com. This is home to Nova Scotia's oldest professional repertory company.

Lunenburg (902)

Lunenburg Opera House, 290 Lincoln St, tel: 640-6500; www.lunenburgoperahouse.com. A century-old landmark in the midst of a mammoth restoration, but still hosts art exhibitions and small concerts.

Ontario

Mississauga (905)

Living Arts Centre, 4141 Living Arts Dr, tel: 306-6000/1-888-805-8888, email: lac.boxoffice@livingarts.on.ca; www.livingartscentre.ca. Just a 20-minute drive west from downtown Toronto, the performing, visual, and digital arts are presented in this dynamic center.

Niagara-on-the-Lake (905)

Set in one of the best-preserved 19th-century small towns in Canada, the **Shaw Festival** is devoted to performing the works of George Bernard Shaw and his contemporaries. Expert productions with renowned actors draw large crowds, especially on weekends. Try to make prior arrangements and reservations as early as possible.

The festival runs from April through November. For more information write to the Shaw Festival, Box 774, 10 Queen's Parade, Niagara-on-the-Lake, ON L0S 1J0, or call 905-468-2172 for the box office in Niagara-on-the-Lake, or 1-800-511-7429 from the rest of Canada and the US; www.shawfest.com.

Ottawa (613)

National Arts Centre, 53 Elgin St, tel: 947-7000/1-866-850-arts, email: info@nac-cna.ca; www.nac-can.ca. The focus of Ottawa's performing arts scene. The center has three auditoriums: the 2,300-seat opera house, home to the acclaimed National Arts Centre Orchestra and guest performers; the 950-seat theater for its French- and English- language plays; and the studio, a theater for experimental works, seating 300.

Ottawa Little Theatre, 400 King Edward Ave, tel: 233-8948, email: boxoffice@ottawalittletheatre.com; www.ottawalittletheatre.com, has a fine resident company.

Stratford (519)

The annual **Stratford Festival** (early May–November) draws over a half-million theater-goers from around the world to this town on the banks of the Avon River. Three fine theaters perform Shakespearean, classic, and modern dramas.

Tickets go on sale in late February. Write to the Festival Theatre Box Office, Box 520, Stratford, ON N5A 6V2, tel: 1-800-567-1600 toll-free from Canada and the US, email: orders@stratfordshakespearefestival.com; www.stratfordfestival.ca.

Toronto (416)

To check out what's happening in Toronto, look in the daily (or better, the weekend) editions of the *Globe and Mail* or the *Toronto Star*, or pick up a free copy of *Now* or *Eye* (both weekly). Toronto offers world-class performances year round. Note that queues for tickets in Toronto form early on weekends. Book ahead, if you can.

Air Canada Centre, 40 Bay St, tel: 815-5500; www.theaircanadacentre.com. One of the city's newest venues, it hosts a variety of concerts and ice shows as well as professional sports teams, including the Toronto Maple Leafs and the Toronto Raptors.

Buddies in Bad Times Theatre, 12 Alexander St, tel: 975-8555, www.artsexy.ca. An influential professional company promoting gay and lesbian theater.

BELOW: it's showtime in Toronto.

Canon Theatre (formerly Pantages), 244 Victoria St, tel: 872-1212; www.mirvish.com. A 2,000-seat theater, restored to its original 1920s opulence, that hosts musical crowd-pleasers such as *Chicago* and *The Producers*.

Can Stage, The Bluma Appel Theatre, 27 Front St E and **Berkeley Street Theatre**, 26 Berkeley St, tel: 368-3110; www.canstage.com. Offers works of broader appeal at its Front St location, riskier productions on Berkeley St.

Distillery Historic District, 55 Mill St, tel: 364-1177, email: wg@thedistillery district.com; www.thedistillerydistrict.com. Toronto's newest center for arts, culture, and entertainment is based in Canada's largest 19th-century distillery, now converted into studios, cafés, and home to six dance, theater, and opera venues.

Elgin and Winter Garden Centre, 189 Yonge St, tel: 314-2901; www.heritagefdn.on.ca. Beautifully restored to its original vaudeville-era glory and now hosts a variety of musical shows and drama.

Factory Theatre Lab, 125 Bathurst St, tel: 594-9971, email: info@factory theatre.ca; www.factorytheatre.ca. Produces experimental plays.

Four Seasons Centre for the Performing Arts, 145 Queen St W, tel: 363-8231/1-800-250-4653; www. fourseasonscentre.ca. The new home of the Canadian Opera Company and the National Ballet of Canada. The multimillion-dollar building opened in June 2006, the first theater in Canada built specifically for opera and ballet.

Hart House Theatre, 7 Hart House Circle, tel: 978-8668; www.harthouse.ca. Part of the University of Toronto, this historic theater in the center of the downtown campus has been mounting first-rate productions for the past 90 years.

Lorraine Kimsa Theatre for Young People, 165 Front St E, tel: 862-2222; www.lktyp.ca. Offers fine children's drama.

Massey Hall, 178 Victoria St, at Shuter, tel: 872-4255; www.masseyhall. com. Toronto's Victorian grande dame plays second fiddle to Roy Thomson Hall, but still attracts international stars and musical groups to suit all tastes.

Molson Amphitheatre, Ontario Place, tel: 260-5600; www.livenation. com/venue/molson-amphitheatre-tickets. There's room for an audience of 16,000 here, with 9,000 under the canopy roof. Summertime rock, jazz, and dance performances all take place here.

Princess of Wales Theatre, 300 King St W, tel: 872-1212/1-800-461-3333; www.mirvish.com. A spectacular modern theater designed to accommodate major international productions.

Royal Alexandra Theatre, 260 King St W, tel: 872-1212; www.mirvish.com. The "Royal Alex," with its baroque decor, hosts the latest plays from Broadway and London, as well as local productions.

Roy Thomson Hall, 60 Simcoe St, tel: 872-4255; www.roythomson.com. This concert hall, opened in 1982, is designed so that all 2,800 members of the audience sit within 34 meters (110ft) of the stage. It is the winter home of the excellent Toronto Symphony Orchestra and Mendelssohn Choir.

Sony Centre for the Performing Arts, 1 Front St E (at Yonge), tel: 393-7469; www.sonycentre.ca. The Sony Centre hosts visiting performers and companies and was the home of the Canadian Opera Company and the National Ballet of Canada until their move to the Four Seasons Centre for the Performing Arts in 2006. Renovations to the space are currently underway with an anticipated reopening by 2010.

St Lawrence Centre for the Arts, 27 Front St E, tel: 366-7723/1-800-708-6754; www.stlc.com. Just east of the Sony Centre, its modern theater showcases classic and contemporary drama, with an emphasis on Canadian playwrights and local talent. It is home to the Canadian Stage Company.

Second City, 51 Mercer St, tel: 343-0011/1-800-263-4485; www. secondcity.com. New home in the entertainment district for Toronto's well-known satirical comedy group.

Soulpepper Theatre, The Young Centre, 55 Mill St, Building 49, tel: 866-8666; www.soulpepper.ca. Based in the Distillery Historic District, one of the city's most reputable companies offers classical repertory.

Tarragon Theatre, 30 Bridgman Ave, tel: 531-1827, email: info@tarragon theatre.com; www.tarragontheatre.com. Produces excellent works, with an emphasis on Canadian drama.

Theatre Passe Muraille, 16 Ryerson Ave, tel: 504-7529, email: info@passe muraille.on.ca; www.passemuraille.on.ca. Innovative and experimental productions.

Toronto Centre for the Arts, 5040 Yonge St, tel: 733-9388; www.tocentre. com. This state-of-the-art performing arts center has a main 1,800-seat theater for major international musicals, a 1,000-seat recital hall, and a 250-seat experimental studio theater.

Prince Edward Island

Summer theater is a tradition on the island with performances in a number of locations. Particularly noteworthy are the **Victoria Playhouse** in Victoria (tel: 658-2025; www.victoriaplayhouse. com) and the **Kings Playhouse** in Georgetown (tel: 652-2053/1-888-346-5666; www.kingsplayhouse.com).

Charlottetown (902)

The Confederation Centre of the Arts, 145 Richmond St, Charlottetown, tel: 566-1267/1-800-565-0278; www.confederationcentre.com. Houses a museum, art gallery, and theater. In summer, two theatrical

What's On Listings

Besides local newspapers, most cities have publications, usually free, which provide up-to-the-minute information on theater, concerts, clubs, festivals, and anything else of interest to locals and visitors. Some of the main publications, both in print and/or on-line are:
• *Where Magazine* www.where.ca – distributed through hotels in Halifax, Ottawa, Toronto, Muskoka, Winnipeg, Calgary, Edmonton, Canadian Rockies, Vancouver, Victoria, Whistler, and Yukon.
• www.dose.ca covers Toronto, Vancouver, Edmonton, Calgary, and Ottawa.
• *Eye Weekly* and *Now Magazine* are Toronto-area weeklies that both provide on-line coverage as well:

www.eyeweekly.com and www.nowtoronto. com.
• *The Georgia Straight* is by far the best way to find out what is happening in Vancouver – it is produced every Thursday and updated daily online at www.straight. com.
• *Montréal Mirror* and *Hour Magazine* in Montréal, also on-line at www.montrealmirror.com and www.hour. ca respectively.
• *The Coast* in Halifax.
• *Uptown Magazine*, an on-line source of what's on in Winnipeg, at www.uptownmag.com
• *Prairie Dog Magazine*, Regina's only news, arts, and entertainment magazine, free distribution throughout Downtown.

productions are presented simultaneously (with some matinée performances), one of which is perennial favorite, the *Anne of Green Gables* musical.

Québec
Québec offers limitless opportunities for cultural diversions and entertainment. To find out what's on, contact the local travel bureau, but newspapers can be helpful too. As a general rule, call ahead for program information, especially concerning movies and plays, the majority of which will be in French but some also in English.

Montréal (514)
The weekend editions of *Gazette* and *La Presse* are the two mainstream publications that update Montréalers on what's happening around town. For a wider range of alternative arts and entertainment listings, consult *Mirror* and *Hour* (both English) and *Voir* (French), all available free of charge throughout the city.

Centaur Theatre, 453 rue St-François-Xavier, tel: 288-3161; www.centaurtheatre.com. Performances in English from October through June.
Place des Arts, corner of rues Ste-Catherine and Jeanne-Mance, tel: 1-866-842-2112, email: billets@pda. qc.ca; www.laplacedesarts.com. Holds five halls, offering the finest in performing arts: Salle Wilfrid-Pelletier, home to the acclaimed Montréal Symphony Orchestra, Montréal Opera Company, and Les Grands Ballets Canadiens.
Segal Centre at The Saidye, 5170 Côte Ste-Catherine, tel: 739-2301; www.segalcentre.org. Performances in English. Théâtre Maisonneuve features chamber music and plays. Studio-théâtre primarily showcases francophone song, while Cinquième salle, the center's newest performance hall, hosts a variety of vocal, musical, dance, and dramatic performances. Théâtre Jean-Duceppe is home to a famous Québec drama group.

Québec City (418)
Grand Théâtre du Québec, 269 blvd René-Lévesque E, tel: 643-8131; www. grandtheatre.qc.ca. Two concert halls host classical concerts, variety shows, dance, and theater productions.
Théâtre Capitole, 972 rue St-Jean, tel: 418-694-4444; www.lecapitole.com. Québec City's largest theater.
Théâtre Petit-Champlain, 68 rue du Petit-Champlain, tel: 692-2631; www. theatrepetitchamplain.com. A unique theater where patrons pay a cover

charge to view French-language productions in a licensed cafe.

The Laurentians
In the summertime, this resort area hosts a number of theater productions, many outdoors. For information write to: Association Touristique des Laurentides, 14142 rue de La Chapelle, RR1, Mirabel, PQ J7J 2L8 or tel: 450-224-7007/1-800-561-6673; www.laurentians.com.

Saskatchewan
Regina (306)
Conexus Arts Centre (formerly the Saskatchewan Centre of the Arts), 200A Lakeshore Dr, tel: 525-9999/1-800-667-8497; www.conexusartscentre.ca. This is the home of the Regina Symphony, and where Regina's major dance, theater, and symphony performances are held.
Globe Theatre, 1801 Scarth St, tel: 525-6400/1-866-954-5623; www. globetheatrelive.com. In the converted former City Hall, this is home to Regina's professional acting company, which features eight performances between September and April.

Museums and Galleries

Most Canadian museums and art galleries offer extended hours on one or more nights a week, and sometimes free admission at certain times as well. It's best to check with each one individually, but here are a few examples:

Toronto's **Royal Ontario Museum** charges a nominal fee on Friday nights, 4.30–9.30pm.

In Montréal, the **Montréal Museums Pass** gives free access to 34 Montreal-area museums and attractions, along with public transit, in a package good for three consecutive days. For details, check at www.museesmontreal.org/site/museums pass.htm.

Out west, the **See Vancouver Card** includes Victoria and places beyond both cities, providing admission to around 50 attractions including the Art Gallery of Greater Victoria, the Maritime Museum of British Columbia, the Museum of Anthropology, and the Vancouver Aquarium. For more information, visit www.seevancouvercard.com.

The Québec City **Museum Card** offers a three-day package, with unlimited access to the city's 10 museums, two one-day bus passes, and rebates for services and attractions such as Parc Aquarium du Québec, various cruise lines, some

restaurants and cafes, and some museum boutiques.

Toronto's **CityPass** covers six attractions including the Royal Ontario Museum, the Art Gallery of Ontario, and the Ontario Science Centre. For further details, visit www.citypass.com/ city/toronto.html.

Comedy Venues

The comedy club scene in Canada is thriving, and has been for decades – many of the most famous "American" comedians are actually Canadians who cut their teeth in these Canadian clubs. Two of the big names are Yuk Yuks Comedy Club and The Second City (listed below), but there are countless clubs across the country, most easily found through the What's On listings for each city.
Yuk Yuks Comedy Club, Century Plaza Hotel, 1015 Burrard St, Vancouver, tel: 604-696-9857; www. yukyuks.com. Popular stand-up venue with numerous locations across Canada including Halifax and Toronto.
The Second City, 51 Mercer St, Toronto, tel: 416-343-0011; www. secondcity.com. Comedy theater chain with venues across North America.

For "serious" comedy fans, here are some of the top comedy fests:
Just For Laughs Comedy Festival/ Festival Juste Pour Rire, Montréal, July (www.hahaha.com).
We're Funny That Way, Canada's International Queer Comedy Festival, held each May in Toronto (www.were funnythatway.com).
FunnyFest Calgary Comedy Festival in May (www.funnyfest.com).
The CBC Winnipeg Comedy Festival held each April, claims to bring together more comedians than any other similar event in the country. (www.winnipegcomedyfestival.com).
The Canadian Comedy Awards and Festival takes place in October in a different city every year, an annual celebration of the best Canadian comedic talent in stand-up, television, and film (www.canadiancomedy.ca).

Movies

There are several major movie theater chains that show first-run movies across Canada, including AMC Theatres, Alliance Atlantis Cinemas, Cineplex, and Rainbow Cinemas. Larger cities (and some small ones) also support small independent cinemas where you can see second-run, alternative, underground, experimental, and less mainstream

films. Local entertainment guides will list these theaters, but here are a few for cinema buffs to note:
In Vancouver, **Fifth Avenue Cinemas** (2110 Burrard St; tel: 604-734-7469; www.festivalcinemas.ca); **Pacific Cinematheque** (1131 Howe St; tel: 604-688-3456; www.cinematheque.bc.ca).
In Winnipeg, **Cinematheque** (304-100 Arthur St; tel: 204-925-3456; www.winnipegcinematheque.com).
In Toronto, **Cinematheque Ontario** (Art Gallery of Ontario, 317 Dundas St W; tel: 416-968-3456); **Bloor Cinema** (506 Bloor St W; tel: 416-516-2331); **Revue Cinema** (400 Roncesvalles; tel: 416-531-9959).
In Montréal, **Cinémathèque Québécoise** (335 blvd de Maisonneuve Est; tel: 514-842-9763); **Ex-Centris** (3536 blvd Saint-Laurent; tel: 514-847-2206).

NIGHTLIFE

Alberta

In Alberta's resort areas (and, to a lesser extent, in Calgary and Edmonton), hotels generally offer the most popular hot-spots, but a little exploration can take visitors off the beaten path to watering-holes which cater mainly to the locals. Some bars and "beer parlors" are laid-back, but many have a free-spirited (and sometimes raucous) Western atmosphere. The provincial drinking age is 18.

Calgary (403)

In addition to theater and a few interesting bars, Calgary is famous for its rollicking two-step music and western dance clubs. The hottest spot for going out is all along 17th Avenue SW.
Beat Niq Jazz & Social Club, 811–1 St SW, tel: 263-1650; www.beatniq.com. Different bands play nightly in this eclectic New York-style jazz spot.
Cowboy's, 1088 Olympic Way SE, tel: 770-2200; www.cowboysniteclub.com. The most popular cowboy bar in town, close to Stampede Grounds and Saddledome, handy for drinks before and/or after. Live bands.
Ship and Anchor, 534 17th Ave SW, tel: 245-3333; www.shipandanchor.com. Best summer patio in town, great people-watching location on trendy 17th Ave.
Tubby Dog, 103 1022 17 Ave SW. Imaginative hot dogs. A great place to relax and watch eclectic videos before heading out on the town. Open very

late on weekends.
Vintage Chophouse & Tavern, 320-11 Ave SW, tel: 262-7262; www.vintagechophouse.com. Live blues and jazz on weekends in this upscale lounge, with its cozy booths and leather club chairs.
Wildwood, 2417–4 St SW, tel: 228-9113; www.wildwoodgrill.ca. A brewpub with a full range of fresh, handcrafted beers. Upscale dining upstairs, pub downstairs.
Wine Bar Kensington, 1131 Kensington Rd NW, tel: 257-1144; www.winebarkensington.com. Relaxed wine bar in trendy Kensington with a revolving list and tasty snacks, open until 2am on weekends,

Edmonton (780)

For nightlife Edmonton relies mostly on festivals, opera, and theater groups, with a few notable nightclubs and a popular jazz scene. Here's a sampling:
Blues on Whyte, 10329 Whtye Ave, tel: 439-5058; www.bluesonwhyte.ca. An R&B club.
Druid, 11606 Jasper Ave NW, tel: 454-9928; www.druidpub.ca. An Irish pub, complete with a "runic" stone, 18 draft beers, 30 malt beers, and a wide assortment of Irish whiskeys. Entertainment ranges from live bands to DJs and dancing.
Yardbird Suite, 11 Tommy Banks Way, tel: 432-0428; www.yardbirdsuite.com. One of Edmonton's best and longest-running jazz venues.

British Columbia

British Columbia's legal drinking age is 19. Nightlife includes bars, cafes, casinos, comedy clubs, dance clubs, and music clubs, in addition to arts offerings.

Vancouver (604)

Events information is available in the *Georgia Straight* (free) newspaper found in cafes throughout Vancouver.
Backstage Lounge, Arts Club Theatre, 1585 Johnston St, tel: 687-1354; www.thebackstagelounge.com. Popular Granville Island hang-out with live bands on weekends. Waterside patio.
The Cellar Restaurant/Jazz Club, 3611 W Broadway, tel: 738-1959; www.cellarjazz.com. Intimate hub for Vancouver's best jazz musicians.
Commodore Ballroom, 868 Granville St, tel: 739-7469. 1929 dance hall restored to its art deco glory, with massive dance floor.
Dover Arms, 961 Denman St, tel: 683-1929. Pub-crawling venue for British-style pub enthusiasts.

Irish Heather, 217 Carrall St, tel: 688-9779; www.irishheather.com. Properly poured Guinness along with a shebeen or whiskey house serving almost 100 whiskeys.
Steamworks Brewery, 375 Water St, tel: 689-2739. Some of best beer in town served in convivial downstairs pub with harbor views.

Victoria (250)

Perhaps due to the preponderance of retirees, Victoria's nightlife is rather quiet and hotel bars are possibly your best bet.
Boom Boom Room, 1208 Wharf St, tel: 381-2331. High-energy dance music for the young crowd.
Herman's Jazz Club, 753 View St, tel: 388-9166; www.hermannsjazz.com. Everything from Dixieland to big band music with dancing in this long-established pub-style club.
Hugo's Lounge & Brewpub, 625 Courtney St, tel: 920-4844. The hottest music, every night – from R&B to tech-house, deep house, funk, hip-hop, soul, and all current hot tracks – a block from the Inner Harbour.
Spinnakers Brew Pub, 308 Catherine St, tel: 386-2739; www.spinnakers.com. Victoria's most extensive menu of microbrews and a waterfront patio.
Sticky Wicket, 919 Douglas St, tel: 383-7137. Super-popular nightclub featuring rooftop volleyball courts.
The Upstairs Lounge, 15 Bastion Square, tel: 385-5483; www.upstairscabaret.ca. Dishes up jazz, live rock, and blues.

Whistler

Whistler was designed to be a party town and what is trendy one week is passé the next – the best bet is to walk through the village and listen for the loudest bar. Or, ask one of the liftees from Australia doing his year abroad for the best place to go.
Garfinkel's, Unit 1, 4308 Main St, tel: 932-2323; www.garfswhistler.com. Live bands and Top 40.

Manitoba

Minimum drinking age is 18.

Winnipeg (204)

The performing arts have perhaps been Winnipeg's strong suit for nightlife, with the dance club scene exploding more recently. The Exchange area has numerous clubs with personalities that evolve quickly with the music scene.
Your best bet is to check it out for yourself. Some of Winnipeg's nightlife

can also be found at the downtown hotels.

Ampersand, 114 Market Ave, tel: 942-6274. A huge nightclub.

The Cavern Club, 112 Osbourne St, tel: 284-7201. Live music in trendy Osbourne Village. Popular British-style pub located upstairs.

The Empire, 436 Main St, tel: 943-3979. A unique hotspot in a heritage building, with two lounges, and a cabaret for dancing.

Finn McCue's, 210-25 Forks Market Rd, tel: 944-8118. Spacious Irish pub, with a great view over The Forks, live music most weekends.

Palomino Club, 1133 Portage Ave, tel: 722-0454; www.palominoclub.ca. Live music from country rock to classic rock. Closed Tuesdays.

New Brunswick

New Brunswick's legal minimum drinking age is 19. Most large hotels have bars and some have nightspots.

Fredericton (506)

Boom!, 474 Queen St, tel: 463-2666. A celebrated gay club where people of all orientations come to dance the night away.

Dolan's Pub, 349 King St, tel: 454-7474. A cheerful Irish tavern, with live music on Thursday, Friday, and Saturday from some of the best in East Coast talent.

iRock, 339 King St, tel: 444-0121. Part of Sweetwaters, but geared to the 25+ crowd; Fridays are oldies night.

James Joyce Irish Pub, The Lord Beaverbrook Hotel, 659 Queen St, tel: 450-9820. Filled with mementoes of Joyce from books to his photo, the pub is a popular watering-hole for locals.

Lunar Rouge, 625 King St, tel: 450-2065. A local favorite, with more than 50 whiskeys and 14 draft beers on offer.

Sweetwaters, 339 King St, tel: 444-0121. One of Fredericton's most upbeat dance clubs, with four giant screens, five bars, and two dance floors.

Moncton (506)

Oxygen Night Club, 125 Westmorland St, tel: 854-0265. One of Atlantic Canada's hottest dance clubs, with live bands.

Saint James' Gate, 14 Church St, tel: 1-888-782-1414. Live jazz and blues.

Sasha's, 196 Robinson Court, tel: 854-8748, A tapas and martinis lounge, with jazz on Saturday nights.

ABOVE: performing at the Montréal Jazz Festival.

Saint John (506)

Look for pubs in the Market Square area, or try:

Happinez, 42 Princess St, tel: 634-7340. An intimate, friendly wine bar within exposed brick walls. Good atmosphere.

O'Leary's Pub, 46 Princess St, tel: 634-7135. A popular venue for traditional and East Coast artists.

Shuckers Bar, Delta Brunswick Hotel, 39 King St, tel: 648-1981. Enjoy cocktails in their relaxing lounge.

Studio 54, 9 Sydney St, tel: 693-5454. Dance to the best of 70s, 80s, and current music.

Newfoundland and Labrador

Newfoundland's legal drinking age is 19. In St John's, nightlife happens in the Water and Duckworth Street area, as well as in the bars of all major hotels. Outside the capital, hotels are the centers of nightlife.

St John's (709)

Bridie Molloy's, 5 George St, tel: 576-5990. Place to go for traditional Newfoundland music and excellent pub grub.

Erin's Pub, 184 Water St, tel: 722-1916. Popular spot for folk music, especially Irish.

The Fat Cat, 7 George St, tel: 739-5554. A great contemporary blues club.

The Ship Inn, 265 Duckworth St, tel: 753-3870. Draws a bohemian crowd,

with poetry readings, jazz, blues, and reggae.

Trapper John's, 2 George St, tel: 579-9630. Downhome atmosphere and some of the best live music in St John's.

The Northwest Territories (867)

Northwest Territories' legal drinking age is 19, and bar closing time is 1am. Many native communities are completely dry by law (check first before flying anywhere with alcohol), but the rest of the territories more than makes up for them. In short, most watering holes are wild establishments. Licensed hotels generally sport a lounge.

Nova Scotia

Nova Scotia's watering holes stay open until midnight or 2am depending on classification, and the drinking age is 19. Most taverns in the province's small towns welcome travelers, but a word of caution: many have acquired a rough-and-tumble atmosphere unsuited to quiet drinkers.

Halifax (902)

Most nightlife is centered in the downtown area, with Argyle Street as its focus. The clubs can be crowded on weeknights and absolutely packed on weekends. Here is a selection:

Bearly's House of Blues & Ribs, 1269 Barrington St, tel: 423-2526. The city's premier blues club.

Economy Shoe Shop Cafe & Bar, 1663 Argyle St, tel: 423-7463. A small cafe that expanded to include The Backstage, The Diamond, and The Belgium Bar, it has become the hangout for the city's creative types. Jazz on Monday nights.

Granite Brewery, 6054 Stairs St, tel: 422-4954. A deservedly popular brewpub.

Lower Deck Good Time Pub, Privateers' Warehouse, Historic Properties, 1869 Upper Water St, tel: 425-1501. Traditional maritime music.

Reflections Cabaret, 5184 Sackville St, tel: 422-2957. A gay and lesbian bar, and one of the hottest nightclubs in town.

Ontario

Ontario possesses a set of liquor laws that are, in part, remnants from its prohibitionist past. Many restrictions are being eased but:
• all carry-out alcohol is marketed through provincially owned outlets

including: The Beer Store for beer, and Liquor Control Board of Ontario (LCBO) stores for liquor, wine, and specialty beers. Many are open seven days a week. Check the phone book for the nearest one.

• you may not go out in public with an open bottle of booze or opened case of beer.

• licensed establishments can serve liquor from 11am–2am seven days a week.

• The legal drinking age is 19. Though the old laws remain, Ontario has long since shed its reputation for having a dull nightlife, as evidenced below.

Ottawa (613)

Ottawa's nightlife becomes more vibrant every year, especially in the ByWard Market area, which draws a youngish crowd.

Barrymore's Music Hall, 323 Bank St, tel: 565-9999. In a former vaudeville theater, Barrymore's is long established as one of the top live music venues in the city. Retro 90s night on Thursday, Retro 80s on Sunday.

Caliente Latin Club, 110 York St, tel: 562-0698. Always hopping, with a variety of Latin dance themed nights, along with free dance lessons on Friday evenings.

Irish Village, 67 Clarence St, tel: 562-0674. Four great pubs share the same kitchen and a huge courtyard patio; an imaginative menu and a wide range of beers.

Lieutenant's Pump, 361 Elgin St, tel: 238-2949. A popular, English-style pub, with 16 beers on tap.

Rainbow Bistro, 76 Murray St, tel: 241-5123. Live music nightly, largely – but not only – the blues.

Suite34 Bar & Lounge, 34 Clarence St, tel: 789-7770. An ultra cool spot to hang out, including a hugely

popular rooftop patio when weather permits.

Toronto (416)

This entire book could be spent describing Toronto's nightlife. Yorkville and nearby Bloor Street clubs draw a younger, stylish crowd. Queen St East and West, as well as the Theatre District, offer an ever-growing assortment of bars and clubs. The Yonge/St Clair and Yonge/Eglinton area bars cater to single, young professionals, while Yonge St south of Bloor is home to gay bars and heavy-metal emporiums. Downtown hotel lounges draw a youngish to middle-aged crowd, while the increasingly gentrified Annex neighborhood (immediately north and west of the University of Toronto) has sprouted numerous imported English pubs. For listings of events, check *Now* or *Eye* free weekly newspapers. Here are a few samplers, by category.

Pubs and Patios

Duke of York, 39 Prince Arthur Ave, just north of Bloor St, tel: 964-2441. Three floors, including a plush basement lounge popular with the "after work" crowd, and a non-smoking floor.

Madison Avenue Pub, 14 Madison Ave, just east of Spadina, tel: 927-1722. A sprawling Victorian house that lends itself to socializing, with two pool rooms, 12 bars, a five-level patio, and 150 drafts on tap.

Ye Olde Brunswick House, 481 Bloor St W, at Brunswick, tel: 964-2242. A long-established party spot famous for its draft beer. Mix of live bands and DJs. A favorite with the student crowd.

Quieter Lounges

The Comrade, 758 Queen St E, tel: 778-9449. Located in up-and-coming

Leslieville, with tin ceilings, leather couches and exposed brick walls decorated with vintage Communist-era posters and Asian-inspired art.

Panorama, 55 Bloor St W, at the top of the Manulife Center, tel: 967-0000. The city's highest patio with close to the best city view.

Jazz and Blues

Dominion on Queen, 500 Queen St E, tel: 368-6893. In Corktown, this long-established pub is a local favorite, with jazz and blues six nights a week, as well as comedy acts and poetry nights.

Gate 403, 403 Roncesvalles, tel: 588-2930. A neighborhood café that offers good jazz, every night.

The Pilot, 22 Cumberland St, tel: 923-5716. A stalwart on the scene for many years, this is where jazz enthusiasts head on weekend afternoons.

Rex Hotel Jazz and Blues Bar, 194 Queen W, tel: 598-2475. A hive of musical activity, presenting many of Canada's top musicians in 17 acts every week.

Silver Dollar Room, 486 Spadina, tel: 763-9139. Possibly the pre-eminent blues club in town.

Bars, Clubs, and Discos

Cameron House, 408 Queen St W, tel: 703-0811. An arty bohemian hangout hosting local musicians.

Hugh's Room, 2261 Dundas St W, tel: 531-6604. A comfortable, spacious 240-seat addition to the folk scene, presenting blues, folk, jazz, and bluegrass musicians from far and wide.

Lula Lounge, 1585 Dundas St W, tel: 588-0307. A cultural cornerstone for the Latin and Brazilian community, it is beloved by arts connoisseurs, concert-goers, salsa aficionados, and tapas devotees.

M Lounge, 241 Richmond St W, tel: 595-5559. A large dance club in the nightlife district, with a sleek wood-and-marble interior and private booths for bottle service.

Revival, 783 College St, tel: 535-7888. In a former Baptist church turned Polish legion, Revival combines Pan-Asian cuisine with live jazz, soul, Latin, and blues.

The Docks, 11 Polson St, tel: 461-3625. A huge 8.4-hectare (21-acre) complex that includes three nightclubs – The Deep End, Tides, and Aqua Lounge. Open nightly in summer; weekends only from autumn through Victoria Day.

The Drake Hotel, 1150 Queen St W, tel: 531-5042. A hip lounge with a

BELOW: live jazz in a hip Vancouver hangout.

rooftop patio and an 'underground' space for indie entertainment; a place to be seen.

The Feathers, 962 Kingston Rd, tel: 694-0443. An excellent line of fine whiskeys plus a few house beers in a British-style pub.

Wide Open, 139A Spadina Ave, tel: 727-5411. A long, narrow bar with a cozy lounge at the back. Local art graces the walls. An eclectic range of music.

Gay Scene

Fly Nightclub, 8 Gloucester St, tel: 410-5426. Hugely popular, with frequent line-ups. Two chill-out lounges downstairs and a cavernous dance space upstairs, where DJs play house, tribal, and circuit music.

Zelda's, 542 Church, tel: 922-2526. An outrageously zany restaurant, bar, and drag cabaret where eccentricity rules supreme, in the heart of the Gay Village.

Prince Edward Island

P.E.I.'s legal drinking age is 19.

Charlottetown (902)

The Gahan House Pub and Brewery, 126 Sydney St, tel: 626-2337. The only brewpub on the island. Housed in a former convent, it offers great ales and ambience.

Olde Dublin Pub, 131 Sydney St, tel: 892-6992. Sells imported draft beer from Scotland and Ireland. Some live entertainment.

Peakes, 11-C Great George St, tel: 368-1330. Always action-packed, with the Island's largest outdoor waterfront patio, summer concerts from May to October, and a lively nightclub year-round.

Summerside

Crown & Anchor Tavern, 195 Harbor St, tel: 436-3333. Varied menu; weekend entertainment.

Québec

The drinking age in Québec is 18. Bars close at 3am.

Montréal (514)

The major hotels house lavish nightclubs, which feature discos, cabaret shows, comedies, and other entertainment. With the growth in popularity of micro-brewery beers, produced by small, independent breweries, there are many bars along the St-Laurent strip between Sherbrooke and Mont-Royal, as well as along rue St-Denis, to try a wide

range of these beers. Most clubs and bars are located in the downtown area, where explorers can sample the chic rue Crescent scene, rue Ste-Catherine's red-light district, or trendy rue Bishop.

Here are a few starting points for a night out in the city:

Altitude 737, 1 Place Ville Marie, 43rd Floor, tel: 397-0737. Chic disco lounge and restaurant, with breathtaking views from its rooftop terrace.

Bily Kun, 354 ave du Mont-Royal E, tel: 845-5392. A popular hangout for jazz and blues enthusiasts.

Else's, 156 rue Roy E, tel: 286-6689. A neighborhood favorite that offers homey, unpretentious, and convivial atmosphere. Great selection of ales and scotches.

Foufounes Electriques, 87 rue Ste-Catherine E, tel: 844-5539. A massive three-floor industrial space full of electric atmosphere and hard rock pulsing through the night.

Funky Town, 1454 rue Peel, tel: 282-8387. A retro disco club that plays the best of the '70s for anyone ready to boogie.

House of Jazz, 2060 Aylmer, tel: 842-8656. The place to enjoy performances by seasoned musicians, an extravagant decor, and the famous saxophone beer pitcher.

La Sala Rossa, 4873 blvd St-Laurent, tel: 284-3804. Once a left-wing social club that hosted the likes of Paul Robeson and Eleanor Roosevelt; now the place to see indie bands before they hit the big time.

Newtown, 1476 rue Crescent, tel: 284-6555. A tri-level club/resto/bar partly owned by race-car driver Jacques Villeneuve (its name an intentional play on his own name).

St Sulpice, 1680 rue St-Denis, tel: 844-9458. The city's largest patio, plus three floors of entertainment, including a lively dance club.

Québec City (418)

The city sports few clubs, but many small cafes and bars. Stroll rue St-Jean to find sidewalk cafes, while rue Ste-Anne offers rather more expensive fare.

Bar St-Laurent, 1 rue des Carrières, tel: 266-3919. Soft lighting and panoramic views make this one of the most romantic bars in the city, in Château Frontenac.

Boudoir Lounge, 441 rue de L'Eglise, tel: 524-2777. East meets West in this Asian-inspired restaurant, lounge, and club.

Chez Maurice, 575 Grande Allée E, tel: 647-2000. An avant-garde setting and hip music frequently draw visiting celebrities.

L'Inox, 37 quai St-Antoine, tel: 692-2877. A popular brewpub in the Lower Town.

Saskatchewan

There are a few nightspots in the province, particularly in Regina and Saskatoon, but in most cases, meals figure as prominently as entertainment. In smaller towns, the nightlife tends to center around the hotels and resorts. Saskatchewan's drinking age is 19.

Regina (306)

Applause Feast and Folly Theatre, Regina Inn, 1975 Broad St, tel: 791-6868; www.applausedinnertheatre.ca. Relaxed dinner theater.

Bushwakker Pub and Brewing Company, 2206 Dewdney Ave, tel: 359-7276; www.bushwakker.com. In addition to nine flagship ales and lagers, 20 seasonal beers are produced on site, served with Canadian syle pub fare, which includes burgers, pizza, Greek food, and even jambalaya.

Soho Restaurant and Club, 2300 Dewdney St, tel: 359-7772; www.sohoregina.ca. Upstairs dance club Friday and Saturday.

Saskatoon (306)

Amigos Cantina, 632 10th St, tel: 652-4912; www.amigoscantina.com. Mexican decor and food. Eclectic live music several times weekly.

The Bassment, 245–3rd Ave S, tel: 683-2277. The city's premier jazz club, featuring the best of local and touring jazz.

The Yukon (867)

The drinking age is 19; bar closing-time is 2am. Most hotels have restaurants and lounges, and in the summer, when Yukon swells with visitors, the nightlife is raucous.

Dawson City (867)

Bombay Peggy's Inn and Pub, 2nd Ave at Princess St, tel: 993-6969; www.bombaypeggys.com. Popular pub in a gold rush era restored building, featuring microbrew beer as well as extensive martini list.

Diamond Tooth Gertie's Gambling Casino, 4th and Queen St, tel: 993-5525. Canada's first legal gambling casino. Honky-tonk pianist and cancan girls, all in the gold rush spirit.

Palace Grand Theatre, King St and 2nd, tel: 993-6217. A musical-spoof-comedy revue from mid-June to mid-September.

Whitehorse (867)

Frantic Follies, Westmark Whitehorse Hotel, 201 Wood St, tel: 668-2042; www.franticfollies.com. Rollicking gold rush revue nightly, late May–end Sep.

FESTIVALS

Across Canada, the national holiday of July 1st is celebrated with parades and parties. Smaller cities tend to have more interesting parades, which often boast floats from community groups and civic services like the fire and rescue groups. It's not as focused on patriotism as the American July 4th activities, but there are fireworks and a festive feeling prevails.

Alberta

July and August (Banff)

Banff Arts Festival
Professional dance, opera, and music presented by artists from around the world, as well as showcases of the visual arts. www.banffcentre.ca

First weekend of July (Vegreville)

Ukrainian Pysanka Festival
A folk fair in this center of Ukrainian settlement. Camp in the shadow of the world's largest Easter egg, standing over 10 meters (30ft) tall. www.pysankafestival.com

Second week of July (Calgary)

Calgary Stampede and Exhibition
The most famous annual Canadian event – 10 days of raucous western showmanship and celebration, with rodeo events, chuck-wagon racing, and more. Make hotel reservations well in advance (by some estimates, Calgary's population doubles at this time), and book tickets for main events as soon as possible. Tel: 403-261-0101/1-800-661-1260; www.calgarystampede.com

Late July (Edmonton)

Capital Ex
Formerly known as Klondike Days, the renamed festival focuses on celebrating Edmonton today, including Global Connections and Northwest Originals. www.capitalex.ca

July (Drumheller)

The Canadian Badlands Passion Play
Set in an acoustically superb natural amphitheater, the similarity of the site to the Holy Land enhances the drama. A hugely popular affair that draws people from across North America every year. www.canadianpassionplay.com

Mid-August (Edmonton)

Edmonton's International Fringe Theatre Festival
Fabulous Fringe event, second only to Edinburgh in size. www.fringetheatreadventures.ca

British Columbia

January (Squamish)

Brackendale Winter Bald Eagle Festival and Count
The bald eagle count takes place throughout January, with volunteers encouraged to participate, on well-organized tours, including on rafting trips. www.brackendaleartgallery.com

April (Whistler)

World Ski and Snowboard Festival
North America's largest annual snow sports and music celebration – serious skiing and snowboarding competitions for 10 days straight, film, music, and partying every night. http://wssf.com

May (Vancouver)

Vancouver International Children's festival offers a week of entertainment for kids of all ages – it's been around for more than 30 years, so it is a bit of an institution. www.childrensfestival.ca.

First week in July (Williams Lake)

Williams Lake Stampede
Five thousand spectators come to watch top contenders in one of Canada's best rodeo events. www.williamslakestampede.com

Mid-July

Vancouver Folk Music Festival
Folk musicians from all over the world come to Jericho Beach for this three-day music festival. www.thefestival.bc.ca

Mid-July (Kimberley)

Julyfest
A celebration of all that "Canada's highest city" has to offer, including the Canadian bocce championships and extreme skateboard racing. www.kimberleyjulyfest.com

Late July (Vancouver)

The HSBC Celebration of Light
Held annually, this international pyrotechnics competition attracts hundreds of thousands to any space close to English Bay. www.celebration-of-light.com

Early August (Penticton)

Peach Festival
Five-day spectacle includes fireworks, floats, lumberjack shows, lots of live music, and the Peachfest Square Dance Festival. www.peachfest.com

Late August (Vancouver)

Pacific National Exhibition
Features parades, exhibits, sports, entertainment, and logging contests, along with the usual 4-H competition for raising the best farm animals. www.pne.ca

Early October (Okanagan Valley)

Okanagan Wine Festival
A 10-day festival including vineyard tours, lunches, dinners, and other events focused on wine, food, education, and the arts. www.owfs.com

Manitoba

February (St Boniface)

Festival du Voyageur
The lively francophone community celebrates the early fur traders. www.festivalvoyageur.mb.ca

Late June (Winnipeg)

Cool Jazz Winnipeg Festival
For 11 days, downtown Winnipeg rocks to some of the world's best jazz, blues, funk, and urban music, bringing locals Downtown in droves. www.jazzwinnipeg.com

Mid-July (Winnipeg)

Winnipeg Folk Festival
The internationally acclaimed folk music festival is held over five days in a provincial park 34km (20 miles) outside the city, featuring bluegrass, folk, and world music. www.winnipegfolkfestival.ca

End of July (Austin)

Manitoba Threshermen's Reunion and Stampede
Antique tractor races, sheep-tying, and threshing demonstrations. www.ag-museum.mb.ca

August (Dauphin)

Canada's National Ukrainian Festival
Music, fun, and plenty of food for all. www.cnuf.ca

First week in August (Gimli)

The Icelandic Festival of Manitoba
Gimli, the largest Icelandic community outside of Iceland, celebrates its heritage. www.icelandicfestival.com

ABOVE: playing ball on St Kitts Beach, Vancouver.

August (Winnipeg)

Folklorama
This two-week, city-wide festival features the food, dancing, crafts, and culture of 40 different ethnic groups. www.folklorama.ca

New Brunswick

Mid-July (Kings County)

Kings County Covered Bridge Festival
A celebration of the 16 covered bridges in Kings County, from home-baked teas to canoe and bicycle tours. www.coveredbridgevic.com

Mid-July (Shediac)

Shediac Lobster Festival
Five days of delicious seafood and lively entertainment. www.shediac lobsterfestival.nb.ca

Late July–early August (Edmundston)

La Foire Brayonne
The most popular festival in this area of New Brunswick, the mythical République du Madawaska. The local French-speaking population engages in three days of celebrations. Visitors enjoy the local food and the weaving and other crafts. www.foirebrayonne.com

End of July–early August (Newcastle)

Miramichi Folk-Song Festival
Offers a fascinating introduction to the exuberant local ballads. www. miramichifolksongfestival.com

First Monday in August

New Brunswick Day
Barbecues, games, and live entertainment.

Mid-August (Caraquet)

Festival Acadien de Caraquet
A huge two-week celebration of Acadian culture, this festival begins

with prayers for the fishing fleet, and is attended by hundreds of Acadian and francophone singers, musicians, actors, dancers, artists, and writers. www.festivalacadien.ca

Early September (Sussex)

Atlantic International Balloon Fiesta
Around 180 balloon flights take place over the lush valleys of Kings County. The festival also includes an antique car show, helicopter rides, and amusement rides. www.atlanticballoon fiesta.ca

Mid-September (Fredericton)

Harvest Jazz and Blues Festival
Musicians from across Canada turn Fredericton into New Orleans of the North, playing jazz, blues, and Dixieland. www.harvestjazzandblues.com

Newfoundland and Labrador

June–mid-September (Trinity)

Rising Tide Theatre
A festival of plays, dinner theater, concerts, and special events in outdoor venues all around Trinity Bight, bringing the area's colorful, and not-so-distant past to life. www.rising tidetheatre.com

1 July (St John's)

Newfoundland and Labrador Folk Festival
Folk groups, dancers, and storytellers from around the province gather in Bannerman Park to provide a taste of the traditional Newfoundland lifestyle. www.nlfolk.com

Late July (Twillingate)

Fish, Fun, and Folk Festival
One of the province's largest folk festivals, on the scenic northeast coast, this family-oriented gathering

celebrates Newfoundland's culture and food. www.fishfunfolkfestival.com

End of July–early August (Gander)

Festival of Flight
Honoring the area's role in aviation history, this popular festival offers a wide range of events, from a daring demolition derby with car-crashing thrills to the popular Festival of Flight parade and Newfoundland's biggest kitchen party. www.gandercanada.com

End of July–early August (St John's)

George Street Festival
Six nights of outdoor entertainment and parties at George Street pubs and taverns. www.georgestreetfestival.com

First Wednesday in August (St John's)

Royal St John's Regatta
The regatta on Quidi Vidi Lake is the oldest sporting event in North America, but get up early – the rowing's over before breakfast. The city closes down and general festivities continue for the rest of the day. (If it rains, the race – and festivities – will be postponed until the following week.) www.stjohnsregatta.org

Nova Scotia

May–June (Annapolis Valley)

Apple Blossom Festival
Dancing, parades, and entertainment celebrate the blossoming apple trees. www.appleblossom.com

End of June–early July (Halifax)

The Royal Nova Scotia International Tattoo
An annual extravaganza that presents more than 2,000 of the best military and civilian international and Canadian performers. www.nstattoo.ca

Mid-July (Antigonish)

Antigonish Highland Games
This action-packed Scottish festival features caber tossing (log throwing) and a continuous display of Highland dancing, with hundreds of marching bagpipers. www.antigonishhighlandgames. com

Mid-August (Halifax)

Halifax International Busker Festival
Street performers from around the world provide 11 days of music on the waterfront in downtown historic Halifax. www.buskers.ca

Mid-August (Lunenburg)

Lunenburg Folk Harbor Festival
A popular festival featuring acoustic music performed by some of the best of Canadian talent, dances, and

workshops in a range of venues, from tents to a Victorian bandstand, an old opera house, and the wharf. www.folkharbour.com

Early October (Across Cape Breton)
Celtic Colours International Festival
A nine-day, Cape Breton Island-wide celebration of Celtic culture, featuring artists from around the world and across Canada, along with some of Cape Breton's finest singers, players, dancers, and tradition-bearers. www.celtic-colours.com

The Northwest Territories

Late March (Yellowknife)
Caribou Carnival
This three-day festival celebrates spring, such as it is, in the Arctic, featuring Inuit and Dene northern games, ice-sculpting, and the Annual Canadian Championship Dog Derby, a three-day, 230km (143-mile) dogsled race. www.cariboucarnival.net

20 June (Yellowknife)
Raven Mad Daze
Celebration of the summer solstice, with entertainment in the streets. www.solsticefestival.ca

20 June (Yellowknife)
Midnight Classic Golf Tournament
Fun tournament at the Yellowknife Golf Club takes advantage of the midnight sun. www.yellowknifegolf.com

Mid–late July (Inuvik)
Great Northern Arts Festival
Artists celebrate Inuit culture, 10 days of activities including workshops. www.gnaf.org

Nunavut

Last two weeks of April (Iqaluit)
Toonik Tyme Festival
A popular festival celebrating the return of the sun, includes northern games, snowmobile races, and a memorable community feast. Tel: 867-975-8510; www.tooniktyme.com

Ontario

Mid-February (Ottawa)
Winterlude
Extravagant carnival features ice-sculpting, snowshoe races, ice-boating, and other wintertime fun. www.capcan.ca/winterlude

May–November (Stratford)
Stratford Festival
See section on Performing Arts, page 373. www.stratfordfestival.ca

May (Ottawa)
Canadian Tulip Festival
Over three million tulips highlight this festival, which also offers parades, regattas, craft shows, etc. www.tulipfestival.ca

May–October (Niagara-on-the-Lake)
Shaw Festival
See section on Performing Arts, page 373. www.shawfest.com

Mid-June (Toronto)
Luminato
A ten-day international festival of arts and creativity, held at indoor and outdoor locations citywide. www.luminato.com
Pride Week
One of the largest Prides in the world, with a seven-day celebration of Canada's inclusiveness, including an arts and cultural program. www.pridetoronto.com

July 1 (Ottawa)
Canada Day
Countrywide celebrations; the largest takes place in Ottawa with concerts, street entertainment, and fireworks over the Ottawa river.

Early July (Toronto)
Toronto Fringe Festival
Toronto's largest theatre festival with over 150 international theatre companies performing all over the city. www.fringetoronto.com

Mid-July–early August (Toronto)
Toronto Caribbean Carnival
The city's West Indian community celebrates with singing, dancing, and parades, mostly on Toronto Islands, creating a Mardi Gras atmosphere. www.caribana.com

Late July (Oakville)
Canadian Open Golf Championship
Glen Abbey Golf Club hosts one of golf's top five tournaments. www.rbccanadianopen.ca

Early August (Maxville)
Glengarry Highland Games
Canada's second-largest Highland gathering. www.glengarryhighlandgames.com

Early August (St Catharines)
Royal Canadian Henley Regatta
The largest rowing regatta in Canada. Draws competitors and spectators from throughout the continent. www.henleyregatta.ca

Early August (Manitoulin Island)
Wikwemikong Annual Cultural Festival and Pow Wow
Well over 40 years old, this pow wow initiated the restoration of the traditions of dancing and drumming in Ontario. On the August civic holiday weekend, dancers, drummers, and singers travel to the Wikwemikong Pow Wow from across North America. www.wikwemikongheritage.org

Mid-August–Labor Day (Toronto)
Canadian National Exhibition
The largest and oldest exhibition of its kind in the world, featuring air shows, big-name entertainment, and all sorts of exhibits. All this takes place for three weeks at Exhibition Place on Lake Shore Boulevard. www.theex.com

Early September (Toronto)
Toronto International Film Festival
A 10-day showcase of the best in global filmmaking. www.tiff.net

Early September (Guelph)
Guelph Jazz Festival
Considered to be one of the premier

BELOW: the Canadian Tulip Festival in Ottowa.

jazz festivals in North America. www.guelphjazzfestival.com

First Saturday in October (Toronto)
Nuit Blanche
An extraordinary celebration of contemporary art, in galleries, museums, and countless unexpected places from sunset to sunrise. www.scotiabanknuitblanche.ca

Mid-October (Kitchener/Waterloo)
Oktoberfest
This famous Bavarian celebration attracts over a half-million festive partygoers to the area's 30-odd beer halls and tents. www.oktoberfest.ca

Late October (Toronto)
Canadian Aboriginal Festival
Beneath the SkyDome, Canada's largest Aboriginal event features up to 1,000 dancers and singers, as well as arts and crafts and the Aboriginal Music Awards. www.canab.com

Prince Edward Island

Mid-June–Labor Day (Charlottetown)
Charlottetown Festival
The Confederation Center hosts a very fine series of concerts, theater, and film. www.confederationcentre.com

Early July (Charlottetown)
P.E.I. Jazz and Blues Festival
A well-attended four-day event that takes over much of downtown Charlottetown, featuring musicians from across the country and around the world. www.jazzandblues.ca

Mid-July (Summerside)
Summerside Lobster Carnival
Five days of fairs, parades, and lobster suppers. www.exhibitions-festivals peiae.com/summersidelobstercarnival.html

Early August (Tyne Valley)
Tyne Valley Oyster Festival
Fiddling, dancing, and oyster-shucking contest. Oysters, presented all sorts of different ways, are featured on the menus of the Oyster Suppers. www.exhibitions-festivalspeiae.com/tynevalley oysterfestival.html

Québec

Early February (Québec City)
Carnaval de Québec
Québécois engage in 11 days of revelry, heightened somewhat by the ubiquitous "Cariboo," a concoction of whiskey, sweet red wine, and other surprises. There's a parade, ice-sculpture contests, and even a canoe

race on the frozen St-Laurent. www.carnaval.qc.ca

Mid-January–early February (Montréal)
La Fête des Neiges
Winter carnival, including costume balls, ice-sculptures, and outdoor sports events held on the islands in the river. www.fetedesneiges.com

Early April (Province-wide)
Sugaring-off Parties
Festivities accompany the collection of maple tree sap. www.bonjourquebec. com (then enter "sugaring off" in the search box).

Early May to Late September (Montréal)
Tam Tams
Perhaps the largest spontaneous gathering in the world, Montréalers gather every Sunday on Mont-Royal's east slope to play drums, have picnics, throw frisbees, and enjoy the summer sun. www.tamtamsmontreal.net/ english.html

Mid-June (Bromont)
International Bromont
On the site of the 1976 Equestrian Olympics, a World Cup equestrian competition takes place in the Eastern Townships. www.international bromont.org

June–August (Mont Orford)
Festival Orford
Performances of the Jeunesses Musicales du Canada draw international talent and are presented throughout the summer in Mont Orford Park's music center. www.arts-orford.org

Mid-June–early October (Montréal)
International Flora Montréal
Gardening enthusiasts flock to the Quays of Old-Port Montréal to visit the 45 gardens and learn about the latest trends in gardening and landscaping. www.floramontreal.ca

24 June
Fête Nationale
Provincial holiday. www.fetenationale.qc.ca

Early–mid-July (Québec City)
Québec City Summer Festival
Free concerts and lively shows throughout the city. www.infofestival.com

Late June–early July (Montréal)
Montréal International Jazz Festival
A mammoth jam, with over 300 free shows, besides the ticketed events. www.montrealjazzfest.com.

Mid-July (Montréal)
Just for Laughs Festival
The world's largest comedy festival. Offers more than 2,000 shows, including 1,300 free events. www.hahaha.com

Mid-July–mid-August (Val-David)
1001 Pots
An enormous exhibition of ceramics, showcasing 25,000 original pieces by more than 100 ceramicists. www.1001pots.com

Mid-August (St-Jean-sur-Richelieu)
St-Jean-sur-Richelieu International Balloon Festival
A family-oriented summer festival, this is the biggest gathering of hot-air balloons in Canada. www.montgolfieres.com

Late August (Montréal)
18th-century Public Market
A trip back in time, to Montréal's first public market. Rain or shine, festivities take place in Place Royale and in the streets around the Pointe-à-Callière Museum of Archeology and History, as farmers, craftspeople, and entertainers recreate the 18th-century market. www.pacmuseum.qc.ca

Late August/early September (Montréal)
Montréal Film Festival
Over 350,000 people flock to this event every year. www.ffm-montreal.org

September–end October (Montréal)
The Magic of Lanterns Festival, Montréal Botanical Gardens
Hundreds of lanterns, in an amazing variety of shapes and colors, light up the Chinese Garden each fall, each one handmade in Shanghai by Chinese craftspeople. www2.ville. montreal.qc.ca/jardin/en/propos/lanternes.htm

Early October (Montréal)
Black and Blue Festival, Montréal
Gay festival featuring a wide variety of shows, artistic displays, sports activities, and a parade. www.bbcm.org

Saskatchewan

February (Prince Albert)
Prince Albert Winter Festival
A much-enjoyed winter festival including dogsled races, the Ol' Tyme Fiddler's showdown, a contemporary country music concert, and a children's carnival. www.princealbertwinterfestival.com

First week of August (Saskatoon)
Saskatoon Exhibition
This is a popular, week-long fair of

contests, historical displays, horse racing, and livestock exhibitions. www.saskatoonexhibition.ca

First weekend in August (Regina)

Buffalo Days Exhibition
This seven-day exhibition focuses more on the midway and live entertainment than buffalo.

Mid-August (Regina)

Regina Dragonboat Festival
Dragonboat festivals have taken Canada by storm and Regina is no exception. Join the 20,000 spectators who come out to see the prairie version of a 2,000-year-old Chinese tradition.

The Yukon

Last week in February (Whitehorse)

Yukon Sourdough Rendezvous
Native-born Yukoners call themselves "sourdoughs" after the famous biscuits. Now, to qualify as a sourdough, you must have spent one winter in Yukon. Their rendezvous is a week-long bash celebrating the Klondike days. It includes such local traditions as dogsled races, packing sacks of flour, log toss, and axe throw, along with drinking heavily at the nightly cabarets. www.yukonrendezvous.com

Early June (Haines Junction)

Kluane Mountain Bluegrass Festival
In a stunning location, just outside world-renowned Kluane National Park, bluegrass is performed by both international and local musicians. www.kluanemountainbluegrassfest.com

Third weekend in August (Dawson City)

Discovery Days
Parades, dancing, races, and general merriment to celebrate the anniversary of the discovery of gold near Dawson City. www.dawsoncity.ca

Mid-August (Dawson City)

Yukon Riverside Arts Festival
Part of Discovery Days, this festival features artists from across the Yukon and Northwest Territories, showcasing their work in parkland beside the Yukon river. www.kiac.org

SHOPPING

Alberta

Handicrafts stores in Edmonton and Calgary as well as Banff, Jasper, and other tourism centers offer a range of Western and Northern specialties including furs, and wood and stone carvings made by native peoples. A number of tourist information centers around the province offer garments designed and made in Alberta.

With more than 800 stores, the West Edmonton mall has pretty much anything a shopper could want, with other activities for the non-shoppers in the family (a 13-screen movie complex including IMAX, skating rink, a water park, mini-golf amongst others).

British Columbia

Vancouver

For chic galleries, boutiques, and import shops head to Robson Street. Granville Island has an extensive selection of locally produced arts and crafts. Circle Craft has a broad spectrum, while other smaller shops specialize in unique items. At its entrance, **Leona Lattimer** (1590 West 2nd Ave; www.lattimergalleries.com) is one of several reputable stores representing First Nations artists where you can find masks, bent wood boxes, lithographs, and prints, as well as exquisite jewelry. Nearby, at **Robert Held Art Glass** (2130 Pine Street; www.robertheld.com), you can learn about glass blowing and watch the artisans at work.

Victoria

The emphasis for visitors is on specialty shops which offer Canadian handicrafts as well as goods imported from Britain and Asia. Government Street is very touristy (much of what you see is not local at all), but there are gems along the way to Trounce Alley, Market Square, and Bastion Square, which together offer a wide range of arts and crafts and souvenirs. For First Nations art and clothing, **Hill's Native Art** at 1008 Government Street is a must-see.

Manitoba

If it's sold in Manitoba, chances are it can be bought in Winnipeg. Wander through Osborne Village (behind the Legislative Building) to find artisan and specialty shops. **The Forks Market** (tel: 888-942-6302; www. theforks.com), at the junction of the Red and Assiniboine rivers, is where vendors sell ethnic foods, produce, and baked goods. It is also popular for crafts and jewelry.

New Brunswick

Fredericton's highly respected New Brunswick College of Art and Design is one reason for this province's high-quality crafts, including yarn portraits, blown glass, wood sculptures, pottery, and pewterware. These goods are also available in St John and Moncton, while Fredericton is especially well-known for such pewter shops as **Aitkens Pewter** (408 Queen St, tel: 506-453-9474; www.aitkenspewter.com) and **Pewter Originals** (580 Reid St, tel: 506-454-6986). Tourism New Brunswick (see Tourist Offices page 396) has a directory of arts and crafts at www.tourismnewbrunswick.ca.

Newfoundland and Labrador

Aside from the run-of-the-mill handicrafts, Newfoundland is famous for its Labradorite jewelry, seal-skin products, and Grenfell cloth parkas. For a huge variety of shops, browse along Duckworth and Water streets in St John's.

Northwest Territories

The N.W.T. is now a major producer of Canadian high grade Polar Bear diamonds and custom-made jewelry featuring nugget-size raw gold. The territory's Dene and Inuit people operate co-operatives, which produce soapstone sculptures, ivory carvings, delicate tapestries, and intriguing prints. These are all available at lower prices than elsewhere in Canada, since there are no shipping costs and the lowest taxes, although genuine items are still pretty expensive.
The Gallery of the Midnight Sun (5005 Bryson Dr, tel: 867-873-8064) has a good selection of native arts and crafts.
Trapper's Cabin (4 Lessard Dr, Latham Island, tel: 867-873-3020), is the nearest to an old-time frontier store that Yellowknife offers.

Nova Scotia

Nova Scotia is known for its crafts, and Tourism Nova Scotia (see page 397) will send a booklet containing the names and addresses of outlets on request.

Halifax

Halifax is the largest retail center east of Montréal. Scotia Square and other shopping malls contain

ABOVE: window display on Robson Street, Vancouver.

representatives of most Canadian retail chains, along with local businesses. The Historic Properties district houses numerous craft shops, while outlets in the Spring Garden Road area offer a wide variety of regional goods and imports from Britain and around the world.

Nunavut

The Inuit's long history in art and crafts has been well documented, and their sculptures, prints, jewelry, and ceramics can be seen in museums, art galleries, and stores throughout Canada. Cape Dorset is one of the main centers for this activity and much can be seen at the **West Baffin Eskimo Co-operative Store** (tel: 867-897-8827). Soap stone carvings, paintings and other crafts are also sold in numerous stores in Iqaluit, including **Jessie Oonark Crafts** (tel: 867-793-2428) on Baker Lane, **DJ Sensations** (626 Tumitt Plaza Building, tel: 867-979-0650), and **Northern Country Arts** (1555 Federal Rd, tel: 819-979-0067).

Ontario

For craft shopping check out the **Ninavik-Native Arts** in Jordan Village on the Niagara peninsula (3845 Main St, tel: 905-562-8888/1-800-646-2848; www.ninavik.com), **Canada's Four Corners** (93 Sparks St, tel: 613-233-2322) in Ottawa, the **Cornerstone** (255 Ontario St, tel: 613-546-7967; www.cornerstonefinecrafts.ca) artists' co-operative in Kingston, or the **Bookstore Cafe** (Junction County Roads 1 & 4, tel: 613-378-1102; www.bookstorecafe.ca) in Camden East for an imaginative array of local artists' work. There is an extensive collection

of Inuit art and handicrafts at the **Eskimo/Inuit Art Gallery** (12 Queen's Quay W, tel: 416-366-3000) in Toronto.

For antiques browse Queen St (East and West), Yorkville, or Markham Village.

Sunday flea markets in Burlington and Hamilton offer some good finds. In Hamilton, visit the restored shops in Hess Village and browse through some rare displays.

Ottawa

Some very classy gift stores are to be found here, perhaps catering to the international diplomatic corps as well as to regular tourists. **Canadian Geographic** (tel: 613-745-4629), a long-established and much revered institution, operates a store in its head office at 39 McArthur Ave, with numerous items of interest for naturalists. **The Snow Goose** (83 Sparks Street Mall, tel: 613-232-2213; www.snowgoose.on.ca) specializes in Inuit and Indian arts and artifacts.

Ottawa has at least three commendable shopping areas. **Sparks Street Mall** (tel: 613-230-0984; www.sparksstreetmall.com) is a central, pedestrian-only stretch lined with specialty shops and assorted vendors. The **Rideau Centre** (tel: 613-236-6565; www.rideaucentre.net) also lies Downtown. Its three floors offer over 180 stores, including the major department stores. Cross the walkway to **ByWard Market** (55 ByWard Market Sq, tel: 613-562-3325; www.byward-market.com), which also houses several fascinating artisan shops and is worth a visit.

Toronto

Stories have been told of travelers who came to Toronto and stayed for months browsing through the city's myriad shops, stores, boutiques, and stalls. A word to the wise: bring a good pair of walking shoes with you.

Yorkville and **Bloor St W** offer the latest in European and North American fashion. The trendy cafes and chic boutiques are pricey, but surprisingly unintimidating.

Walk south from Bloor along eclectic Yonge St to find bookstores, army-surplus retailers, audio/video outlets, jewelry stores, and more, including the famed **Eaton Centre** (tel: 416-598-8560), whose 300 diverse stores stretch from Dundas to Queen St.

From Queen St South lie the skyscrapers of the downtown core. Underneath winds a subterranean maze of interconnected shopping

centers where you can find everything from the practical (florist, liquor, and drug stores) to the stylish (hair salons, fashion boutiques). Interesting furniture stores, antique shops, and secondhand clothiers dot Queen St West to Bathurst.

Further south still and moving east to Jarvis and Front streets, is **St Lawrence Market** (tel: 416-392-7120), considered by many to be the city's best fresh produce market. Moving north again, venture west through bustling **Chinatown** to vintage stores, bars and restaurants, produce vendors, European butchers, and West Indian music shops.

Trek north to **Honest Ed's** (Bloor St W at Bathurst, tel: 416-537-1574; http://honesteds.sites.toronto.com), a discount department store with a garish three-story sign announcing its presence. Now deceased, owner Ed Mirvish has created a more sedate shopping area next door on Markham St south of Bloor: **Mirvish Village** is a renovated Victorian mews lined with galleries, bookstores, and restaurants.

Of note outside the downtown area are some good shopping malls: **Yorkdale** (3401 Dufferin St, tel: 416-789-3261), **Scarborough Town Center** (Hwy 401 between Brimley and McCowan, tel: 416-296-0296; www.scarboroughtowncentre.com), **Fairview Mall** (1800 Sheppard Avenue E, tel: 416-491-0151; www.fairviewmall.ca), and **Sherway Gardens** (25 The West Mall, tel: 416-621-1070; www.sherwaygardens.ca). All are accessible by public transit; Scarborough Town Center by subway and then LRT (Light Rapid Transit).

Prince Edward Island

The island offers little in the way of fashion goods, but its crafts – leatherwork, wood carvings, weaving, and pottery – are excellent. The Prince Edward Island Crafts Council (tel: 902-892-5152; www.peicraftscouncil.com) gives information on P.E.I. handicrafts and where to find them. One of the larger outlets is **The Dunes Studio Gallery** (Brackley Beach, tel: 902-672-2586; mid-May–mid-Oct), which also has a fine restaurant.

Québec

Québécois crafts such as patchwork quilts and Inuit carvings and drawings are popular items, but shop around and ask questions to be sure that what you buy is genuine. Price is often a good indicator: authentic crafts tend to cost more than the mass-produced variety.

The major department stores of cosmopolitan Montréal and Québec City will carry the latest fashions, and the smaller shops and boutiques will offer an intriguing range of styles and merchandise to the persistent browser. Shopping hours vary with the season or locale.

Montréal

The Underground City, a sprawling system of subterranean passages linking business complexes, offers theaters, hotels, restaurants, and shops, all underground and connected to the Métro. Rue Ste-Catherine is home to the major department stores, while Sherbrooke Street features high-fashion outlets. Smaller or more specialized boutiques dot the downtown area, both above ground and below. Visitors in search of handicrafts should visit any of **Le Rouet Boutiques**, **Métiers d'Art**, or the **Canadian Guild of Crafts** (1460 Sherbrooke St W, tel: 514-849-6091). Also well worth a look are **Atwater Market** (tel: 514-937-7754) and **Jean Talon Market** (tel: 514-277-1379), each with stall after stall of fresh fruits and vegetables, cheeses, meats, breads, and pastries.

Québec City

Although Montréal offers substantially more shopping opportunities, a sizeable antiques district has formed around rue St Paul in the recently restored Basse-Ville. For the right price, dealers will part with Victorian furnishings, Québec furniture, and various colonial objects.

Saskatchewan

Among the many prairie native arts and crafts are examples of birchbark-biting art made with the teeth and unique to this part of the world. Saskatoon's best shopping for Canadian merchandise is at **The Trading Post** (226–2nd Ave, tel: 306-653-1769), which carries a wide range of beadwork. **The Handmade House** handicraft store (710 Broadway Ave, tel: 306-665-5542; www.handmadehousesk.com) specializes in crafts. In Regina the **Mackenzie Art Gallery** (3475 Albert St, tel: 306-584-4250; www.mackenzieartgallery.ca) has a small outlet.

The Yukon

Unique native arts and crafts, including moose-hair tufting and locally made jewelry crafted from gold

nuggets, are available from hotel-lobby crafts stores. Other than the federal Goods and Services Tax, there are no sales taxes in the Yukon. **The Yukon Gallery** (201B Main St, tel: 867-667-2391; www.yukongallery.ca) is Whitehorse's finest visual-arts commercial outlet and **North End Gallery** (118–1116 First Ave, tel: 867-393-3590; www.northendgallery.ca) has a good selection of Inuit and First Nation art.

SPORTS

Alberta

Skiing

Alberta is renowned for its excellent alpine skiing in the Canadian Rockies. The season runs from November through May; the best months are January and February. Superb slopes can be found at Lake Louise, with additional ski areas are Nakiska in Kananaskis Country, Marmot Basin in Jasper National Park, and Sunshine Village, Mount Norquay, and Mystic Ridge in Banff National Park.

For ski and snowboard classes and the chance to ride a bobsled, visit the **Canada Olympic Park** (tel: 403-247-5452; www.winsportcanada.ca) at Calgary. During the summer the park transforms into a center for mountain-biking and other activities.

Water Sports

Canoeing and **rafting** opportunities abound throughout the provincial and national parks. **Canadian Rockies**

Rafting (tel: 1-877-226-7625; www.rafting.ca) offer river excursions for those who like to float gently down a stream.

Fishing

Alberta is a fisherman's fantasyland. Certain species can be caught year round, but a license is required. (The national parks have their own regula-tions.) For details and a sport-fishing guide and regulations, contact the Alberta Sustainable Resource Development Information Center at 1-877-944-0313, locally 780-944-0313, or visit the website for Alberta Government Sustainable Resource Development at www.srd.gov.ab.ca. Fishing and hunting regulations vary between the national parks, so check the listings at www.pc.gc.ca or phone 1-888-733-8888 to find out the rules covering a specific park.

Hunting

Hunting of any kind is prohibited in Alberta's national and provincial parks. In other specified areas, waterfowl, and some big game can be hunted, but check out the regulations with Alberta Sustainable Resource Development Information Center, tel: 780-944-0313/1-877-944-0313 or visit the website at www.srd.gov.ab.ca.

British Columbia

Golf

Golf courses abound here, and many public courses are both affordable and relatively easy to get tee times. Vancouver and Victoria's mild climate allow golfing year round.

Spectator Sports

Hockey is Canada's favorite sport. Children start playing it as soon as they can skate, so the country is filled with organized leagues. Canadians avidly follow their National Hockey League teams, including the Vancouver Canucks, Calgary Flames, Edmonton Oilers, Toronto Maple Leafs, and Montréal Canadiens. The season lasts from October through June. Canadian Hockey Association, tel: 403-777-3636/613-562-5677, www.hockey canada.ca.

Canadian football, very similar to the American variety, is very popular. Contact the Canadian Football League, tel: 416-322-9650, www.cfl.ca for tickets or check each team's website.

In summer you'll find professional **baseball** is also popular. The Toronto Blue Jays are Canada's only surviving professional Major League baseball team, but there are double A and triple A teams. Baseball Canada, tel: 416-341-1000, http://oronto.bluejays.mlb.com

Other sports are popular too. Canada's national sport is **lacrosse**, a hard-hitting game that originated with North America's natives. For a further glimpse of Canadiana, try **curling** (a bit like bowling on ice), where only the rocks are hard hitting. **Basketball** and **volleyball** draw more interest yearly. **Cricket** and **soccer** have their adherents and **rugby** is played vigorously in some parts. In summer, central B.C. and Alberta become **rodeo** country.

ABOVE: putting for glory in Mont Tremblant, Québec.

Mountaineering/Hiking

British Columbia's mountain ranges are a challenge to climbers, who should check with the provincial and national parks for details. There are well-marked trails which are used in winter by cross-country skiers and snowshoers. Check Tourism B.C.'s website, www.hellobc.com, for information on hiking and mountaineering experiences. Under hiking, there are overviews of popular walking and hiking trails in B.C.

Water Sports

Sailing is a popular pastime all along the coast. Contact Victoria or Vancouver tourism offices or local yacht clubs for advice on renting boats. **Canoeing** and **sea-kayaking** are highly popular; contact Tourism B.C. (www.hellobc.com) for rental and route information. Or, consider signing up for a package with an experienced operator to take you to the most exciting places.

The Sunshine Coast region between North Vancouver and Powell River, and the lower east coast of Vancouver Island lay claim to some of the warmest **sea-water swimming** and **scuba diving** in Canada. More great swimming and **boating** can be had in the Okanagan Valley Resort areas. There is even surfing off the west coast of Vancouver island.

Fishing/Hunting

For anglers, British Columbia's lakes and streams offer bass, char, perch, and trout. B.C. is famous for its salmon, best sought in the waters up and down the coast. The halibut fishing around Prince Rupert is unparalleled. Rivers yield the famous fighting steelhead, and interior lakes can produce mammoth trout. Hunters come to B.C. in search of moose, caribou, deer, bear, and waterfowl. Secluded resort camps around Prince George reward those who make the long drive with excellent fishing and hunting. Camps farther north offer still better opportunities. Required non-resident hunting and fishing licenses can be obtained from local outfitters or through park rangers. For more information on both fishing and hunting, contact the B.C. government Fish and Wildlife website, www.env.gov.bc.ca/fw.

Skiing

Excellent ski slopes dot B.C. from the Coast Mountains to the Rockies. Whistler and Blackcomb are the most famous, a resort boasting the largest ski area in North America, the host mountain resort of the 2010 Olympics. Other major resort areas include Big White and Silver Star in the Okanagan Valley; Red Mountain in the Kootenays; the Panorama and Fernie Alpine Resort in the Rockies; and Forbidden Plateau on Vancouver Island. Closer to Vancouver, Cypress Bowl, Grouse Mountain, Hemlock Valley, and Mount Seymour can be seen from Vancouver, so it is entirely possible to sail in the afternoon and ski at night.

Manitoba

Summer Sports

Golf and **horseback riding** are popular in the summer, as is nearly every water sport. Provincial authorities have cleared challenging hiking trails, including the exciting "Amisk" trail in Whiteshell Provincial Park.

Fishing/Hunting

Manitoba offers both summer and winter fishing seasons for those in pursuit of trout, northern pike, walleye, and arctic grayling. Hunters come to Manitoba in search of black bear, deer, and moose. Non-Manitoban residents must obtain hunting licenses and be accompanied by a licensed Manitoban resident. For more information visit www.manitoba.ca or contact the Manitoba Conservation Office Box 22, 200 Salteaux Crescent, Winnipeg, MB R3J 3W3, tel: 204-945-7257/1-800-214-6497.

Winter Sports

Manitoba is increasing its wintertime recreational facilities. Many of Manitoba's provincial park trails are utilized for **cross-country skiing**. Growing numbers of resorts offer **tobogganing**, **snowmobiling** and, of course, **skiing** opportunities.

New Brunswick

Tourism New Brunswick provides extensive information on sports and recreation.

Golf/Boating

In the summer, New Brunswick's 40-plus golf courses are rarely too crowded. Boating is popular, both out on the ocean and on the gorgeous, if tame, St John River.

Fishing/Hunting

In the more remote areas of northern New Brunswick, hunting for deer and small game can be arranged, with the proper licensing. Deep-sea fishing charters usually originate from Caraquet, while the rivers of the Miramichi and Restigouche valleys are renowned for their Atlantic salmon fishing. Tourism New Brunswick can provide more information on outfitters (see Tourist Offices page 396).

Winter Sports

For winter sports enthusiasts, **alpine and cross-country ski trails** can be found in New Brunswick's parks, both provincial and national. **Snowmobiling** is also popular.

Newfoundland and Labrador

The province offers many challenges to the outdoor enthusiast, from canoeing and kayaking to skiing.

Newfoundland is a **fisherman's** paradise unequaled in eastern Canada, although the province has stringent regulations and bag limits. Pike, bass, salmon, and trout abound in inland rivers and lakes, while offshore tuna fishing can be great. For experienced **hunters**, with a licensed guide, Newfoundland has moose and caribou seasons. The Tourism Department will put you in touch with the right authorities.

The Northwest Territories

Water Sports

Canoeing and **rafting** in the Northwest Territories can be an adventure. Only expert canoeists should attempt such rivers as the Dubawnt or South Nahanni; nevertheless, most lakes and tamer rivers are suitable for beginner or intermediate paddlers. Remember the scourge of the north: black flies and

mosquitoes. When planning a canoe trek, bring plenty of repellent, netting and sun block, as well as warm, waterproof clothing.

Many lodges and camps offer canoe vacations and packages, usually supplying all the necessary equipment and supplies, or travelers can bring their own, or rent locally.

Fishing/Hunting

Hunters come to the Northwest Territories in search of big game: moose; caribou; black, brown, grizzly, and polar bear (fortunately for the animals most hunters merely photograph their prey). Licensed guides must accompany non-resident hunters. Check in the Explorer's Guide (available online at www.explorenwt.com) about season, limits, outfitters, and guides.

Although hunting is above average, fishing is the favorite pastime in the Northwest Territories. Northern pike, arctic grayling, trout, and the delicious arctic char are major sport fish. Although one can fish from the roadside or canoe, serious anglers stay at fishing camps or lodges, or make arrangements with an outfitter and air charter. Even so, fish mature so slowly in these cold northern waters, that many outfitters follow a "catch and release" program where fish are set free after being weighed and photographed

Winter Sports

In the North, winter can last more than 6 months; as a result this area boasts a diverse selection of winter sports. **Ice-fishing, snowshoeing, skiing**, and **dog-mushing** (sledding) are very popular. Equipment can be rented locally. Many lodges and resorts stay open year round.

Although perhaps not a sport in the strict sense of the word, the Territories are among the best places in the world to view the Aurora Borealis (Northern Lights) – they are visible all year round, but most spectacular between September and April. They are a major tourist attraction.

Nova Scotia

Winter sports enthusiasts will probably head for neighboring provinces for their abundant wintertime sporting opportunities, but the province comes into its own in summer. Tourism Nova Scotia's Doer's and Dreamer's Travel Guide (available at www.novascotia.com) gives details of what is available.

Canoeing enthusiasts hold Nova Scotia's rivers, both tame and wild, in high regard and the more sheltered coastline is great for **sea-kayaking**.

Fishing/Hunting

Fishing and hunting are highly controlled, but it is well worth buying a license. Salmon and trout fishermen enjoy the rivers, while others pursue bigger prizes, particularly bluefin tuna, out on the ocean. A variety of game is available to hunters, including bear, white-tailed deer, rabbit, pheasant, duck, and grouse.

Nunavut

With winter lasting from October through June, snow season adventures for the snow enthusiast abound. **Dogsledding**, either mushing the dogs and caring for a team or just enjoying the ride, is one way to experience Nunavut. **Snowmobiling** is also a popular way to travel on a wildlife-spotting trip.

In the spring, **cross-country skiing** in Nunavut's parks offers opportunities to see wildlife such as caribou and arctic hare.

Water Sports: Activities should be arranged through one of Nunavut's outfitters. There is **sea-kayaking** around icebergs in the fjords of Baffin Island, **canoeing** and **rafting** on rivers such as Baffin Island's **Soper** or **Coppermine** rivers, and awe inspiring wildlife, fish, and archeological sites.

Fishing here is an angler's dream, since the fish are abundant and large. No ultrasonic lures are needed here. High oxygen levels in Nunavut's waters mean that large fish feed near the surface in relatively shallow waters. There are lodges and tent camps for experienced anglers, and

BELOW: cycling the Kettle Valley Trail.

Participant Sports

Canada's vast outdoors is perhaps its finest attraction. Consult the individual provinces for more details about the activities listed below.
Hiking All over Canada, particularly on provincial and national park trails. More information at Canada Trails, www.canadatrails.ca, and Trans Canada Trail, tel: 514-485-3959/1 800-465-3636, www.tctrail.ca
Rafting and Canoeing Every province, especially Ontario, B.C., Yukon, and the Northwest Territories. Try Paddling Canada for more information on canoeing, tel: 1-888-252-6292, www.paddlingcanada.com
Sailing Throughout Canada, especially on the coasts and Great Lakes. Canadian Yachting Association, tel: 613-545-3044, www.sailing.ca
Diving The Broken Islands Group and Sunshine Coast in B.C., the Nova Scotia coast and Georgian Bay, Ontario.

Golf Every province, especially southern B.C. and Ontario. For information on where to golf across Canada, provincial and national golf associations are listed here: www.canadatrails.ca or visit www.canadagolfguide.com
Tennis All of Canada, but especially in resort areas. Tennis Canada can provide a list of provincial tennis associations, tel: 416-665-9777/514-273-1515, www.tenniscanada.ca
Fishing and Hunting Throughout Canada, but regulations, licensing, and seasons differ between provinces. Fishing, but not hunting, is permitted in most provincial and national parks.
Mountain Climbing Alberta, B.C., Yukon. Contact The Alpine Club of Canada, tel: 403-678-3200, www.alpineclubofcanada.ca
Alpine/Downhill Skiing Alberta, B.C., Québec, Ontario. Canadian

Snowsports Association, tel: 604-734-6800; www.canadaskiandsnowboard.net
Cross-country Skiing Throughout Canada, particularly in the provincial and national parks. Cross Country Canada, tel: 403-678-6791, www.cccski.com, has information on the provincial offices.
Snowmobiling All over Canada, especially in Ontario, Québec, the Yukon, the Northwest Territories, and Nunavut. For information on provincial requirements and associations contact Canadian Council of Snowmobile Organizations, tel: 807-345-5299, www.ccso-ccom.ca
Other recreation activities include skating, snowshoeing, ice-fishing, hang-gliding, sky diving, horseback riding, windsurfing, water skiing, nature study, and photography.

day trips for interested novices. Grizzly bear hunts are legendary here.

Hikers have miles of trails to explore in Nunavut's various parks, from the mountains of Auyuittuq National Park to the willow forest of Katannilik Park. One option is to trace the steps of the Franklin expedition when searching for the Northwest Passage.

Two of the main attractions for **mountaineers** flocking to Nunavut over the past few years are the 1,000-meter (3,280ft) west face of Mount Thor and the 800-metre (2,624ft) South Peak of Mount Asgard, both in Auyuittuq National Park, although there are many other challenging mountains in this park and elsewhere in Nunavut, including around Sam Ford Fiord/Clyde River area on north Baffin Island.

Ontario

Travel Ontario publishes a range of activity guides: Adventure Guide lists canoeing, hiking, biking, and snowmobiling package tours; Cruise Ontario outlines boating, sailing, and cruising opportunities; Fish Ontario covers the wide range of fishing opportunities; and Snow Country Guide is geared toward snowmobile enthusiasts but also includes information on skiing, ice fishing, and other winter outdoor experiences. Some other useful addresses and/or contacts are:

Ontario Tourism Marketing Partnership Corporation, 10 Dundas St E, Suite 900, Toronto, Ontario, Canada M7A 2A1, tel: 1-800-668-2746; www.ontariotravel.net.
Ministry of Natural Resources, tel: 1-800-667-1940; www.mnr.gov.on.ca.
Sports Alliance of Ontario, 3 Concorde Gate, Toronto, Ontario, M3C 3N7, tel: 416-426-7000; www.sportalliance.com
Resorts Ontario, 29 Albert St, Orillia, ON L3V 5JP, tel: 705-325-9115/1-800-363-7227; www.resorts-ontario.com.

Hiking

Over a dozen magnificent trails slice through Ontario. The most famous is the Bruce Trail, which winds 740km (460 miles) along the Niagara Escarpment, from near Niagara Falls to the Bruce Peninsula. Contact: Bruce Trail Association, Box 857, Hamilton, ON L8N 3N9, tel: 905-529-6821 or 1-800-665-HIKE, www.brucetrail.org.

Algonquin Provincial Park offers many **wilderness trails**. The most beautiful ones are the Western Uplands Trail, divided into several loops ranging from 32 to 82km (20 to 51 miles), and the Highland Trail, divided into two – 19 and 35km (12 and 22 miles). Contact: Algonquin Provincial Park, Box 219, Whitney, ON K0J 2M0, tel: 705-633-5572; www.algonquinpark.on.ca; email: info@algonquinpark.on.ca

The Rideau Trail follows the Rideau Canal for 186 miles (300km) from

Kingston to Ottawa. Contact: Rideau Trail Association, Box 15, Kingston, ON K7L 4V6, tel: 613-545-0823, www.rideautrail.org; email: info@rideautrail.org.

Trails of various length meander their way through most Ontario provincial parks. Pukaskwa National Park, on the north shore of Lake Superior, has rugged paths, which are not for novices.

Fishing/Hunting

A raft of regulations await anglers and hunters in Ontario, but the rewards are plentiful. Although most North American freshwater fish can be found in Ontario, the province is known particularly for its muskellunge, bass, walleye, pike, and trout. Hunters come in search of animals including deer, moose, pheasant, and black bear.

Hunting and fishing are seasonal. For maps and more information about licensing and outfitters contact the Ministry of Natural Resources Information Center, 300 Water St, PO Box 7000, Peterborough, ON K9J 8M5, 1-800-667-1940; www.mnr.gov.on.ca.

True aficionados charter a plane and pilot to fly to a northern locale, where the fishing and hunting are unparalleled. Contact Travel Ontario for a list of fly-in services. Resorts Ontario also lists fishing packages.

Water Sports

With access to one-third of the world's fresh water, including over 400,000 lakes and innumerable rivers and streams, Ontario is a water sports heaven. Canoeing enthusiasts can enjoy Ontario's rivers and lakes from mid-May through October. The best known, albeit still remote, routes lie in Algonquin and Quetico provincial parks. The Ottawa River and some provincial parks lay claim to excellent white-water canoeing and rafting, which grow yearly in popularity. For a list of outfitters visit Paddling Ontario at www.paddlingontario.com.

Lake Huron's Georgian Bay, the Muskoka Lakes, 1,000 Islands, and the Trent-Severn Waterway are all excellent boating areas. Many marinas rent motorboats, sailboats, and water-skiing equipment.

Ontario's beaches offer excellent swimming. Of note are the "cottage country" lakes of central Ontario and Georgian Bay (especially Wasaga Beach). Sandbanks Provincial Park, on the edge of Lake Ontario, is home to three of Ontario's largest and sandiest beaches, each of them great for swimming, windsurfing, sailing, and boating.

Scuba divers love Georgian Bay, a graveyard of sunken vessels (equipment can be rented from outfitters in Tobermory).

Other Summer Sports

Ontario has nearly 400 **golf courses**, many open to the public. **Horseback riding** is also a favorite, while one of the best ways to see Ontario is from a **bicycle**.

Skiing

A popular downhill skiing haunt in southern Ontario is the Blue Mountain range near Collingwood.

BELOW: mountain-biking in Whistler.

Otherwise, try the northern slopes around Sault Ste Marie and Thunder Bay. The latter is known for its titan ski jumps.

Ottawa is blessed with three **alpine and cross-country skiing** areas less than 32km (20 miles) away in Québec: Mont Cascades (tel: 819-827-0301), Camp Fortune (tel: 819-827-1717) in Gatineau Park, and Edelweiss Valley (tel: 819-459-2328). More challenging slopes await at Mont Ste-Marie (tel: 819-467-5200), 100km (60 miles) north. Remember: Ottawa is but a short drive from the Laurentians.

The Ontario Snow Resorts Association (125 Napier St, PO Box 575, Collingwood, ON L9Y 4E8, tel: 705-443-5450, email: osra@skiontario.on.ca; www.skiontario.on.ca) and Travel Ontario can help with accommodations and packages. For the latest snow conditions, tel: 1-800-ONT-ARIO or, for a recorded message, 416-314-0998. For information about cross-country skiing, tel: 1-800-ONT-ARIO or, for a recorded message, 416-314-0960.

Cross-country skiers will find superb trails throughout the province, tel: 1-800-461-7677.

Other Winter Sports

Snow-mobiling was invented in this part of the world and remains immensely popular here. Trails criss-cross the Georgian Bay and Muskoka/Algonquin Park regions, but can be found all over the rest of the province as well. For information on snow conditions for snowmobiling, tel: 1-800-ONT-ARIO.

For anglers who can't wait for warm weather, Ontario has an **ice-fishing** season. The province's hiking trails are often suitable for **snowshoeing**.

Québec

Each of the 20 tourist regions has a list of sports and recreation activities, including **skiing**, **boating**, **hunting**, and **fishing**. Write to: Tourisme Québec (see Tourist Offices, page 397). www.bonjourquebec.com

Summer/Winter Sports

Canoeing and **hiking** are popular in the summertime, particularly in the lake-strewn forests of the Canadian Shield. **Canoeists** will find that provincial parks offer the best excursions. Québécois have also cleared over 1,200 trails for **cross-country skiing** and **snowshoeing**, and 30,000km (18,600 miles) for **snowmobiling**.

Fishing/Hunting

Québec's rivers and lakes are renowned for their excellent fishing. It is claimed that there are more fish in Québec than in any other country! Deep-sea excursions and trips to northern fly-in camps are popular with aficionados. Tourisme Québec (www.bonjourquebec.com) can provide details of licensing, seasons, limits, and packages.

Skiing

An average of 200cm (78 inches) of snow falls on Québec's downhill slopes between October and April, making the province a skiers' paradise. In the Charlevoix region, Le Massif has the highest vertical drop in Eastern Canada and is renowned for its snow-fall, which averages close to 22ft (7 meters) per season. Enquire at resorts about weekend or week-long packages, which often include lodgings, meals, lift tickets, lessons, and more.

The Eastern Townships

Skiing

The Eastern Townships Mont Orford is the place to ski. Call or write to Magog-Orford Tourist Information, 55 Cabana, Magog, PQ J1X 2C4 (tel: 819-843-2744/1-800-267-2744) to plug into a highly organized network of facilities that offer a variety of accommodations and packages.

Québec City Region

From Québec City, skiing 1,000-meter (3,050ft) high Mont Ste-Anne can be a one-day excursion by bus or car. Call the Parc du Mont Ste-Anne (tel: 418-827-4561/1-888-827-4579; www.mont-sainte-anne.com) for details of the well-groomed downhill and cross-country trails just 40km (25 miles) from the Old City walls.

The Laurentians

Just northwest of Montréal, this region offers a plethora of superb hotels and resorts, which, incidentally, are the favorite destination of the **golf** and **tennis** set in the summer.

Mont Tremblant

The largest complex here, by far, is Tremblant, tel: 819-681-2000/1-866-356-2233; www.tremblant.ca. For complete information on the whole area, write to the Bureau touristique de Mont Tremblant, www.mt-tremblant.com.

Ste-Adèle

For general information you can call the Bureau Touristique des Pays-d'en

Haut, tel: 1-800-898-2127, or call the Tourist Information office 450-227-3417. Le Chantecler, tel: 1-888-916-1616; www.lechantecler.com, is a very popular ski resort.

Saskatchewan

The people of Saskatchewan love **curling**, and nearly every small town has a bonspiel in January/February. **Hiking** and **cross-country skiing** are popular, especially through parks.

Water Sports

Saskatchewan has more than 100,000 lakes, so water sports are a favorite. Among them, **canoeing** is probably the best. The province has laid out more than 50 canoe routes, for amateur and veteran alike. Canoe outfitters can put together a package to suit any need by arranging the necessary lodgings, food, and equipment rentals.

Fishing/Hunting

Hunters will find large game as well as several species of wildfowl available in Saskatchewan. For fishermen, the province's northern lakes and streams offer an abundance of catch, including trout, northern pike, walleye, and arctic grayling. For information about fly- or drive-in camps, outfitters, licenses, canoeing etc., as well as on other sports and recreation opportunities, contact Saskatchewan Environment and Resource Management, 3211 Albert St, Regina, SK S4S 5W6, tel: 306-787-2847; www.environment.gov. sk.ca/licences.

The Yukon

Canoeing

Yukon is a haven for canoeists of intermediate level or better. The Stewart and Yukon Rivers are fairly tame. The Klondike and Big Salmon, conversely, can be challenging and treacherous. In any event, non-residents must register with the Royal Canadian Mounted Police (RCMP) for safety reasons, and they will be required to show they have adequate equipment and supplies.

Hiking

Hiking is popular, though Yukon's jagged terrain means that this often entails rock or mountain climbing as well. Kluane National Park is a favorite for this, but Tourism Yukon can give more detailed information about hiking and climbing throughout the territory.

Fishing/Hunting

Essentially a wilderness, Yukon is perfect for fishing and hunting. Obtain a license from an outfitter, find a suitable spot, then cast for trout, arctic grayling, salmon, and northern pike. Some of the best fishing spots lie just off the main roads although some people prefer to fish at the more obscure fly-in camps and lodges.

The Yukon Vacation Guide has details of fishing and fishing lodges. Big game and bird hunting is possible during the prescribed season (usually in fall). Non-resident hunters must be accompanied by a licensed guide. For further information on regulations, seasons, limits, and outfitters, write to the Yukon Fish and Game Association, Department of Environment, Suite 14078 – 4th Avenue Whitehorse, Yukon Y1A 1H1, tel: 867-667-4263; www.yukonfga.ca.

CHILDREN'S ACTIVITIES

From east to west, Canada has an abundance of family-friendly attractions to entertain all age groups. Here are just a few examples.

In Newfoundland, take a ride on one of the many locally operated tour boats from the fishing village of Witless Bay out to the **Witless Bay Ecological Reserve** – four small islands that are home to millions of seabirds that come to shore to nest and raise their young. Hundreds of humpback whales feed here in summer, making it one of the best whale-watching areas anywhere. For more information contact the Park and Natural Areas Division, tel: 709-635-4520; www.env.gov.nl.ca.

Just outside Annapolis Royal in Nova Scotia, the **Upper Clements Park** (Upper Clements, tel: 902-532-7557; www.upperclementspark.com) is one of Atlantic Canada's largest amusement parks, with 26 rides including Rollercoaster, Waterslide and Flume ride.

In Québec City, visitors to the **Parc Aquarium du Québec** (1675 Ave des Hôtels, tel: 418-659-5264; www.sepaq. com/paq/en) explore the ecosystems of the St Lawrence River and Canadian waters, all the way to the North Pole. Along the way, they observe 10,000 fresh- and salt-water fish, and marine mammals such as walruses, seals, and polar bears.

In Toronto, **Black Creek Pioneer Village** (1000 Murray Ross Parkway,

near Steeles Ave and Jane St, tel: 416-736-1740) transports visitors to a typical 18th century village, to experience the lifestyle of the early residents of Ontario through many hands-on demonstrations and period activities.

Both Toronto and Montreal have excellent science museums with interactive exhibits and IMAX films; **Ontario Science Centre** (770 Don Mills Rd, tel: 416-696-1000/1-888-696-1110); **Montreal Science Centre** (333 de la Commune St W, tel: 514-496-4724/1-877-496-4724).

In Hamilton, the **Parks Canada Marine Discovery Centre** (57 Guise St E, tel: 905-526-0911) introduces visitors to Canada's national marine conservation areas. Through riveting interactive displays – such as tests on navigating the Great Lakes – and lively guides, all age groups absorb the importance of conserving Canada's marine heritage.

The **Manitoba Children's Museum** (45 Forks Market Rd, tel: 204-924-4000; www.childrensmuseum. com) is not your traditional museum. There are no "Do Not Touch" signs and each of the six galleries – from the high-tech secrets of the Live Wire Gallery to the magic forest of The Tree and Me – is designed for hands-on fun.

Just outside Saskatoon, for extraordinary insight into the First Nations history and culture, the **Wanuskewin Heritage Park** (RR #4, Penner Rd, tel: 306-931-6767/1-877-547-6546; www.wanuskewin.com), is hard to beat. There are 19 interactive sites showing summer and winter camps, bison kills, and tipi rings. Northern Plains people provide interpretive programs including tipi-making (with try It yourself activities), a medicine walk to find medicinal herbs, and history and archeology sessions. The restaurant offers a wide range of foods, including bison, elk, and venison, along with more familiar offerings.

Drive Alberta's Icefields Parkway, from Lake Louise to Jasper, and be sure to stop for a **Snocoach** ride. Huge buses with tank-like rollers glide onto the Athabasca Glacier, or just walk around on your own. It's an experience no one ever forgets.

In Vancouver, a day spent in Stanley Park Is perfect for children of all ages. The Vancouver Aquarium is as entertaining as it is educational. For sheer unadulterated fun, the water park is a perfect spot.

A–Z

A HANDY SUMMARY OF PRACTICAL INFORMATION, ARRANGED ALPHABETICALLY

A dmission Charges

There is an unlimited supply of museums and art galleries that cover a variety of themes. Although many charge admission, discounts are available for children, students and senior citizens.

Canada's 'Doors Open' (www. doorsopencanada.ca) scheme grants the public access to historic buildings that are normally closed or ones that have admission charges.

B udgeting for Your Trip

The daily costs for an average traveler in Canada vary considerably across the country. In the large cities – Vancouver, Toronto, and Montréal – the comfortable daily cost should be about $200 ($125 for hotel, $10 for breakfast, $20 for lunch, $35 for dinner, and $10 for public transport). Accommodations and food costs generally decrease away from the main centers, except in the far North. Gasoline prices increase away from the main centers. A thrifty traveler in the city – and an average traveler in more rural areas – might get away

with about $80–115 per day ($50–75 for accommodations, $30 for restaurant food, or as little as $20 self-catering and $10 for fares). For extravagant luxury in the city – and in hot spots such as Banff, Whistler, and Mont Tremblant – you could pay $700–800 per day ($300–500 for accommodations, $25 for breakfast, $75 for lunch, as much as $200 for dinner and $100 for taxi fares).

C hildren

North America generally, including Canada, is strongly oriented toward accommodating family travel. Many hotels have excellent packages for children that often include children under a certain age staying free of charge, and most restaurants will produce children's menus and a supply of paper and wax crayons to keep them happy. Shopping malls and parks frequently have children's play areas. Restaurants and movie theaters will also provide booster seats for smaller children. Across the country there are hundreds of attractions geared toward children, from toddlers to teens.

Climate

It is difficult to generalize about the Canadian climate. Most visitors come during the summer, when temperatures average around 24°C (75°F). During July and August, however, the mercury can climb into the 90s on the prairies and in southern Ontario. In northern Canada, summer temperatures stay at 15°C (65°F) during the day, but can drop close to freezing at night. Don't forget to pack some protection against mosquitoes and other biting insects, especially if you are traveling in the early summer.

Canadian winters have been slightly exaggerated in popular lore. Winter temperatures average between −5°C and 10°C (10°F and 25°F) from the Maritimes through southern Ontario. It gets colder and windier from northern Québec through the Rockies, with temperatures ranging from −18°C to −5°C (0°F to 10°F). In the Yukon, Northwest Territories, and Nunavut the mercury can drop to as low as −40°C (−40°F). On the balmy southern coast of British Columbia (B.C.), however, warm

CLIMATE CHART

Ottawa

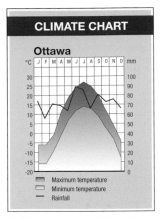

Maximum temperature
Minimum temperature
Rainfall

Pacific currents generally keep the temperature above freezing during the winter.

Snowfall varies throughout Canada. Skiers can sometimes take to the slopes and trails by late November, and the snow lasts generally until April or even May in the mountains.

Crime and Safety

Generally speaking, Canada is one of the safest countries to visit. Its large cities, like any others, have areas that are best not visited, and it is not unusual to see homeless men and women on the streets, but they generally pose no threat to safety. Being aware of one's surroundings is always important.

Anyone in an emergency situation should phone 911, and the call is forwarded to police, fire department, or ambulance, depending upon the reason for the call.

In case your documentation is stolen, it's a good idea to have two photocopies of your passport identification page, airline tickets, driver's license, and the credit cards that you plan to bring with you. Leave one photocopy of this with family or friends at home; pack the other in a place separate from where you carry your valuables.

Pickpockets are not unheard of, especially in crowded places like a busy subway station, but it is not a huge problem in Canada, and simply requires people being mindful of how they carry their wallets or any other valuable item, such as a camera.

The Canadian government has an excellent website providing information on traveling safely in Canada, with tips as wide-ranging as driving with cell phones, reporting collisions, child safety seats, and current health notices. Visit www.safecanada.ca.

Customs Regulations

Canada's customs requirements for vacation visitors are fairly simple. Personal effects for use during the stay may be brought into the country. There is no problem with bringing rented cars from the US, but drivers should always carry a copy of the contract with them in the car (this is also important if stopped by police for any reason).

Hunting rifles and shotguns can be brought into Canada, but with restrictions. Consult the Canadian Firearms Program website: www.rcmp-grc.gc.ca/cfp-pcaf Limits on duty-free tobacco, alcohol, and personal gifts are like those in other countries. For more details on customs regulations and what you can bring to Canada, contact: Canada Customs and Border Services tel: 204-983-3500 or 506-636 5064 from outside Canada and 1-800-461-9999 from inside Canada; www.cbsa-asfc.gc.ca.

Pets require a veterinary's certificate of good health and vaccinations, etc. Many foods and plants are prohibited, so check the rules before arriving. The Canada Border Services Agency website has full details: www.cbsa-asfc.gc.ca

Citizens of the UK may bring home, duty-free: 200 cigarettes or 50 cigars; 4 liters of wine and 1 liter of liquor; and additional goods totaling no more than £340 (Cdn$600).

Each American citizen who spends more than 48 hours in Canada may return with $800 worth of goods, duty-free. Some airports and border points feature duty-free shops, offering liquor and other goodies at good prices. Americans should direct their questions to any US customs office or visit its website at www.cbp. gov, while travelers from other countries should contact the customs office in their own country for information on what they can bring back.

D isabled Travelers

The Canadian Transportation Agency offers an on-line guide for disabled visitors traveling by air in Canada, which can be accessed at www.cta-otc. gc.ca. Another useful on-line source for people with disabilities is www.pwd-online.ca.

Airlines, buses, and trains all offer wheelchair assistance, although you should allow extra time before commencing your journey. Taking a wheelchair on the train requires advanced notice so it is recommended to call VIA Rail 48 hours beforehand (toll free tel: 1-888 842-7245, www.viarail.ca).

Disabled access, especially for those in wheelchairs, can be found in almost every public building across Canada, and most museums, tourist information centers, and visitor attractions have taken steps to make access easier. Hotels, especially those affiliated with chains, generally provide disabled accommodation and toilet facilities. Many national and provincial parks offer alternative trails that are accessible to disabled travelers. And designated spaces for disabled drivers are generally found at parking lots in cities, at shopping malls, and in the parking lots of large stores.

BELOW: the colorful flags of Canada's 13 provinces.

TRANSPORTATION

ACCOMMODATIONS

EATING OUT

ACTIVITIES

A – Z

LANGUAGE

Electricity

Canada operates on 110 volts in common with the US. Sockets accommodate plugs with two flat or two flat and one round pins, so an adaptor is required for the use of European appliances.

Embassies and Consulates

While foreign visitors are traveling in and across Canada, they may need to contact their own country in case of an emergency. Consulates can be most helpful, for example, if a passport is stolen or if a message needs to be relayed quickly back home. The following list gives details of all the consulates located in the major Canadian cities.

British Columbia
Australia 888 Dunsmuir St, Ste 1225, Vancouver, tel: 604-684-1177.
France 1130 West Pender St, Ste 1100, Vancouver, tel: 604-681-4345.
UK 1111 Melville St, Ste 800, Vancouver, tel: 604-683-4421.
US 1095 West Pender St, 21st Floor, Vancouver, tel: 604-685-4311.

Ontario
Australia 175 Bloor St E, Ste 1100, Toronto, tel: 416-323-1155.
France 2 Bloor St E, Suite 2200, Toronto, tel: 416-847-1900.
UK College Park, 777 Bay St, Ste 2800, Toronto, tel: 416-593-1290.
US 360 University Ave, Toronto, tel: 416-595-1700.

Québec
France 1501 McGill College, Bureau 1000, Montréal, tel: 514-878-4385.
UK 1000 de la Gauchetière Ouest, Ste 4200, Montréal, tel: 514-866-5863.
US 1155 rue Alexandre, Montréal, tel: 514-398-9695.

Emergencies

Visitors are urged to obtain **health insurance** before leaving their own country. Anyone using prescription medicine should bring an adequate supply with them, as well as a copy of the prescription in case it needs to be renewed. Travelers requiring medical attention needn't worry – Canadian hospitals are known for their high medical standards.

In an emergency requiring the **police**, an **ambulance** or **firemen**, immediate help can be summoned in Canada's major cities by dialing **911**. Emergency telephone numbers are listed in the front of all local telephone directories. If caught in a legal bind, foreign visitors can contact their consulates, a partial listing of which is shown in the Embassies and Consulates section.

Etiquette

Good manners are valued: hold doors open for people following you; don't jump the queue; let people get off public transport before you get on; offer your seat to older passengers or pregnant women; on escalators, stand on the right, walk past on your left. If you are a smoker, ask the people around you if it's OK to light up. Smoking is banned in most public places.

Gay and Lesbian Travelers

Canada is one of the world's more gay-friendly countries, and in July 2005 became the fourth country to recognize gay marriage, after the Netherlands, Belgium and Spain. Vancouver, Toronto and Montréal's Pride Weeks draw the biggest crowds, but all of Canada's main cities host an annual Pride Week – and Canadian tourism bureaus are increasingly dedicating sections of their web sites to gay and lesbian tourists.

For a comprehensive, all-in-one spot to start research, **Travel Gay Canada** (www.travelgaycanada.com), provides Canada-wide information on hotels, events, and travel packages.

BELOW: all dressed up for the Gay Pride Parade in Vancouver.

Health and Medical Care

As visitors to Canada are not eligible for health care in any of the provinces or territories, it is important to be covered by a health insurance policy for the duration of any time spent in Canada. It may also be advisable to ensure the policy covers emergency evacuation with a medical escort to your country of residence.

If you are entering Canada with prescription drugs and syringes used for medical reasons, be sure to keep the medication in its original and labeled container to avoid problems. Syringes should be accompanied by a medical certificate that shows they are for medical use and should be declared to Canadian Customs officials. You should carry with you an extra prescription from your doctor in the event your medication is lost or stolen and to attest to your need to take such prescriptions.

Internet

More and more coffee shops offer free wireless internet access if you have a laptop. For free access to the Internet, visit any public library. Note that usually there is a time limit for usage of a library's computer. Most hotels and airports have business centers where you can access emails and the Internet, usually for a fee. To find an Internet cafe in many communities across Canada, visit: www.world66.com/netcafeguide.

Media

Newspapers and Magazines
The *National Post* and *The Globe and Mail* are distributed throughout Canada. *La Presse* is the ranking Québec daily. Newsstands sell major American, British, and French newspapers and magazines. Canada's largest news magazine, *Maclean's*, is published weekly.

Radio and Television
The Canadian Broadcasting Company (CBC) operates two nationwide television networks (French and English), along with an all-news network. CTV Global broadcasts two others. Regional and provincial networks, along with independent and US broadcasters, account for the rest.

Cable networks enable viewers to see programs produced in all parts of Canada and the US, along with a sampling of programs from the UK, Australia, France, and other countries. The majority of large cities originate at least one multilingual or ethnic channel.

CBC operates a national radio network, both AM and FM, in English and French. There are hundreds of private stations that fill the airwaves with news and music.

Money

The Canadian and US dollars have a different rate of exchange. All dollar prices quoted in this book are in Canadian dollars.

There is no limit to the amount of money visitors may bring to, or exchange in, Canada. To get the best rate, exchange your money before leaving home. Canadian banks and foreign exchange bureaux will convert funds for a fee. US funds are readily accepted by many department stores and hotels, etc., but may not offer the most advantageous rate.

Credit Cards, Debit Cards, and Traveler's Checks

Major credit cards are widely accepted in Canada. Car rental companies prefer credit cards to cash.

Traveler's checks still offer a safe way to carry funds, but they are fading in popularity as bank debit and credit cards are preferred. Ask your bank about overseas charges. If you do buy traveler's checks, buying them denominated in Canadian dollars saves the expense of exchanging upon arrival. Just countersign and show proper identification, and they will be accepted as cash. American Express, Thomas Cook, and Visa traveler's checks are widely accepted.

Opening Hours

Standard business hours for stores are 10am–6pm, or 9pm in many large cities. Stores in many parts of the country are open for more limited hours on Sunday.

Drug and convenience stores generally close at 11pm but some operate for 24 hours. Banking hours vary greatly; the majority of banks now open long hours, which may include Saturday, and also, in some instances, Sunday. Bank machines are readily available.

Banks, schools, government offices, and many beer and liquor stores close on national holidays. Hotels, restaurants, and most retail outlets stay open. See the section on Festivals (see pages 380–4) for further information and listings of provincial holidays and festivals.

Postal Services

Stamps may be purchased at Canada's post offices (open Monday–Friday during business hours) or from many local convenience and drug stores.

Canada Post and a number of international courier companies provide express services across the country and to foreign destinations. Canada Post, along with other private establishments, can also send faxes from coast-to-coast or internationally. Canada Post locations are listed in the business section of the telephone directory.

Public Holidays

Each province has public holidays (check with the local tourist board) in addition to the following national holidays:

January 1 New Year's Day
July 1 Canada Day
First Monday in September Labor Day
Second Monday in October Thanksgiving Day
December 25 Christmas Day
December 26 Boxing Day (except Québec)

The Provinces

Alberta: (abbreviated Alta)
Capital: Edmonton
Size: 661,190 sq km
(255,310 sq miles)
Area Code: Calgary and Southern Alberta 403; Edmonton and Northern Alberta 780
Postal Address: AB
British Colombia: (B.C.)
Capital: Victoria
Size: 947,800 sq km
(365,980 sq miles)
Area Code: Vancouver and southwestern section 604 and 778; remainder, including Vancouver Island 250
Postal Address: BC
Manitoba: (Man)
Capital: Winnipeg
Size: 649,950 sq km
(250,970 sq miles)
Area Code: 204 unless stated
Postal Address: MB
New Brunswick: (N.B.)
Capital: Fredericton
Size: 73,440 sq km
(28,360 sq miles)
Area Code: 506 unless stated
Postal Address: NB
Newfoundland and Labrador: (Nfld)

Capital: St John's
Size: 405,720 sq km
(156,600 sq miles)
Area Code: 709 unless stated
Postal Address: NF
Northwest Territories: (N.W.T.)
Capital: Yellowknife
Size: 1,171,920 sq km
(452480 sq miles)
Area Code: 867
Postal Address: NT
Nova Scotia: (N.S.)
Capital: Halifax
Size: 55,490 sq km
(21,430 sq miles)
Area Code: 902 unless stated
Postal Address: NS
Nunavut:
Capital: Iqaluit
Size: 1,900,000 sq km
(733,600 sq miles)
Area Code: 867
Postal Address: NU
Ontario: (Ont)
Capital: Toronto
Size: 1,068,580 sq km
(412,610 sq miles)
Area Code: Toronto 416 or 647, Ottawa 613, plus several others for smaller communities: 807, 705,

226, 519, 905, 289, 705
Postal Address: ON
Prince Edward Island: (P.E.I.)
Capital: Charlottetown
Size: 5,660 sq km
(2,190 sq miles)
Area Code: 902 with Nova Scotia
Postal Address: PE
Québec: (P.Q.)
Capital: Québec City
Size: 1,540,680 sq km
(594,900 sq miles)
Area Code: Montréal 514 or 438; Québec City and Eastern Québec 418; Southern Québec 450; rest of Québec 819
Postal Address: PQ
Saskatchewan: (Sask)
Capital: Regina
Size: 652,330 sq km
(251,880 sq miles)
Area Code: 306
Postal Address: SK
The Yukon:
Capital: Whitehorse
Size: 483,450 sq km
(186,680 sq miles)
Area Code: 867 with the Northwest Territories and Nunavut
Postal Address: YK

Time Zones

Canada straddles six time zones. Daylight saving time begins the second Sunday in March and ends the first Sunday in November but is not observed in Saskatchewan.

Pacific Standard Time
(8 hours behind GMT) the Yukon, B.C. (Alaska Time is one hour behind the Yukon).
Mountain Standard Time
(7 hours behind GMT) Alberta, western N.W.T.
Central Standard Time
(6 hours behind GMT)

Saskatchewan, Manitoba, central N.W.T., western Nunavut.
Eastern Standard Time
(5 hours behind GMT) Ontario, Québec, eastern N.W.T., eastern Nunavut.
Atlantic Standard Time
(4 hours behind GMT) New Brunswick, P.E.I., Nova Scotia, most of Labrador.
Newfoundland Standard Time
(3½ hours behind GMT; half an hour ahead of Atlantic Standard Time) Newfoundland (including part of Labrador).

Movable Feasts:
Good Friday
Monday preceding May 24 (Victoria Day, the Queen's birthday)

Religious Services

Roman Catholics are by far the largest religious group, with Protestants in second place. Muslims, Sikhs, Hindus, Buddhists, and Jews are also represented. Any hotel concierge will direct you to the nearest place of worship.

In Vancouver, Christchurch Cathedral has weekday services with holy communion at 12.10pm, and at 8am and 10.30am on Sunday.

S tudent Travelers

Students traveling within Canada can take advantage of discounts in many areas. For traveling around, VIA Rail and Greyhound offer student discounts and in most cities there are hostels and university residences for the budget traveler.

A good source of on-line information is provided by the ISIC, the International Student Identity Card, at www.isic.org, which covers places and services across Canada.

T elephones

The telephone system in Canada is similar to that in the US. Payphone costs begin at 25 cents, but they can be hard to find. For collect or other operator-assisted calls, dial "0" then the number you wish to reach. Dial "1" (Ottawa +613, Montréal +514 or +438, Vancouver +604 or +778, Victoria +250, Winnipeg +204, Toronto +416 or 647, Québec City +418) for long-distance calls charged to the originating phone.

The first pages in public phone books explain everything you need to know, including emergency numbers, North American area codes, and long-distance country codes.

Toll-free Numbers

Any phone numbers beginning with 1-800, 1-866, 1-877 or 1-888 are toll-free if dialed within North America from a land line.

Tourist Information

One of the smartest things you can do upon arrival in Canada is to go to the nearest tourist information center. Aside from being able to answer questions, they distribute travel brochures and maps on areas of interest to you. Each province and territory also has a toll-free number for tourist information (see the following list). For general information on traveling in Canada you can contact:
Canadian Tourism Commission
Suite 1400, Four Bentall Centre, 1055 Dunsmuir St, Box 49230, Vancouver, British Columbia V7X 1L2, tel: 604-638-8300; www.canadatourism.com

Canadian consulates in foreign countries also provide some travel information. See the Useful Addresses section *(page 398)* for further details. Some provinces maintain tourist offices in foreign cities.

Alberta

Travel Alberta publishes accommodations and campground guides. Updated annually, they list approved hotels, motels, camp-grounds, and resorts. For this, and more specific information, contact:
Travel Alberta
Box 2500, Edmonton, AB T5J 2Z4, tel: 780-427-4321/1-800-252-3782;

www.travelalberta.com
Calgary Convention and Visitor Bureau
200–238–11th Ave SE, Calgary, AB T2G 0X8, tel: 403-263-8510/1-800-661-1678; www.tourismcalgary.com

For comprehensive information about the provincial capital, contact:
Edmonton Tourism
3rd Floor, World Trade Centre Edmonton, 9990 Jasper Avenue, Edmonton, AB T5J 1P7, tel: 780-424-9191/1-800-463-4667; www.edmonton.com

British Columbia

For information about traveling in British Columbia, call or write to:
Tourism British Columbia
Box 9830, Station Provincial Government, 3rd Floor, 1117 Wharf St, Victoria, BC V8W 9W5, tel: 250-356-6363/1-800-435-5622; www.hellobc.com

Most communities operate Travel InfoCenters at least during the tourism season. In the major cities they are:
Tourism Vancouver
Plaza Level, 200 Burrard St, Vancouver BC V6C 3L6, tel: 604-683-2000; www.tourismvancouver.com
Tourism Victoria
812 Wharf St, Victoria, BC V8W 1T3, tel: 250-414-6999/1-800-663-3883; www.tourismvictoria.com

Manitoba

The provincial government distributes the free *Manitoba Vacation Planner*, which will direct you to accommodations and campgrounds, and contains a fishing and hunting guide. The planners are available from any provincial information center or from:
Travel Manitoba
155 Carlton St, Winnipeg, MB R3C 3H8, tel: 204-927-7800/1-800-665-0040; www.travelmanitoba.com

New Brunswick

For road maps, assistance in choosing accommodations, and suggestions for itineraries in New Brunswick contact:
Tourism New Brunswick
Box 12345, Cambellton, NB E3N 3T6, tel: 506-457-6701/1-800-561-0123; www.tourism newbrunswick.ca

Newfoundland and Labrador

For complete information about traveling in Newfoundland write to:
Department of Tourism, Culture and Recreation
PO Box 8700, St John's, NF A1B 4J6,

tel: 709-729-0862/1-800-563-6353; www.newfoundlandlabrador.com

Northwest Territories

This territory distributes a yearly *Explorers' Guide*, a listing of hotels, lodges, restaurants, and activities. This, and more information, is available from:

NWT Tourism
Box 610, Yellowknife, NWT X1A 2N5, tel: 867-873-7200/1-800-661-0788; www.explorenwt.com

Nova Scotia

For information about Nova Scotia:
Tourism Nova Scotia
PO Box 456, Halifax, NS B3J 2R5, tel: 902-425-5781/1-800-565-0000; www.novascotia.com

Nunavut

Canada's newest territory produces its own *Arctic Traveler* and further information is available from:
Nunavut Tourism
Box 1450, Iqaluit, NWT X0A 0H0, tel: 867-979-6551/1-866-686-2888; www.nunavuttourism.com

Ontario

It takes a comprehensive travel bureau to describe and explain all that this province has to offer but Ontario Travel fits the bill. To contact them, call toll-free from Canada or the continental US 1-800-668-2746 (English) or 1-800-268-3736 (French). Write to:
Ontario Tourism Marketing Partnership Corp.
10 Dundas St E, Suite 900, Toronto, ON M7A 2A1; www.ontariotravel.net

Ontario Travel booklets and brochures explain nearly every facet of traveling the province. Among these are:
• The road map
• The *Ontario Travel Discovery Guides*, which feature all the coolest places to play and stay, including information on winter destinations and experiences.
• Individual event guides for spring and summer, with dates, locations, and brief event descriptions.
• Individual experience guides for spring and summer, outlining all that the province has to offer at this time of year.

Ontario Travel also operate a number of travel information centers, open year round; most have currency exchanges. The five listed here are all at border points; there are others at St Catharines, Fort Erie, Fort Frances, Sarnia, and Barrie.
• Cornwall, 903 Brookdale Ave, at the

Seaway International Bridge.
• Niagara Falls, 5355 Stanley Ave, Hwy 420, west from Rainbow Bridge.
• Sault Ste Marie, 261 Queen St W, at the International Bridge.
• Windsor, 1235 Huron Church Rd, east of the Ambassador Bridge.
• 110 Park St E, at the Windsor/Detroit Tunnel.
• The *NOTO* Ontario Outdoor Adventure Guide, which covers the 12 regions of Ontario with information on its diverse outdoor adventure experiences from canoeing to hiking, biking, snowmobiling, etc www.noto.net

Algoma Kinniwabi Travel Association
485 Queen St E, Ste 204, Sault Ste Marie, ON P6A 1Z9, tel: 705-254-4293/1-800-263-2546; www.algoma country.com

Almaguin Nipissing Travel Association
1375 Seymour St, Box 351, North Bay, ON P1B 8H5, tel: 705-474-6634/1-800-387-0516; www.ontariosnearnorth.on.ca

Cochrane Témiskaming Travel Association
PO Box 920, 76 McIntyre Rd, Schumacher, ON P0N 1G0, tel: 705-360-1989/1-800-461-3766; www.ontarioswildernessregion.com

Georgian Triangle Tourist Association
30 Mountain Rd, Collingwood, ON L9Y 5H7, tel: 705-445-7722/1-888-227-8667; www.collingwoodthebluemountains.com

Muskoka Tourism
Hwy 11, Kilworthy, ON P0P 1G0, tel: 1-800-267-9700; www.discover muskoka.ca

Niagara Falls Tourism
5400 Robinson St, Niagara Falls, ON L2G 2A6, tel: 905-356-6061/1-800-563-2557; www.niagarafallstourism.com

Niagara Parks Commission
Queen Victoria Pkwy, Box 150, Niagara Falls, ON L2E 6T2, tel: 905-356-2241; www.niagaraparks.com

North of Superior Tourism Association
920 Tungsten St, Suite 206A, Thunder Bay, ON P7B 5Z6, tel: 807-346-1130/1-800-265-3951; www.nosta.on.ca

realontario.ca
Aaron Merrick Block, Ste 200, 104 St Lawrence St, PO Box 730, Merrickville, ON K0G 1N0, tel: 613-269-4113; www.realontario.ca

Northwest Ontario's Sunset Country
Box 647W, Kenora, ON P9N 3X6, tel: 807-468-5853/1-800-665-7567; www.ontariossunsetcountry.ca

Ottawa Tourism
130 Albert St, Ste 1800, Ottawa, ON

K1P 5G4, tel: 613-237-5150/1-800-363-4465; www.ottawatourism.ca
Tourism Kingston
209 Ontario St, Kingston, ON K7L 2Z1, tel: 613-548-4415/1-888-855-4555; www.kingstoncanada.com
Tourism Toronto
207 Queen's Quay W, Ste 590, Toronto, ON M5J 1A7, tel: 416-203-2500/1-800-499-2514; www.see torontonow.com
Convention and Visitor Bureau of Windsor, Essex County, and Pelee Island
333 Riverside Dr. W, Ste 103, Windsor, ON N9A 5K4, tel: 519-255-6530/1-800-265-3633; www.visit windsor.com/main.htm

Prince Edward Island

The **Visitor Information Centers** at Confederation Bridge and Wood Islands ferry terminal are extremely helpful. For advance information on what's on offer on the island you can write to:
Tourism PEI
Box 200, Charlottetown, PE C1A 7N8, tel: 902-368-4444/1-800-463-4734; www.tourismpei.com

Québec

Québec is divided into 17 regional tourist associations, each of which is eager to offer information and tours to visitors to the region. Contact:
Tourisme Québec
Box 979, Montréal, QC, H3C 2W3, tel: 514-873-2015/1-877-266-5687; www.bonjourquebec.com

For information on Montréal contact:
Montréal Infotouriste Centre
174 Notre-Dame St E, Old Montréal or

BELOW: Whistler resort in B.C. caters for all tourists' needs.

Sidebar tabs: TRANSPORTATION · ACCOMMODATIONS · EATING OUT · ACTIVITIES · A – Z · LANGUAGE

Useful Addresses

Travelers who want to plan ahead can do so by writing to the Canadian embassy or consulate in their own country for information. Listed below are the addresses and telephone numbers of a selection of Canadian tourist information centers:

Australia Canadian High Commission in Canberra, Commonwealth Avenue, Canberra ACT 2600, tel: +61 2 6270 4000/1 613 944 9136; www.australia.gc.ca
There are Canadian consulates in Sydney, Melbourne and Perth, see above website for further details.
France Canadian Embassy, First Secretary for Tourism, 35 Ave Montaigne, 75008 Paris, tel: +33 1 44 43 29 94; www.france.gc.ca

UK Canadian High Commission Consular and Passport Section, Canada House, Trafalgar Square, Pall Mall E, London SW1Y 5BJ, tel: +44-207-258-6600; www.unitedkingdom.gc.ca
US Embassy of Canada, 501 Pennsylvania Ave NW, Washington, DC 20001, tel: 202-682-1740, www.washington.gc.ca
There are Canadian consulates in every major American city, including:
• 1251 Avenue of the Americas, New York 10020-1175, tel: 212-596-1628.
• 2 Prudential Plaza, Ste 2400, 180 North Stetson Ave, Chicago, IL, tel: 312-616-1860.
• 1501 4th Ave, Suite 600, Seattle, WA, 98101, tel: 206-443-1777.

1255 Peel St in the Downtown, tel: 514-873-2015/1-877-266-5687; www.tourisme-montreal.org
Québec City Tourism
835 ave Wilfrid-Laurier, Québec, QC G1R 2L3, tel: 418-641-6290/1-877-783-1608; www.quebecregion.com

Saskatchewan

The Saskatchewan Vacation and Accommodations Guides list and rate accommodations and provide additional information concerning campgrounds, parks, resorts, and outfitters. For further details contact:
Tourism Saskatchewan
1922 Park St, Regina, SK S4N 7M4, tel: 306-787-9600/1-877-237-2273; www.sasktourism.com

The Yukon

Tourism Yukon provides a wealth of information for visitors to the territory. Its useful publication Yukon Vacation Guide lists lodgings, restaurants, service stations, and campsites. Road maps and other brochures can be obtained by contacting: Box 2703, Whitehorse, Yukon, Y1A 2C6, tel: 1-800-661-0494; www.travelyukon.com

Tour Operators

Canada

With the effectiveness of the internet in marketing, there are many Canadian-based tour operators who serve visitors from all over the world, particularly for specialty adventure packages for the north.
For hiking, biking, and kayaking in Rocky Mountains, Western Canada, Newfoundland, the Arctic:

Gap Adventures
19 Charlotte St, Toronto, Ontario M5V 2H5, tel: 1-800 708-7761; www.gapadventures.com
Adventure Canada
14 Front St S, Mississauga, Ontario L5H 2C4, tel: 905-271-4000/1-888-888-2682, UK Toll Free: 0-808-101-0935; www.adventurecanada.com

USA

There are many Canadian tour packages offered by US tour operators; the USA Travel Industry Guide to Canada has extensive listings. For more information, or to order a brochure visit: www.canadatravelguides.ca or visit the Canadian Tourist Board's website: http://us.canada.travel.
The following list of tour operators gives a flavor of the destinations and activities that Canada has to offer:
Arctic Odysseys
3409 E Madison, Seattle, WA 98112, tel: 206-325-1977/1-800-574-3021; www.arcticodysseys.com
Travel America
8719 West Greenfield Ave, Milwaukee WI 53214, tel: 414-258-4886/800-686-4114; www.travelamericatours.com
World on Skis
250 Moonachie Rd, 4th Floor, Moonachie NJ 07074, tel: 866-678-5858/201-228-5300; www.worldonskis.com
The following tour operators offer vacations with limited impact on the Canadian environment:
Black Spruce Tours has customized tours to the Maritime Provinces, Québec, Newfoundland, and Labrador. Contact:

Fred Vidito, 58 Woodland Drive, Sag Harbor, New York 11963, tel: 631-725-1493; www.blacksprucetours.com
For hiking, biking, and kayaking in Rocky Mountains, Western Canada, Newfoundland, the Arctic:
Gap Adventures
364 Avenue of the Americas, New York, NY 10011-8402, tel: 212 228 6655/888 800 4100; www.gapadventures.com
Northern Lights Expeditions offers camping and lodge-based sea-kayaking tours.
PO Box 4289, Bellingham WA 98227-4289, tel: 800-754-7402/360-734-6334; www.seakayaking.com

UK

For further details on UK tour operators, look in Canadian Travel Planner, which can be obtained by calling the Visit Canada Centre at tel: 0870-380 0070 or emailing visitcanada@dial.pipex.com or www.canada.travel.
For tours to **Canada's North**:
Arctic Experience/Discover the World
8 Bolters Lane, Banstead, Surrey SM7 2AR, tel: 01737-218 800; www.discover-the-world.co.uk/en/destinations/canada
For tours to **B.C.** and **Alberta** for 18 to 35 year olds:
Contiki Holidays
Wells House, 15 Elmfield Rd, Bromley, Kent BR1 1LS, tel: 0845-075-0990; http://contiki.co.uk
Ski trips to Québec, Ontario, Manitoba, Alberta, B.C., and the Yukon are the focus of:
Frontier Ski/Frontier Adventures
6 Sydenham Ave, London SE26 6UH, tel: 020-8776 8709; www.frontier-ski.co.uk
Travelpack
73–77 Lowlands Rd, Harrow, Middlesex HA1 3AW, tel: 0844-493 0402; www.travelpack.com
Offers escorted tours, coach and rail tours, self-drive itineraries, adventure and city packages across the country.
Eco-tours to Newfoundland, New Brunswick, Québec, Manitoba, British Columbia, the Yukon, Northwest Territories, and Nova Scotia are offered by:
Windows on the Wild
2 Oxford House, 24 Oxford Rd North, London W4 4DH, tel: 020-8742 8299; www.windowsonthewild.com
Committed **anglers** may want to consider:
Anglers World Holidays
46 Knifesmithgate, Chesterfield, Derbyshire S40 1RQ, tel: 01246-221 717; www.anglers-world.co.uk

V isas and Passports

US citizens traveling by air between the US and Canada must present a current passport or other approved travel document; a birth certificate and photo ID are no longer sufficient. Amtrak also requires a current passport, if traveling by rail between the US and Canada For those traveling by land, rules are constantly changing, so it's important to check with both Canadian and American border regulatory agencies (what may be sufficient to enter Canada may not be sufficient to return to the US). Residents of other countries must carry a passport. In some cases a visa is also required. For more information, call 1-800-992 7037 (outside Canada); 1-888-242 2100 (within Canada), or visit www.cic.gc.ca.

Until recently, crossing the Canada-US border has been relatively simple. American visitors to Canada did not need a passport to cross in either direction. Visitors were sometimes asked to verify their citizenship and therefore carried one of the following documents: birth certificate, naturalization certificate, Green Card, or passport. Photo identification was also required in the form of a driver's license or other photo ID.

However, in April 2005, the US government announced the Western Hemisphere Travel Initiative, which will require all travelers, including US citizens, to present a passport or acceptable alternative when entering the United States. This rather draconian measure was launched on December 31, 2006 for air and sea travel, and on December 31, 2007 for land-border crossings. Given the probable impact on trade and tourism, the Canadian government and border communities on both sides are extremely concerned, and urging the US to consider a more pragmatic approach to border security.

Citizens of other countries need a valid passport; no visas are required of the citizens of most British Commonwealth or European Union countries. Prospective visitors who are in any doubt about which documents they will need, should check with their travel agent or the nearest Canadian consulate.

Visitors may be asked to produce return tickets and possibly evidence that they have the funds to support themselves while in Canada.

Non-Canadian visitors going from Canada to the US, however briefly, will require a passport with at least six months' validity. Visitors from some countries may also require a visa. Check this with a travel agent or the nearest US consulate before leaving home.

W hat to Wear

Visitors to urban and resort areas from Europe or the US should be perfectly comfortable in the clothes they wear at home under similar circumstances. Visitors planning a canoeing or hiking trip should bring suitable layers of clothing, including warm and waterproof garments, as weather conditions change rapidly.

In winter, wind chill can reduce ambient temperatures, leading to frostbite. Tourists planning to ski, hike, or take part in any other outdoor activity should wear very warm clothing and be prepared to cover exposed skin. Canadians wear both synthetic and non-synthetic clothing in layers to retain heat.

Women Travelers

Canada is probably one of the safest countries in the world for women to travel alone. With so many women traveling on business, hotels and restaurants are fully accustomed to seeing women on their own and are becoming increasingly sensitive to safety issues. Provided a female traveler follows a common-sense-based code of conduct, the chances of running into a problem should be minimal.

Some city hotels have recently introduced "singles" tables in their dining rooms, at which hotel guests can ask to be seated – this is a civilized way to encounter other single travelers in a "safe" environment. The hotel's concierge is also likely to be a reliable source of information on suitable or safe places to go and acceptable routes to get there. There are places where single women at night will feel out of their comfort zone, and personal theft of articles, particularly purses in restaurants, is on the increase. The safest thing to do is place your handbag on your lap while sitting in a restaurant.

Weights and Measures

Canada uses the metric system.
1 centimetre (cm) = 0.394 in
1 kilometre (km) = 0.621 miles
1 liter = 0.22 UK gallon
1 liter = 0.26 US gallon (g)
1 kilogram = 2.2 lbs

BELOW: many tour packages feature a cruise of Canada's shores.

TRANSPORTATION

ACCOMMODATIONS

EATING OUT

ACTIVITIES

A – Z

LANGUAGE

L ANGUAGE

UNDERSTANDING THE LANGUAGE

English

Though officially bilingual, English is the language of choice throughout most of Canada outside Québec and some relatively small sections of the Atlantic Provinces, Ontario, and Manitoba. Canadians speak with their own distinct accent, but written Canadian English is very similar to that of Great Britain. Americans will note the British spellings, often in such words as "labour" and "centre," and usage, such as "railway" instead of "railroad."

Newfoundland English

Newfoundlanders speak a dialect all of their own. The accent is vaguely Irish, but the idioms and expressions are truly unique:
"Go to the law with the devil and hold court in hell" – the odds are against you
"To have a noggin to scrape" – an extremely difficult task
"Pigs may fly but they are very unlikely birds" – a vain hope
"in a hobble" – not worrying
"he is moidering my brains" – he is disturbing me
"Long may your big good jib draw" – good luck

French

Pronunciation

Even if you speak no French at all it is worth trying to master a few simple phrases. The fact that you have made an effort is likely to get you a better response. Pronunciation is key; they really will not understand if you get it very wrong. Remember to emphasize each syllable, not to pronounce the last consonant of a word as a rule

(this includes the plural "s"), and always to drop your "h"s. Whether to use "vous" or "tu" is a vexed question; increasingly the familiar form of "tu" is used by many people. However, it is better to be too formal, and use "vous" if in doubt. It is important to be polite; always address people as Madame or Monsieur, and address them by their surnames until you are confident first names are acceptable.

Learning the pronunciation of the French alphabet is a good idea and, in particular, learn to spell your name.

Montréal claims to be the second-largest French-speaking city in the world, after Paris. Some 52 percent of the city's residents and 68 percent of those in the metropolitan area are French-speakers (francophones), with 17 percent and 12 percent English-speakers (anglophones) respectively.

Unique to Montréal is joual, a patois whose name is derived from French for horse: cheval. The earthy dialect flourishes among the city's working class and in the work of playwright Michel Tremblay.

Pronunciation of mainstream French also differs. Accents distinguish French in Québec from French in Paris or Marseilles.

The Inuit Language

There is little available literature on the Inuktitut Inuit language, largely because the Inuits don't want "the whites" to take their language away. The best guide to the language and culture is *The Inuit of Canada*, published by The Inuit of Taparitsat, 170 Laurier Avenue W, Ste 150, Ottawa, Ontario K1P 5V5, tel: 613-238-8181.

Québec's francophones form sounds deep in the throat, lisp slightly, voice toward diphthongs, and bend single vowels into exotic shapes. It has also incorporated some English words, such as "chum," as in mon chum or ma chumme, and blonde, for girlfriend, while le fun is a good time.

Even if you don't speak much French, starting a conversation with "Bonjour," is likely to evoke a positive response. Some shopkeepers hedge, with an all-purpose: "Bonjour-Hi."

French Words and Phrases

How much is it? *C'est combien?*
What is your name? *Comment vous appelez-vous?*
My name is... *Je m'appelle...*
Do you speak English? *Parlez-vous anglais?*
I am English/American *Je suis anglais/américain*
I don't understand *Je ne comprends pas*
Please speak more slowly *Parlez plus lentement, s'il vous plaît*
Can you help me? *Pouvez-vous m'aider?*
I'm looking for... *Je cherche*
Where is...? *Où est...?*
I'm sorry *Excusez-moi/Pardon*
I don't know *Je ne sais pas*
No problem *Pas de problème*
Have a good day! *Bonne journée!*
That's it *C'est ça*
Here it is *Voici*
There it is *Voilà*
Let's go *On y va/Allons-y*
See you tomorrow *A demain*
See you soon *A bientôt*
Show me the word in the book *Montrez-moi le mot dans le livre*
At what time? *A quelle heure?*
When? *Quand?*

What time is it? *Quelle heure est-il?*
yes *oui*
no *non*
please *s'il vous plaît*
thank you *merci*
(very much) *(beaucoup)*
you're welcome *de rien*
excuse me *excusez-moi*
hello *bonjour*
OK *d'accord*
goodbye *au revoir*
good evening *bonsoir*
here *ici*
there *là*
today *aujourd'hui*
yesterday *hier*
tomorrow *demain*
now *maintenant*
later *plus tard*
right away *tout de suite*
this morning *ce matin*
this afternoon *cet après-midi*
this evening *ce soir*

On Arrival

I want to get off at... *Je voudrais descendre à…*
What street is this? *Quel est le nom de la rue?*
How far is...? *A quelle distance se trouve…?*
airport *l'aéroport*
train station *la gare de train*
bus station *la gare routière*
bus stop *l'ârret de bus*
platform *le quai*
ticket *le billet*
return ticket *aller-retour*
toilets *les toilettes*
This is the hotel address *C'est l'adresse de l'hôtel*
bed *le lit*
key *la clé*
air conditioned *air climatisé*

Dining Out

Table d'hôte *(the "host's table") is one set menu served at a set price.*
Prix fixe *is a fixed price menu.*
A la carte *means dishes from the menu are charged separately.*
breakfast *le petit déjeuner*
lunch *le déjeuner*
dinner *le dîner*
meal *le repas*
first course *l'entrée/les hors d'oeuvre*
main course *le plat principal*
made to order *sur commande*
drink included *boisson comprise*
wine list *la carte des vins*
the bill *l'addition*
fork *la fourchette*
knife *le couteau*
spoon *la cuillère*
plate *l'assiette*
glass *le verre*

Emergencies

Help! *Au secours!/A l'aide!*
Stop! *Arrêtez!*
Call a doctor *Appelez un médecin*
Call an ambulance *Appelez une ambulance*
Call the police *Appelez la police*
Call the fire brigade *Appelez les pompiers*
Where is the nearest telephone? *Où est le téléphone le plus proche?*
Where is the nearest hospital? *Où est l'hôpital le plus proche?*
I am sick *Je suis malade*
I have lost my passport/purse *J'ai perdu mon passeport/porte-monnaie*

napkin *la serviette*
ashtray *le cendrier*

Viande (Meat)

bleu **rare**
à point **medium**
bien cuit **well done**
grillé **grilled**
agneau **lamb**
bifteck **steak**
boudin **sausage**
brochette **kebab**
caille **quail**
canard **duck**
carré d'agneau **rack of lamb**
chateaubriand **thick steak**
entrecôte **beef rib steak**
faisan **pheasant**
farci **stuffed**
faux-filet **sirloin**
foie **liver**
foie de veau **calf's liver**
foie gras **goose or duck liver pâté**
grillade **grilled meat**
hachis **minced meat**
jambon **ham**
lapin **rabbit**
lardons **cubes of diced bacon**
magret de canard **breast of duck**
oie **goose**
perdrix **partridge**
pintade **guinea fowl**
porc **pork**
poulet **chicken**
poussin **young chicken**
rognons **kidneys**
rôti **roast**
veau **veal**

Poissons (Fish)

anchois **anchovies**
anguille **eel**
bar (or loup) **sea bass**
cabillaud **cod**
calmars **squid**
coquillage **shellfish**
coquilles Saint-Jacques **scallops**
crevette **shrimp**

fruits de mer **seafood**
homard **lobster**
huître **oyster**
langoustine **large prawn**
lotte **monkfish**
moule **mussel**
raie **skate**
saumon **salmon**
thon **tuna**
truite **trout**

Légumes (Vegetables)

ail **garlic**
artichaut **artichoke**
asperge **asparagus**
avocat **avocado**
champignon **mushroom**
crudités **raw vegetables**
épinards **spinach**
frites **French fries, chips**
haricots verts **green beans**
lentilles **lentils**
oignon **onion**
poireau **leek**
pois **pea**
poivron **bell pepper**
pomme de terre **potato**
salade verte **green salad**

Dessert/Dessert

clafoutis **baked batter and cherries**
coulis **purée of fruit or vegetables**
crème anglaise **custard**
crème caramel **caramelized custard**
crème Chantilly **whipped cream**
fromage **cheese**
gâteau **cake**
tarte tatin **upside down tart of caramelized apples**

Drinks

drinks *les boissons*
coffee *café*
...with milk or cream *au lait or crème*
...decaffeinated *déca/décaféiné*
...black espresso *express/noir*
...American filtered coffee *filtre*
tea *thé*
milk *lait*
mineral water *eau minérale*
fizzy *pétillante*
non-fizzy *plate*
fizzy lemonade *limonade*
fresh lemon juice served with sugar *citron pressé*
fresh squeezed orange juice *orange pressée*
fresh or cold *frais, fraîche*
beer *bière*
pre-dinner drink *apéritif*
with ice *avec des glaçons*
sparkling wine *vin pétillant*
house wine *vin de maison*
local wine *vin régional*
after-dinner drink *digestif*
cheers! *santé!*

TRANSPORTATION
ACCOMMODATIONS
EATING OUT
ACTIVITIES
A – Z
LANGUAGE

FURTHER READING

Canada has a strong literary tradition (*See Art and Performance chapter, page 99*). Among the best-known writers are Robertson Davies (*Fifth Business*), Margaret Atwood (*The Handmaid's Tale*), Carol Shields (*The Stone Diaries*), Douglas Coupland (*Generation X*), Margaret Laurence (*The Diviners*), Mordecai Richler (*The Apprenticeship of Duddy Kravitz*), and Alice Munro (*The Love of a Good Woman*). For those who want a taste of the wild, Jack London's books, *The Call of the Wild* and *White Fang* are classics.

General

Black Robe by Brian Moore. This novel by an Irishman and one-time reporter for the *Montréal Gazette* was the inspiration for a 1991 film directed by Bruce Beresford. It's the harrowing tale of a proselytizing 17th-century Jesuit missionary struggling with the brutality of life among the native peoples of northern Québec. First published in 1983, it has recently been reprinted in paperback. (Penguin, 2006.)

The Book of Negroes by Lawrence Hill. This book won the Commonwealth Writer's Prize in 2008. The novel is set in the 18th century and tells the story of a young black girl who escaped from the US to Nova Scotia, and her trials and tribulations in Canada. (HarperCollins Publishers 2007.)

The Call of the Wild (1903) is one of Jack London's best-loved master-pieces. It is an adventure story set in the Yukon gold rush, and fully captures the unquenchable spirit of Buck, a kidnapped dog trying to survive in the harshest of environments. (Reprint, Wordsworth Editions.)

The Apprenticeship of Duddy Kravitz by Mordecai Richler. This is one of his best-known novels. Set in Montréal, it is about an opportunistic, amoral young Jew's determination to fight his way out of the working-class neighbor-hood of his youth. (Washington Square Press, reprint edition 2003.)

Beautiful Losers by Leonard Cohen. Although the world-famous singer/ songwriter is best known for his music, the Montréal native started his career as a poet back in the 1960s. He has written well over a dozen books, some better than others. Beautiful Losers examines the three cultural forces (French, anglo, and native) that have shaped the city. (Vintage, 1993.)

I Married the Klondike by Laura Beatrice Berton is a memoir of her life in the mining town of Dawson City in the Yukon, from her arrival as a single, 29-year-old kindergarten teacher in 1907, at the end of the gold rush, to her reluctant departure as a wife and mother in 1934. (First printed 1955, Harbour Publishing reprint, 2005.)

Innovation Nation: Canadian Leadership from Java to Jurassic Park by Leonard Brody, Ken Grant, and Matthew Holland. Designed to cut through traditional Canadian modesty, this book looks at how over 30 Canadian innovators have redefined the landscape of business in the global technology sector. (Wiley Publishers, 2002.)

Random Passage by Bernice Morgan. An epic story of an Irishwoman, Mary Brundle, and her perilous odyssey from a harsh English workhouse to the remote Newfoundland outport of Cape Random – a struggling settlement forced to be a community through the sheer will to survive. (Breakwater Books, 1992, reprinted 2000.)

Still at the Cottage by Charles Gordon. A funny yet affectionate look at cottage life, one of the enduring elements of the Canadian psyche. (McClelland & Stewart, 2006.)

This is my Country, What's Yours? A Literary Atlas of Canada by Noah Richler. Originally a CBC radio documentary, Noah Richler interviewed the who's who of Canadian literature about the places and ideas that are most meaningful to their work, to create a bold cultural portrait of contemporary Canada. (McClelland & Stewart, 2006.)

The Two Solitudes by Hugh MacLennan. This novel, first published in 1945, has become such a classic that the title has moved into common parlance to describe the linguistic and cultural conflicts between Canada's two founding nations. (McGill-Queen's University Press, reprinted 2006.)

BELOW: locks at the Trent-Severn Waterway, a popular way to travel around.

Who has Seen the Wind by W.O. Mitchell. First printed in 1947, this is a classic tale of a boy growing up on the Prairies of Saskatchewan during the Depression years. Mitchell presents an evocative glimpse of small-town life and death as seen through a child's eyes. (McClelland & Stewart, reprint edition 2000.)

History

Canada: A People's History, Vol. I and II by Don Gillmor, Achille Michaud, and Pierre Turgeon. These richly illustrated books tell the epic story of how Canada came to be the nation we know, from its earliest days. (McClelland & Stewart, 2001 and 2002.)

The Arctic Grail: The Quest for the Northwest Passage and the North Pole, 1818–1909 by Pierre Berton. One of Canada's most popular chroniclers, Berton's wonderful storytelling style and excellent research brings to life the explorers who traveled the Arctic, often with disastrous results. (McClelland & Stewart, 1989.)

Passages: Welcome Home to Canada, foreword by Michel Ignatieff, is an anthology of essays by immigrants – now public figures and authors – to Canada. It examines the concept of home and how the experience of being an immigrant is increasingly the binding Canadian experience. (Doubleday Canada, 2002.)

The Toronto Story by Claire MacKay. An ongoing documentation of Toronto's history, brought to life in a warm and humorous style with wonderful illustrations. (Annick Press 1997, updated 2002.)

A Flag for Canada: The Illustrated Biography of the Maple Leaf Flag by Rick Archbold. Since its birth in February 1965, the red-and-white Maple Leaf has become one of the world's great flags. This intriguing story reflects the history of the country as seen through the evolution of Canada's national symbol. (Stanton, Atkins, & Dosil 2008.)

Language

French Fun: The Real Spoken Language of Quebec by Steve Timmins. Written by an Ontario translator who now lives in Montréal, it takes a humorous look at the colorful idioms in common use. (John Wiley & Sons, 1995.)

The Dictionary of Newfoundland English, edited by G.M. Story, W.J. Kirwin, and J.D.A. Widdowson. First published in 1982 to widespread acclaim, this historical dictionary focuses on the varieties of English spoken in Newfoundland over the last four centuries. An entertaining book, it offers a wide view of the island's unique culture. (University of Toronto Press, 1998, reprinted edition 2002.)

Travel Literature

Welcome Home: Travels of an Innocent in Newfoundland by David McFadden. A poet and traveler rambles through Newfoundland, his love of a good chat shared with the many people he meets – who are happy to share their own stories. (McClelland & Stewart, 2003.)

Smalltown Canada by Stuart McLean. A well-known author and radio host takes his readers on a cross-country tour of small-town life in seven communities across Canada, presenting a humorous, rich portrait of the people and their history. (Penguin, 2002.)

Beauty Tips from Moose Jaw by Will Ferguson. A humorous account of the writer's 3-year journey around Canada using every mode of transportation – from helicopter to canoe –

Send Us Your Thoughts

We do our best to ensure the information in our books is as accurate and up-to-date as possible. The books are updated on a regular basis using local contacts, who painstakingly add, amend and correct as required. However, some details (such as telephone numbers and opening times) are liable to change, and we are singularly reliant on our readers to put us in the picture.

We welcome your feedback, especially your experience of using the book "on the road". Maybe we recommended a hotel that you liked (or another that you didn't), or you came across a great bar or new attraction we missed.

We will acknowledge all contributions, and we'll offer an Insight Guide to the best letters received.

Please write to us at:
Insight Guides
PO Box 7910
London SE1 1WE
Or email us at:
insight@apaguide.co.uk

imaginable. (Canongate Books Ltd, 2005.)

The Good Life: Up the Yukon Without a Paddle by Dorian Amos. The story of a couple from England who decide to sell up and move to Canada in search of a better life and the people and problems they come across before finding the dream they were looking for. (Eye Books, 2004.)

City of Glass: Douglas Coupland's Vancouver by Douglas Coupland. The cult author turns his pen to his home town. (Douglas & McIntyre, 2003.)

Passage to Juneau: A Sea and Its Meaning by Jonathan Raban. Raban documents his 1,000 or so mile journey from Seattle up the Inside Passage to Alaska. (Picador, 2000.)

Sacré Blues: An Unsentimental Journey Through Québec by Taras Grescoe. A spicy, irreverent examination of a unique part of North America, with nary a mention of a politician. It explores the heart of contemporary Québec and how it relates to its neighbors. (Macfarlane Walter & Ross, 2001.)

Other Insight Guides

Insight Guides

The 190-title Insight Guides series is the main series in the Insight stable, known for its superb pictures, in-depth background reading, detailed maps, excellent coverage of sights, and comprehensive listings section.

There are a number of **Insight Guides** to North America. Current titles include *Alaska*, and *USA On The Road*.

Insight City Guides

Insight City Guides are written by locally-based writers, who show you how to make the most of the city. There are Insight City Guides to North American cities including *Boston*, *Chicago*, *Seattle*, and *Vancouver*.

Insight Fleximaps

There are also **Insight Fleximaps**, with clear cartography, travel information, and a laminated finish, available for *Montréal*, *Toronto*, and *Vancouver*.

TRANSPORTATION

ACCOMMODATIONS

EATING OUT

ACTIVITIES

A – Z

LANGUAGE

ART AND PHOTO CREDITS

AKG London 50
Alamy 70
Alberta Tourism 7BR, 8BL, 128, 258/259, 261B, 290, 292R, 293, 295/T, 299
Andrzej W 142T
Archives Canada 22/23, 28, 33, 38, 39, 40, 41, 42, 43, 49, 55R, 56, 90
AWL 89, 333
Axiom 160
Ottmar Bierwagen 139T
Canada House 58/59, 99, 100, 110, 113, 115, 159, 172
Canadian Tourism Commission 102
Circque du Soleil 87L, 187
James Colbourne 92R
Corbis 25M/T, 26, 72, 73L, 84R, 85, 103, 251, 255R, 256, 257, 291, 310T, 311L
Fotolibra 250
Bruce Fritz 314
Getty 71, 74, 88, 95, 98, 205L, 238T, 243, 244, 248L/R
D Gordon 153
Image Ontario 9ML, 15B/T, 19, 80/81, 82, 116, 117, 121L/R, 126/127, 129B, 132, 133T, 134/135, 136, 139, 141, 144L/R, 147, 148/149, 150, 151, 155/T, 161L/R, 162L, 164, 166, 167, 168, 170, 171, 173L, 174/T, 175T, 346, 402
Istockphoto 3B, 5B, 6MR, 7ML, 133B/M, 158, 179, 191, 195T, 199, 202L/R, 203, 205R, 212, 214T, 219R, 220L/R, 244T, 247, 249, 279, 297, 308, 309, 316/317, 318, 319B/T, 320/321, 334, 335/T
Alexander Keiths 120
LauBrau 204
Maid of the Mist 6ML
Manitoba Tourism 6B, 18, 261M, 311R, 313/T, 315,
Mary Evans Picture Library 24B/M, 46L, 49, 53, 57, 63, 66, 163
Metropolitan Toronto Library 62
New Brunswick Tourism 10/11, 122/123 210/211, 214, 216, 218, 221, 222, 223, 225, 226L/R, 227, 228

Nova Scotia Department of Tourism 7MR, 17L, 129T, 230R/T, 234L/R, 235, 236L/R, 237, 238, 239,
APA Richard Nowitz 106, 178, 181/T, 182, 183, 184, 186, 190, 194, 195, 197, 198, 200
Office de Tourisme Canadien de la Communauté Urbaine de Québec 47
Ontario Archives 27, 30, 52, 54L/R, 55L, 60/61, 64, 65, 67, 91
Ontario Ministry of Tourism 173R, 175
Photolibrary 8BL, 9B/T, 246R, 248T, 277R, 281, 292L, 298, 330, 331, 336, 337
Pictures Colour Library 185, 213, 215L/R, 217L/R, 219L, 254, 310
Princess of Wales Theatre 107, 140L, 373
Province of British Columbia 278
Carl Purcell 86
Government of Québec 31, 34, 87R, 114
Lizzie Rainbow 144T
David Ramsay 232
Rex Features 75, 105
Robert Harding 201, 255, 339
Saskatchewan Tourism 303, 304L/R, 305, 306, 307
Sinoda 382
Société Régionale de Développement de Portneuf 24T
Courtesy of St Jacob County 169
Cylla von Tiedemann 146
APA Tim Thompson 4T, 7BL, 8BR, 9MR, 12/13, 14, 20, 21, 112, 118R, 119, 124/125, 137, 140R, 145, 260, 261T, 262/263, 264, 265, 267, 268, 270/271, 274, 275, 276, 277L, 280R, 282, 283, 284, 285, 311L, 312L/R, 340, 348, 281, 385, 388, 394
TIPS 16, 78/79, 83, 157, 228T, 203L, 242, 252, 255T, 280L, 288/289, 294, 296,
Topfoto 29, 31, 44, 46R, 104, 106, 142,
Young/Vancouver Public Library 36/37
Joe Viesti 45, 176, 177

Vancouver Playhouse 96/97
D Wilkins 162R
Leanna Rathkelly/Whistler Resort Assn 269
Wulfsohn/South Light 111
Yukon Tourism 2/3, 17R, 92L, 93, 94, 118L, 319M, 322, 323, 325, 326, 327

PHOTO FEATURES

76/77: APA Tim Thompson 76/77, 76BR, Manitoba Tourism 76BL,Yukon Tourism 77BL, Image Ontario 77BR, New Brunswick Tourism 77M, Istockphoto 77TR.

108/109: Fotolibra 108/109, TIPS 108BL/BR, 109M/T, Istockphoto 109BL, Canadian Museum of Civilization 109BR.

188/198: New Brunswick Tourism 188/189, 189BL/BR, APA Tim Thompson 188BL, 189BR, Manitoba Tourism 189T.

240/241: Nova Scotia Department of Tourism 240/241, Photolibrary 240BL/BR/T, 241BR, Istockphoto 241TR, TIPS 241M, Ansgar Walk 241BL

286/287: Photolibrary 286/287, Istockphoto 286BL, Nova Scotia Department f Tourism 286BL, Palleala 286BR, Manitoba Tourism 286M, 287BL, TIPS 287BR, Image Ontario 287T

328/329: TIPS 328/329, 328M, Manitoba Tourism 328B, Corbis 329M, Image Ontario 329BL/BR, Saskatchewan Tourism 329T

Map Production:
Polyglott Kartographie

© 2010 Apa Publications GmbH & Co. Verlag KG (Singapore branch)

Production: Tynan Dean, Linton Donaldson